Jill Pavich

Cambridge International AS Level

English General Paper

Coursebook

CAMBRIDGE
UNIVERSITY PRESS

CAMBRIDGE
UNIVERSITY PRESS

University Printing House, Cambridge CB2 8BS, United Kingdom

One Liberty Plaza, 20th Floor, New York, NY 10006, USA

477 Williamstown Road, Port Melbourne, VIC 3207, Australia

314–321, 3rd Floor, Plot 3, Splendor Forum, Jasola District Centre,
New Delhi – 110025, India

103 Penang Road, #05-06/07, Visioncrest Commercial, Singapore 238467

Cambridge University Press is part of the University of Cambridge.

It furthers the University's mission by disseminating knowledge in the pursuit of
education, learning and research at the highest international levels of excellence.

Information on this title: www.cambridge.org/9781316500705

© Cambridge University Press 2018

First published 2018

20 19 18 17 16 15 14 13

Printed in Mexico by Litográfica Ingramex, S.A. de C.V.

A catalogue record for this publication is available from the British Library

ISBN 978-1-316-50070-5 Paperback

Additional resources for this publication at www.cambridge.org/9781316500705

Cambridge University Press has no responsibility for the persistence or accuracy
of URLs for external or third-party internet websites referred to in this publication,
and does not guarantee that any content on such websites is, or will remain,
accurate or appropriate. Information regarding prices, travel timetables, and other
factual information given in this work is correct at the time of first printing but
Cambridge University Press does not guarantee the accuracy of such information
thereafter.

....

....

All exam-style questions and sample answers in this title were written by the author.
In examinations, the way marks are awarded may be different.

Past exam paper questions throughout are reproduced by permission of Cambridge
Assessment International Education.

Contents

How to use this book   iv

Introduction   vi

1   Overview of the Cambridge International AS Level English General Paper   1

1.1   Syllabus outline   2
1.2   Core course knowledge   12
1.3   Reading comprehension   35

2   Understanding and applying   64

2.1   Summarising and explaining what you read   65
2.2   Planning and organising responses   83
2.3   Skills review and practice   97

3   Analysing and evaluating   116

3.1   Argumentative writing   117
3.2   Exploring issues through discursive writing   142
3.3   Skills review and practice   164

4   Essential language skills   184

4.1   Use of English   185
4.2   Parts of speech that add detail   199
4.3   Essential parts of speech   214
4.4   Adding complexity to your writing   236
4.5   Reviewing, editing and revising   250

5   Skills review and further study   268

5.1   Reviewing your writing skills   269
5.2   Reviewing your reading comprehension skills   279

Glossary   285

Index   288

Acknowledgements   294

How to use this book

Throughout this book you will notice particular features that are designed to help your learning. This section provides a brief overview of these features.

In this chapter, you will learn about:

- the key skills that you will need to develop during the course
- the content of the syllabus and what it aims to achieve
- the benefits of taking the AS Level English General Paper course
- how you will be assessed
- the types of questions that you will need to answer.

Learning objectives indicate the important concepts within each chapter and help you to navigate through the coursebook.

KEY TERM

Effective communication: using language accurately to express your thoughts or opinions about a topic while remaining sensitive to your audience's feelings and experiences.

Key terms are important terms in the topic that you are learning. They are highlighted in **black bold**. The glossary at the back of the book contains clear definitions of these key terms.

ARTICLE GLOSSARY

wrath: anger
evictions: sending people away from their homes or land
dissent: expressing disagreement
fostered: encouraged
repression: controlling people by force

Important terms in articles and book extracts are highlighted in **blue bold** and defined in **Article glossaries** following the article or extract.

KEY SKILLS

There are several types of sentence structures: *simple, complex, compound* and *complex-compound*. In Chapter 4.4, you will learn how each is formed.

Key skills boxes identify key skills that are required in a chapter and show you where in the book you can find more help on developing these key skills. Opportunities to review your key skills occur in every unit, but Unit 5 has a particular focus on reviewing your writing and reading comprehension skills, and is helpful to refer to throughout the course.

TIP

Errors in your writing can quickly affect your message, and damage your credibility as a writer. Make sure you allow yourself time to edit errors in grammar, spelling and punctuation before you share or submit your writing.

Tip boxes contain helpful guidance.

DID YOU KNOW?

The first video ever uploaded to the popular video website YouTube was an 18-second clip by founder Jawed Karim on 23 April 2005. In the video, he is at the zoo talking about elephants.

The first video ever to go 'viral' was posted in 2006 by American vlogger Gary Brolsma, who is featured lip-synching the 'Numa Numa' lyrics made popular by Moldovan band, O-Zone.

Did you know? boxes contain interesting facts to add useful context to the topics that you are learning.

Activities provide opportunities for you to practise what you have learned.

→

ACTIVITY 7

1 Identify five stakeholders who might have a perspective on the question about issuing travel bans.

2 Identify reasons why each stakeholder might agree or disagree with this issue. Remember to keep context in mind while you are considering these perspectives.

Exam-style questions help you to become familiar with the style of question you will encounter in examinations.

EXAM-STYLE QUESTIONS 1

This activity will introduce you to the types of reading comprehension questions you will meet in this course. Answer questions **1–5**.

1 From the passage, give two reasons why languages are lost. **[2]**

2 In no more than 50 of your own words, summarise Peter Austin's arguments for wanting to preserve dying languages. **[5]**

3 Why do you think *parents decide not to teach their children their heritage language*? In your own words, explain why families are likely to perceive it as a *hindrance* (line 19). **[4]**

4 In your own opinion, what do you think is the most important reason why we should save dying languages? Using evidence from the passage and your knowledge of the present day, justify your answer. **[8]**

5 (i) Explain the meanings of the following words as they are used in the passage. You can write your answer as a single word or a short phrase. **[3]**

imperiled (line 6)

degrade (line 13)

teeter (line 45)

(ii) Use the words in three **separate** sentences to illustrate their meanings as used in the passage. Your sentence content should stand apart from the subject matter of the passage. **[3]**

Total marks: 25

Summary

Key points to remember from this chapter:

- Learning different ways to structure your sentences can help you use detail to clarify your message. It can also add a sense of style to your writing.
- To express a complete thought, most sentences will contain a subject, verb and complement.
- Direct and indirect objects can be found after action verbs, whereas predicate nominatives and predicate adjectives appear after linking verbs.
- There are four types of sentences: simple, complex, compound and complex-compound.
- Conjunctions are powerful tools in writing because they can help you coordinate ideas and structure sentences.
- Commas are not strong enough to hold two independent clauses together. Instead, you should use a semicolon or a full stop.
- Learning to identify clauses will help you avoid errors such as run-ons and misplaced modifiers.

At the end of each chapter, a **Summary** box lists the key points that were covered in the chapter.

Introduction

What is the Cambridge International AS Level English General Paper?

The Cambridge International AS Level English General Paper syllabus encourages you to think critically about modern issues as a means of developing your skills in reading and writing. It also seeks to strengthen your ability to communicate in English.

To help you meet the aims of the syllabus, the course will target the following core skills:

- reading
- writing
- application of information
- analysis and evaluation.

How will you be assessed?

A common misconception about this course is that it is a test of knowledge. As the following diagram suggests, however, Cambridge International AS Level English General Paper is a *skills*-based syllabus. You will *not* be assessed on your level of knowledge. You will write about a range of different topics throughout the year, but you will be assessed on your ability to:

communicate in written English

analyse and evaluate information

select and apply information

The course will build and assess your skills in written communication and reading comprehension. Here is a brief overview of what to expect.

Written communication

Throughout the course, you will practise responding to a range of essay subjects. In an assessment situation, you will have 1 hour 15 minutes to plan, organise, support, write and refine your essay.

The syllabus sets out three broad topics, which each contain a number of suggested areas to explore. The topics are:

- economic, historical, moral, political and social
- science, including its history, philosophy, ethics, general principles and applications; environment issues; technology and mathematics
- literature, language, the arts, crafts and the media.

Reading comprehension

You will encounter two types of reading material during the course:

- prose
- sources requiring logical reasoning.

You will be asked reading comprehension questions which relate to these materials. For example, you may be asked to:

- summarise information
- put information into your own words
- identify key ideas and details
- make inferences
- draw conclusions
- examine options
- offer your opinion.

In an assessment situation, you will have 1 hour 45 minutes to read and respond to the material.

Why study for the Cambridge International AS Level English General Paper?

This is a skills-based course, which can help you become a stronger critical reader, writer and thinker. These skills can transfer to most other academic fields you are studying, therefore the Cambridge International AS Level English General Paper can be a valuable foundation for your educational experience across all disciplines. The skills you practise in this course are *required* at university level, *valued* in the professional world, and *necessary* for citizens living in 21st-century society.

The Cambridge International AS Level English General Paper course can help you to:

- develop your own opinions
- analyse the opinions of others
- evaluate the quality, value or significance of ideas before judging them.

We are all shaped by our own experiences and hold different values, so not everyone sees the world in the same way. Learning how to address today's issues (and the opinions surrounding them) in a sensitive and mature way can therefore improve your approach to global conversation. It is hoped that success in this course will inspire you to play an active role in global society and, as you do so, you may help to make positive changes in the world around you.

How is this coursebook structured?

The approach in this book is built on the assumption that good readers make good writers. The following diagram shows how the book helps you to use reading skills to improve your writing:

Reading comprehension   **Essay writing**

Reading comprehension		Essay writing
understand detailed information, identify key words	UNDERSTAND →	understand the key words of an essay question
identify and summarise issues, express information in one's own words	APPLY →	apply appropriate knowledge as evidence to support a point; make sure information is relevant
analyse and respond to information; interpret by making inferences and drawing conclusions	ANALYSE →	interpret the meaning of information; draw inferences and understand implications; examine points of view
use both text and one's own knowledge to justify ideas; choose between different points of view	EVALUATE →	assess evidence, ideas and opinions in order to form a reasoned conclusion
organise information; communicate clearly	COMMUNICATE →	organise/structure information deliberately for effect; communicate clearly

The main aim of this coursebook is to teach you how to think critically about contemporary issues, and how to respond to them in a way that clearly communicates your ideas and opinions:

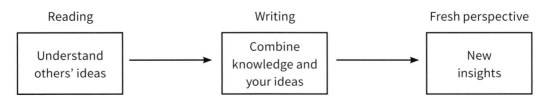

Reading → Writing → Fresh perspective

Understand others' ideas → Combine knowledge and your ideas → New insights

How can this coursebook help you?

The best way to feel confident about meeting course expectations is through careful preparation. This book provides information and guidance to help you do this. Each chapter is organised around a learning theme which is related to the topics listed within the course syllabus. The main chapter themes are as follows:

Chapter	Theme
1.2	Language and communication
1.3	Celebrity culture
2.1	Visual arts
2.2	The individual and society
2.3	Technology, gender and education
3.1	Food, water and other essential resources
3.2	Tradition versus modernity
3.3	Government priorities
4.1, 4.2	Literature
4.3	Poetry in the modern world
4.4	Media as literature
4.5	What makes a person 'great'?

The Cambridge International AS Level English General Paper course aims to build your general knowledge and awareness of today's issues. Nevertheless, it would be impossible to cover all possible topics in a single year! Your teacher may therefore develop topic areas related to those in the syllabus, but it is *your* responsibility to pay attention in your study of other disciplines such as science, maths, history and the arts so that you develop and reinforce your knowledge and understanding of these subjects. Remember: you may be asked to write about any of the topic areas listed in the syllabus for this course, so it is important to develop your general knowledge as much as you can!

The skills you learn in the Cambridge International AS Level English General Paper course will apply to the critical tasks in other disciplines. This coursebook will help to inspire good reading which, in turn, will inspire good writing. Since communication is a key skill in a globally-connected society, your hard work in this course will be well worth the effort!

Unit 1:
Overview of the Cambridge International AS Level English General Paper

Chapter 1.1
Syllabus outline

The Cambridge International AS Level English General Paper syllabus will challenge you to think critically and creatively about complex global issues.

Learning objectives

In this chapter, you will learn about:

- the key skills that you will need to develop during the course
- the content of the syllabus and what it aims to achieve
- the benefits of taking the AS Level English General Paper course
- how you will be assessed
- the types of questions that you will need to answer.

A Topics and key skills

In your Cambridge International AS Level English General Paper course, you will study topics from across the curriculum. The course will help you to develop both your writing and critical reading skills.

The course will prepare you to do two types of tasks:

- to *write* essays about contemporary society (i.e. society today)
- to *read* information critically and to respond to questions that challenge your logic and understanding.

TIP

There is a list of Cambridge International AS Level English General Paper topics later in this chapter in Section *D Course content*.

The 'key skills' are the core abilities you will develop in this course. These will help you to become a competent reader and writer as well as a critical thinker and problem-solver. The course will help you to develop a number of important key skills in both reading and writing:

Reading

- Can you:
  - understand the question being asked or the text you are reading?
  - understand detailed written information presented in different ways (e.g. texts, data, charts, lists)?
  - understand the use of English words and phrases as they are used in different contexts?
  - acquire a wide-ranging vocabulary from what you read?

Writing

- Can you:
  - use knowledge and information appropriately to support your argument?
  - express ideas in clear and accurate written English?
  - present ideas in a structured way?
  - write appropriately for a variety of purposes?
  - demonstrate range in vocabulary and control over grammar and other mechanics?

Application of information

- Can you:
  - summarise key text in your own words?
  - select appropriate information to use in your written responses?
  - pair reasons with relevant examples to support your point(s)?
  - recognise different viewpoints?
  - explain the ideas of others in your own words?

Analysis and evaluation

- Can you:
  - analyse data?
  - interpret meaning from the text you read or the knowledge you gain?
  - make inferences from what you read or learn?
  - assess various points of view and decide between them?
  - develop ideas in a logical way?
  - understand the consequences of actions?
  - offer workable solutions to real world problems?
  - make judgements supported by evidence?

B Syllabus aims and objectives

The Cambridge International AS Level English General Paper syllabus is intended to enable you to:

- develop understanding and use of English language in the context of contemporary topics
- encourage and appraise a broad range of topics
- develop a wider awareness and knowledge of contemporary issues through reading
- develop independent reasoning skills
- develop the skills of interpretation, analysis, evaluation and persuasion
- develop skills in writing structured and developed arguments, and present reasoned explanations
- develop the ability to present a point of view clearly, and consider and reflect upon those of others.

There are three assessment objectives (AOs) that correspond with these aims. To meet these objectives you will need to show that you can:

- select and apply information (AO1)
- analyse and evaluate information (AO2)
- communicate using written English (AO3)

3

The table shows examples of the kind of tasks that you may do during the course, and the assessment objective that each task will meet.

Example task	AO1	AO2	AO3
Give reasons for the increasing popularity of start-up businesses. (*reading comprehension task*)	✓		
How effective are consumer boycotts? (*essay/writing task*)	✓	✓	✓
By considering both the advantages and disadvantages, explain which of the options is most suitable. (*reading comprehension task*)		✓	
Analyse the need for classes like art, music and drama in the school curriculum. (*essay/writing task*)	✓	✓	✓
What does the expression *paring down* mean as it is used in the material? (*reading comprehension task*)			✓
Examine the advantages and disadvantages of travelling in today's society. (*essay/writing task*)	✓	✓	✓

C Course benefits

The skills that you will develop in this course can be applied to any subject. They may also help you to:

- meet the entrance requirements for universities, since many universities place a high value on critical thinking skills
- become more aware of contemporary 'real world' issues
- communicate effectively with others about these issues.

Effective communication is a skill that is essential to everyone, everywhere. It is a skill that enables you to change the world around you. Communicating effectively can help you discuss issues, articulate ideas and voice your opinions. Essentially, this course gives you the skills you need to find your own voice in an increasingly globalized society.

KEY TERM

Effective communication: using language accurately to express your thoughts or opinions about a topic while remaining sensitive to your audience's feelings and experiences.

D Course content

Writing essays

One of the main focuses of the course will be essay writing. You will usually be given a choice of essay questions, which are organised by the following topics:

- economic, historical, moral, political and social
- science, including its history, philosophy, ethics, general principles and applications; environmental issues; technology and mathematics
- literature, language, the arts, crafts, and the media.

Demonstrating critical thought

A good essay will show knowledge of the topic area, but it will also discuss that information on a more critical level. So as well as selecting appropriate information to include in your essay, you will need to analyse it.

It may help if you think of this as the 'input' and 'output' of your essay.

INPUT ⟶	OUTPUT
(the information, facts or knowledge that you use to support the points you are making)	(your informed opinion about the information (i.e. the input), why it is relevant to your point and/or whether there are other points of view)

By sharing these thoughts with your audience, you are actively and critically interacting with the information that you present in your essay.

KEY TERM

Prompt: a question or instruction which encourages you to respond.

ACTIVITY 1

Read the paragraph, which responds to the following essay **prompt**: *How far do you agree that traditional stories are worth preserving?* With a partner or independently, identify the 'input' and 'output' in the paragraph.

Traditional stories should be preserved because they have the ability to influence behaviour. In fables, for example, characters' actions and the consequences of choices they make culminate in a moral lesson learnt by the end of the story. For children especially, these characters serve as examples for how to act and how not to act. This serves an important purpose as they develop a sense of self and establish their own values. A classic case of such stories are Aesop's *Fables*, which have a timeless ability to influence moral behaviour. One tale, 'The lion and the mouse', teaches its audience that 'a kindness is never wasted'; and 'The fox and the goat' teaches us to 'look before we leap'. Based on the popularity of these fables, it stands to reason that traditional stories can play a significant role in how we think and act, which certainly makes them worth saving.

Storytelling is a timeless tradition in many cultures. What kinds of stories does your culture value and to what extent are these traditions maintained?

Choosing topic areas for essays

The course title, 'Cambridge International AS Level English General Paper', means that the essays you write will be on *general* academic topics from science to maths, literature to history, media, culture and beyond. For example, you may be asked to write about:

- the value of art or the quality of cinema
- the relevance of graffiti
- the benefits of research technology
- truth in advertising
- ethical concerns surrounding genetically modified crops.

Would any of these areas interest you? Would you like to write about them? If not, there are plenty more to choose from. Look at the following list for the full range of topic areas that you could be asked to write about in this course.

Economic, historical, moral, political and social

- The role and value of history in modern society
- Wars, conflicts and terrorism
- The state and its institutions
- Political systems, leadership, nationalism and forms of government
- The role of international organisations
- The provision and politics of aid
- Justice and the justice system; prison and rehabilitation
- The role of the individual in society
- Family, marriage and partnerships, social pressure, class and social attitudes
- Globalisation and its impacts

- Wealth and equality in society
- Population and migration
- Education
- Welfare
- Sport and leisure
- Work and employment
- Industry and commerce
- Freedom of speech, thought and action
- Human rights
- Animal welfare
- Matters of conscience, faith and tolerance

Science, including its history, philosophy, ethics, general principles and applications; environmental issues; technology and mathematics

- Medical and scientific advances and their ethics
- Drug testing, manufacture and provision
- Diet, health education and provision of healthcare
- Space exploration and its associated industry
- Information and communications technology
- Surveillance and privacy
- Environmental concerns
- Natural disasters including mitigation and management
- Rural and urban concerns
- Food and water security
- Transport, travel and tourism
- The uses and applications of mathematics

Literature, language, the arts, crafts, and the media

- Literature
- Non-fiction writing
- Language
- Performing arts
- Visual arts
- Applied arts
- Arts institutions and venues
- Traditional arts and crafts; heritage
- Print and digital media
- Advertising
- Censorship and freedom of the media and the arts

There should be something of interest here for everyone. The essays that you write during the course will always be based on the topic areas in the list. You will always have a number of essay questions, so you will be able to choose what you want to write about.

KEY SKILLS

In this course, you will focus mainly on developing your reading and writing skills, not on your direct knowledge of specific topics. However, it is part of your responsibility as a learner in this course to apply the knowledge you are learning in other subject areas (e.g. sciences, history, languages or media) to the skills you are practising for the AS Level English General Paper. For example, knowledge gained from a science class on the use of pesticides could be used for a writing task such as:

Are pesticides the answer to the problems facing the business of global agriculture?

Answering comprehension questions

Besides essays, the other main focus of the course will be comprehension questions. You are provided with materials and required to:

- explain and interpret information
- respond to the material by writing a persuasive text that expresses an opinion and justifies a conclusion
- demonstrate understanding of how language features are used
- analyse and evaluate the material.

Depending on the type of material, you may be asked to find the solution to a problem using common sense and logic. For example, you might need to choose the most appropriate renovation for a building; in this case, you might be given data, costs and/or a list of considerations to take into account before arriving at a decision.

Comprehension questions may ask you to demonstrate understanding of a prose piece such as a speech, email or news article. A question following a text like this, for instance, might ask you to put ideas from the text into your own words to show understanding. You may also be asked about language specifically: for example, the definition of a word in context or the meaning of a colloquial (informal) phrase.

KEY SKILLS

> The comprehension questions can help you improve the skills you need to meet the essay-writing assessment objectives of *understanding, analysing, evaluating, applying and communicating.*

Comprehension questions may ask you to do any of the following:

- summarise ideas in different types of material
- make inferences about the meaning of a text
- analyse the reasoning of an argument
- develop arguments of your own in response to a text or other material
- discuss the implications of an issue
- suggest a way of solving a problem.

The comprehension questions may cover a wider range of topic areas than the essay topic areas list that you have already looked at. You will use the skills you have learnt in the course to understand and analyse the information presented in the material, then provide relevant answers to the questions that follow. Most questions will be based on your immediate comprehension of the material; however, some questions may allow you to use knowledge outside the reading to further support your answer.

 KEY SKILLS

> The material you will read for comprehension practice can be up to 900 words long.

In their book about reading comprehension, *Mosaic of Thought*, Ellin Keene and Susan Zimmermann define synthesis as the process of organising the different pieces of information to create 'a *mosaic* … a [new] meaning, a beauty greater than the sum of each shiny piece'.

Comprehension skills

The material for comprehension questions may consist of:

- statistics
- diagrams
- maps
- tables
- notes
- listed information.

By practising comprehension questions, you will develop the skills needed to persuade your audience to accept any argument that you put forward. You will learn to evaluate the various solutions to a problem or issue before deciding which one works best.

Practising comprehension questions will also help you to develop the critical skill of **synthesising** information. After analysing several pieces of information, you might reorganise this input in a new way, creating fresh understanding of the issue.

KEY TERM

Synthesise: create new ideas or understanding by combining knowledge from different sources in fresh ways.

For comprehension questions, the material may also be printed or online texts, such as:

- reports
- reviews
- essays
- scripts (e.g. dialogue, recorded conversations)
- speeches
- descriptions.

As you practise answering comprehension questions, you will learn how to read text closely and carefully in order to recognise differences in key features like tone and style. By doing this, you will develop the ability to 'read between the lines' and interpret the deeper meaning beneath the material itself. Practising with comprehension questions will also help you improve your own writing skills, because you will need to summarise and communicate information in your own words.

ACTIVITY 2

Here are some criterion-based statements, which summarise the expectations for writing an effective essay. With a partner or in a small group, consider the meaning of the underlined terms, then rewrite the statements in your own words.

The essay:

a is fully relevant and offers a range of effective examples which respond to the question

b analyses possible meanings of the question

c defines the scope of the response

d features a consistently appropriate register when discussing the issue

e uses a wide range of vocabulary

f uses a variety of language features

g uses language in a controlled way

h is cohesive, coherent and engaging

i links ideas together in a convincing way

j analyses a range of arguments in order to reach a supported conclusion

k is well-organised.

TIP

Terms such as 'scope', 'cohesive' and 'register' may be difficult to understand. Putting these terms into your own words can help you become more comfortable with the language of the criteria. This will make it easier for you to write with these standards in mind.

E Expectations and assessment

Criteria for assessing essays

Assessing an essay is quite different from assessing responses to a question that offers multiple choices but has one fixed answer. For example, what do you think:

- distinguishes an *impressive* essay from an *average* one?
- makes a response *adequate* rather than *underdeveloped*?
- is the difference between a *clear* range of examples and a *reasonable* range?

Distinctions like these can be difficult and subjective sometimes. However, if you understand the criteria necessary for a strong essay, you will have a greater chance of communicating ideas effectively and satisfying the objectives of this course.

To assess essays as fairly as possible, it is helpful to use a *criterion-referenced* marking system. This means there is a fixed set of criteria, or standards, that an essay is judged against.

The table contains a more complete set of criteria for assessing the effectiveness of an essay.

Criteria for assessing an essay

	Select and apply information (AO1)	Analyse and evaluate information (AO2)	Communicate in written English (AO3)
Effective	• Fully relevant • Clear use and range of examples • Applies evidence and examples appropriately	• Considers possible interpretations of the question • Defines essay scope • Considers a range of perspectives • Strong line of reasoning • Offers a judgement based on both evidence and personal view	• Communicates ideas clearly • Consistently appropriate register • Wide range of vocabulary and style • Controlled, accurate use of language • Ideas are well-organised and cohesive
Competent	• Uses examples to illustrate, though some are more relevant and appropriate than others	• Demonstrates an understanding of the question • Offers some perspective regarding the issue, though not as varied • Argument is generally logical • Regular use of evidence to support the line of reasoning • Some judgement is passed, but it may be too broad or irrelevant	• Communication is generally clear • Register is generally appropriate • Uses everyday vocabulary • Generally controlled use of language, though not always accurate • Errors are present but do not impede communication • Coherent • Organisation may be inconsistent
Developing	• Lacks examples, or examples lack connection to points raised	• Lacks understanding of the question • Forms a basic conclusion, though it lacks insight • Weak line of reasoning • Does not offer judgement or draw conclusions about the information shared	• Inconsistent communication; frequent errors impede communication • Basic or limited vocabulary • Language lacks control and accuracy • Response may be fragmented or disorganised

What influence does fashion have in your life?

To what extent does fashion determine our health and/or happiness?

Fashion can symbolise many things such as happiness and good health. Some people are dedicated followers of fashion and it could be because they believe it helps their mental as well as physical well-being. Certain colour schemes can symbolise certain things such as happiness and joy, and some even believe that image affects the overall health of an individual.

One way that fashion can determine health or happiness is that the shapes, patterns and colours can portray certain emotions. Some colours have underlying meanings or feelings associated with them. For example, some prisons have started painting the inside of cells pink because it instils calmness and encourages calm behaviour. Some symbols or patterns therefore encourage certain behaviours, which could be a reason why some people are so into fashion since it can make them feel good, happy and even healthy.

However, health and happiness are always dependent on the image of clothing or styles of fashion. While in some cases it may make an individual feel better about his or her appearance and overall health, it can be a psychological thing. For some people, for example, sports are very enjoyable to play or watch and can clear the head of the individual. For others, however, sports are a waste of time and they can get bored watching or playing no matter what it is. The same goes for fashion: while some people love it and use it for relaxation others dislike it and think it's a waste of time, proving that it is an individual thing whether image determines happiness and healthiness.

Another reason fashion may have an effect on mental or physical state might be because the nicer you look, the nicer you feel. For example, if you dress up in a beautiful wedding dress, you feel loved and important, which makes you feel happy, which makes you feel better healthwise. On the other side of the spectrum, if you were to look like a mess with ragged clothing and messy hair, with people staring at you and pointing, it could take a toll on your mental health because having people criticise you can make you feel bad about yourself. Lots of times feeling down about yourself can lead to physical complications as well, such as the way depressed people often feel physically sick.

In conclusion, people may be dedicated to fashion because it can make them feel better about themselves when they look nice. On the other hand, it may just be a psychological thing. Either way, however you look at it, happiness makes you feel good, and you need a way of achieving happiness, and for some, it is fashion.

Criteria for assessing reading comprehension questions

Some reading comprehension questions ask you to develop your own explanation, argument or other set of ideas. For example, a question might ask you to look at several options before arguing which one is the best. In this case, there is no 'wrong' answer, provided that you develop and explain your choice. Therefore, you will be assessed based on specific criteria about *how* you answered the question.

Other questions, however, will be looking for answers that can be found in the reading material. For example, a question might ask:

> Which two brands did consumers like most?

The two brands in question will be clearly mentioned in the material. When a question has a specific answer like this, your response will be assessed on the *content* of the answer.

In addition to the information provided in the question itself, you will be told how many marks are available for each comprehension question that you answer. This will give you an idea of how detailed your response should be. As a general rule, those questions worth only 2 or 3 marks should be brief in comparison to those worth 8 or 10 marks.

 KEY SKILLS

Chapter 5.2 offers more tips for understanding how to answer comprehension questions as well as possible.

Summary

Studying for the Cambridge International AS Level English General Paper helps students to:

- think about issues
- sympathise with, as well as challenge, opposing viewpoints
- understand and apply ideas which are relevant to the issue
- analyse and evaluate different perspectives
- express these ideas effectively through fluent use of the English language.

As a student in this course, you will:

- explore a variety of global issues and be able to discuss them on a mature level
- learn how to communicate your thoughts and opinions clearly by using precise language, good sentence structure and thoughtful, logical organisation.

The skills you will learn in this course will be valuable in your study of other subjects and later as part of your university-level study.

Chapter 1.2
Core course knowledge

Effective communication is built on your understanding of both your audience and your purpose for writing. Take note of the core knowledge presented in this chapter, which explores the theme of *Language and communication*.

Learning objectives

In this chapter, you will:

- learn to write for a specific purpose and audience
- break down essay questions to better understand what is being asked
- get to know different approaches to writing
- become familiar with the common errors made by young writers
- find out how reading skills can improve your writing
- practise critical reading and writing skills
- select a style of writing that best matches your level of knowledge

A Core knowledge

There are a number of key points that you need to remember as you start out on your Cambridge International AS Level English General Paper course. You will refer back to this 'core knowledge' throughout your course. Here are a few key points to remember:

- you are expected to use a style of writing that matches your audience and purpose
- awareness of common writing errors can help you communicate more clearly
- a clear understanding of the task will help you write a more focused response
- the tone and structure of your writing will vary depending on the task
- you can become a better writer by observing the way others write (i.e. by critical reading).

You will explore these ideas briefly in this chapter and then in more detail in later chapters.

B Considering audience, register and purpose

Think about the kind of language you use when communicating in the following situations:

- at lunch with a group of friends
- during a presentation in front of your peers
- in an essay that your teacher assigned
- in a text message to a parent or family member.

You will notice that the way you communicate when speaking is probably quite different from when you are writing. Your language may change depending on *who* you are writing to, as well. For example, consider the following scenario. You are supposed to meet a friend for coffee, but she hasn't arrived yet. You send a text message to ask whether or not she will make it. Your message might look something like this:

> hi, where r u? 3pm still ok? lmk.

This kind of approach to language is most characteristic of personal conversation. Therefore, this memo would be most appropriate if you were speaking to a good friend. But what if you were meeting an acquaintance for coffee, or someone who was interviewing you for a job? How might you amend this message?

Perhaps it might look something like this:

> Hello, Charlotte. I'm writing to enquire about your intentions for coffee this afternoon. At your earliest convenience, please advise. Regards, Sally

It sounds awkward to speak in such a structured way to a close friend or relative, but it makes sense to organise your ideas in this way when you are communicating with a person of authority or someone you do not know so well. If you were in Sally's position, you might even change the medium of your message entirely, from a text message to a more formal email! Ask yourself who your audience is. This will affect how you write to them.

 KEY TERM

Audience: the person/people that you are speaking to or writing for; for example, in a writing competition your audience would be the competition judges, while your audience in this course is usually your teacher.

Clearly, there is a need for both formal and informal styles of communication. However, there are some situations where one **register** is more appropriate than the other. In order to decide whether to use a formal or informal communication style, consider the **purpose** of your message, who your audience is and what your audience will expect.

 KEY TERMS

Register: type pf language used for a particular purpose or in a particular setting.

Purpose: your reason for writing/speaking; for example, your purpose may be to persuade someone to agree with you about something.

How formal should your language be? Your register will depend on your audience and your purpose for speaking and writing.

Keep in mind that your audience may be just your own teacher. If you are reviewing your work with classmates or offering feedback to others in a writer's workshop activity, your audience might be a group of students or the whole class. If you post your writing on the internet, your ideas may reach a much wider audience.

In this course, you will be writing for an academic audience. You should therefore always use a scholarly register if you want them to take you seriously.

ACTIVITY 1

When we communicate in social settings, we tend to use colloquialisms or other informal phrases (i.e. slang). If you use this register when you are writing for a global audience, however, your audience may not understand your message if they are not familiar with the colloquialisms you use.

How could the following statements be changed to make communication more appropriate for an academic audience?

1   The results of the study were *patchy* and *mixed up*.

2   I think you have great ideas, so I don't mean to *rain on your parade*, but the management is not going to accept them.

3   Paolo had participated in tennis tournaments for many years, but he knew this year would be his *last shot at* a title.

4   Montoro used to be a busy and successful town for young artisans, but its *glory days* are now long gone since the closing of the city centre shops.

5   Local businesses accused officials of *turning a blind eye* to the problem.

Can you think of statements which are commonly spoken in your region that are appropriate for informal conversation, but perhaps inappropriate for writing?

C Use of English

Since the essays that you will write are academic and formal, you should always follow conventional rules for spelling, grammar and punctuation to make your writing successful. In order to deliver a clear and concise message that your audience can understand and appreciate, make sure that your writing does not contain errors that might confuse your readers.

Here are some of the errors that young writers tend to make when using English:

- misuse of punctuation (e.g. apostrophes, commas)
- non-agreement of subject and verb, or pronoun and antecedent (i.e. the noun phrase that the pronoun relates to)
- confusion between parts of speech (e.g. adjective and adverb)
- sentences not separated by punctuation, or incomplete sentences
- wrong position of modifiers (e.g. adjectives, adverbs).

TIP

Errors in your writing can quickly affect your message, and damage your credibility as a writer. Make sure you allow yourself time to edit errors in grammar, spelling and punctuation before you share or submit your writing.

You will learn more about these and other rules for grammar, spelling and punctuation in Unit 4. Get into the habit of editing your work: this is an important step in communicating effectively.

ACTIVITY 2

Test yourself! Read the following statements and decide whether they are grammatically correct.

1   It is the countries responsibility to provide language support for immigrants.

2   If someone arrives early to the discussion group, they should wait by the door.

3   The Office of Bilingual Affairs is on the second floor; this is where you can sign up for classes.

4   The participants in last week's fundraising event will receive a free ticket to the Multicultural Fair this is an annual event that takes place in the spring.

5   For example, students who are travelling to Dubai.

Discuss your answers with a partner.

Now that you have thought about why a formal, grammatically accurate approach to writing is necessary, let's consider a few other essential skills that you will need in order to be an effective writer in this course.

D Understanding the task

As part of the Cambridge International AS Level English General Paper course, you will write for a variety of different purposes. As you respond to reading comprehension questions, for example, you might write to explain your observations about a text or justify inferences you make about the material. You may also be asked to share your own logical reasoning in response to text, which would require you to write with a more argumentative purpose in mind.

In responding to essay questions, you will be assessed on your ability to develop a well-reasoned argument in response to questions concerning modern issues. This may involve arguing a distinct position or investigating the topic more objectively before passing judgement. No matter what your purpose is for writing, you will need to practise structuring ideas in order to achieve your goal. This coursebook will therefore help you develop:

- **expository writing** skills, so you can explain ideas in response to reading material, and to help you summarise information when presenting evidence in essays
- **argumentative writing** skills, so you can establish and reason through a clear position on a topic or issue
- **discursive writing** skills, so you can analyse multiple points of view surrounding a debatable issue before passing judgement on it.

TIP

It is important to keep in mind that while you will not write expository essays in an exam situation, you will still need to know how to explain your ideas in order to develop a point or argument. Learning how to write for expository purposes can therefore serve as a building block to help you achieve a higher purpose later in the course when writing essays.

KEY TERMS

Expository writing: when your purpose is to *explain* something to the reader by presenting it clearly and sharing details and facts, to educate and inform your audience.

Argumentative writing: when your purpose is to *argue* something by developing a line of reasoning in order to arrive at a logical conclusion; the aim is to convince your audience either to accept your position or even to take action.

Discursive writing: when your purpose is to *explore* an issue by considering objectively various points of view before arriving at an evidence-based conclusion.

KEY SKILLS

In Chapters 2.2, 3.1 and 3.2 you will learn more about the features and characteristics of writing to explain, argue and discursively investigate.

One of the key differences in writing for different purposes lies in **tone**. For example, if you are writing to explain, your tone might be confident because you are knowledgeable about what you are sharing.

Meanwhile, if you are writing to convince your audience, your tone might be:

- persuasive
- determined
- **biased**.

This is the kind of tone you will need to adopt when taking a stand on issues in this course. If you approach an essay with more of an investigative (discursive) purpose in mind, however, your tone will shift to appear more:

- **objective**
- unbiased
- analytical.

KEY TERMS

Tone: the attitude of the writer towards their subject or audience.

Biased: having a tendency to believe one aspect of an argument more than others as a result of one's personal opinions and/or prejudice.

Objective: not influenced by personal feelings or opinions when presenting an argument.

Command words

There are a number of **command words** you should become familiar with. These words indicate how you are expected to respond to a reading comprehension or essay question. Think about how your response might change as you read through the following tasks:

- Identify the importance of grammatical accuracy in today's society.
- Evaluate the importance of grammatical accuracy in today's society.
- Consider the importance of grammatical accuracy in today's society.

What words change the nature of the question in each? You may have noticed that words like 'identify,' 'evaluate' and 'consider' make a difference to how you should respond to these tasks.

There are a number of command words and phrases like these that you will encounter while taking this course. Review the table below to begin familiarising yourself with these.

Command word	What it means
Analyse	examine in detail to show meaning, and to identify elements and the relationship between them
Assess	make an informed judgement
Compare	identify/comment on similarities and/or differences
Consider	review and respond to given information
Contrast	identify/comment on differences
Demonstrate	show how or give an example
Describe	state the points of a topic/give characteristics and main features
Develop	take forward to a more advanced stage or build upon given information
Discuss	write about issue(s) or topic(s) in depth in a structured way
Evaluate	judge or calculate the quality, importance, amount or value of something
Examine	investigate closely, in detail
Explain	set out purposes or reasons / make the relationships between things evident / provide why and/or how and support with relevant evidence
Give	produce an answer from a given source or recall/memory
Identify	name/select/recognise
Justify	support a case with evidence/argument
State	express in clear terms
Suggest	apply knowledge and understanding to situations where there is a range of valid responses in order to make proposals
Summarise	select and present the main points, without detail

You may also come across phrases like *to what extent*, which encourage balance and evaluation.

TIP

Whether you are answering a reading or writing task, read the question carefully to make sure you understand what you are being asked to do. This will help you write a focused response that satisfies the requirements of the task. If a question asks you to *examine* an issue, but you only state what the issue is, you would not be satisfying the task required. Meanwhile, if a question asks you to simply *identify* the main points of an issue, but you analyse each point in detail, you will have wasted a lot of time and energy!

KEY TERMS

Command words: terms that indicate how you are expected to respond to a question.

Qualifier: a word or phrase used to limit the meaning of a word; it maximises or minimises the value of the word.

Aside from command words, there are other words or phrases that can help you understand the nature of the question. **Qualifiers** like 'always', 'ever' or 'only' suggest, for example, that a grey area exists around the issue being discussed. These words are a reminder that the task may require a consideration of multiple perspectives in your response. Here are a few examples of questions that use qualifiers to inform the approach you should take in your response:

- Is colloquial language <u>only</u> appropriate in spoken form?
- Is slang <u>ever</u> appropriate in the workplace?

As you work through this course, remember to pay close attention to the command words and qualifiers in each question. These play a key role in how you shape your response.

Any of the command words or phrases in the list above might appear in a comprehension question. Here are some common question stems you might encounter as a reader in this course:

- Identify two pieces of evidence the author uses to …
- Explain briefly what the author means when she says …
- What do you think is meant by the reference to … in paragraph …?
- In your own words describe the disadvantages of …
- Analyse the relationship between the points made in paragraphs … and …
- Suggests reasons why … might occur. Justify your response by using evidence from the reading material provided.
- Consider why the author chose to include …
- Compare … against …
- Give at least two reasons why option … would not work as the best solution to the problem.

Any combination of these command words may appear at any point to formulate both reading comprehension and essay questions.

E Choosing your approach to the essay task

The essays you write in this course will need to be drafted in the form of an argument. Depending on the question being asked and what you know about it, you will structure your arguments in different ways. However, this coursebook will share two basic approaches to writing an argument that can help you develop your point of view on an issue. These approaches include:

- argumentative
- discursive

Using a traditional (argumentative) approach

Depending on the essay topic you choose, you may have a clear point of view, or **perspective**, on the issue right away. If this is the case, you might take a more traditional approach to writing your argument in which you would:

- make your position clear in the beginning of the essay
- use a tone that indicates you have a bias towards the issue
- develop a fair and logical line of reasoning to support your position
- show an awareness of views which are different from your own.

Using a discursive (investigative) approach.

What happens, however, if you do not have a clear position at the start of the essay? You will develop your position differently! In using a discursive approach, you would:

- begin your essay by considering the many points of view that surround the issue, without showing bias towards one
- carefully analyse each point of view
- wait until the end of the essay to offer your position on the matter, after all information has been examined.

 KEY TERM

Perspective: a point of view or opinion about a problem, situation or issue.

17

KEY SKILLS

Ignoring the perspectives of others can seriously impact the quality of an argumentative essay by weakening both its logic *and* its credibility. See Chapter 3.1 for more information on how to use logical reasoning effectively.

Putting an essay question into your own words can help you understand the task and therefore make decisions about how you will approach the essay. Read the following question:

Assess the benefits of video conferencing against more traditional ways of conducting business.

Now look at the 'train of thought' of two students who are deciding how to respond to this question:

Student A

It looks like I need to compare the benefits of one form of communication over the other in order to decide which one is better.
↓
Hmm … I like the idea of video conferencing because it's so convenient these days but meeting face-to-face the traditional way is really important, too.
↓
I can think of several, reasonable situations that support both modes of communication, so it's hard to say …
↓
If I'm going to give a strong answer to this question, I'll need to sort through the evidence for both sides before I make a decision on this.
↓
It's settled … I'll need to *evenly investigate* this topic before I pass judgement!

Student B

It looks like I need to compare the benefits of one form of communication over the other in order to decide which one is better.
↓
Well, I definitely think traditional methods for conducting business, like meeting in person, are better than meeting online!
↓

So if I'm going to give a strong answer to this question, I think I'll share my perspective on traditional ways of conducting business because I have a lot to say about it – I just need to make sure I acknowledge those who might disagree with me.
↓
I can do that! I have a few thoughts on why video conferencing can be better, or at least why people *think* it is.
↓
I'm going to *take a position* on this topic!

Notice that Student B knows his/her position on the topic right away, whereas Student A is not so sure. These two writers will need to organise their ideas in different ways as a result of how they feel going in to the issue.

ACTIVITY 3

A 'think-aloud' is a helpful mental strategy where learners say their train of thought aloud as it comes to them. This is a useful way to organise your ideas. Complete the following think-aloud activity with a small group of no more than five participants.

For each of the essay questions **1–5**:

a Put the task into your own words.
b Think about what you know about the topic and how you feel about it.
c Decide which approach you would use if you were asked to respond to this question.
d Justify your decisions where appropriate.

Choose an approach which best aligns with your knowledge and understanding of the issue. As long as you answer the question in a way that thoughtfully and maturely addresses the topic, your response will be on the right track!

Essay questions

1 'Minority languages still have value in the modern world.' Discuss.
2 'The textbook still has value in 21st-century society.' What is your view?
3 To what extent are social media sites and/or blogs only for entertainment and nothing else?
4 Evaluate whether gaming should be considered a sport.
5 Assess the idea that an uncensored press is dangerous.

F Key elements of an essay

Constructing an essay requires several key components, which provide a scaffold to support the essay's conclusion.

In the past, you may have learned how to write essays that explain a process or an idea through the development of details and examples, often referred to as an expository essay. In Cambridge International AS Level English General Paper essays, you will be writing arguments as opposed to explanations. Unlike responses to reading, your essays will take up several pages, ranging from 600 to 700 words in length, so it is important to learn different ways to structure your ideas. Specifically, this coursebook will teach you two different ways to frame an argument: argumentatively and discursively.

While argumentative and discursive essays may differ considerably in tone and **shape**, they share elements that are common to any essay. Specifically, each argument should include:

- an introduction that presents your main idea (**thesis**)
- several body paragraphs developing arguments related to the main idea (thesis) and using appropriate **evidence**
- a reasoned conclusion which should make a personal judgement on the arguments rather than just summarising.

KEY TERMS

Shape: the way the writer organises writing to develop a point or provide information.

Thesis: a summary of the main idea, which makes the intentions of an essay clear to the reader; this idea should be supported by evidence during the course of the essay.

Evidence: the factual information that supports your reasons; evidence may appear in the form of examples, data (i.e. statistics), case studies, expert opinions or logic

The tone of an essay should match your purpose for writing it. If you are writing to convince, for example, it would not be appropriate to use an objective tone.

The shape of your essay will also depend on your intentions. For example, if you are writing about the problems associated with grammar and modern text messaging and how this could be resolved, the body of your essay might consist of a list of problems, each followed by a possible solution. This would effectively convey this information.

The sections that follow briefly introduce the standard key components of an essay (introduction, body and conclusion). They also explain how the tone and shape of your essay can change depending on the approach you take. Later, in Chapters 3.1 and 3.2, you will learn about these components in more detail.

The introduction

No matter how you approach your essay, the basic components of your introduction will remain largely the same. The following may be a useful reference for you:

Key features of an introduction

An introduction may, in any combination:

- introduce the topic by using key words from the essay question
- briefly consider possible meanings of the question before settling on your definition of terms
- determine the scope of your essay
- explain why the issue matters or why it is worth reading about now (**context**)
- present the main idea of the essay (**thesis**).

KEY TERM

Context: the circumstances and information you need to know in order to fully understand an issue.

Banksy, an anonymous graffiti artist known for his satirical street art, uses his work as a form of expression regarding serious political and social views. To understand a piece of street art by Banksy, it is essential to know the larger context surrounding the issue in focus.

KEY SKILLS

Strategies for establishing context are explained in Chapter 2.1.

When writing essays in this course, you will be expected to use logic to reason through the topic or issue. As you have learnt, one way to do this is by taking a clear position and defending your argument. If you aren't sure how you feel about the issue, however, you can choose a more discursive approach by weighing multiple arguments surrounding the issue before arriving at a judgement.

For example, depending on how you feel about the question, you might:

- argue in favour of the topic
- warn about its dangers or criticise its problems
- explore fairly the benefits and risks associated with it
- invite the audience to consider the issue with you via unbiased discussion.

KEY SKILLS

Unit 3 explores argumentative and discursive approaches to essay-writing in depth.

No matter which approach you choose, you could start either essay in a similar way: by briefly introducing the topic and establishing its importance to the reader. However, once you do this, you will need to make more significant changes to your thesis, which is what sets the *tone* of your essay.

ACTIVITY 4

Read the introductory paragraphs below, each of which begins a response to the following essay question:

> In today's society, to what extent does the use of accurate grammar still matter?

With a partner, or as a whole class, consider the following:

1. In what ways are these introductions similar?
2. How are they unique?
3. How would you describe the tone of each?
4. What seems to be the writer's intention for each? How do you know?

Introductory paragraph 1

In a modern world, where digital tools like email, texting and social media platforms are always present, it might seem as though the rigid structures of formal grammar are no longer important in our day-to-day communication. The high-speed nature of text messaging often leaves out punctuation like apostrophes and commas; and the brevity of Twitter forces us to be creative with this system which uses few words. Despite these short cuts which we consider digitally acceptable, accurate grammar is still a necessary part of our modern world. Whether spoken or written, good grammar is directly associated with professional credibility and trust, so being accurate still matters when communicating today.

Introductory paragraph 2

Today's technology helps businesses communicate through digital tools like email, texting and social media platforms. Social media is essential for marketing and team collaboration tools like Asana are crucial for encouraging productivity and meeting deadlines. While content can be more important than form when using these applications, co-workers and consumers alike expect the use of accurate grammar in the business setting as well. Therefore, depending on your audience and purpose, accurate grammar may be necessary when communicating in today's business world, though not always.

We will now look in detail at the key features of an introduction.

Thesis statements

The thesis statement is a one-sentence summary that expresses the main idea of your essay. You can always amend this statement later if the direction of your essay shifts, but having a draft of it at this stage helps immediately to structure your essay.

A thesis statement makes your intentions clear to the audience and sets the tone for how you plan to treat the issue. It also gives your essay a clear focus. Everything you write in your essay will relate back to this claim and its intentions. This makes it the most essential component of any introduction.

Depending on the style of essay, every thesis is different, but here are some general rules to remember when drafting a thesis statement.

Guidelines for drafting a thesis statement

A thesis statement:

- uses the same terms as the essay question
- serves as the guide for all reasons and evidence to follow in your essay
- is a one-sentence summary of your essay's content
- may change as your essay takes shape (i.e. you can change the wording of your thesis later or make it more specific when you revisit it in the conclusion).

ACTIVITY 5

On your own, practise writing a thesis statement by selecting an exam-style essay question from the list at the end of this chapter. Use the previous guidelines to help you through this process.

When drafting your thesis statement, the main rule to remember is that you should avoid a long list of reasons. Read the following example and think about why this approach is problematic.

> In today's society, the use of accurate grammar is still necessary because it builds credibility, upholds academic values, ensures clear communication, maintains traditional systems, and makes the world a better place.

Having too many ideas listed in a row makes this thesis sound awkward, too long or even disjointed. In fact, it may prove more useful to offer a broader thesis to start with, then tighten your thesis by the conclusion, once all evidence has been considered. Read the example thesis statements below, which do not list specific reasons but still clearly communicate the main idea of the essay.

Argumentative thesis

While some people claim that accurate grammar is no longer necessary in a digitally driven era, it still serves a very important purpose in the professional world.

Discursive thesis

Accurate grammar still matters in modern communication, though not always.

 KEY SKILLS

Notice how these thesis statements are different in tone. A discursive thesis statement in the introduction usually has a less urgent tone than an argumentative one, for instance (see Chapters 3.1 and 3.2 for more information on these differences).

> **TIP**
> If an essay question asks about 'you' or 'your' country/region/world, it is acceptable to use 'I' or 'me' in the introduction and/or conclusion. However, it is not necessary to use 'I' in the body of your essay because your evidence should take precedence over your opinion. As a general (prescriptive) rule, phrases such as 'I think' or 'I feel' should also be avoided. Although these are grammatically correct, they can affect the strength (force) and credibility of your message.

Look back at the practice thesis you wrote for Activity 5. Do you now want to make any changes? Remember, however, that there is no single 'right answer' to this task, though you should make sure your thesis ideas are:

- clear
- connected
- easy for the audience to follow.

Writing your thesis statement first can make it easier to develop the rest of the introduction around it. In other words, now that you know what your main point is, you might be in a better position to explain the context and define terms.

The thesis statement is a feature that is specific to the introduction. However, the other features of the introduction are not a sequence of individual steps, as with the thesis. Nor are they a checklist to follow in any particular order. Instead, these elements often merge or overlap with each other. For example, you could introduce your topic to the audience and explain why it matters at the same time.

Introducing the topic

Introducing the topic is the easiest step in writing an introduction because you can use the key words from the essay question to help you start. Do not feel that you are being lazy or unimaginative by using these words – they can be helpful by reminding you to focus on the task. For example, the essay question that we have been considering is:

> In today's society, to what extent does the use of accurate grammar still matter?

So you might find it helpful to use some variation of the following key words in your introduction:

- accuracy
- grammar
- still matters / doesn't matter
- today's society.

Defining terms and setting limits

As you introduce the topic for your reader in the introduction, you should define key words from the question and indicate what limits you will place upon them (see Chapter 2.2 Section *E Deconstructing questions* for more information on setting limits to your essay). For example, the concept of *accurate grammar* might need clearer definition.

How might you define some of the other words in the question, such as what is meant by *today's society*? Does *today's society* refer to your immediate environment / geographic location (e.g. the US state of Florida, Malaysian society, in the East or West), or does it invite a broader interpretation (e.g. 21st-century, global society)?

It is important that you define any key words in your introduction to stop your readers from making assumptions of their own. This can avoid the potential for confusion.

The next step is to set limits to your essay. If you were in an exam situation, for example, you would be allowed only 1 hour 15 minutes to write your essay. If you were responding to a question asking you about the extent to which modern communication brings us together, you would hardly be able to address every form of modern communication we use today! And even if you did, it would not be possible to do so in much depth. Instead, you would need to narrow the range of coverage to address a few selected sub-categories within 'modern communication':

> Modern communication can encompass a range of mediums, from emails to text messaging, and even social media posts. This essay will address video conferencing exclusively, and the extent of its ability to bring us together.

Taking time to make decisions like this may help you to find just the balance you need to address the topic in a lively and engaging way, within a time limit.

Giving a sense of 'why this topic matters'

In other writing, you may have been instructed to provide a 'hook' in the introduction to your essay, to grab the reader's attention and encourage them to read on. There are several common 'attention-grabbing strategies'. For example, you could try starting with:

- a well-known quotation
- some persuasive data
- a familiar reference
- a hypothetical scenario.

22

When used well, these strategies can be effective in engaging your audience.

In this section, however, you will explore a different strategy for grabbing the interest of your audience. If your audience members are going to invest the time in reading your essay, they want to be assured that there is something worthwhile to gain from it. By establishing a *case* for why a topic/issue is important, you will give your readers a reason to continue reading. Otherwise, they might not bother reading your essay because of your failure to present the *prima facie* for reading it.

> **DID YOU KNOW?**
>
> *Prima facie* is an expression from the Latin language meaning 'at first sight'. In modern English, it might be best translated as 'at face value'. In most democratic courts of law – both civil and criminal – significant evidence to support a case must be given at the start. If not, the case may be dismissed.

We will now look at two ways of explaining why your essay topic is valuable, which is also part of developing *context*. Keep in mind that, because of the timed nature of the writing task, this is meant to be a brief part of your introduction.

Past-to-present development

Ask yourself: when did the issue first start and how has it changed since then? How can you illustrate its recent development or the momentum it has gained? You should explain to your audience the growing need to understand this issue. Why now? If you can show how the issue is relevant to them, your readers will be more likely to listen to what you have to say.

> **ACTIVITY 6**
>
> Which of the following past-to-present opening lines is more effective and why? Discuss with a partner.
>
> > Technology has existed since the Neolithic Era when metal tools became widespread, and its progress over time has led to major advances in the way we communicate.
>
> > Once companies like IBM and Apple coined the term 'smartphone' in the early 1990s, it was clear that communication would never be the same again.

When using past-to-present development as your hook, it is important to establish the time frame, but take care in doing this. Students commonly use opening statements such as, 'since the dawn of man' or 'since primitive times' to show how something came to be, but going back this far is probably unnecessary. Instead, think about when the topic became relevant in contemporary society.

Local-to-global significance

Another way to keep the attention of your audience is to emphasise the global significance of your topic. If you can show how this issue matters to everyone, everywhere, members of your audience are more likely to want to know more about it. This strategy also allows you to consider your topic from different viewpoints, where possible, rather than just from your own local perspective.

> **ACTIVITY 7**
>
> Return to the thesis statement you wrote earlier for Activity 5. Using the skills and strategies you have learnt in this section, practise drafting your introduction. When you have finished, look at how you have incorporated the key features of an introduction described earlier in this section.

The body: supporting your thesis

The body of an essay contains information that supports an essay's thesis, or main claim. Specifically, it will add two new important elements to your essay:

- reasons to support the thesis
- **evidence** to support the reasons.

> **KEY TERM**
>
> **Evidence:** the factual information that supports your reasons; evidence may appear in the form of examples, data (i.e. statistics), case studies, expert opinions or logic.

Evidence is especially important because an audience expects proof if they are going to believe someone else's ideas and/or opinions. Meanwhile, 'empty claims' (statements for which there is no evidence) generally do not make a good impression on an audience.

In any argument, evidence can present itself in a number of ways: through exemplification, as data, or in the form of a case study, a testimonial or informed opinions from credible stakeholders (see Chapter 2.2 Section *C Generating ideas for your essay*). Remember that you will be expected to provide evidence to support your points in both the writing and reading comprehension tasks in this course.

KEY SKILLS

> The body (support) paragraphs of an essay contain several reasons and evidence. See Chapter 3.1 to find out what other elements are needed in the body paragraphs of an argumentative essay so that it achieves its purpose to argue.

The way you organise the body of your essay is essential to a logical response. No matter what type of argument you are writing, you should present supporting ideas in a way that is clear and easy to follow. Points should connect logically and follow on from one paragraph to the next.

Activity 8 continues to address the same essay topic as the introductory paragraphs did:

> In today's society, to what extent does the use of accurate grammar still matter?

ACTIVITY 8

Depending on your approach, body paragraphs will serve different purposes. Read the sample paragraphs that follow.

1 Compare the tone and shape in each example.
2 Discuss how each example achieves its aim of taking a position or investigating objectively.

Body paragraph 1: argumentative

Although it is still possible to communicate despite errors, political leaders especially can harm their own credibility by ignoring accuracy in grammar. When former United States President George W. Bush asked of the education system: 'Is our children learning?', the audience certainly knew what he meant, but this slip damaged his position as an authority in the matter; it challenged his credibility as a chief decision-maker for education. Meanwhile, national leaders who use words deliberately can have a lasting impact on their audience. In fact, political activists like Nelson Mandela and orators like Winston Churchill successfully influenced civil movements and wars, respectively, just by using stylised grammar to improve their rhetoric. Clearly, we might be free to relax our grammar as we wish, but our specific attention to it can make a long-lasting difference on the sociopolitical landscape.

Social rights activist and former South African President Nelson Mandela led his country out of apartheid. Mandela is well known for the eloquence of his 1964 speech to the courts in Pretoria, which had accused him of sabotage. His skilful use of words also helped him attract positive publicity for his cause in his autobiography, *Long Walk to Freedom*, which he wrote while still in prison.

Body paragraph 2: discursive

Depending on the medium, accurate grammar may or may not matter when communicating online. If, for example, a student needed to email a professor regarding a homework task, the letter would likely be formal, including a proper greeting, complete sentences and a closing, followed by the writer's full name. If this same individual were writing to a professor via Twitter, however, the circumstances would immediately change: tweets aim to use as few words as possible to convey a message, and they often contain creative abbreviations and spellings. The email might read:

> Dear Professor Marks,
>
> For the weekend homework, do we need to hand in the original article used when writing our summary?
>
> Thank you, in advance, for responding.
>
> Sincerely, John Doe, Period 6 English

Alternatively, a tweet might read:

> @prof_marks, 4 wknd hmwk, do we need 2 include article? Thx! #pd6eng

Both are accepted by the professor as appropriate. Since situations like these are common in the digital era, it appears that accurate grammar still matters, but it is largely dependent upon context.

During Activity 8, you may have noticed the following points in each of the paragraphs:

- The argumentative paragraph uses concrete examples to support the claim being made. However, since the aim is to *convince* the reader, the writer uses contrasting examples and changes tone in order to favour one example over the other.

- In the discursive example, both points of view are mentioned just as they are in the argumentative paragraph. However, the writer does not place emphasis on one side over the other. Instead, the discursive approach uses a more unbiased tone, considering each side equally without yet making a judgement.

The following list may be a useful reference for you:

Key features of a body paragraph

A good body paragraph:

- stays focused on the thesis, without digressing
- makes reasons clear
- offers evidence to support reasons
- uses **transitions** to show relationships among ideas within a paragraph
- uses transitions to connect ideas from one paragraph to the next.

 KEY TERM

Transitions: words or phrases that connect one idea to another, e.g. *however, in addition, likewise, for example, in fact.*

Body paragraphs will be structured differently, depending on the choices you make when planning your essay.

In the next sections, you will learn more about the following key strategies:

- maintaining focus
- using topic sentences and transitions
- linking evidence to claims.

KEY SKILLS

These strategies for writing body paragraphs can also help you respond to other types of writing tasks in this course. Your response to comprehension questions should also demonstrate the qualities of focus and organisation, for example, while making the relevance of your evidence clear.

Maintaining focus

Using key words from the essay question is a useful strategy for getting started and establishing the focus of your essay. Using these terms consistently throughout the body of your essay can help you keep ideas connected. The use of key words can be helpful:

- when introducing a new reason to support the thesis
- after evidence is presented, to connect it back to your thesis.

Avoid overusing these terms, however. Complete Activity 9 to better understand why a fresh expression of ideas is necessary.

ACTIVITY 9

Look at the two different drafts of responses to the essay question:

> How far do you agree with the notion that wordless music is meaningless?

With a partner, discuss whether Student A or Student B uses the words from the question most effectively to maintain focus. Give reasons for your choice.

Student A

Wordless music is very valuable in many circumstances. A popular place where wordless music exists is in movies. Wordless music completes a movie. Without a soundtrack, a movie wouldn't be as intriguing, but it needs to be wordless so you can hear the characters. The first known use of wordless music in a movie surfaced in Paris when the Lumière family played their piano at screenings of their own films at the Grand Café in Boulevard de Capucines in 1985. Within a few months, several London theatres embraced wordless music and incorporated orchestras to add quality to their film. Today, musical directors across the globe are winning awards for their wordless approach to music in movies, thus demonstrating its value and meaning just like music with words.

Student B

Music without words is very valuable in many circumstances. A popular place where wordless music exists is in movies. Background tunes complete a movie; without a soundtrack, a movie wouldn't be as intriguing. The first known use of music in this way surfaced in Paris when the Lumière family played their piano at screenings of their own films at the Grand Café in Boulevard de Capucines in 1985. Within a few months, several London theatres embraced the same approach and incorporated orchestras to add quality to their show. Today, musical directors across the globe are winning awards for instrumental pieces in movies, thus demonstrating both value and meaning in music without lyrics.

Using topic sentences and transitions

Topic sentences have an important purpose – to guide the reader through the main points of the essay.

In your topic sentences you should:

- clearly state your reasons
- use transitions to show how your ideas relate.

Each time you introduce a new reason to support your thesis, the topic sentence should be used to make this clear to the reader. Without a signal, the audience may lose their way and miss the connection to your next point.

 KEY TERM

Topic sentence: a sentence that identifies the main idea of the paragraph.

Topic sentences should also use transitions to connect your thoughts. These transitions can be used to indicate:

- comparison/contrast
- cause/effect
- conclusion.

The following table provides lists of transitional words and phrases that are useful for indicating relationships between ideas.

Exemplification	Addition/ similarity	Contrast/ limitation	Emphasis/ intensification	Concession	Qualification
in particular	in addition	yet	indeed	but even so	almost
specifically	additionally	however	of course	however	never
as an illustration	furthermore	in contrast	without doubt	but still	always
another key point	moreover	on the other hand	in fact	nevertheless	sometimes
the most compelling evidence	besides	on the contrary	undoubtedly	nonetheless	occasionally
notably	in similar fashion	at the same time	by all means	though/although	in part
including	likewise	in spite of / despite	certainly	notwithstanding	maybe
such as	also	even so	surely	be this as it may	frequently
namely	similarly	in reality	more importantly	admittedly	rarely
in fact	equally important	but still	above all else	albeit	although
to demonstrate	coupled with	unlike	besides	despite	perhaps
to explain	not only … but also	while	truly	in spite of	nearly
for instance	comparatively	albeit	remarkably	this	often
for example		even though / although	regrettably	granted	likely
considering		alternatively		regardless of	
		regardless			
		whereas			
		conversely			

When used appropriately, transitions act as effective signposts for the reader. If they are overused, however, they can become a distraction. One way to avoid the overuse of transitions is to make them invisible. Instead of relying on words like those in the list above, **seamless transitions** (i.e. smooth transitions without obvious connecting words) use the concepts within the essay itself as a link from one thought to another. This is demonstrated in the activity that follows.

KEY TERM

Seamless transition: a movement from one idea to another without the use of standard transitional words or phrases (examples of standard transitional words and phrases are *in addition, furthermore, meanwhile*).

ACTIVITY 10

Read the first essay in Chapter 2.1 Section *D Using expository skills in an argument*, which concerns the purpose of cartoons. In the topic sentence of each body paragraph, identify the concepts the writer uses to seamlessly transition from the ideas in one support paragraph to the next. Be prepared to share your observations with the class.

Linking evidence to claims

No matter what style of essay you are writing, the body paragraphs should always contain a combination of reasons and evidence. Evidence is only relevant, however, if it has a clear connection to the main claim, or thesis. The best way to make this connection for the readers is by talking them through it. This commentary is called 'output'.

KEY SKILLS

Look back to Chapter 1.1 for a review of 'input' and 'output'.

'Output' can improve your response because it helps you to justify that your ideas are relevant. Keep in mind, though, that you should not just put a phrase like '… and this is why X is relevant to Y' at the end of each paragraph. This is not usually enough to make the connection clear. Your commentary needs to be point-specific in order to be meaningful.

Here are some questions to keep in mind that will help you to link evidence to your point:

- Why is this information important? Why does it matter in light of the question?
- What does this evidence/example imply?
- What are the consequences of thinking this way or looking at a topic/issue this way?
- You have just described what something is like, or how you see it, but *why* is it like that?
- You have just said that something happens – so *how* or *why* does it happen? How does it come to be the way it is?
- How is this idea related to the reason you gave in support of your thesis?
- Does it truly support your thesis? If so, how does it do that despite what others might think?

KEY SKILLS

Chapter 3.1 will go into greater depth on linking claims, reasons and evidence.

The following list may be helpful in linking your evidence to your reasons and/or thesis:

Words and phrases for linking evidence to your point		
confirms	affirms	indicates
attests to	is congruent to	relates
connects	correlates	associates
shows	is evidence of	signifies
demonstrates	corroborates	testifies
pertains to	applies	aligns
allies with	equates to/with	clarifies
exhibits	is evidenced in	

ACTIVITY 11

Return to the introduction you wrote earlier in this chapter. Using the strategies you have learnt in this section, draft one or two body paragraphs to follow your introduction. Refer back to the key features of a body paragraph earlier in this section.

The conclusion

Despite the common assumption, the conclusion of your essay is much more than a re-statement of your points. Instead, it is an evaluation of the evidence you have presented. The insights you offer demonstrate your ability to think critically.

The conclusion is usually one paragraph in shorter essays like the ones you will write in this course; however, if complex solutions are presented, it can extend to more than one paragraph. The following list may be a useful reference for you:

Key features of a conclusion

A good conclusion:

- signals the end of the essay
- restates your thesis
- draws conclusions about the issue based on the evidence you presented
- offers fresh new ideas, insights or alternate ways of thinking as a result of the input you shared

A strong conclusion may also:

- consider implications and consequences of accepting or denying your position
- offer solutions and/or make value-based judgements when appropriate.

TIP

While it is acceptable to use transitions like 'in conclusion' or 'to summarise', there are other, more subtle ways to signal closure in the final paragraph(s) of your essay. Try experimenting with the following alternatives:

- clearly
- evidently
- apparently
- therefore
- it appears that
- the evidence seems to suggest
- after considering
- a closer look reveals.

The conclusions you draw offer your perspective after careful analysis of the issue, so your personal view should be evident. However, be careful not to let personal biases dominate. If your insights aren't a **reflection** of the evidence, they may not be **relevant**! No matter how you feel (emotionally) about the issue by essay's end, take care to provide a *logical* response to the information you shared.

 KEY TERMS

Reflection: a thought, idea or opinion formed after careful consideration of information or experience.

Relevant: directly related to the issue being discussed.

Activity 12 will help you understand the importance of drawing relevant, evidence-based conclusions.

ACTIVITY 12

1   Review the list of evidence below in response to the following essay prompt:

> How far do you agree with the idea that wordless music is meaningless?

2   Based on the evidence and your own perspective, what kind of conclusion would you draw about wordless music? Take some time to discuss this with a partner or with the whole class.

Evidence

1   Ludwig Van Beethoven's music has affected the lives of many people for over 200 years; pieces like *Für Elise*, the 'Moonlight' Piano Sonata and the Fifth Symphony are all in the top 100 masterpieces of classical music today, yet they contain no words.

2   Background music in movies is essential for building intense or dramatic scenes, hinting at character or other instances of **foreshadowing**, and developing emotion in the audience; the Golden Globe Awards offer a category for 'best instrumental'.

3   Country music is known for its clever storytelling; without words, songs such as Patsy Cline's 'I Fall to Pieces' would not be as effective in demonstrating her feelings of sadness.

4   Rhythmic beats of tribal Africa are often used in religious ceremonies (e.g. traditional drumming in Ghana).

5   Rap music is known for its frank and open style of storytelling; songs often reveal a hard and painful life that not everyone experiences.

6   According to the Center for New Discoveries in Learning in California, USA, listening to wordless music with 60 beats per minute (e.g. music by Mozart) can increase learning potential; activities that activate both the left and right sides of the brain, such as playing an instrument, can make the brain more capable of processing information.

 KEY TERM

foreshadowing: a literary device in which the writer hints at what is going to happen, so that the reader can predict what is to come.

Beethoven wrote some of the most iconic and popular music in the Western musical tradition, but much of it does not use any words.

Passing judgement

Whether you write your essay using an argumentative approach or a discursive one, you will need to have offered a clear perspective on the issue by the conclusion. Perhaps you are wondering, however: *if a discursive essay is supposed to explore both sides of the issue objectively, why would it choose one side in the end?*

A writer might not yet have a firm perspective on an issue at the start of this kind of essay. However, after genuinely exploring the issues in the body paragraphs, the discursive writer has an obligation to the audience to make a decision in the closing paragraph. In fact, your audience *expects* you to give your own evidence-based opinion at the end because it helps them challenge or validate their own. If you do not offer your perspective, you may risk your credibility as a writer. In addition, the essay task requires you to write an argument, and arguments require position-taking at some point.

Until you arrive at that judgement, however, the tone of your conclusion will continue to reflect your initial approach. If you broach the topic objectively to start, for example, your conclusion will not take on a biased tone until you have made your decision. Activity 13 will help you to better understand the subtle difference between conclusions from different types of arguments.

> **ACTIVITY 13**
>
> Read the two sample conclusions, which address the question:
>
> > In today's society, to what extent does the use of accurate grammar still matter?
>
> With a partner, discuss the similarities and differences between them.

Conclusion 1: argumentative

Clearly, there is a link between good grammar skills and professionalism. Good grammar still plays an important role in how we build relationships and how we present ourselves to others, particularly in the business world. Although it may be true that our attitude toward grammar is changing because of technological progress, a professional approach to the way we speak is still expected. And while it is true that speech can depend on context, there is no denying that the words we use communicate our level of respect for our audience. Therefore, good grammar should be used in every situation because good grammar is certainly good for business.

Conclusion 2: discursive

Clearly, the ways we communicate with one another will continue to evolve in the digital era, and the traditional rules of grammar are bending with each turn we take. Accurate grammar can be a powerful tool in formal contexts, such as on the political stage or in the professional world, and it establishes our credibility to an audience that is sometimes sceptical. However, in a world where texting and abbreviation are the norm, our language is not necessarily wrong if grammatically inaccurate. It therefore appears that to keep up with the present, where we are willing to sacrifice form for content, grammatical accuracy shouldn't matter as much today as it traditionally has in the past.

29

KEY SKILL

You can find further help on how to write an effective conclusion in Chapters 3.1 and 3.2.

Review of key elements

Now that you have been introduced to the foundational elements of an essay, it is useful to look at a complete sample essay to see how all these elements contribute to the whole. By deconstructing the elements of an essay, you will be able to offer more quality feedback to your peers and it will eventually help you to self-evaluate your own work. Your ability to identify the key elements of an essay will enable you to share suggestions for revision that stretch beyond grammatical considerations.

ACTIVITY 14

Turn to Chapter 2.1 Section *D Using expository skills in an argument* and locate the same essay you read for Activity 10 in this chapter, which discusses the purpose behind cartoons. Make a copy of the essay and complete the following tasks using multi-coloured highlighters/pens (or an alternative set of annotations) and the checklist below.

1 Identify the basic elements of an essay.
2 Consider what the essay does well and where it could be improved.
3 Note your observations in the margin.

Be prepared to share your observations with your teacher and the class.

Checklist

Introduction:
☐ Introduce topic (blue)
☐ Provide context (use brackets to indicate)
☐ Define scope / interpret key terms (green)
☐ Thesis (yellow)

Body:
☐ Use key words from the question (yellow)
☐ Provide reasons and explanation (pink)
☐ Provide evidence to support reasons (orange)
☐ Use transitions to link ideas (purple, use pink arrows to indicate seamless ones)
☐ Connect evidence back to reason and/or claim (black arrows)

Conclusion:
☐ Signal ending (purple)
☐ Freshly restate thesis (yellow)
☐ Offer new insights based on evidence presented (underline)
☐ Look to the future and consider consequences (indicate with asterisks)
☐ Provide closure (use brackets to indicate)

G Benefits of critical reading

Think back to the wide-ranging list of possible essay topics for the Cambridge International AS Level English General Paper in Chapter 1.1 Section *D Syllabus outline*. There may have been some that you found interesting, but there were probably others that you did not. Ask yourself why you did not like some of the topics.

For example, if you were uninspired by a subject like *Rural and urban concerns*, perhaps this is because you do not know very much about it. Reading as widely as possible will play a crucial role in helping you build your knowledge. The more you read, the more choice you give yourself when selecting essay questions.

Seeing how others share their ideas in written texts can help you communicate your own. This combination of knowledge and 'know-how' (skills) will help you write successful and engaging essays. Being a critical reader is therefore an important step to becoming a critical writer.

TIP

When a question asks for an answer 'in your own words', you are expected to use the information in the material to develop ideas for your answer. However, your answer should avoid including any quotations from the material.

Read the article 'Why we must save dying tongues', which is about the danger of losing minority languages. After reading the article, answer the exam-style questions.

Why do you think minority languages are worth saving?

WHY WE MUST SAVE DYING TONGUES

Over the past century alone, around 400 languages – about one every three months – have gone extinct, and most linguists estimate that 50% of the world's remaining 6,500 languages will be gone by the end of this century. Today, the top ten languages in the world claim around half of the world's population. Can language diversity be preserved, or are we on a path to becoming a monolingual species?

Since there are so many imperiled languages, it's impossible to label just one as the rarest or most endangered, but at least 100 around the world have only a handful of speakers – from Ainu in Japan to Yaghan in Chile. It can be difficult to find people who speak these languages, too.

One such case is Marie Smith Jones, who passed away in Alaska in 2008, taking the Eyak language with her. Or, in the case of the pre-Columbian Mexican language Ayapaneco, the last two surviving speakers refused to talk to each other for years. Without practice, even a native language will begin to degrade in the speaker's mind.

Languages usually reach the point of crisis after they are displaced by a socially, politically and economically dominant one, as linguists describe it. In this scenario, the majority speaks another language – English, Mandarin, Swahili – so speaking that language is key to accessing jobs, education and opportunities. Sometimes, especially in immigrant communities, parents will decide not to teach their children their heritage language, perceiving it as a potential hindrance to their success in life.

Endangered tongues

For these reasons and others, languages are dying all over the world. Unesco's *Atlas of the World's Languages in Danger* lists 576 as critically endangered. The highest numbers occur in the Americas. 'I would say that virtually all the [minority] languages in the US and Canada are endangered,' says Peter Austin, a professor of Field Linguistics at the University of London. 'Even a language like Navajo, with thousands of speakers, falls into that category because very few children are learning it.'

If measured in proportion to population, however, then Australia holds the world record for endangered languages. When Europeans first arrived there, 300 aboriginal languages were spoken around the country. Since then, 100 or so have gone extinct, and linguists regard 95% of the remaining ones as being on their last legs. Just a dozen of the original 300 are still being taught to children.

But does it matter whether a seemingly obscure language spoken by a few people in one isolated corner of the world goes out of existence?

Some people argue that language loss, like species loss, is simply a fact of life on an ever-evolving planet. But there are many counterarguments. According to Mark Turin, an anthropologist and linguist at Yale University, 'We spend huge amounts of money protecting species and biodiversity, so why … shouldn't [language] be similarly nourished and protected?'

What's more, languages are conduits of human heritage. Writing is a relatively recent development in our history (written systems currently exist for only about one-third of the world's languages), so language itself is often the only way to convey a community's songs, stories and poems. *The Iliad* was an oral story before it was written, as was *The Odyssey*. 'How many other traditions are out there in the world that we'll never know about because no one recorded them before the language disappeared?' Austin says. Without language, cultures themselves might teeter, or even disappear.

Wealth of wisdom

Minority languages contain an accumulated body of knowledge, including geography,

85 zoology, mathematics, navigation, astronomy, pharmacology, botany, meteorology and more. In the case of Cherokee, that language was born of thousands of years spent inhabiting the southern Appalachia Mountains. Cherokee

90 words exist for every last berry, stem, frond and toadstool in the region, and those names also convey what kind of properties that object might have – whether it's edible, poisonous or has some medicinal value. 'No culture has a monopoly on human genius, [so] we never

95 know where the next brilliant idea may come from … we lose ancient knowledge if we lose languages.'

Finally, languages are ways of interpreting the world; different languages provide unique ways

100 to think and problem-solve. Because of this, they can provide insight into neurology, psychology and the linguistic capacities of our species. For instance, speakers of Cherokee can use different suffixes to indicate whether a noun is toward or

away from them; uphill or downhill. It's a much 105 more precise way of dealing with the world than English. 'There's a misconception that these languages are simple just because many are unwritten,' Turin says. 'But most have an incredibly complex grammatical system that far 110 exceeds that of English.'

Scramble to save

For all of these reasons, linguists are scrambling to document and archive the diversity of quickly disappearing languages. Their efforts include 115 making dictionaries, recording histories and traditions, and translating oral stories.

But as a Cherokee elder notes: 'It's all well and good that y'all want to do this, but remember, they didn't take it away overnight, and you're not 120 going to get it back overnight.'

Abridged and adapted from an article by Rachel Nuwer, BBC, June 2014

TIP
Consider the number of marks shown in brackets after each question below. This will help you decide how long each response should be.

TIP
Prose comprehension texts usually include line numbers in the margin, and questions may direct you to specific parts of the text using these line numbers.

EXAM-STYLE QUESTIONS 1

This activity will introduce you to the types of comprehension questions you will meet in this course. Answer questions **1–5**.

1 From the text, give two reasons why languages are lost. **[2]**

2 In no more than 50 of your own words, summarise Rachel Nuwer's arguments for wanting to preserve dying languages. **[5]**

3 Why do you think parents decide not to teach their children their heritage language? In your own words, explain why families are likely to perceive it as a hindrance (line 34). **[4]**

4 In your own opinion, what do you think is the most important reason why we should save dying languages? Using evidence from the text and your knowledge of the present day, justify your answer. **[8]**

5 (i) Explain the meanings of the following words as they are used in the text. You can write your answer as a single word or a short phrase. **[3]**

imperiled (line 11)

degrade (line 23)

teeter (line 80)

(ii) Use the words in three **separate** sentences to illustrate their meanings as used in the text. Your sentence content should stand apart from the subject matter of the text. **[3]**

Total marks: 25

KEY SKILLS

Look ahead to Chapter 1.3 to learn more about the other type of comprehension questions you will meet in the course, which require you to use *logical reasoning* to show your understanding.

H Practising what you have learnt

Now you have worked through this chapter and considered each part of the writing process, it is time to write your own essay.

This essay will help you and your teacher to assess the strengths and weaknesses of your writing. You can return to this essay later in the course to help you assess your progress.

EXAM-STYLE QUESTIONS 2

Read the list of essay questions and decide which topic area you would like to write about. Then write an essay that demonstrates an understanding of the basic essay elements outlined in this chapter. You may use knowledge gained from this chapter and/or you can use your own knowledge to support your ideas.

Remember to take into account:

- purpose
- audience
- register.

You should also remember to think carefully about:

- what the question is asking
- what specific knowledge or information you need to support your ideas or views
- the kind of approach you need to take in order to effectively express the ideas you have in mind.

You have 1 hour 15 minutes to draft your essay. Don't forget to allow yourself time at the beginning to generate and plan your ideas, and at the end to check your work for errors.

Essay questions

1 To what extent does modern communication bring us together? **[30]**

2 'Schools should be teaching computer coding, not handwriting.' What is your view? **[30]**

3 To what extent is social media the preferred mode of communication in today's society? **[30]**

4 Which do you prefer and why: the written or spoken word? **[30]**

5 Argue the benefits of digital communication against more traditional methods. **[30]**

6 In advertising, how valid is it to say that visual images do more to communicate than words? **[30]**

7 'Today's era can be explained in two words: digital overload.' What is your view? **[30]**

8 Explain and evaluate the appeal of medical technology as it applies to your society. **[30]**

9 'We are as we speak.' Discuss this view. **[30]**

10 How far would you agree that dance is a form of communication? **[30]**

ACTIVITY 15

Swap essays with a partner. Using the Criteria for assessing an essay in Chapter 1.1 Section *E Expectations and assessment*, decide whether your partner's essay is:

- effective
- adequate
- developing.

Point out specific examples that justify your decision.

Summary

Key points to remember from this chapter:

- When you communicate, it is important to consider the *purpose* of your message and who your intended *audience* is. This will help you decide whether to use a *formal* or *informal* communication style.

- In this course, you will be writing for an academic purpose. You should therefore always use an appropriate *formal* style and tone of communication in order to be taken seriously by your audience.

- It is important to read the question carefully and consider every word. If you understand the task clearly, you will write a more focused response.

- The reading activities in your course will help you develop stronger writing skills.

- Understanding the structure of an essay and its essential components will help you write a successful response.

- Essay questions often contain certain terms (e.g. command words) which can help you understand the nature of the task.

- Command words help you understand what is expected of you in your response, and signal words can also be a helpful guide.

Chapter 1.3
Reading comprehension

How far do you agree that celebrities influence society in a positive way?
This chapter will explore issues associated with *Celebrity culture*.

Learning objectives

In this chapter, you will learn how to:

- observe the work of other writers to help improve your own writing
- set a purpose for your reading
- use close reading and other strategies
- apply critical comprehension skills to text
- demonstrate reading comprehension through both logical reasoning and analysis of prose.

A Introduction

The 17th-century English poet and playwright Ben Jonson once wrote:

> For a man to write well, there are required three necessaries, – to read the best authors, observe the best speakers, and much exercise of his own style …
> It is fit for the beginner and learner to study others and the best. For the mind and memory are more sharply exercised in comprehending another man's things than our own …
>
> *From* Timber, or Discoveries Made upon Men and Matter

Re-read Jonson's words carefully. What is he saying?

Jonson, who was a contemporary of Shakespeare, believed that if a writer wants to improve, 'it is important to observe the work of others and practice often'. Following this advice, this course will help you to improve your writing skills by reading the work of other writers.

If you can understand what you read, then you will be able to:

- use the knowledge you have gained to support your own ideas
- apply the structure and style that others use to your own writing.

B Setting a purpose for your reading

When you begin watching a movie, the first 15 minutes are critical. They determine whether you will continue watching or give up and watch something else. If you have seen the movie trailer (the one- to two-minute preview of the storyline), you are more likely to watch the whole movie because the preview gives you an idea of what to expect (i.e. the genre, who the main characters are, their motivations, high points in the plot, etc.). In highlighting the movie's key features, a trailer establishes a purpose for you to watch more!

Reading is no different. Without a purpose, you can quickly lose interest, and your mind may wander to the many other things competing for your attention. If you set goals for your reading, you are more likely to read through to the end.

The first step in setting a purpose for reading is to scan the text to identify its main features. This will help you to know

what to expect (rather like a movie trailer). During this process, make a note of features such as:

- headings
- sub-headings
- images or graphics
- captions
- footnotes.

Once you have scanned the text for its main features, start thinking about the following questions, which give you a purpose for reading the text. Keep these questions in mind to keep you focused as you read.

Purpose-setting questions

Questions to consider *before* you begin reading:

- What is the topic of the text?
- When was it written?
- What issue(s) will be addressed?
- What conclusion(s) might the author reach about the issue(s)?

Questions to consider *during* reading:

- What reasons does the author give for their statements or belief?
- Is the author using facts, theory, opinions or faith? Remember:
  - *Facts* can be proved.
  - *Theory* needs to be proved and should not be confused with fact.
  - *Opinions* may or may not be based on strong reasoning.
  - *Faith* does not need to be proved, by its nature.
- Has the author used neutral or emotive words (words which express feelings)? When reading critically, you should look beyond the language to see if the *reasons* are clear.
- What seems to be the writer's intellectual position (e.g. conservative, liberal, Marxist, nationalist, feminist)?
- What assumptions does it make?

Questions to consider *after* reading:

- What does the text leave out? Whose perspective, experiences and attitudes are *not* considered?
- Do you accept the arguments made by the author? Why / Why not?

Questions adapted from the University of Manchester's Faculty of Humanities Study Skills website

---

ACTIVITY 1

Choose an article in this coursebook. If possible, choose one about a topic that you are unfamiliar with or that would not normally interest you. Apply the 'Purpose-setting questions' to the article and make notes. These kinds of questions can help to increase your interest and engagement with the text, because you are thinking *critically* about the material.

C Strategies for close reading

What makes a 'good' reader? Speed is usually associated with success when it comes to reading. When processing difficult text for comprehension, however, it is quite the opposite. You are more likely to understand difficult text if you read with a close and critical eye, sometimes called **close-reading**.

 KEY TERM

Close-reading: a thoughtful, critical analysis of a text, which focuses on both structure and meaning to develop a deep, precise understanding.

Since you have limited time available in class, you might feel under pressure to speed-read a text. In an exam situation where results are very important, you can feel especially pressured to read quickly. You may rush through the reading process in order to start writing and to avoid missing out on marks.

But just as you need to understand an essay question before you begin writing your answer, you also need to understand the reading material before you can answer questions about it! Several close-reading strategies can help you read and understand better, and respond more effectively to the questions that follow. These strategies are explained in the following sections.

Reading actively to build comprehension

Reading text carefully may seem to slow you down, but a critical approach can help you better comprehend what you are reading. If you casually skim-read information, this will not be enough for you to properly understand

the meaning of the material. It may also make it more difficult to produce an informed and effective response to what you have read.

Instead, interacting directly with the material can help you identify specific elements of the text that you might otherwise not notice. If you mark the text with annotations such as circling, underlining or even writing a note in the margin occasionally, you are drawing attention to important information. Slowing down the process also helps you to see patterns, which can lead to new ideas and critical insights.

Reading *actively* can help you understand the text on a deeper level. It will help you engage with the text more effectively than just reading passively. Making notes as you read can help keep you focused while reading particularly long texts. If you interact with the material in this way, you are more likely to connect ideas within the text and to link these with your own experiences.

As you read, you could write down:

- notes to explain meaning
- synonyms for unfamiliar words
- challenges to opinions that are expressed
- examples to support points that are made
- connections to your own experiences or wider knowledge
- questions about the text.

This kind of intellectual engagement can help you develop your critical thinking skills and deepen your appreciation for the issues that are explored. The more you understand a topic, the more effectively you will be able to respond to it.

Making connections

Reading text closely and carefully gives you time to think about how the ideas within the text connect. It can also help you see how these ideas or examples connect with your own experiences or with those of society as a whole. Being able to apply the ideas from a text to your own life and experience is one way of making information more memorable. This is a key skill for a critical thinker.

ACTIVITY 2

Actively read the following article about an Olympic athlete's impact on the politics of his country. Interact with the text by making connections to the events described. How can you relate your own knowledge and/or experiences to his story? To stimulate these connections, ask yourself:

1   Have you seen a situation similar to this before, either in your own country or abroad?

2   Is this event opposite or contradictory to something else that you have read about or experienced personally? What surprises you?

3   Have you ever personally experienced this?

4   Have people in your society ever experienced this?

In addition to connecting the text with your own knowledge and experiences, make additional notes and/or annotations such as the ones suggested in the bulleted list offered in this section. Then answer the comprehension questions in Activity 3.

An Ethiopian runner makes a brave gesture of anti-government protest at the Olympic finish

Defying Olympic rules and risking the **wrath** of his country's government, Ethiopian runner Feyisa Lilesa made a political gesture in support of the Oromo people after competing in a marathon during
5   the last weekend of the Olympic Games in Brazil.

Lilesa, who won a silver medal, crossed his arms to make an 'X' at the finish line and during medal presentation. The sign is used by the Oromo people and their supporters in their protests against their
10   repression by the Ethiopian government.

The International Olympic Committee, however, bans political protests. Tommie Smith and John Carlos, for example, two black athletes from the United States, were famously expelled after they did a black power
15   salute in the 1968 Games.

Lilesa, who told reporters that if he returns to Ethiopia he would be killed, plans to seek asylum in Brazil, the US or Kenya.

The Oromo people have been protesting since
20   November 2015. The protest in Oromia, Ethiopia's largest administrative region, started when students asked the government to stop its plan to expand the capital city Addis Ababa into Oromia's surrounding farm lands. The students believe that the controversial
25   expansion would result in mass **evictions** of farmers mostly from the Oromo ethnic group.

The government argued the plan was meant only to facilitate the development of infrastructure such as transportation, utilities and recreation centres.

30 Although the government has scrapped the plan to expand Addis Ababa, the protesters are demanding action on the greater questions of self-rule, freedom and identity. For example, the students want Oromo to be made a federal language. Oromo, the language 35 of the Oromo people, is the most widely spoken language in Ethiopia and the fourth largest African language. However, it is not the working language of the federal government.

Both Oromia and Amhara regions are challenging the 40 dominance of the Tigray ethnic group in Ethiopia's politics. The Tigray make up 6% of the population, but have an overwhelming hold on power in the country, while the Oromos, who are the country's largest ethnic group, representing 34%, and the Amharas at 45 27%, have very little representation in key government positions.

Dissent, both physical and virtual, is not tolerated in Ethiopia. Early this month, security forces used live bullets to disperse protesters in Oromoa and 50 Amhara, another administrative region, killing about 100 protesters, according to news sites and social media reports.

On April 25, 2014, nine bloggers and journalists were arrested in Ethiopia on accusations of 'inciting public 55 disorder via social media' and 'receiving support from a foreign government'. The detainees had all worked with Zone9, a collective blog that **fostered** political debate and discussion.

After Lilesa made headlines with his gesture, one Facebook user observed that the Olympics have 60 exposed two things about the state of politics in Ethiopia: **repression** and favouritism.

Given Lilesa's decision not to return home for fear of his life, Ethiopians online raised US$54,433 in less than 24 hours to help him seek asylum. 65

The Ethiopian government officially says the runner will not be prosecuted over his protest gesture but 'will be conferred a heroic welcome along with his team members'.

Endalk, an Ethiopian free speech advocate in 70 exile and a Global Voices author, reacted to the government's statement by saying (on social media): *Ethiopian gov't is saying please come home so that we will torture you, nothing else #oromoprotests.* 75

While the Ethiopian government spokesperson congratulated Lilesa, state TV did not show footage of him at the finish line.

Abridged from an article by Ndesanjo Macha in De Birhan, August 2016

ARTICLE GLOSSARY

wrath: anger

evictions: sending people away from their homes or land

dissent: expressing disagreement

fostered: encouraged

repression: controlling people by force

ACTIVITY 3

Answer the comprehension questions 1–5.

1 Give two reasons why Feyisa Lilesa may be punished for his gesture at the Olympics. **[2]**

2 In your own words, explain why the Oromo people are protesting. **[3]**

3 If the average cost of living in the United States is $28 458 per year, explain why it might be a good idea for Feyisa to seek asylum there. Use evidence from the text to justify your response. **[2]**

4 What is the tone of Endalk's comment on social media (lines 73–75)? Justify your answer. **[3]**

5 Re-read the last paragraph of the text (lines 76–78). How do the words and actions of the Ethiopian government seem to conflict? **[4]**

Re-reading

In this course, you will be asked to read challenging material. When you come across a particularly challenging section, there are three steps you can take to help you understand it:

1 Read ahead – the text will probably offer further information to clarify what you do not understand.

2 Re-read the challenging section a second time, now that you have read ahead for more information.

3 Make a note in the margin to clarify or simplify the section of text, once you understand it better.

Notes like these can easily provide a quick reference that you can return to when you begin drafting your responses to comprehension questions. Also, careful note-taking is characteristic of a critical reader and thinker. This not only helps you meet the needs of this course, but can also help you develop the skills and qualities which are required at university level.

'Chunking' information

When you are dealing with longer texts, it can be useful to break down the information into smaller, more digestible chunks. A simple way of doing this is to divide the text into three sections: beginning, middle and end. Consider each section, one at a time, before attempting to process the message of the entire article. As you read each section, ask yourself:

- What has happened? Who or what was involved?
- How is the information structured?
- How does it link up with what comes before it?
- Where is it likely to lead next?

Once you understand the content of these smaller sections, you can put these ideas together to help you see the bigger picture and the purpose of the article.

ACTIVITY 4

Practise breaking down longer texts into sections or chunks which are easier to manage. Read the article 'Bollywood influence on fashion trends waning?', which is about the influence of celebrity culture on fashion. For each section, identify:

- 'what it *says*' (i.e. the *main point or idea being expressed*)
- 'what it *does*' (i.e. the function of the section in the whole structure of the article, e.g. gives background information, contains a view that opposes the one in the previous section, etc.).

TIP

Titles of large works, such as books and films, are often indicated by using italics. Smaller works, like poems, titles of articles or chapter titles, are indicated by using quotation marks. The text about Bollywood will mention several Indian film titles, which are easy to identify in this way.

Bollywood influence on fashion trends waning?

Whether it is Madhubala's Anarkali look in *Mughal-e-Azam* or Kareena Kapoor's T-shirt and **salwar combo** in *Jab We Met*, Bollywood has inspired fashion trends down the ages. But that influence seems to be **waning** due to a variety of reasons, including greater exposure to the West and the move towards more realistic cinema, say designers.

There is also the constant fear of criticism, which has restricted filmmakers from attempting to set fashion trends.

According to veteran designer Ritu Kumar, people were earlier not so exposed to fashion. So every new and unique garment seen on the big screen set a trend. This is no longer the case.

'Initially, costumes, which were not everyday wear for the normal population, did cause a stir and led to fashion influences as the market was

To what extent does culture influence fashion?

starved of such designer wear. But this has largely changed,' says Kumar, who is yet to design for a Bollywood film.

Kumar, who designed the costumes for Deepa Mehta's *Midnight's Children*, hopes the scenario improves, stating, 'The industry still seems to design for individuals. When more **holistic** designing for a complete film is taken up, the fashion scene in India will mature further.'

In the past, Bollywood has given memorable styles to **the masses**. Remember the 1960 period drama *Mughal-e-Azam* when actress Madhubala, playing the slave-girl character Anarkali, **sported** long flowing **kurtas and churidars**? Almost five decades later, the same character is responsible for the 'Anarkali **kameez**', which is the current **rage**, with everybody from homemakers to hip Bollywood actresses wearing it.

In 1994, Madhuri Dixit **left a mark** with her green embroidered **choli** paired with a white **lehnga** and a purple embroidered **sari** in *Hum Aapke Hain Koun*. Women **lapped up** the styles at family weddings. There are so many similar instances. There were Rani Mukerji's *Bunty Aur Babli* suits and then the sari, of course, **redefined** over and over again with movies like *Chandni*, *Main Hoon Naa* and *Dostana*.

But new trends are now few and far between.

'The main reason for this is that a lot of stylists of celebrities or films are playing safe with **ongoing** trends in fashion. They are primarily using outfits which are in fashion, avoiding the risk of fashion **faux pas**. Thus they are unable to create a new trend,' says designer Pria Kataaria Puri.

'Earlier, film costumes were not designed according to what everyone was wearing or according to international trends but were rather 'filmy' or **outlandish**, rule breaking; and if they worked well, it became a new trend. To create a style, one has to create costumes that are unusual,' she adds.

Costume designer Payal Saluja, who has worked on Vishal Bhardwaj's *Maqbool*, *Ishqiya*, *Saat Khoon Maaf* and now *Matru Ki Bijlee Ka Mandola*, says the move towards realistic filmmaking in Bollywood has changed the scene.

'Stories are becoming real and connectable for the audience these days. So, the clothes also need to be **in tandem**. Clothes should never be stronger than the character because then the viewer will only remember the clothes. So it is first important to think of blending costumes into the narrative rather than create fashion trends,' says Saluja.

According to designer duo Meera and Muzaffar Ali, one of the leading names in the world of fashion, 'Costumes (today) are left to stars' **whims** and their **sycophant** designers and colours that suit a cameraman.'

'Anything and everything in Bollywood can set a trend amidst mindless people who know no better. What concerns me is the style of the film,' says Muzaffar Ali, director of the classic *Umrao Jaan*.

His wife Meera adds: 'There were some **yesteryear** stars who had a body language which made what they wore extremely attractive. They somehow caught the fancy of the audience by getting the colour and mood right … women had a story on their face and they knew how to tell it more effectively through their performance.'

Adapted from an article in India Today, *November 2012*

ARTICLE GLOSSARY

salwar: loose trousers (typically worn by women in South Asia)

combo: combination

waning: decreasing

holistic: taken as a whole

the masses: the ordinary people

sported: wore (in a way that draws attention)

kurtas and churidars: South Asian-style clothing

kameez: South Asian-style long shirt

rage: something which is extremely popular but only for a short time

left a mark: made an impression

choli, lehnga, sari: South Asian-style clothing

lapped up: accepted with enthusiasm

redefined: interpreted in a new way

ongoing: continuing

faux pas: embarrassing mistake in social manners

outlandish: very strange

in tandem: in the same way, together

whim: sudden or unusual wish

sycophant: acting to try to please somebody in order to gain advantage for yourself

yesteryear: from the recent past

Challenging ideas and assumptions

You have probably heard this advice before: *don't believe everything you read*. Why do you think this age-old advice still stands? In today's world, online media allows anyone to publish information. For this reason, you can never be sure that what you are reading is entirely accurate, objective or unbiased. One person cannot be the sole authority on a subject. His or her voice is only one perspective, shaped by circumstance, and therefore likely to emphasise or omit information depending on those experiences.

Therefore, if you want to fully comprehend a reading text, it is important that you learn to challenge the assumptions and perspectives of other writers when necessary. You can do this by asking yourself questions such as:

- Do you believe what the writer believes? Should you?
- How or why is the writer in a position to know?
- Would anyone else disagree with their view? On what basis?
- What could be missing from the discussion that the writer presents? What does the discussion fail to consider?

Readers engage with text on a critical level when they take time to challenge the ideas and assumptions presented. This is a more advanced skill, so you will practise and develop this later in the course (see for example Chapter 2.1 Section *C Generating ideas for your essay*).

D Essential reading comprehension skills

One of the aims of this course is to improve your reading comprehension skills. Some of the skills you will need to practise are listed here, along with the syllabus objectives (see Chapter 1.1).

Understanding	• determining the main idea of a piece of text • identifying key details • determining the author's purpose • identifying tone and emotion

Applying	• selecting relevant text evidence • connecting informational text with prior knowledge • explaining prose in your own words to show comprehension • summarising information
Analysing	• considering perspective • using text to make inferences • making comparisons • considering the role and effect of words and phrases in context
Evaluating	• using evidence to pass judgement • using outside knowledge to pass judgement
Communicating	• using logical reasoning to argue a point • write responses that are clear and cohesive

To help you understand how each of these comprehension skills are assessed, read the following texts and do the activity which follows them. The texts consist of a series of interdepartmental memos from a law firm. The emails are about legal action which is to be taken against a local celebrity.

Email 1

TO: info@iswaranatlaw.com
FROM: PR Rep for Cooper Sands
SUBJECT: (Untitled)

Greetings,

I am contacting you because my client, Cooper Sands, has recently fallen into unfortunate circumstances. As you may know, Mr Sands is the lead vocalist for the internationally popular punk band, Sights and Sands. Following their concert last weekend, Mr Sands was arrested for an arson incident that took place at his hotel, placing him allegedly at fault for the damage. I assure you that, as a well-respected musician who has been in the music business for two and a half years, my client has an excellent reputation for using his best possible judgement at all times, particularly when representing his home town. (This is with the exception of his arrest in 2011 for inciting violence while on stage. I assure you that this was not intentional or premeditated.) We are seeking your immediate legal counsel with the hope that your law firm will represent Mr Sands in the matter. I have attached the official police report along with Mr Sands' statement, which testifies to his innocence.
We look forward to hearing from you.

Sincerely,
Toddrick Eloi, PR Manager and
Communications Director

Email 2

TO: julie.paremen@iswaranatlaw.com, philo.latreaux@
iswaranatlaw.com, warren.hernandez@
iswaranatlaw.com
FROM: Malik Iswaran
SUBJECT: (Untitled)

I'm writing to the three of you to find the perfect fit for a case we recently received here at Iswaran at Law. Following recent allegations against him, celebrity icon Cooper Sands seeks counsel from our team of legal reps. As the owner of this firm, I took the liberty of meeting with Mr Sands personally to get a better sense of his case. Following my consultation with him and his PR manager, and a subsequent meeting with my partner, our law firm has agreed to take on the case. As we see it, Cooper is not directly responsible for the incident. Since this is such a 'textbook' case, I will be forwarding representation responsibilities to our junior team. I've attached a detailed set of my own notes for you to read, along with Mr Sands' statement. Please advise.

MI

Email 3

TO: malik.iswaran@iswaranatlaw.com
FROM: philo.latreaux@iswaranatlaw.com
SUBJECT: (Untitled)
Mr Iswaran,

I believe I'm the best candidate to take on Mr Sands' case. With nine years of experience at this firm, I have no doubt that I will represent us well (plus, I'm a huge fan of his music, so this would be the opportunity of a lifetime!). I am still finishing off the Milo case, which should be finished by mid-February, but I may be able to speed it up to the start of the month, as long as the Records department keep to my schedule for document processing (sigh …).
One query, if you don't mind, sir … I took the liberty of looking up the police report (it wasn't attached to your memo … a mere oversight, I'm sure). I couldn't help noticing that the fire extinguisher which put out the fire came from the 18th floor. Meanwhile, both fire extinguishers from the East Wing of Floor 16, where the fire occurred, were found in the swimming pool below. I can't help wondering why this is?
I look forward to sorting this out before we proceed.
Thank you,
Philo

Email 4
TO: malik.iswaran@iswaranatlaw.com
FROM: julie.paremen@iswaranatlaw.com
SUBJECT: (Untitled)

Senior Attorney Iswaran,
I hope I am the first to respond to your query, as I am deeply interested in taking on this case. I've followed the story since it broke last weekend and I am keen to see the related details and various perspectives regarding Sands' innocence. I've looked through the documents at length and have already started drafting a potential brief for your perusal (see attachment).

I know this is my first year at Iswaran at Law, but I am confident that my academic training and professional development make me a prime candidate for the cause. If, indeed, Mr Sands did not commit the offence (which I genuinely believe), then I think I can complete this case rather quickly. My meticulous attention to detail, ability to think critically and my hard-line approach to questioning all but guarantee that I'll defend the sound reputation you've built over the years here at Iswaran at Law.

I ask that you please consider me for the position. I promise I won't let you down.

Most genuinely,
Julie Paremen, JD

Email 5
TO: malik.iswaran@iswaranatlaw.com
FROM: warren.hernandez@iswaranatlaw.com
SUBJECT: (Untitled)

Dear Mr Iswaran,
I recently spoke with Ms Paremen about the Sands case. I'm just as interested as she is, but I know she has already put in considerable work to lead the case. If I'm too late in responding, or if I'm overstepping my boundaries here, I apologise, but I'd like to give the case a 'go', if possible.
Julie and I are both in agreement that Philo is not fit for the position (no offence to him). He's knee-deep in the Milo case with no end in sight. Not to mention, I don't think he cares if Sands is guilty-as-charged (which I think he is!), as long

as he gets that autograph he wants from his favourite singer, right?!

Joking apart, I'd love to be the rep for this one. I don't have any cases on my plate right now, so I have the time to dedicate. More time than Julie, even … she seems a little overwhelmed with the renovations she's doing to the new house she purchased over the holiday break.

If you're intent on making her lead, though, I would be satisfied with teaming up with Julie as the alternative. As this is her first year at the firm, and since I've been in the profession (thought not under you) for some 18 years, I think you'd agree I have a lot of experience to offer.

I'd love to hear your thoughts on the matter.

Cheers,
W

Email 6
TO: philo.latreaux@iswaranatlaw.com
FROM: malik.iswaran@iswaranatlaw.com
SUBJECT: (Untitled)

Mr Latreaux,
Thank you for taking note of the unusual fire extinguisher issue. At Iswaran at Law, we applaud that level of meticulous concern. I assure you, however, that my partner and I went into the matter during our face-to-face interview with Mr Sands, and it appears that all is well after all. The East Wing extinguishers were under recall, so they did not work when needed. This is why they were discarded over the balcony, while another was found on Floor 18 to put out the fire.

Provided that you stick with the protocol in my notes, everything should hold up in court. Note well that we've represented elite figures such as Mr Sands on far more delicate matters in the past. It is my intention to award you the case on the strict condition that you can stick to the outline I've set as your superior. Do hurry through the Milo case, so we can proceed. You're a marvel in the courtroom, Mr Latreaux.

Regards,
M

ACTIVITY 5

Answer the following comprehension questions, which are grouped according to the skill you will need to use. Write your ideas on a separate sheet of paper.

Understanding

1   For each email, decide on an appropriate subject line.
2   Using information from the material, give two qualities or characteristics of each of the following candidates. Justify your responses for each.
    a   Philo Latreaux
    b   Julie Paremen
    c   Warren Hernandez
3   Give *two* characteristics that all email correspondents (including Malik Iswaran) collectively share.
4   Look at the use of brackets (parentheses) in Email 3 from Philo Latreaux to Malik Iswaran. In one word or a short phrase, describe the tone of these statements.
5   Review the context of Email 4. Using your own words as far as possible, explain the purpose of paragraph 2.
6   Re-read Email 5. How would you describe the tone:
    a   at the beginning of the memo?
    b   at the end of the memo?
Justify your reasoning for each by pointing to evidence from the text.

Applying

1   Briefly explain why Toddrick Eloi is emailing Iswaran at Law.
2   Using your own words, explain Philo's cause for doubt of Sands' innocence, as outlined in Email 3.
3   Using evidence from the material and your knowledge of the present day, explain the challenges that celebrities face once they are on public view.

Analysing

1   Briefly explain the differences between Julie's and Warren's approach in responding to Malik Iswaran's proposal. Justify your answer, using the material and your own knowledge/opinion.
2   What do you learn about Malik's character from the emails? Answer in about 60 words, giving justifications for your answer.
3   Infer reasons why Malik might have taken on the Sands case.
4   Explain briefly what Malik means when he says Sands' situation is a 'textbook' case.
5   Analyse the sign-off phrases that the candidates use in the first five emails (Sincerely, etc.). What does each seem to suggest? In roughly 80 words, compare their approaches.

6   What do the following expressions mean, as used in Email 5?
    a   overstepping my boundaries
    b   give [the case] a go
    c   no end in sight
    d   on my plate
7   Using context as a clue, offer one synonym for each of the words as they are used in Email 4.
    a   keen
    b   perusal
    c   allegations
    d   meticulous
    e   hard-line
8   Use each of the words from question 7 in a separate sentence to illustrate their meaning as used in the email. Your sentences should not deal with the same topic as the email scenario.
9   What is Malik's tone in paragraph 2 of Email 6? Justify your answer with at least two expressions that he uses.

Evaluating

1   Explain which candidate is most suitable for the position, considering the positive and negative aspects of each. You should limit your discussion to the candidate you have chosen and not refer to the others. Use your own words.
2   Considering the positive and negative aspects of each candidate, explain which one is least suitable for the position. You should limit your discussion to the chosen candidate and not refer to the others. Use your own words.
3   Choosing ONE of the employees from the email thread, explain what you would have done better in response to your boss's advertisement of the position.
4   Do you think Cooper Sands is innocent? Defend your position.

Communicating

1   If you were applying for the same position as Julie, Philo and Warren, how would you set yourself apart? What qualities do you possess that could contribute to this line of work and/or this case specifically?
2   In your own opinion, what is one advantage and one disadvantage of being a defence lawyer?
3   Because of recent events, Cooper Sands is preparing for a radio interview on a popular, celebrity gossip news programme. Imagine that you are his PR manager and suggest at least three relevant questions you would use to prepare him for this. Be creative in your approach to questioning.

In the next section of this chapter, you will learn more about the reading comprehension skills introduced in the email activity. You will also be introduced to the various types of material and questioning featured in this course. The aim is to help you develop your critical thinking and reading comprehension skills.

Understanding main ideas and key details

The **main idea** of a text is the central message the writer wishes to convey. **Key details** are the specific pieces of information used to support the main idea. Later, you will learn how details break down further into *reasons* and *evidence*. For now, we will consider details more generally.

To explore how details are part of bigger ideas, complete the following activity.

KEY TERMS

Main idea: the writer's central message.

Key details: specific information to support the main idea.

KEY SKILLS

The way a writer develops the main idea and key details of a piece depends upon their purpose for writing. Learn more about essay development in Chapters 2.3, 3.1, 3.2, and 5.1.

ACTIVITY 6

Scenario 1

A newspaper article usually focuses on a central main idea, but remember that evidence in longer texts can be divided into smaller subsections, with subheadings. In this scenario, a newspaper columnist is writing a story about whether the media should have the right to probe into the personal lives of celebrities. Read each of the details she plans to include in her article. Which article subsection should the detail be featured in? (The first one has been completed for you as an example.)

Main idea: The media has no right to probe into the lives of celebrities	Subsections of the article			
Details	Celebrities fight back	Legal situation	Protecting privacy	Other opinions
Article 3 of the Universal Declaration of Human Rights states that 'everyone has the right to life, liberty and security of person'. Celebrities are no exception.		✓		
Companies like InkBlot are offering services to help celebrities who are harassed by the paparazzi. They will get rid of imperfections in our digital footprint, but for a cost. Sports figure Halo Gordon had to pay the equivalent of $50 000 to remove incriminating photos found in his private social media account which suggested potential use of performance-enhancing drugs.				
The paparazzi have sometimes provoked celebrities to violence. Consider last month's incident where teen actress Suki Bowser intentionally ran over the foot of a journalist as he tried to photograph her leaving popular night club, Renegade.				
In defence of the media, fashion designer Mikhail Marks mentioned in an interview: 'The minute you steal that place in the public eye, you sign an invisible contract that hands over your personal world. Even the brand of pet food you use goes public. It doesn't matter if you asked for it. You just have to deal with it.'				

Scenario 2

Just like news articles, scientific reports also break down long texts into smaller subsections. In this scenario, a psychologist is drafting a report regarding the influence of celebrities on teenage appearance. Review the details of her findings. Then decide in which section of her report each detail should appear.

Main idea: Celebrity culture sets examples that can have irreversible effects on the health of adolescents	Subsections of the article			
Details	Fad diets	Eating disorders	Case study	Further research
Dysmorphia (dissatisfaction with one's own body weight) has more than doubled in the past three years. According to MedHealth Journal, many young adults respond by bingeing, which may damage their health sometimes irreversibly.				
New studies in cognitive behavioural therapy show promising results in treating eating disorders, though no superior approach for this form of illness has been identified so far.				
Singer-songwriter Viola has total confidence in the lemon-water and kiwi detox that she uses before concerts: 'It gives me the look I want, and it's great for my skin.'				
At her high school, an astonishing 74% of girls in Walker's class reported that dieting was nothing new to them. This may partly explain the outcome of her situation.				

Identifying key details

Observing how others organise details can help you become a better writer. As a writer in this course, you will need to be able to determine which details are relevant to your point when you are drafting an essay or a reading response. If you select the wrong details, your message can easily get lost or lose focus. As you work through this course, you will learn how to identify details in the work of others. You will also learn how to use details effectively in your own writing and how to eliminate unnecessary information when possible.

However, writers or speakers may sometimes use irrelevant details *on purpose*. They may try to evade a point or deliberately avoid giving certain information as an unfair way of strengthening their argument.

Think back to musician Cooper Sands' situation in Activity 5. What if he were guilty of setting fire to hotel property but did not want to wreck his reputation by admitting it? What might he do when questioned by a police officer about the incident? Here are two examples to illustrate how Mr Sands might offer irrelevant details to avoid admitting his guilt.

Example 1

Officer: Mr Sands, there is a theory that you nearly burned down the entire 16th floor the other night. Is that true?

Cooper Sands: With all due respect, Officer, what really *is* 'theory' anyway? Other than an abstract set of ideas intended to give a clever explanation of something. I mean, it's offensive that you're basing my guilt on *general* principles independent of the thing in question. Let me tell you about a time when 'theory' really got Elvis Presley into legal trouble …

Example 2

Officer: Mr Sands, did you have something to do with the fire on the 16th floor last night?

Cooper Sands: No, sir. I am a famous musician. Everyone knows my work and I've worked really hard to get where I am. I have four platinum records. Four! I am innocent!

What does the musician seem to be doing in these examples? How is he attempting to use irrelevant details in each situation to avoid the point?

KEY SKILLS

In the first example, Cooper Sands' strategy to avoid the officer's question is called a 'red herring fallacy' (see 'Recognising weaknesses in arguments' in Chapter 3.1 Section *B Understanding arguments*). In the second example, he uses something called a 'non-sequitur' to keep away from the point (i.e. where a conclusion is supported by weak or irrelevant reasons).

It is important to be able to identify key details, while also understanding their relationship to the main point and to other details. This is a skill you need to develop in order to be a good critical thinker, reader and writer. The practice activities later in this chapter will develop your ability to recognise relevant details and eliminate *extraneous* ones.

DID YOU KNOW?

The suffix –*ous* means 'possessing' or 'full of'. What do you think is the meaning of 'extraneous' as used in this context?

Making inferences

Informational text does not always explicitly tell you what it means to say. It is sometimes necessary for the audience to **infer**, or guess, the meaning.

As a reader, you infer (make inferences) all the time, probably without even realising you are doing it. Inferring is a natural part of your critical thought process. However, you may sometimes make incorrect inferences. This is because when you infer, you are forced to 'read between the lines'. Sometimes this can suggest a meaning that is not as accurate as one that is explicitly stated. Practice with inferring ideas can therefore help you to reduce the chance of missing the point when you are reading.

KEY TERM

Infer: to draw conclusions from evidence given.

Skimming headlines

Every time you skim-read news headlines, you are simultaneously making inferences about the content. This is the mechanism that helps you decide what to read and what to ignore.

Consider the following headlines, which appeared in the 'Style' section of a popular magazine. What can you infer about the content of each article from its headline? Why?

1 Platinum album promise loses shine
2 Wannabe wardrobes: D-listers compete
3 All's fair in race and runways
4 Football starters let their hair down
5 Street style: a new avenue in Perth

Images and inferences

There is an old proverb that says: 'A picture is worth a thousand words.' Words are certainly not the only way we can communicate information. Images can also offer a wealth of input. Without words, however, much is left to the imagination, making 'a thousand' different interpretations possible. This is why images are a great way to practise mastering the reading comprehension skill of *inference*. Just as with text, you can 'read' pictures for meaning and draw conclusions about them.

As an example, look carefully at this image.

- What do you see happening in the photo?
- Based on what you see, what guesses can you make about what is happening?

- What evidence from the image leads you to believe this?

Here are a few examples of possible inferences you might make from the photo:

Objective observation: a man with his hand up is walking through a crowd of people.	
Inference	**Evidence**
The photo appears to be at an official institution such as a court of law.	• architecture of the building (i.e. white pillars, Roman design, grand steps leading up to entrance) • professional attire (suit and tie, neutral tones)
The man does not want attention.	• His right hand appears to be pushing the woman in the long coat away. • He is using his left hand to cover his face. • He is glancing down. • He appears to be ignoring the woman speaking behind him.
The man may be a lawyer who has lost a case, or he may have just been charged with a crime.	• He is wearing a suit and tie. • He seems to be frowning. • Although his mouth isn't quite visible, he does not appear to be smiling.
The man might be a well-known figure or perhaps he has become a figure of interest as a result of the events surrounding him.	• There is a group of journalists attempting to interview him on camera.

ACTIVITY 7

View images A–D carefully. Make a list of inferences from each, identifying evidence from the photo. Create a chart to organise your ideas, like the chart for the previous photo.

A

C

B

D

Identifying the author's purpose

Another key comprehension skill is the ability to identify the author's *purpose*. In other words, why is the author bothering to write about the topic, or what is the intention? Remember that authors may choose to write about a topic in order to:

- inform
- argue
- entertain.

However, among these broad intentions there may be more specific purposes. What is the author writing to inform you *about*, for instance? A more targeted reason for writing could be to *educate* the reader about the rights of private citizens. It is important to be able to identify precisely *why* the author is writing, in order to truly comprehend their message. To help you practice this skill, complete Activity 8 below.

Understanding tone and emotion

The term 'tone' (see Chapter 1.2 Sections *D Understanding the task* and *F Key elements of an essay*) is most commonly used to refer to the pitch of a person's voice when speaking. Consider, for example, when an angry parent might say: 'Don't take that tone with me, young lady!' When someone speaks, it is relatively easy to pick up from their tone of voice how formal, respectful, or perhaps sarcastic, the individual is being.

In a piece of writing, however, tone can be much more difficult to identify, as the reader is not actually hearing the author's voice. For example, how would you describe the tone of the microblog entries from Activity 8?

Since you cannot actually hear the writer, you must rely on the words to *infer* what his or her tone is. In establishing tone, writers must first consider their audience. Who will they be speaking to and in what circumstances? Should the tone be formal or informal? Serious or light-hearted?

ACTIVITY 8

Social media is a well-known channel for expressing ideas and opinions. It can be used to celebrate victories, throw light on issues, complain about setbacks and share life experiences. Read the following microblog posts below, each of which aims to share a thought in 45 words or fewer. Working in pairs, determine the author's specific purpose for sharing each message. (Hint: ask yourself: why did the author write this post?)

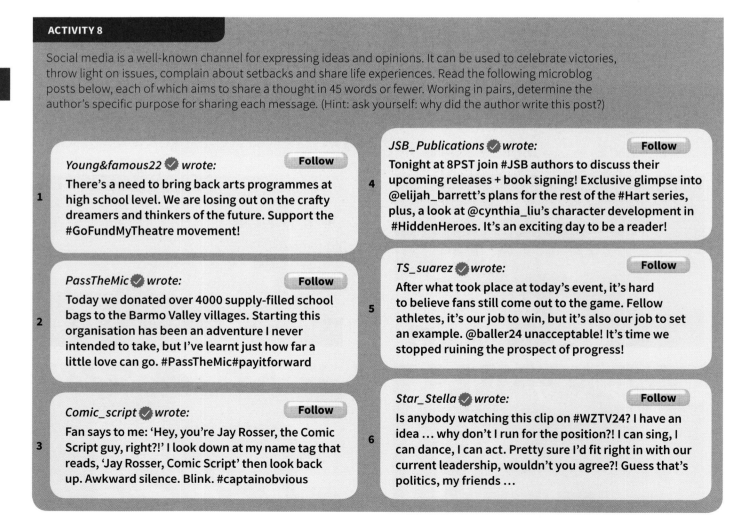

Young&famous22 ✅ *wrote:*   [Follow]

1   There's a need to bring back arts programmes at high school level. We are losing out on the crafty dreamers and thinkers of the future. Support the #GoFundMyTheatre movement!

PassTheMic ✅ *wrote:*   [Follow]

2   Today we donated over 4000 supply-filled school bags to the Barmo Valley villages. Starting this organisation has been an adventure I never intended to take, but I've learnt just how far a little love can go. #PassTheMic #payitforward

Comic_script ✅ *wrote:*   [Follow]

3   Fan says to me: 'Hey, you're Jay Rosser, the Comic Script guy, right?!' I look down at my name tag that reads, 'Jay Rosser, Comic Script' then look back up. Awkward silence. Blink. #captainobvious

JSB_Publications ✅ *wrote:*   [Follow]

4   Tonight at 8PST join #JSB authors to discuss their upcoming releases + book signing! Exclusive glimpse into @elijah_barrett's plans for the rest of the #Hart series, plus, a look at @cynthia_liu's character development in #HiddenHeroes. It's an exciting day to be a reader!

TS_suarez ✅ *wrote:*   [Follow]

5   After what took place at today's event, it's hard to believe fans still come out to the game. Fellow athletes, it's our job to win, but it's also our job to set an example. @baller24 unacceptable! It's time we stopped ruining the prospect of progress!

Star_Stella ✅ *wrote:*   [Follow]

6   Is anybody watching this clip on #WZTV24? I have an idea … why don't I run for the position?! I can sing, I can dance, I can act. Pretty sure I'd fit right in with our current leadership, wouldn't you agree?! Guess that's politics, my friends …

It is important that you, as the reader, interpret these intentions accurately in order to understand the writer's message clearly. Awareness of tone is therefore a key strategy in comprehending text. In this section of the chapter, you will learn about the different registers of tone that writers use.

Specific registers of tone

The following list can give you a good idea of the range of *emotion* available when you are determining the author's attitude. Of course, there are many more possibilities.

vibrant	whimsical
affectionate	candid
approving	amused
light-hearted	conversational
nostalgic	reverent
playful	sympathetic
humorous	
detached	pessimistic
reflective	exasperated
straightforward	naïve
judicious	satirical
uncertain	objective
mistrustful	pragmatic
forceful	irreverent
urgent	sarcastic
abrasive	cold
bitter	stern
cavalier	mocking
condescending	severe
disdainful	threatening

Read the following quotations about the quality of punk rock music. Try using the words in the list, or words of your own, to identify the tone being used in each.

1   The Sex Pistols, who were responsible for launching the punk rock movement in the 1970s, challenged traditional attitudes with their unmelodious music and rebellious style.

2   It's ridiculous that they scratched graffiti all over their London apartment. Who in their right mind would consider awarding this heritage status?

3   Calling the 'artwork' in their Denmark Street apartment 'graffiti' seems strange … don't you find graffiti outside?

4   All that racket! If punk rock hadn't dug its own grave, I would have done it myself!

5   It's a shame the punk rock movement was short-lived. There is so much promise in sticking out your tongue at mainstream society and authority figures once in a while, don't you think?

Reflect for a moment on your process for describing the tone in the quotations. How did you arrive at your answers? What helped you decide, for example, the tone used in quotation 4?

The word 'racket', as used to describe the sound of punk rock, has a negative **connotation**. This suggests that the author of quotation 4 has a poor attitude toward this type of music. The writer of quotation 1 doesn't seem to particularly like punk rock either, but is much more reserved when describing the music as *unmelodious*. Careful attention to word choice can therefore help you determine the tone of a piece of writing.

 KEY TERM

Connotation: the underlying emotion produced by a word or phrase.

Read the following interview transcript, then do the exam-style questions that follow. This will give you further practice in identifying tone.

Extract 1

Please note that sections marked with a line [_____] have been left blank deliberately.

Introduction

Belle, an 18 year old student at Esperanza Academy, is attending a careers interview with her class teacher, Mr Forti. She is hoping for some insightful guidance as she is very undecided about further study and which career path to follow.

Mr Forti: Hi Belle! Take a seat. Now, tell me, what are you intending to do with regards to a career?

Belle: Well… you see… the problem is I haven't got a clue and I'm really stressing about it, Sir. Could I _____?

Mr Forti: Come, come, Belle. That's not the attitude I expect from a student like you! I just read in the
5 newspaper the other day that there is a shortage of forensic accountants. It sounded like a really interesting job – you look back over a company's books so you get to see the internal workings of an organisation in fine detail. Combing through all their records does sound so absorbing, doesn't it? Don't you agree?

Belle: Er… the problem is, Sir, that… you remember… I wasn't doing that well in my mathematics
10 tests earlier this year and so you arranged for me to have extra tuition at lunchtime from Mrs Harvanto. By the way, she's really good and I am regaining my confidence slowly but surely, but not enough to consider a career so dependent on being brilliant at mathematics.

Mr Forti: Hmm, in that case, how about… (*running his finger down a list of professions on his desk in front of him*)… financial advisor?

15 Belle: (*in a tone of exasperation mixed with disappointment*) Sir!

Mr Forti: Oh yes, of course. OK then, let me think… a colleague was only talking about his son yesterday who works in logistics and loves it so much that he is climbing the corporate ladder at an astonishing rate. What would you say to that?

Belle: I don't know, Sir. What exactly do you mean by logistics? I've never even heard of that
20 before. Has it got something to do with being logical?

Mr Forti: (*appearing suddenly very flustered*) Right… perhaps not then. Let me put my thinking cap on. We need to go in another direction, don't we? Ah, another idea has just come to me! Someone I caught on a TV programme recently was extolling the virtues of a career in the field of design. How does that sound to you? Apparently there are lots of different types of
25 design too – graphic, interior, fashion, product, car, aeronautical, marine – the list is endless. And what's more, there is a worldwide demand for such skills.

Belle: That does sound interesting, but I gave up design technology and art years ago, so I don't think that would be a realistic option for me, do you?

Mr Forti: (*looking mildly irritated now*) No, I suppose not. Swiftly moving on then. My niece is
30 thoroughly enjoying her studies in retail management. She is on the graduate programme of a multinational organisation, and, when she finishes it, the world will be her oyster. She will be highly qualified, have work experience under her belt, be able to travel extensively, and there are lots of opportunities for promotion as there are plenty of successful companies in this area. What's not to like?

35   Belle: Sorry, Sir, but, although that sounds amazing and congratulations to your niece, I don't think it is really me. I can't say I relish the whole shopping experience because I find shops, department stores and malls a bit claustrophobic, especially when I get caught up in crowds of shoppers pushing and shoving. It just doesn't interest me, I'm afraid. Though, now I'm talking it out with you, I would say my people and communication skills are among my

40   strong points.

      Mr Forti: (*becoming frustrated*) Remind me, Belle, what your favourite subject is again.

      Belle: Oh, Sir, I absolutely adore English. You do know, don't you, that I am in the Debating Society, the Book Circle and the Drama Club too? And I'm getting excellent feedback from my information technology teacher too. She thinks that my PowerPoint presentation is first

45   rate and she wants me to show it at Speech Day.

      Mr Forti: (*triumphantly*) I've got it! What would you say to a career in _____?

      Belle: Phew, what a good idea! Thank goodness you suggested that, Sir. I was beginning to

_____.

Cambridge International AS Level General Paper 8001/23 Insert Passage 2, November 2015

EXAM-STYLE QUESTIONS 1

Answer the comprehension questions **1–6**.

1   How would you describe Belle's tone in line 2. Why do you think this is? Explain. **[2]**

2   Explain why Belle's tone changes in line 15. Justify your response by using evidence from the text for support. **[3]**

3   Review lines 29–34:

    a   Why do you think Mr Forti is 'looking mildly irritated'? Explain using your own words. **[2]**

    b   Despite his mild irritation, how would you describe Mr Forti's tone in this segment? Justify your answer. **[2]**

4   Using your own words, explain how Belle's tone changes from the beginning of her conversation with Mr Forti to the end. **[4]**

5   Think critically: what career do you think Mr Forti suggests for Belle at the end of the extract? Justify your answer. **[6]**

6   Does a university degree still have value? Argue your case. You may use knowledge outside the exercise. **[6]**

Total marks: 25

Words and phrases in context

Another key skill for reading comprehension is the ability to work out the meaning of words you don't know using information from the context in which they appear. Consider the following simple sentence. As is stands, the meaning of the word *impecunious* may be difficult to work out:

> Parker lived an *impecunious* lifestyle.

Now read the word within its wider context. Using the surrounding information, can you work out what *impecunious* means?

> Before his rise to literary stardom, Lance Parker had seen his fair share of suffering. After the death of his only parent, he became a runaway teen at 15, spending many a night in shelters and halfway homes. In this *impecunious* lifestyle that he never intended, Parker struggled to find food and safety on a daily basis. He had very few possessions, which he kept in a white, plastic garbage bag, but one thing Parker was never seen without was a one-subject, spiral notebook. It was always folded in half, carefully tucked in his back pocket, unless he was furiously scrawling away on its pages. Most of his work was born in these dollar-store journals. Today, he's published 14 novels, four of which have reached the top of the best-seller list.

KEY TERM

Context clues: information surrounding an unknown word, which helps you understand its meaning.

When you are trying to work out an unfamiliar word, sometimes the clues to its meaning can be found in the sentence itself or in the sentences before or after it. At other times, however, you might need to look at the *overall* meaning being conveyed in the sentence or paragraph in which the word appears.

A helpful strategy for working out the meaning of a word is to use **context clues** to replace the unknown word with a synonym. This way, you can check if the word fits without altering the author's original message. For example:

> Celebrities live in trendy *metropolitan* areas like Tokyo, Milan and New York City.

What word could replace 'metropolitan'? What clues in the sentence help the reader know what 'metropolitan' means? Notice that the sentence gives examples which illustrate the definition of the word. This is one way of creating context for the reader. Clues like this make communication clearer.

There are several different kinds of context clues that can help you determine the meaning of unfamiliar words.

Examples

The sentence or paragraph (such as the one above) offers an illustration of the term through the use of examples. These are usually signalled by words like: *such as*, *other*, *include*, *these* and *for example*.

Definitions

The explicit definition of the word is built into the sentence or paragraph. It is usually signalled by words like: *is* and *means*. For example:

> A *rogue* state is a nation that refuses to follow rules set by the international community.

Restatements

A follow-up sentence or phrase breaks down or simplifies a point that has just been made, using more difficult terms. This is usually signalled by words like: *or*, *that is*, *in other words* and *which is*. For example:

> The team took a more *pragmatic* – that is, a practical – approach to the case this time.

Contrast

The word is compared to its opposite; by showing what it is *not*, the reader can figure out what it *is*. This is usually signalled by words like: *unlike*, *but*, *not*, *in contrast to*, *opposite*, *apart from*, *while*. For example:

> Unlike Juanita, with her careless and extravagant spending habits, Tomas is much more *frugal* with his money.

Cause/effect

The word is placed in relationship to its cause or outcome, which hints at its meaning. This is usually signalled by words like: *so*, *that*, *so that*, *because*, *in order to*. For example:

> The mayor *allocated* a quarter of the funds to building a new road, so there won't be so much congestion on the existing roads.

ACTIVITY 9

Using a dictionary, look up the definitions of the following words. Using the methods for creating context clues just described, write a sentence for each word.

1 amorphous
2 ostensible
3 paucity
4 tangential
5 ubiquitous

An awareness of context clues will not only help you be a better reader, but it can help you write better, too. By embedding context clues into your own work, you are providing support for your audience, which builds your credibility and increases the chances of effective communication.

Making comparisons

An important part of critical thinking involves your ability to compare. As you can imagine, this kind of analysis leads to a judgement, or evaluation, of the things you are comparing.

Consider this example. A celebrity is interested in building an environmentally-friendly school that focuses on science as a key field of study. He or she will be re-purposing a former building and has narrowed down the options to the following abandoned spaces:

Option 1: an old shopping mall on a major waterway

Option 2: a former bed and breakfast on top of a remote mountain

Option 3: an ageing grain silo on farmland

Option 4: a run-down steel mill just outside a large city.

In order to make the best decision, the celebrity would need to compare each location against the other to see which one has the best features, amenities and accessibility to meet the needs of the school's vision and its students.

ACTIVITY 10

Think about Options 1–4. Pick two that you think would be most appropriate for an environmentally-friendly school that focuses primarily on the sciences. Now write a response that compares one against the other before making a decision on which of these two is better.

Throughout this course, you will meet questions like this, which involve *logical reasoning* to show comprehension. A scenario, along with several options or potential solutions, may be provided for you to analyse and evaluate. There are some useful strategies to learn when approaching this kind of question, and these strategies can help you compare effectively and think critically.

Comparatives and superlatives

The process of making a comparison between a number of items can be complex. Using key words called **comparatives** and **superlatives** can help you organise and express your ideas when you are responding to critical reading tasks that ask you to compare.

Look back at the four options from which the celebrity has to choose. If you were comparing these options in terms of size, you might use comparative and superlative words to express your point:

> This campus is *larger* than that one. (comparative)
>
> This campus is the *largest* one in the area. (superlative)

 KEY TERMS

Comparatives: adjectives or adverbs used to compare differences between the two objects they describe.

Superlatives: adjectives or adverbs used to describe an object which is at the upper or lower limit of quality.

These words are usually adjectives or adverbs that add *–er* or *–est* to the end of a word, but they can also be combined with words like: *more, less, the most, the least*. As a general rule, you would use:

- *–er* and *–est* endings when the word has one or two syllables (e.g. *Ask the <u>older</u> children to carry the <u>heavier</u> boxes.*)
- 'more', 'less', 'most' or 'least' when the word has three or more syllables (e.g. *This is the <u>most accessible</u> entrance in the building.*).

However, consider the following example. Which do you think is correct?

1 *The ground is <u>more even</u> at the farm location than it is on the mountain top.*

2 *The ground is <u>evener</u> at the farm location than it is on the mountain top.*

As with many language rules, exceptions always exist. This example challenges the rule about the number of syllables: 'even' has only two syllables, yet it uses 'more even' instead of 'evener' (since the latter sounds awkward). Most two-syllable adverbs can take either form, but they tend to take the 'more' form more readily, which appears to contradict the rule. For example:

> Demolition work at the mountaintop site went *more smoothly* today than it did last week.

Notice that while the adverb 'smoothly' is two syllables, it takes on the word 'more' instead of the *–er* ending when comparing. We choose the appropriate

55

comparative form for adverbs mainly according to how they sound.

> **TIP**
> Reading your writing aloud is a helpful strategy when you are editing your work.

As a general rule, use *comparative* forms when comparing *two* things. For example:

> This is the <u>larger</u> of the *two* campuses.
>
> The old mall is significantly <u>more expensive</u> *than the steel mill option.*

Use *superlative* terms to compare *three or more* things. For example:

> This is the <u>largest</u> of the *four* options.
>
> The old mall property is the <u>most expensive</u> one *of all.*

	Number of things compared	Form	Examples
Comparative	two	–er	smarter
		more	healthier
		less	more engaging
			less troublesome
Superlative	three or more	–est	the smartest
		the most	the healthiest
			the most engaging
		the least	the least troublesome

> **TIP**
> Avoid using both *–er* and 'more' at the same time. This creates a double comparison, which is grammatically incorrect and sounds very odd (e.g. *more livelier*).

Again, as with any language, there are always exceptions to grammar rules. The irregular forms of comparison include the following:

Original word (base word)	Comparative	Superlative
good	better	best
well	better	best
a little	less	least
some	more	most
much	more	most
many	more	most
bad, badly	worse	worst

 KEY SKILLS

Unit 4 will help you develop your grammar, spelling and punctuation skills.

ACTIVITY 11

Read through the paragraph. Complete each space with an appropriate comparative or superlative term. (Hint: to maximise your learning experience, be creative in selecting vocabulary.)

> For the most part, the bed and breakfast is the (1) _____ of the four options, but it is also the (2) _____ to get to, too. Driving to the silo each day, for instance, is (3) _____ than a day's trek up the mountain. Meanwhile, when it comes to space, the steel mill has the (4) _____ potential. It is (5) _____ than the mall! The land is (6) _____ than the farmland, however, and has the (7) _____ layout overall.

Knowing how to use comparatives and superlatives appropriately will help you express ideas clearly when making comparisons. It will also help to improve your use of English, which is another important aspect of this course.

ACTIVITY 12

Re-read your response to Activity 10. Circle or highlight any comparative or superlative terms you used.

- Did you use these terms enough, and appropriately?
- If not, how could you use the knowledge from this section to revise your work? Edit your writing to include the use of comparative and superlative terms where necessary.

Demonstrating understanding

Developing active reading habits and practising key reading skills can help you to understand what you read. One of the best ways to demonstrate this understanding is to summarise information in your own words. Comprehension questions may ask you to summarise points from a text. For example, a question might ask you to 'summarise the drawbacks of X as outlined in paragraph 2 of the reading material'. It is unlikely that you will be asked to summarise an entire text.

You will also be using your summarising skills when developing arguments. When you offer input (evidence) to support your thesis, you *summarise* the information for the reader. Then you explain how that information relates to the point you are arguing.

KEY SKILLS

You will have the opportunity to practise your summarising skills in Chapter 2.2.

E Types of reading comprehension

You will encounter several types of reading materials during this course. They aim to develop your ability to think critically about information as well as language.

As outlined in this chapter, you will work with news articles, speeches, dialogue/scripts, data charts and infographics, bulleted lists and different types of correspondence.

As you read, you will be expected to demonstrate your understanding in two ways. Comprehension questions will require you to show comprehension through either:

- logical reasoning, or
- analysis of prose.

Logical reasoning and everyday problem-solving

Have you ever had to decide where to go on holiday? Ever planned a club event and had to find ways to raise money? Or perhaps you are deciding which university to attend once you finish school?

In choosing a university, you might focus on the facilities available and what courses the university offers. What else might you take into account? For example, what if the university you like *least* is the one your parents prefer? How might external factors like this therefore influence your choice? Problem-solving can become a complicated process because of the internal and external factors involved.

Every time you solve a problem, you engage in critical thinking. As you weigh one option against another, you are analysing its component parts and deciding on their value in order to arrive at a decision. At the same time, you are also taking into account external factors, or context.

Remember the celebrity interested in building an environmentally-friendly school? When comparing the options, geographical features certainly need to be taken into account. What other factors might the celebrity need to take into account? Take some time to discuss this with a partner.

57

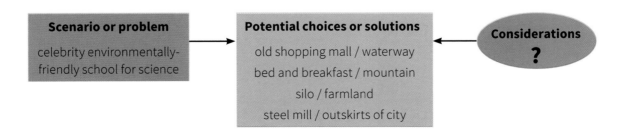

You will find that the problem-solving questions you encounter in this course are similar to the kinds of decisions that you (or people in your society) make every day. Therefore, the decision-making skills you develop in this course can be very useful in your everyday life!

Carefully read the information below. Then use it to answer the exam-style questions that follow.

SCENARIO

A popular folk band just became famous with the release of their debut album, *Soul Sunshine*. With the money they have earned, the band members have decided to treat themselves to a holiday. Their aim is to use the time to bond as a group and to get inspiration for their next album. They are planning a seven-day trip in June.

Band budget = $5000 (includes flight and hotel accommodation; all food and leisure activities will be paid individually).

BAND MEMBERS

Taren

- Certified hiking guide, and enjoys outdoor challenges and thrill activities
- Meditates every morning, so he prefers a serene environment
- Prefers his own room, not open to sharing space
- Studied history in college and hopes to write a book one day
- Does not drink or enjoy late evenings out
- Prefers a vegetarian diet but enjoys fish on occasion

Kalif

- Exercises every morning
- Does not like seafood, allergic to shellfish specifically
- Doesn't mind sharing a room and has no preference for bed or cot
- Has just under $300 in cash available for spending
- Does not like being in the sun for too long because he burns easily
- Enjoys night life and considers himself a 'foodie', though he does not cook at all

Bernie

- Gets car sick
- Didn't budget any money for the trip but does not mind using his credit card
- Dreams of producing music some day
- Has never seen the ocean before
- Still recovering from knee surgery; his doctor warned against prolonged walking
- Loves to cook and is a strong advocate for buying locally; has a strict vegan diet

58

HOLIDAY OPTIONS

(A) *Lake Monroe Cabin Community*

A quaint community with simple charm and natural beauty, situated on beautiful Lake Monroe. Independently owned cabins available for weekly rental. At $1050, the 'Simple Life' option includes double bed plus one bathroom with outdoor shower. Or, at $2800, the 'Full Family' boasts one detached bedroom with two double beds, living area with pull-out sofa bed, kitchen and bathroom. The Community's social centre has a pool table, billiards, library and lounge areas. Full schedule of free afternoon and evening activities. Boating and eco-tour excursions are available at a fee. There is a small village five miles west of the Community with mostly small, locally owned shops and one cafe. Car rental is recommended, as no taxi or shuttle service is available in the area. Farmers' market is within walking distance.

(B) *The Mountains at Teralina*

This hotel is packed with luxury amenities including a heated indoor and outdoor pool and hot tub, fitness centre and spa, continental breakfast, three on-site restaurants, two lounges and one nightclub. Each balcony features a two-person hot tub. A popular winter destination, Teralina is also known for its world-renowned summer theme park, a 15-minute drive down the mountain. It features rollercoasters, games and movie-inspired attractions. There is a bustling commercial shopping centre and a string of restaurant chains nearby. Rates average at $175 per night, and typically feature a choice of either two double beds and a smaller bed *or* one double bed and pull-out couch option. On-demand transportation and affordable taxi services readily available.

(C) *Horn Valley Heights*

The Heights is an exclusive high-rise overlooking the vast city lights and endless skyline of Horn Valley. Room options are ready to accommodate every group, ranging from standard, two-double rooms to small studio-style apartments. Rates range from $210 to $495 per night. Serving as the central hub of the region, downtown Horn Valley is home to small individual shops, up-and-coming craft pubs and bistros, and spirited entertainment for the 'young crowd'. The historical West Side is known as Music Lane, where producers like Mic Masterson and Babes Alparez made their millions. Complementary shuttle service to and from the airport. Guests can also enjoy discounted rates for parking at the garage next door.

(D) *Citra Beach 'Stupéfiant' Boutique*

Pearl-white sands and lagoon-like waters are what set Citra Beach apart from any other beach destination around, and this centrally-situated boutique hotel is just as unique. Located on a seven-mile sprawl of private beach property, all 12 guest villas have immediate, beachfront access. At a standard rate of $425 per night, each villa includes two queen-sized beds, sitting area and small kitchen. Luxury extra beds available at $15 per night. Offers family-style eating for all guests, which is included in the cost; all food is made in-house with locally grown products by full-time gourmet staff. Yacht rentals, snorkelling, surfing lessons and parasailing are among the beach attractions available. Bar and live music also available.

Other considerations

1   Free bike rentals are only available at the cabin location. They are available at a daily rate at the beach and city locations. There are no bikes at the mountain location.

2   Annual shark migration patterns occur in the summer months.

3   The road into Horn Valley's historic West End is under construction until October of this year. Some businesses and restaurants have limited days/hours as a result.

4   The only room that does not feature a kitchenette option is the mountain location.

5   For an additional $80 per night, three of the beach villas offer an upgrade of a second floor including sofa bed, balcony and hot tub.

6   Pet day care and animal-friendly services are available at the mountain apartments.

7   Mountain apartment guests get discounted rates into all theme parks, fast-track passes for the most popular rides and attractions, and parking vouchers when visiting local shopping sites.

8   The beach location is a popular wedding destination, so the only week available in June is the same week as Bernie's 37th birthday.

9   Museums exist within walking distance of the beach villa and the city high-rise locations.

EXAM-STYLE QUESTIONS 2

Answer the comprehension questions **1–5**.

1   Give three reasons why Kalif would choose option C and give one point the group might raise to argue against his choice. **[4]**

2   Explain why the band might collectively decide against option B. Justify your reasoning. **[2]**

3   Using both evidence from the text and your own opinion, give two advantages and two disadvantages of travelling with a group. **[6]**

4   After considering the advantages and disadvantages, explain which option you think is most suitable for the entire band. You must restrict your answer to the chosen option and not refer to the other options. **[6]**

5   After considering the advantages and disadvantages, explain which option you think is least suitable for the entire band (since you already ruled out option B for the group in question 2, do not choose this as the basis of your answer for this question). You must restrict your answer to the chosen option and not refer to the other options. **[6]**

Total marks: 25

Data analysis

One way to assess your ability to reason logically is through data analysis. When we think of data, we tend to think of this as numbers and statistics, but data can be represented in numerous ways, such as on charts and in graphics, through images such as maps, and more. It can appear in both quantitative (numerical) and qualitative (categorical) forms.

The activity you just completed was a form of data analysis. The travel and band member profiles plus the list of 'other considerations' are each different sets of data which required you to discern their details before arriving at conclusions about them.

The information you were given contained a mix of quantitative data, such as the expense of something or the budget limits a band member had, and it contained qualitative information, like dietary preferences or medical limitations.

Data is unique from prose, the other type of reading material you will encounter in this course, because of the way in which it is presented: visually, spatially, categorically, or other. Prose, discussed in the next section, involves an ongoing flow of ideas presented all at once, as opposed to separately in sets.

Analysing prose

Analysing data can be challenging, but effective analysis of prose can be equally demanding. Data, like poetry, has a more distinct form. Prose, on the other hand, is continuous and free-flowing writing.

It is useful to compare the kind of questions you will answer for logical reasoning and prose analysis. *Logical reasoning* questions normally focus on:

- analytical comparisons
- problem-solving
- evidence-based judgement.

Prose analysis questions tend to involve:

- identifying elements of writing (i.e. tone, purpose, exemplification, style, structure)
- summarising or paraphrasing information in your own words
- analysing words and phrases in context and their impact on the overall message.

However, each set of skills is used to some extent in both types of questions.

The most common forms of prose you will be asked to analyse include:

- news or magazine articles
- essays
- extracts from works of literature
- speech transcripts
- emails.

To practise your reading comprehension skills, read the following article about travel and 'selfies'. Then answer the exam-style questions that follow.

Travel essay:
Selfies - are they ruining travel?

The Courier | Ute Junker | Sept. 3, 2016

Visiting any of the world's most popular sights, from the Trevi Fountain, to Buckingham Palace, to Old Faithful, is not unlike attending a rock concert; you will find that your view is obscured by a forest of outstretched arms,
5 brandishing camera phones instead of cigarette lighters. The camera phone has become an unavoidable part of the travel experience, one that is both a blessing and a curse, depending on who is wielding it.

There are plenty of travellers ready to sound off on the
10 topic of how the selfie circus is destroying the whole travel experience. Selfie snappers don't even bother setting foot inside monuments half the time, we are told; once they've snapped a suitably attractive shot, they simply move on to the next monument. Grand castles, mighty glaciers,
15 ancient ruins and scenic villages – all are reduced to providing backdrops for "panda travellers", the type that shoots, tweets and leaves.

Personally, I am sceptical of this argument, which tends to be long on invective and short on facts. Photography
20 has been an essential part of the travel experience since the **advent** of affordable cameras. Who hasn't reached for a camera to preserve a pinch-yourself moment in a far-distant land? Would anyone really go to the Taj Mahal and not take a photo? The Grand Canyon? On safari? And once
25 you have a photo, of course you want to show it off. Isn't posting a pic to Instagram just the 21st-century version of inviting friends and family over for a slide night?

I'm not the only one who refuses to join the **condemnation**. At least one senior travel figure argues

that posting photos on social media has brought big 30
benefits for the travel industry. According to Sue Badyari of World Expeditions, all those selfies posted by snap-happy travellers are broadening our collective travel horizons. Badyari has seen a surge of sales in big-ticket adventure trips such as the Inca Trail, the Great Wall Trek, 35
the Kilimanjaro Climb or the trek to Everest Base camp – driven, she says, by images posted on social media.

Destinations closer to home have also benefited from selfie fever. Rottnest Island, a day trip destination from Perth, has seen a boom in visitation thanks to a social media campaign 40
encouraging visitors to take a selfie with one of the island's friendly quokkas. The island has seen a 6 per cent spike in visitor numbers since the campaign was launched.

Not every destination is rolling out the red carpet for selfie snappers, however. In Mumbai, an epidemic of selfie 45
deaths prompted Mumbai's local government to declare 16 selfie-free zones, the *Washington Post* reported this year. That followed a spate of 19 selfie-related fatalities, including three students who stopped for a selfie in front of an oncoming train. 50

The phenomenon is not limited to Mumbai. Similar accidents have happened around the world, including a 17-year-old Russian girl who died falling from a St Petersburg bridge and a 21-year-old Spanish man who died trying to take a selfie atop a train. However, Mumbai is the 55
first place to have introduced such legislation, with fines of 1200 rupees ($24) levied on anyone who steps into the no-go zones, which are principally scenic coastal spots.

60 One of the main reasons selfie snappers aggravate their fellow travellers is their tendency to get in the way. It's a problem that has existed ever since cameras became affordable, but that stretched-arm pose adopted by selfie snappers does intrude further into other people's space than more traditional photo-snapping stances.

65 However, this is merely a symptom of a much larger problem, according to travel photographer Richard I'Anson: the need for better camera etiquette across the board. I'Anson, who leads photography trips to various countries, notes that many people seem to assume that
70 holding a camera gives them a licence to intrude.

"The idea of photography ethics is something I talk about on my photography trips," he says. "As a photographer, I try to do what I do as discreetly as I can; I know I'm intruding on people's privacy. We have to be aware and we
75 have to be sensitive and treat people with dignity."

Yet the issue of ethics is hardly a new phenomenon.

Take Maxime Du Camp, the man behind what was probably the world's first coffee table travel book. Accompanied by one of his friends – a then-
80 unknown writer called Gustave Flaubert – Du Camp took a trip through Egypt and Syria in 1849. Du Camp recorded their travels using an early Calotype camera, and the photographs featured in a book that was published upon his return.

85 In those days, photography required long exposures, which made street scenes impossible to capture.

Instead, Du Camp focused his camera on the area's ancient relics. To give a sense of scale of the massive monuments, Du Camp included the figure of a man in many of his photos. Yet to modern eyes, however, it is
90 outrageous to see someone carelessly clambering over ancient statues.

Despite the lines of etiquette selfies tend to cross, there is another aspect of the travel selfie phenomenon that is often overlooked. One of the reasons that they have
95 taken off, I think, is because other souvenirs have largely lost their lustre. We used to eagerly carry home exotic items from our travels: carved jade from China, camel hair caps from Morocco, carpets from Iran. In today's globalised world, these hard-to-get items have lost their
100 mystique. Chances are, the store down the road stocks something similar; if not, you can always order it over the internet. The glamour-backdrop selfie has taken over as the way to prove your status as an experienced traveller.

However, it's worth remembering that both selfies and
105 souvenirs are, in some ways, a distraction. Travel is not just about what you see and do in a destination; it's about the impact the destination has on you. For ultimately, destinations work on us like **Nietzsche's abyss**: even as we try to capture them with a camera, they are also
110 capturing us.

Abridged and adapted from an article by Ute Junker on
www.traveller.com.au, 3 September 2016

ARTICLE GLOSSARY

advent: the beginning of something

condemnation: very strong disapproval

Nietzsche's abyss: refers to a quote by the German philosopher Friedrich Nietzsche: 'He who fights with monsters might take care lest he thereby become a monster. And if you gaze for long into an abyss, the abyss gazes also into you.'

EXAM-STYLE QUESTIONS 3

Answer the reading comprehension questions **1–8**.

1 Identify two reasons why the travel selfie should be deemed acceptable in today's society, as mentioned in the article. **[2]**

2 Identify two pieces of evidence the author uses to expose the drawbacks of mixing selfies and travel. **[2]**

3 Explain in your own words as far as possible:

   a Sue Badyari's point of view regarding selfies as a part of travel, as stated in lines 31–37. **[3]**

   b the similarities between selfies and souvenirs, as stated in lines 97–104. **[3]**

4 What do you think is meant by:

   a Richard I'Anson's term, 'photography ethics' (lines 71–75) **[3]**

   b the line about Nietzsche's abyss that 'even as we try to capture them with a camera, they are also capturing us' (lines 109–111)? **[3]**

5 What is the author's purpose for including the information about Maxime Du Camp? Explain in your own words. **[2]**

6 Explain, using your own words, how the author's perspective about the travel selfie changes from the beginning of the article to the end. Justify your response. **[3]**

7 Explain the meaning of the following phrases as they are used in the passage. You may write the answer in one word or a short phrase. **[2]**

   a rolling out the red carpet (line 44)

   b to sound off on (line 9)

8 Using context as a clue, determine the meaning of the following words as they are used in the passage. Use a single word for each. **[2]**

   a invective (line 19)

   b aggravate (line 59)

Total marks: 25

F Practising what you have learnt

Read the list of exam-style essay questions, all of which concern the common theme of *Celebrity culture*. Select *one* question from the list. Using your previous experiences as a writer, and any knowledge you have gained in Unit 1, draft an essay.

EXAM-STYLE QUESTIONS 4

Answer questions **1–10**.

1 Evaluate the impact of celebrity culture on people aged over 30 years old. **[30]**

2 How far do you agree that celebrities can be considered role models for young adults? **[30]**

3 How far do you agree that celebrity contributions to charitable causes are beneficial? **[30]**

4 'The paparazzi have no right to interfere with the private lives of public citizens.' What is your view? **[30]**

5 To what extent is the product a reflection of the artist? **[30]**

6 To what extent should people be upset with the high salaries paid out to big name company owners, athletes and/or entertainers? **[30]**

7 To what extent is a formal education necessary? **[30]**

8 Should subjects like art, music and drama be removed from education to make way for core subjects like maths and literacy? **[30]**

9 What do the movies offer that the stage cannot? **[30]**

10 Is gossip ever justifiable? **[30]**

63

Summary

Key points to remember from this chapter:

- Setting a purpose for reading, and reading actively, can help you better understand a text.
- It can help you to read closely and carefully if you mark the text and make connections to, and between, what you are reading and the points you are noting.
- Other reading strategies that support reading comprehension include re-reading, chunking information and challenging perspectives.
- Essential reading comprehension skills include the ability to:
  - identify main idea, details, author's purpose and tone
  - apply information to form new ideas
  - analyse information in order to make inferences or comparisons and to better understand language used when communicating
  - evaluate information in order to draw conclusions and make judgements
  - communicate ideas through logical reasoning and paraphrasing.
- Logical reasoning material may involve everyday problems and/or data analysis.
- Prose comprehension questions tend to focus on elements of writing, words/phrases in context and summary/paraphrase tasks.

Unit 2:
Understanding and applying

Chapter 2.1
Summarising and explaining what you read

The term *art* applies to more than just paintings and sculptures. What qualities does an item need to be considered a work of art? This chapter will feature *Visual arts* as its key theme.

Learning objectives

In this chapter, you will learn about:

■ how information is organised to achieve a purpose
■ how to put information into your own words
■ strategies for summarising information
■ using expository skills to develop an argument.

A Introduction

Writing to inform or explain is a skill you will use often in everyday life. Whether you are emailing a family member or presenting information to work colleagues, the ability to condense ideas and explain them in simple terms is an important skill. It is also a skill you need when writing for academic purposes.

Specifically, in this course, you will need to be able to summarise and explain:

- the ideas of others in response to reading comprehension questions
- evidence or information in an argument before arguing a point or sharing an observation about it.

No matter the purpose, this chapter will help you to develop the foundational skills of summarising and explaining, which will serve as the basis for all the writing you do in the Cambridge International AS Level English General Paper course.

B Understanding how ideas are organised, connected and ordered

To be able to summarise and/or explain something you have read, you first need to understand how the author has organised the information. Writers have several options for organising ideas, many of which you have probably used yourself already. Imagine if you had to explain in your science class where acid rain comes from. Think about how you would structure your ideas in order to convey this message. Or what if your physical education teacher asked you to demonstrate how to perform a particular exercise properly? What order would you put this information in so that your audience can understand you?

Organising ideas

The way you organise your thoughts in any explanation depends on your topic and your purpose. Some of the most common organisational patterns are:

- *compare/contrast* – describing the similarities and/or differences between two or more things

- *problem/solution* – explaining the context of a problem, then giving details of one or more possible solutions
- *cause/effect* – explaining the relationship between two or more things
- *sequence* – describing something in numerical or chronological order
- *reasons* + *examples* – offering a series of points and examples.

Making appropriate choices organisationally will therefore play an important role in this course. Consider, for example, the following reading comprehension question:

> Explain how the tone of the speech changes from the beginning to the end.

Which organisational pattern might you use to accomplish this task? Chances are, compare/contrast seems like the most natural choice in this case because you would need to show how the tone changes, or is *different*, from beginning to end.

Read the article below about visual media in Japan. Observe the author's decisions for organising his explanation based on his topic and purpose for writing. Then complete Activity 1.

ACTIVITY 1

Read the article that follows, then answer these questions.
1   Which organisational structure does the author use?
2   Why do you think the author chose this structure?

Animated fantasy film charms Japan and soars to top of box office

Themes of body swapping, the search for love and a frantic quest to save a town from imminent destruction have combined to propel a Japanese animated film to box office gold.

Your Name, Makoto Shinkai's fantasy film, is about two teenagers drawn together when they appear in each other's dreams, even though they have never met: one, a teenage girl living in a picturesque but unexciting village, and the other, a Tokyo schoolboy. Much of the film's charm derives from their attempts to make sense of their situation and, ultimately, to find each other.

Shinkai has described *Your Name* as his attempt to understand, and perhaps relieve, teenage **angst**. 'I wanted to create something for the generation of young people who **crave** stories like this.'

Your Name is also Shinkai's **homage** to the body-swapping themes of Japanese literature, centuries

before they became a Hollywood **staple**, and because it feeds into modern, Japanese anxiety. The threat of natural, and nuclear, disasters are all too familiar fears in the Japanese **psyche**; this is probably why the film's climax involves the descent of a comet, described as a once-in-a-thousand-year event, the same catastrophic status **afforded** the magnitude-9 earthquake and **tsunami** that destroyed much of Japan's north-east coast in March 2011.

Because of these ingredients combined, *Your Name* has made a tidal impact since its release. It has been seen by more than 8 million people since its debut in August, the **highest-grossing** film in Japan this year, and the ninth highest of all time; and it has earned more than 10 billion yen (£77 million) in box office receipts.

The film has made the 43-year-old Shinkai an obvious candidate to continue the **anime** legacy left by globally acclaimed director, Hayao Miyazaki.

Not only has the success of *Your Name* directly affected the forward path of Shinkai, but it has also made its mark on Japan as well. The painstaking recreations of everyday Tokyo scenes have prompted hordes of fans to descend on locations from the film.

Shinkai's **knack** for knowing his audience's hopes and fears has certainly paid off: 'I can never stand unrivalled like Miyazaki, but ... I am confident of delivering something others can't make.'

Abridged and adapted from an article by Justin McCurry,
The Guardian, September 2016

ARTICLE GLOSSARY

angst: feeling of anxiety about the state of the world
crave: wish for strongly
homage: public honour or praise
staple: regular feature
psyche: soul or spirit

afforded: given to
tsunami: huge sea wave caused by an earthquake
highest-grossing: earning the most money
anime: a style of Japanese film and TV animation
knack: natural skill

Clearly, making deliberate choices about which pattern to use will help the audience to best understand your ideas. Each pattern has its own, unique set of words and phrases, which helps organise the ideas. What words or phrases might appear, for instance, in:

- a response to a comprehension question that asks why the old buildings mentioned in a text should be preserved instead of torn down?
- an essay arguing the consequences of legalising an act like graffiti?

Refer to the table below, which lists signal words for organising information, to help you.

Compare/contrast	Problem/solution	Cause/effect	Sequence	Reason + example
like/unlike	problem/issue	because	first	for instance
similarly	trouble/matter	since	next	for example
in contrast	answer	thus	then	to illustrate
however	solution	therefore	before	
likewise	alternative	as a result	after	
on the other hand		consequently	during	
		if … then	following	

Connecting ideas

In order for information to be organised, the ideas need to be related in some way. One strategy for understanding how ideas connect is to represent them visually.

Read the text 'But I'm not artistic': how teachers shape kids' creative development. Then look at how the ideas are organised and connected, as shown in the visual representation that follows the text.

'But I'm not artistic':
how teachers shape kids' creative development

No doubt most people assume that preschools, more than any other education setting, provide creative environments and experiences that best support children's artistic learning and potential. But this is not always the case.

Some children may not have access to high-quality visual art education. Many early childhood educators lack the self-belief, skills and knowledge needed to provide quality visual arts experiences. They struggle to provide the types of experiences that support young children to access the many benefits of making visual art.

Even educators who value art as a central part of the early childhood curriculum maintain beliefs about the purposes of art that are often confused. Some see art activities as a way to keep children busy. Others use art as a form of therapy or fine-motor development instead of as a tool for communication, problem-solving and meaning-making. Moreover, the experiences offered to children in the name of art often consist of adult-directed crafts and activity sheets – instead of creative and open-ended use of quality art materials. A lack of content knowledge, art skills and confidence causes educators to justify the use of gimmicky commercial materials like glitter, pipe-cleaners and fluorescent feathers. They believe these materials are more fun for children.

Visual art experiences enhance young children's learning and development in many ways. These include intrinsic motivation, enjoyment, positive attitudes, cognitive problem-solving, self-discipline, the development of tools for communication and meaning-making, and fostering creativity and imagination, to name just a few. Creative thinking and the ability to make meaning in many ways also happens to be the key to success in the 21st century. Early childhood experiences with art can therefore affect developing confidence and learning potential throughout a child's education and into adulthood. If an educator's fear or misunderstanding of art stifles a child's individual learning style at a young age, this may prevent them from reaching their full potential later on.

Abridged and adapted from an article in
The Conversation, January 2015

This visual representation is a way of showing the ideas in the text and the relationship between those ideas in a way that you can see easily, using arrows, labels and boxes.

CAUSE/ACTION	EFFECT
Preschool educators lack the visual art knowledge and confidence to provide valuable art experiences.	Children's potential to creatively express ideas may be restricted; lifelong potential for engaged creative learning could be stifled.

ACTIVITY 2

Read the two extracts that follow. Think about which organisational pattern is being used to convey the main idea(s) and important details in each. For each extract, create a visual representation that shows how these ideas all connect.

69

The legalisation of street art in Rio de Janeiro

Extract 1

In Rio de Janeiro, street art is **ubiquitous**. It exists in all corners of the city, from the *favelas* to upper-class neighbourhoods, from residential to institutional. It is bold in scale and aesthetics, and is anything but graffiti. The urban fabric of Rio de Janeiro also figures prominently in the evolving street art scene. The high walls, whether for security or to contain the **topography**, provide **ample** surfaces for painting. But rather than location **dictating** art, the relationship between owner and artist has a direct impact on where street art occurs.

Owners of buildings, both residential and commercial, sometimes invite artists for commissions, which is done to protect from **tagging**, as an aesthetic choice or as an economic choice – painting a **façade** with art may be cheaper than another mode of beautification. In another case, street artists ask permission from the owner.

While the majority of street art continues to be created **illicitly** or at locations with no clear ownership, the existence of these new partnerships marks a striking shift in the production of street art and its relationship with the community. Painted walls turn basic infrastructure into active spots of engagement, creating new informal public spaces that dialogue between residents and their city.

Extract 2

The idea of creating a community is one of the strongest undercurrents I observed in Rio's street

art scene, whether through city-run initiatives, individual projects or local community groups. One strategy is for the city to permit large-scale graffiti on under-utilised walls by limiting 'paint-overs'. The most prominent example is the half-mile stretch along the walls of the Jockey Club situated across from the Botanical Garden (*Jardim Botânico*).

According to Lu Olivero of the AEROSOuL CARIOCA project, Rio's street artists come to this wall to 'make a name for themselves. It is, in my estimation, the largest collection of street art in the city, reserved for only the best. If Street Art had a professional league, the wall at Jardim Botânico would be **the NBA**.'

Some large-scale community projects are initiated by artists, such as the well-known 'Women Are Heroes', where French artist JR famously **canvassed** the Providencia *favela* in Rio de Janeiro with the eyes of women who had lost a loved one in violence with the police, or the colourful façade of the Santa Marta *favela*, an initiative of artists Jeroen Koolhaas and Dre Urhahn, in conjunction with the Let's Colour Project. More often, however, street art occurs as **patches** of small-scale interventions and permanent organisations have **cropped up** to promote the movement and to create opportunities for employment.

Projeto Queto is a community centre founded by Francisco da Silva, the leader of graffiti team Nação Crew, in Sampaoi, a favela in Rio's north zone. Those involved speak of the inspirational potential of graffiti in the *favelas*, along with its ability to establish discipline and structure.

In addition to graffiti workshops, Projeto Queto offers classes in audio production, silk-screening, sewing

and fashion design. Smael Vagner, another member of Nação Crew, believes vocational opportunities are a **by-product** of practising street art: 'Graffiti has created a new horizon for young people that have gone on to become artists and teachers. There are cases in which drug traffickers are now graffiti artists. It's a gateway to a new perspective on life for the poor in *favelas* who don't have other opportunities.'

While it is too soon to tell if these statements are **utopian** hopes, it is clear that the momentum for street art at the community level is strong, and the city and state are **on board** to help create an environment in which it can flourish.

Adapted From posts by Michelle Young in Huffington Post – www.huffingtonpost.com/michelle-young/

ARTICLE GLOSSARY

ubiquitous: found everywhere

topography: natural physical features

ample: plenty of

dictate: control, strongly affect

tagging: graffiti (where graffiti artists add their own mark or 'tag')

façade: front of a building

illicitly: illegally

the NBA: National Basketball Association in North America, considered the top basketball league in the world

canvas: cover with pictures

patches: small areas

crop up: appear without planning

by-product: something unexpected that happens as a result of something else

utopian: idealistic, aiming to be perfect

on board: supportive

DID YOU KNOW?

A *favela* is a low-income, densely-packed community of slum housing in Rio de Janeiro, Brazil. Favelas are home to over 1.5 million people, roughly a quarter of the city's population.

Now that you have had some practice considering how other writers organise and connect their ideas, think about how you might apply this to your own writing. When planning ideas for a response to a reading or writing question, for example, it can also be particularly useful to 'see' these thoughts in a visual way first.

TIP

Mind mapping is a type of visual brainstorm which works particularly well when planning an organisational structure containing reasons plus examples. It can therefore be useful in developing responses to comprehension questions, which sometimes ask you to identify reasons and evidence. These elements are also necessary when writing essay arguments. Mind mapping will therefore be discussed in more depth below.

Consider the following essay question:

> How far do you agree that cartoons are for entertainment and nothing else?

The question is asking you to present an argument considering whether or not cartoons have a purpose beyond mere entertainment. No matter how you approach your argument, you will also need to give fair consideration to both sides in some way.

To ensure that you do this, you can begin planning ideas by using a diagram like the one opposite. Start by drawing a 't-chart' on a blank sheet of paper, intersecting lines to create two columns with headings. Head each column to represent the various sides of the question or argument. Then draw a series of mind maps in each column to visually lay out potential reasons and evidence in support of each perspective.

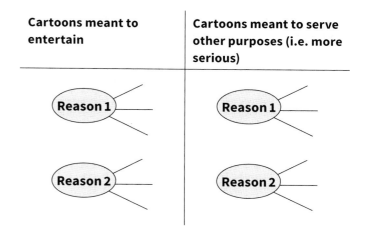

Mind maps are a quick and helpful way to visually organise ideas when communicating a lengthier or more complex response rather than just identifying information. To help you think about how you might organise and connect your own thoughts in responses like this, complete Activities 3 and 4.

ACTIVITY 3

With a partner, continue to generate ideas for the essay question:

> How far do you agree that cartoons are for entertainment and nothing else?

1   Put ideas into a mind map like the one below or create a visual representation of your own. Remember to include concrete evidence to support each of your reasons.

2   Then review your ideas to see which ideas overlap, connect or stand in opposition to one another. Draw arrows to show connections between ideas. As a tip, you might want to make note of what each relationship is so you do not forget once you begin writing.

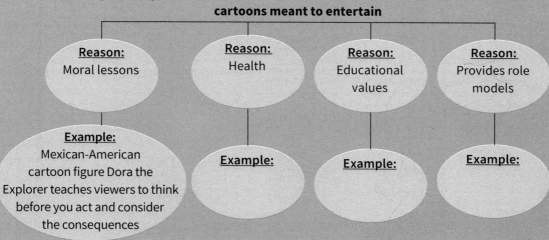

!

TIP

For other strategies for organising ideas, you can also refer back to the 'planning and organising strategy' table in Chapter 2.2 Section *F Organising ideas to show comprehension*.

ACTIVITY 4

1   For the imaginary comprehension questions **a–e** below, think about how you would visually organise ideas if you had to plan responses to each. After carefully reading each question, draw a generic visual representation to illustrate how you might brainstorm and organise ideas for each one. The first one has been done for you.

    a Based on what you read in the opening paragraphs of the reading material, account for the increasing popularity of social media platforms which feature images as opposed to text.

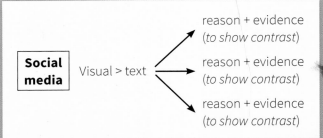

    b Which form of art from Paragraph 2 do you find more useful and entertaining: X or Y? Justify your response.

    c According to the last section of the text, 'art is only for the wealthy'. Using the text or your own outside knowledge, suggest ways the town could make art more accessible for its people.

    d Explain what might happen if graffiti were made legal. Use the information found in paragraphs 4 and 5 to develop your response.

    e What does the theatre offer that the cinema does not? Use the text and your own, outside knowledge to support your answer.

2   For the essay questions **1–5** below:

    a Identify which organisational pattern you would use to organise your response to each. Be prepared to justify your decisions to the class.

    b Select one question which interests you and generate ideas by visually representing them on a separate sheet of paper. Provided your visual meets the purpose of the essay, there is no wrong way to do this!

Essay questions

1   'There is no beauty in modern art.' Discuss with reference to specific examples.

2   Evaluate the role museums and art galleries play in your society.

3   To what extent is the cinema to blame for a declining interest in traditional theatre?

4   Consider the view that instead of preserving old buildings, we should be investing money in new forms of architecture.

5   'Architecture should be more functional than artistic.' How far do you agree?

Ordering ideas

Taking time to consider how you will organise and connect ideas in a response is an important part of communicating clearly. Once you can envision what you want to say and how the ideas relate, there is one final step you can take to ensure that you not only respond clearly but also coherently.

Specifically, the *order* of your ideas plays a role in effective communication. Your points should appear in a logical sequence (as opposed to a randomised order). Take a moment to consider the following, for instance: if someone were reading an argument you wrote, would the response still make sense if they read your points in a *different* order? If the order of your argument's ideas can be moved around without consequence, this is a probably a sign that you haven't thought carefully enough about connecting them in a logical sequence.

> **TIP**
>
> Brainstorming ideas visually is a useful way to think about the order in which you plan to address your points because it helps you to see how the ideas connect.

Instead of appearing in a randomised order, ideas should be deliberately sequenced so that one point builds on from the previous one to create a logical progression of ideas. Look back to Activity 10 in Chapter 1.2, where you were asked to observe the use of seamless transitions in an essay. Think about how the organisation and logic behind this essay would be affected if the support paragraphs were put into a different order.

To help you better understand the importance of order, complete the activity below, which asks you to create a 'photo essay'.

ACTIVITY 5

1 Look at the 'photo essay' below to see how the author deliberately puts the images in a specific order to convey a clear and logical point about his argument concerning traditional arts and crafts. Based on the connections between the photos and the order in which they are placed, can you identify the point the author is trying to make?

2 Select a topic of interest from the list of course topics featured in Chapter 1.1. Develop an argument around the topic using only five photographs to communicate. These can be photographs you take yourself from your local community or professional ones you acquire online. The goal is to arrange the photos in an order that 'builds' ideas logically from one image to the next. Use the photo essay example as a guide.

C Using your own words to explain ideas

Once you can see how information is arranged and how ideas connect, you are in more of a position to explain a text using your own words. This is a key skill in this course, but perhaps one of the most difficult ones to master, so this section offers strategies to help you acquire this skill.

Specifically, there are two ways that can help you explain ideas in this course:

- summarising
- paraphrasing.

Course topic: Traditional arts and crafts

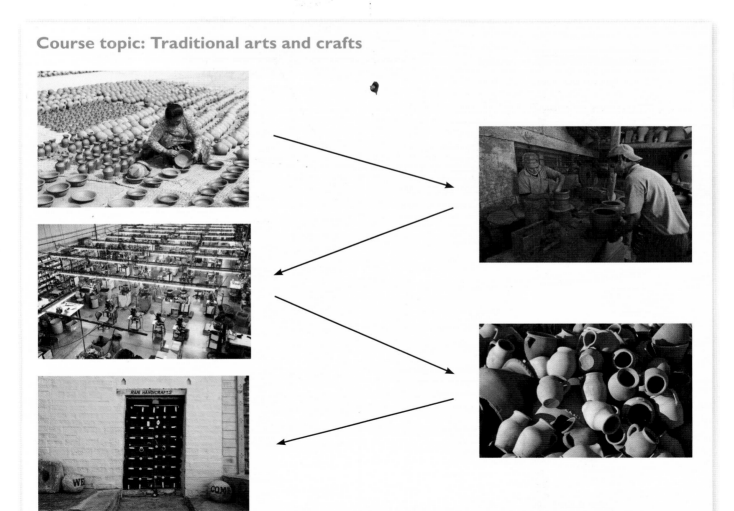

Summarising

When you **summarise**, you use your own words to express the key points of another piece of writing. It can also imply that you express ideas more simply, using fewer words. If you can summarise information, it shows you understand what you are reading.

KEY TERM

Summarise: give a short, clear description of the main points or facts from a piece of writing.

Specifically, a summary:

- restates the central ideas expressed
- covers the content comprehensively, but avoids too many details
- satisfies the audience's basic need to know *who*, *what*, *where*, *why*, *when* and *how*
- presents only information mentioned in the piece of writing.

KEY SKILLS

To summarise information effectively, you need to use key reading comprehension skills such as identifying the main idea and understanding tone. See Chapter 1.3 Section *D Essential reading comprehension skills* to review a full list of these skills.

Comprehension questions in this course will usually ask you to summarise a particular section of text rather than the whole text, but this coursebook will provide you with guidance on both skills.

Summarising is an important skill because the knowledge you gain from reading can be applied to your writing, to expand and reinforce ideas. Combining other ideas with your own can also lead you to new insights about your topic.

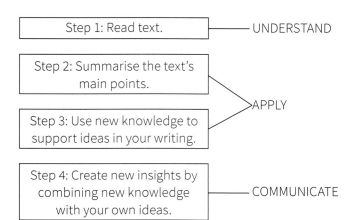

KEY SKILLS

Summarising plays a critical role in developing an argument. You will need to be able to summarise the views of others before you can agree with them or prove them wrong. See Chapters 3.1, 3.2 and 5.1 for more information on developing arguments.

Strategies for writing summaries

In order to summarise ideas, you need to make sure you understand them. Paying close attention to both the content and structure of the material can help you better understand its main message. As you read, pay attention to what the text says and how it is organised. Once you understand the material thoroughly, you can then identify which information to include in your summary.

TIP

Sometimes you will be asked to summarise a few sentences. At other times you might be asked to summarise whole paragraphs or more. Whatever information you are summarising, be sure to communicate the message in your own words, as opposed to 'lifting' words or phrases from the text.

Here are the steps for reading a text closely and carefully:

1. Annotate as you read. Here are some guidelines you can use to annotate, or create your own system:
   - Circle important people or groups. (*Who?*)
   - Put a box around relevant locations and time frames. (*Where? When?*)
   - Use an asterisk (or brackets) to mark any phrases or sentences that express the main idea of the material. (*What?*)
   - Underline any details you think are important to the point. (*Why? How?*)

2. Review what you have read and marked. Also look carefully at subheadings, illustrations and other graphics or organisational elements, and ask yourself:
   - What purpose do they serve?
   - How do they complement the text being summarised?

3. Using a highlighter, distinguish between primary and secondary information.
   - Primary information includes 'big picture' ideas (i.e. reasons) which support the main message.
   - Secondary information contains background information and context.

TIP

The main idea is often mentioned at the beginning or end of a text – or both. Scientists, for example, usually indicate a general direction at the beginning of their research but they don't arrive at their main point until the end of their article, after they have analysed all the evidence. In this case, the main point would not appear until the conclusion.

Paraphrasing

Summarising is one way of expressing the ideas of others, but this can also be done through **paraphrasing**. Whereas a summary is a shortened version of text, a paraphrase maintains the length of the original idea, but expresses it using different words and grammatical structure.

In the *Harvard Guide to Using Sources*, the difference between the two is described like this:

> Whereas a summary provides your readers with a condensed overview of a source (or part of a source), a paraphrase of a source offers your readers the same level of detail provided in the original source. Therefore, while a summary will be shorter than the original source material, a paraphrase will generally be about the same length as the original source material.

A common mistake students make in this course is confusing the act of paraphrasing or summarising with that of **quoting** the reading material. When you quote text, you use the original wording of the author. Under some academic circumstances, such as when writing a research paper or in a literary analysis, quoting text directly may be appropriate. When responding to comprehension questions in Cambridge International AS Level English General Paper, however, you should avoid quoting original wording of a text altogether (unless explicitly instructed otherwise). This is because you need to use your own words to show understanding, not those of the author.

KEY TERMS

Paraphrasing: maintaining the idea of someone's thoughts, observations or ideas, but putting them into your own words.

Quoting: using the exact words from the text (verbatim) to express a thought, observation or idea.

The examples which follow demonstrate the difference between summary, paraphrase, and quotation of the original source.

Original source

For many education advocates, the arts are a panacea: They supposedly increase test scores, generate social responsibility and turn around failing schools. Most of the supporting evidence, though, does little more than establish correlations between exposure to the arts and certain outcomes. Research that demonstrates a causal relationship has been virtually nonexistent.

A few years ago, however, we had a rare opportunity to explore such relationships when the Crystal Bridges Museum of American Art opened in Bentonville, Ark. Through a study of school tours to the museum, we were able to determine that strong causal relationships do in fact exist between arts education and a range of desirable outcomes.

Students who, by lottery, were selected to visit the museum on a field trip demonstrated stronger critical thinking skills, displayed higher levels of social tolerance, exhibited greater historical empathy and developed a taste for art museums and cultural institutions.

Visiting an art museum exposes students to a diversity of ideas that challenge them with different perspectives on the human condition. Expanding access to art, whether through programs in schools or through visits to area museums and galleries, should therefore be a central part of any school's curriculum.

Brian Kisida is a senior research associate and Jay P. Greene is a professor of education reform at the University of Arkansas. Daniel H. Bowen is a postdoctoral fellow at the Kinder Institute of Rice University.

From 'Art makes you smart' by Brian Kisida, Jay P. Greene, and Daniel H. Bowen

Summary

Because a causal relationship between arts education and desirable outcomes such as improved critical thinking and empathy can now be found, schools should be placing greater emphasis on this aspect of the curriculum.

Paraphrase

Researchers at the University of Arkansas and the Kinder Institute of Rice University recently conducted a study at the Crystal Bridges Museum of American Art to see if visiting museums has any academic and/or social impact on students. For the first time, they were able to find more than just a correlation between the two; specifically, they found that a causal relationship exists between exposure to the arts and improved critical thinking skills, empathy and other desirable outcomes. They conclude that schools should therefore focus more on arts education.

Complete the activity below, which will help you practise summarising and paraphrasing information.

ACTIVITY 6

Read the article 'The story of an art fair'. Discuss with a partner what information you would annotate if you had your own copy. Then answer the comprehension questions in Activity 7.

Quotation

A recent study revealed that "strong causal relationships do in fact exist between arts education and a range of desirable outcomes" such as "stronger critical thinking skills…higher levels of social tolerance…greater historical empathy and…a taste for art museums.

Notice that unlike drafting a summary of paraphrase, the quoted response does little to demonstrate the student's comprehension of the text.

The story of an art fair

The Outsider Art Fair (OAF) was founded by New York art fair magnate Sandy Smith in 1993. Smith had been in the business of launching unprecedented art fairs since he established the Fall Antiques Show in 1979. When two of his closest advisors approached him with the idea of an art show entirely comprised of self-taught work – a genre quickly gaining momentum in the art market – Smith decided to give it a shot. At the time, such work was commonly described as 'primitive'. Smith, however, opted for a different descriptor: 'outsider'.

'We named it that because that's what Roger Cardinal called it,' Smith said in an interview with HuffPost, referring to the art historian whose book *Outsider Art* was published in 1972. Cardinal used the term as an English alternative to *Art Brut* – a phrase coined by French artist Jean Dubuffet to mean 'raw art', art that was unmediated by education, culture or ego. 'But nobody knew what outsider art was back then,' Smith continued. 'Many dealers were aghast that we called it "outsider".'

A portrait of the artist

The term is still contested today. The word 'outsider'
is meant to denote artists working not only outside
25 the art world, but outside of mainstream culture,
whether due to physical isolation, incarceration,
mental illness or other singular circumstances. In
such an environment, at least ideally, the creative act is
untethered by artistic precedent or market trends. The
30 outsider artist creates not for fame, or money, or glory,
but for sanity, peace of mind, and survival. At its core,
then, the OAF is a fair that generously and miraculously
and sometimes dangerously shows work that was never
meant to be shown.

35 Of course, the circumstances necessary for an artist to
create truly 'raw' work are hardly ever just right, as few
are wholly isolated from social connections and cultural
associations. Furthermore, many critics who oppose
the term believe the 'outsider' distinction can ghettoize
40 artists who are already disenfranchised enough. It's easy
to imagine how quickly afflictions such as poverty,
mental illness, and physical disabilities can be fetishized
and exploited in the chase for 'pure art'.

But there is something powerful humming in the
45 broad genre of outsider art that is impossible to deny.
Stripped of pretension, irony, and cleverness, the best
outsider artworks use a wholly individualized visual
language brewed in the imagination to probe universal,
unspeakable states that hit the viewer hard.

50 'It has a spiritual dimension to it,' Henry Boxer, an
outsider art dealer told HuffPost. 'That's what I connect
with. There is a very deep space we all have; the
outsiders seem to have direct contact to that.'

Plenty of outsider artists live a lifetime of art without
55 ever selling their work. In fact, this condition is one of
outsider art's identifying factors. For many, it is often 'art
that is not made in order to be sold'. And yet, strangely,
OAF is an art fair that introduced most of America and
the rest of the world to the genre.

60 'It's been easier to open up the field to new discoveries
from all around the world,' OAF Director Becca
Hoffman notes. 'With the knowledge of the fair in the
furthest reaches of the world, we see new artists bringing
work from Japan, Australia, Europe, and South America.
65 The fair has really opened up those boundaries to the
non–Western canon.'

Blurred lines

In terms of related art movements, there's folk art –
decorative or utilitarian objects made by untrained
artisans as part of a communal tradition. While folk art 70
often resembles outsider art in style, the distinction lies
in the context of its creation: was the artist participating
in a traditional ritual or engaged in a solitary surge of
vision?

But there's also a fine line that runs along contemporary 75
art, too. This is because, in part, the success of the
fair itself led more and more contemporary artists
to familiarize themselves with outsider work, and
sometimes pull from its aesthetic.

The owner is well aware of just how porous the 80
boundary separating outsider art from contemporary
art can be. Rather than overzealously guarding the
partition, Edlin uses the OAF to embrace the overlap.
'We look at [outsider art] as part of the greater art world
and less of an island unto itself,' he said. 85

Outside appeal

In an earlier interview, curator Matthew Craven
explained his thoughts on why contemporary artists
were so drawn to the work of outsiders. 'I think what
artists are typically trying to do when you see that 90
'outsider aesthetic' – it's trying to tune out everything
you've learned before, to really approach your work in
a different way,' he said. 'Getting rid of things you've
learned in the past is sometimes a bigger skill than
focusing on the skills you've learned over time.' 95

Much has changed since the OAF's first edition, 25
years ago. The field of outsider art has gone from near
obscurity to a genre that's exhibited at venues from
the Brooklyn Museum to the Venice Biennale.

One thing remains the same, however. Described by 100
OAF Director Becca Hoffman as 'a breath of fresh air'
amongst the sea of contemporary art fairs, the spirit of
the OAF remains intact, perhaps now more than ever.
'There is a warmth,' Harris said when describing the
OAF's magic. 'This is real.' 105

Abridged and adapted from 'The Story Of An Art Fair Whose
Work Was Never Meant To Be Sold' by Pricilla Frank,
Huffington
Post, *January 2017*

ACTIVITY 7

Answer the comprehension questions **1–6**.

1 In your own words, explain how the Outsider Art Fair originated.

2 What is an 'outsider', according to the article? Explain in your own words as far as possible.

3 In your own words, explain the main message of paragraph 7 (lines 54–59).

4 Using approximately 30 of your own words, summarise the section entitled, 'Blurred lines'.

5 Using 150–200 words or fewer, summarise the main points of the material.

6 In one sentence of approximately 40 words, summarise the author's main message.

TIP

A reading comprehension question might ask you to summarise or explain different aspects about a particular text. Lots of practice in putting the ideas of others into your own words is therefore key to success in this course.

D Using expository skills in an argument

The skills of summarising and paraphrasing are an important part of your success in the reading comprehension component of this course, but they play a key role in writing successful essays, too. Since you will not have any reading materials in front of you when writing an essay in an exam situation, you are not expected to quote a source of information word-for-word, so clearly you will need to paraphrase the information to which you may be referring.

Explanation and summary skills can also be used in different ways when writing an essay such as when you are:

• establishing the context of your topic

• offering examples to support a point

• explaining the connection between evidence and claims.

When you use examples in the body of your essay, for example, you first need to *summarise* them, then *explain* their significance to your thesis. Expository skills are therefore a foundational part of your ability to communicate an argument!

ACTIVITY 8

Read the following two essays, which tackle different categories under the chapter's theme and course topic, *Visual arts*. With a partner, identify where in each essay the writer uses expository skills to shape the argument.

How far do you agree that cartoons are for entertainment and nothing else?

When the average American child turns on the television to watch afternoon cartoons, it probably isn't for the purpose of learning something new. Yet without even realising, the seemingly simple adventures of our favourite characters are sometimes the source of our most memorable lessons, from maths to music, even appropriate social behaviour. It is therefore worth arguing that cartoons serve a serious purpose beyond mere
5   entertainment.

Beyond their traditional duty to entertain, stories are usually built around a moral theme – or a lesson learnt – and cartoon stories are certainly no exception to this rule. One of the most classic examples of this occurs in Charlie Brown's 'Thanksgiving' episode, where the moral value of gratitude is taught. During the show, Peppermint Patty invites herself to Charlie Brown's Thanksgiving dinner; yet when she arrives, she complains about the food instead
10   of being thankful for it. Using a situation not uncommon to our everyday lives, a show like this can easily equip its audience with a better understanding of how to treat others, which is a serious lesson to learn.

Not only are important moral messages conveyed through individual episodes, they can also be central to entire characters. Since the behaviour of these figures tends to reflect our own cultural values, children and adults of all ages fall in love with the characters of popular cartoons. In so many instances, a two-dimensional

15 cartoon becomes a 3-D role model we look up to. For example, when the *GI Joe* cartoon was made in the 1980s, viewers admired this soldier's patriotism and commitment to fight against evil. Similarly, He-Man's great strength made him an ideal role model for children, as did She-Ra. Through the choices they make, these characters model traits we admire, such as bravery and mental might, making it plausible that cartoons have a bigger purpose than just leisurely enjoyment.

20   Yet there are other characters whose outlandish behaviours might not seem like they are meant to stretch beyond the realm of fiction. Characters of 'chase' cartoons like *Tom and Jerry*, for example, probably don't teach much in the way of cultural values, yet there is still something to be said about what children can learn in terms of action and consequence. When Wile E. Coyote's absurd inventions to catch the speedy Road Runner fail, or when Pinky and the Brain's grandiose plans to take over the world backfire, children are somehow absorbing

25 Newton's Third Law of Motion: for every action there is an equal and opposite reaction. In this sense, even the most simple-minded scenes can possess something of value when it comes to the way we behave.

    Cartoons teach us many lessons about life, but they can also teach us academic lessons, too. Most viewers, young and old, do not even realise that they are being educated when tuning in to television, but the academic impact is sometimes undeniable. For younger children, consider the 1990s cartoon series, *The Magic Schoolbus*.

30 The purpose of this show was to increase interest in science for girls and minorities, two groups who were falling behind in the subject nationwide. The show covered topics like gravity, the stars, honey bees and the wetlands, among others. The producers wanted to encourage a more balanced interest in science, and their vision proved that entertainment could be merged with serious educational purpose.

    Meanwhile, high-school students can reap the academic benefits cartoons have to offer, too. For struggling

35 readers, it might be difficult to understand the message being expressed in a classic work like Harper Lee's *To Kill a Mockingbird*, for instance; but the *X-Men* cartoon series, which deals with the same issues of racism, segregation and isolation, makes these concepts much more accessible through animation. The characters' struggles with being different clearly demonstrate how serious literary themes underpin modern cartoon entertainment.

40   It might sound like make-believe, but the foundation of many television cartoons is built on the story of our own reality. As a culture, we use the art of storytelling to communicate how we experience the world around us. No matter how outlandish, characters are a reflection of our culture, and their actions therefore serve as both example and non-example for how we should behave. Thus, while television cartoon shows may traditionally be loved for their light-hearted humour, they should also be recognised for the very real wisdom

45 they impress upon us.

79

'With today's technology, anyone can be a photographer.' What is your view?

In today's digital society, many will contend that 'anyone can be a photographer', so to speak. The latest smartphone technology allows users to take photos that achieve the same background blur, or 'bokeh', effect you might get in using a professional DSLR camera. It is also standard for these devices to now feature dynamic range (HDR) image processing, which, again, is what traditionally makes professional photography stand out. What lacks consideration,

Photographer Robert Capa was famous for his war photos.

however, is that real photography requires much more than a bunch of fancy tools. Taking a photo requires the ability to capture an image in an aesthetically pleasing way and the emotional maturity to create a heart-rending experience for the viewer. In short, it requires skillful and creative technique.

More than anything else, the art of photography requires a certain skill set because the artist must know how to manipulate a camera's technology. Without this talent, much is lost in the art form of the photo. One of the most basic skills when taking pictures, for instance, involves the use of mathematical formulas to calculate things such as aperture or shutter speed. Much like Da Vinci's *The Vitruvian Man*, photography has been taken to a scientific level, one that requires careful skill and highly detailed design, which not everybody can do.

Furthermore, photography demands ingenuity in order to achieve the right effect when capturing a subject. Consider the photographic 'rule of thirds' as an example. A guideline for photographers, this technique suggests that if you aim to place the best focus on and around your subject, it should fall into one of the 'thirds' of the picture: top, middle or bottom. This theory exemplifies the enormous care that is taken to bring photography into the realm of art, and it could not be done without the expertise of the modern artist.

While photography requires skill, it is also an art form that needs creative technique to thrive. One must reach deep into the ambiguous to capture something that is truly interesting. One way to look at it is that everyone has seen a tree at some time or another, but it takes the skilled photographer to capture it in such a way that it moves his audience to new (or renewed) emotion.

A photographer whose creative explorations have made this kind of impact is Peter Lik, an Australian artist who is well known for the success of artistic pieces such as *One*. Specifically, his photograph of trees reflecting on a lake has sold for millions of dollars. He has also used his creative vision to explore landscapes previously undocumented, such as volcanoes birthing from the ocean or the inner workings of tunnels in places like the Grand Canyon, United States. While anyone can visit and photograph uncharted territories, it takes a creative eye to capture their emotional rawness and aesthetic beauty.

In a modern world where technology gives us the power of creation at our fingertips, it's not about what we create, but rather how we create it that deems us an artist. Clearly, photography demands skilful technique and a unique perspective in addition to high-tech equipment. Therefore, while anyone can take a picture, not everyone can turn it into art.

E Practising what you have learnt

Putting others' ideas into your own words can be a difficult task, but plenty of practice will help you achieve the aims of this course. Read the article below and complete the exam-style comprehension questions that follow.

Yarnbombing
woolly graffiti in Singapore

Think graffiti, but with yarn instead of spray cans.

The art of yarnbombing started in 2005 when Texan clothes shop owner Magda Sayeg found a creative way of using up half-finished jumpers and scarfs – by putting them on door handles. The craze took off, with artists

5 plastering street signs and even buses with colourful strands of wool made by knitting or crocheting.

Freelance graphic designer and illustrator Kelly Lim, 25, is one such yarnbombing enthusiast here. She first saw it online and was drawn to it because 'yarnbombs are so random and unpredictable ... they add a burst of surprise and excitement in
10 everyday life'.

It helps that Ms Lim can crochet, having taken lessons at seven. However, 'because it was seen as a granny hobby, I was teased by my classmates ... and I guess it affected me enough for me to stop for about a year. I picked it up again later, though.'

15 As a fashion design student at Temasek Polytechnic, she even knitted dresses for her final-year project. Her first yarnbombing project was to cover the handlebars of her bicycle. She went on to yarnbomb several statues, including adding Pikachu caps to the bronze figures along the Singapore River in April 2013.

20 The good thing about yarnbombing is that unlike traditional graffiti, it is temporary. But that also presented a challenge for Ms Lim when she first started. 'The hard part is actually removing the yarn without cutting the wool,' she said.

When coming up with a design, she first considers the colour
25 and, after that, it's 'create as I go along'.

In January, she posted some yarnbombing ideas on her Facebook page. Art lecturer Lucinda Law, 38, contacted her within hours and Ms Lim agreed to undertake her current project: yarnbombing Ms Law's Vespa scooter. So far, after about three days and six to seven balls of yarn, the front part of the scooter is complete, with a design of
30 moss and plants. Ms Law described the result as 'whimsical, witty and well-crafted'.

Ms Lim has turned her skills into a part-time business, but declined to reveal how much she makes from it. She has done commercial work for several shops, yarnbombing items such as a hose reel and even a tree for product displays. She also crochets items such as pouches, coasters and hats, and creates dreadlocks from wool.

Ms Lim proudly wears her crochet pieces and dreadlocks, and often gets curious stares from passers-by.
35 Said Ms Lim: 'Just the other day, I saw this little boy knock into a chair while turning back to gawk at me. I just love kids because they are so honest and don't bother to hide their interest – most of it being good. Even in Tokyo Disneyland, I've had kids wanting to take photos with me, thinking I'm a mascot.'

Meanwhile, retiree Betty Oh, 65, saw Ms Lim when we were doing this interview. She said: 'Very cute and special! You should take up a hairdressing course!'

Phyllicia Wang, The New Paper, *Singapore, April 2016*

'Yarnbombing' is a type of street art that uses colourful patterns of yarn or thread – joined together using either hand-knit or crochet methods – to cover otherwise sterile or dull public spaces.

ACTIVITY 9

When you have read the article closely, answer questions **1–4**.

1 Using information from the first paragraph and using your own words, explain how yarnbombing gained its popularity.

2 Explain how yarnbombing differs from graffiti. Use your own words and outside knowledge to respond.

3 In your own words, explain Lim's interest in yarnbombing as mentioned in paragraph 3 (lines 6–10).

4 Summarise how other people react to Lim's eccentric style. Base your response on the last three paragraphs of the article.

EXAM-STYLE QUESTIONS

Essay questions

1 What do you consider to be the most effective form of street art and why? Defend your position. **[30]**

2 To what extent does art and design play a role in your life? **[30]**

3 How far do you agree that art is anything you can get away with? **[30]**

4 How effectively do schools support visual and performance arts in your region (e.g. art, dance, theatre, film)? **[30]**

5 Evaluate the work of one artist or one writer from your society. **[30]**

6 'Graffiti is appealing to some, appalling to others.' Discuss. **[30]**

7 How far would you agree that visual technology has improved the learning experience? **[30]**

8 Consider the artistic value of animated films and/or comic books. **[30]**

9 Provide the case for social media's move toward image-based content (as opposed to text). **[30]**

10 Which is more visually appealing, a live performance or a cinematic film? **[30]**

Summary

Key points to remember from this chapter:

■ Observing the deliberate choices others make when organising their ideas, and practicing explaining and summarising information from other sources can help you become a better writer.

■ There are a number of different structures you can use to organise your ideas. Pick one that best fits your purpose for writing.

■ Active reading strategies such as annotating the text can help you to understand what the text is about.

■ Brainstorming ideas visually can help you see the connections between ideas before you begin writing.

■ Expository skills can help you develop arguments in several different ways such as explaining context, establishing the basis of an example, and explaining the connection between evidence and your claim.

■ One important reason why expository skills will serve as the basis for developing arguments is because it places a great deal of emphasis on organisation and logic.

Chapter 2.2
Planning and organising responses

As members of society, our personal values and experiences shape the way we see the world. The theme of this chapter is *The individual and society.*

Learning objectives

In this chapter, you will learn about:

■ strategies for generating ideas
■ how to generate ideas in a timed writing situation
■ how to enhance the quality of your ideas through analysis
■ how to organise ideas before drafting your response.
■ analyse and interpret words in a question to determine its scope and limits
■ understand questions that use complex wording or unfamiliar vocabulary.

A Writing to a time limit

Most of the tasks you will face in this course will need to be completed within a time limit. If you are limited by time, you will be working under a certain amount of pressure. This may tempt you to try to *save* time, for example by skimming reading material or questions as opposed to carefully processing each word. Choices like this, however, can have serious consequences on the quality of your response.

There are three important steps that should take place prior to drafting your response to a reading or writing task. You will need to set aside time to:

- **deconstruct** the question
- locate text evidence and/or generate ideas from your own, outside knowledge
- determine how you will organise the ideas in your response.

This chapter will first address how these steps can be accomplished when preparing to write an *essay*; then it will address their usefulness when responding to reading comprehension questions.

KEY TERMS

Deconstruct: break down into individual parts or components; analyse the elements of

B Deconstructing essay questions

In Chapter 1.2 Section *D Understanding the task*, you learnt that most questions in the Cambridge International AS Level English General Paper contain command words (or other phrases) to help you understand the nature of the task. Identifying these can be a good step in the process of deconstructing an essay question. There are other key words in the question, however, that will also need your attention. This section suggests helpful strategies for breaking down writing instructions to make sure you understand what the question is asking you to do.

TIP

Understanding an essay question is a crucial first step in the writing process. Essay ideas can easily lose focus if you do not fully address the question.

Defining scope

At first glance, a word like *art* might make you think of some of the most famous artistic pieces such as the Leonardo da Vinci's *Mona Lisa*, Claude Monet's *Water Lilies*, or the *Nefertiti Bust* by Thurtmose. In this case, 'art' is defined as classic paintings or sculptures. However, if you think more carefully, you will realise that modern graffiti, sound, or even dance can be considered artforms, too.

Consider the view that 'art is anything you can get away with'.

If you can recognise the potential **scope** of a topic and break down words in this way, you can quickly improve the maturity and perceptiveness of your essay because you are thinking critically beyond the obvious. In deconstructing these words, you are working toward defining the scope, or range, of your essay's ideas, which is an important part of any introduction (see Chapter 1.2 Section *F Key elements of an essay*) and a key element of an effective essay (see 'Criteria for assessing essays' in Chapter 1.1 Section *E Expectations and assessment*).

KEY TERMS

Scope: the extent or range of possible ideas; 'defining scope' refers to determining how broad or narrow your essay's coverage will be.

If an essay question asked you to consider the role of artists in your local region, for instance, would you be able to address every type of artist that exists? Definitely not! You would need to set limits to your essay's content by indicating which subcategories you will cover.

Read the essay question that follows. What key words might help you define the scope of your response?

> Assess the ability of technology to ensure human happiness in the present society.

Millions of people worldwide suffer from loss of limbs. Prosthetic limb technology brings new hope to amputees, which is one way that technology has improved happiness for the individual in society.

When deconstructing a question, it is usually good to start with the nouns because these words are often broader than they initially look. For example, at first glance of the question above, the term 'technology' seems very specific – meaning 'computer technology'. However, upon closer examination, you will find dozens of additional subcategories within the term 'technology'. Can you think of some of them? The following diagram may help you.

KEY SKILLS

The nouns which appear in essay questions (such as 'technology') are usually words that you will need to use during the planning phase of your response. To review your understanding of nouns, visit Chapter 4.3.

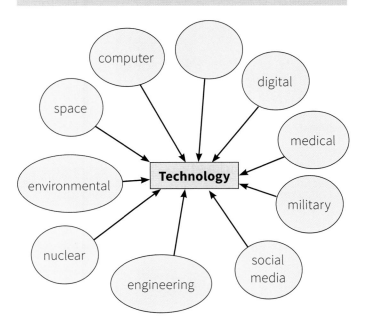

ACTIVITY 1

Look at each of the following **broad terms**. Suggest at least three or four subcategories for each, following the example given.

Example: history = military, environmental, political, African American, legal

1	art	6	research
2	education	7	crime
3	health	8	literature
4	science	9	media
5	human rights	10	communication

The word 'happiness' also opens up a wider range of possibilities than you might think. What *kind* of happiness could you discuss in your essay? For example:

• economic/financial well-being

• social status

• political stability

• environmental balance.

However, the essay question uses some **limiting terms**, too. Specifically, the discussion is restricted to *human* happiness, so you cannot consider anything that is not about *people* (e.g. the well-being of animals or the Earth). The phrase 'in the present' *society* is also an example of a limiting term because it excludes past or future societies.

KEY TERM

Broad terms: any words in an essay question that can be broken down into more specific, subcategories; these terms *broaden* the possibilities of the essay's scope.

Limiting terms: any words in an essay question that restrict the response; these terms *shrink* the possibilities of the essay's scope.

At this point, you have closely considered nearly every word in the essay question.

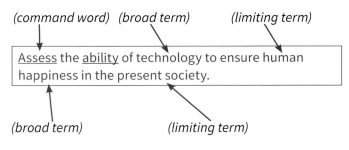

This is a good habit to develop as you work your way through this course. If you miss a single word like 'present', your essay may be too broad; or if you don't see the range of possibility in a word like 'technology', your response may only address the obvious, thus leading to a dull or uninteresting discussion.

Let's look at another example. Read the following essay question:

> To what extent is technology more of a blessing than a curse in the workplace?

After carefully reading the question, identify the following:

- command words or phrases
- broad terms
- limiting terms
- any other words that could improve the focus of your response.

Pepper, a robot programmed to understand human emotions, is now employed as a receptionist in two Belgian hospitals. This humanoid robot accompanies visitors to the correct department and helps patients feel less worried about surgery. Pepper is considered a 'staff member' in a sense. How might this information be used to support or challenge the question about technology's role in the workplace?

Here are a few things you may have noticed:

- The question:
  - asks you to assess the value of technology at a job site

- uses the phrase 'to what extent' to suggest an analysis of multiple views.
- The question is broader than it looks because it includes the following words:
  - 'technology', which can be broken down further into several subcategories
  - 'blessing' and 'curse', which can include any kind of benefit or drawback as long as it relates to the workplace (e.g. economic benefit, social benefit, financial risk)
  - 'workplace', which can include any kind of job or career (e.g. medical field, social work, politics, labour/trades).
- The question is limiting because it includes the phrase 'in the workplace', so conversation about technology is restricted to this setting (e.g. it would not be appropriate to discuss technology in the home).

KEY SKILLS

You will learn more about how to narrow the scope of broad terms later in this chapter by using a brainstorming strategy called the 'hand approach'.

ACTIVITY 2

Deconstruct the essay questions below, which address everyday issues in the lives of different individuals in society. Identify key words (i.e. command words or phrases, broad and/or limiting terms) and consider scope.

Essay questions

1 To what extent should money play a role when deciding on a career?
2 How far do you agree that women enjoy the same rights as men in today's world?
3 'Power attracts the worst and corrupts the best.' What is your view?
4 Assess the moral value of today's political media coverage.

Considering complexity

Not all essay tasks are as straightforward or as easy to break down as the examples in the previous section. Some essay questions are much more complicated because they ask for more than one task to be carried out as part of a single response.

Here is an example of a more complex essay question. Which word makes the writing task more complex?

> How effectively are traditional buildings maintained and supported in your society?

If you chose the word *and*, you are correct! This coordinating conjunction tells you that you need to discuss both:

- how the architecture is *maintained*, and
- how it is *supported* by modern society.

That means you have to address two separate points in your essay.

TIP

Refer back to the question regularly while you are writing to make sure you are answering all parts of it.

Consider how coordinating conjunctions increase the complexity of this next question:

> To what extent are politics influenced by science and/ or technology?

This time, you can discuss either:

- science *and* technology
- science *or* technology.

When options like this are presented, it allows you to control how complicated the content of your essay is going to be.

TIP

Coordinating conjunctions are words such as 'and', 'but' and 'or', which help you connect ideas. To learn more about coordinating conjunctions and how they can add quality to you writing, read Chapter 4.4.

In addition to conjunctions, essay questions will sometimes contain phrases like 'such as', which introduce optional points for discussion; but, as the phrase indicates, it does not *require* them to be discussed.

> Should computer education *such as* coding be compulsory in schools?

If you answer this question, you *may* talk about coding as a form of computer education, but you do not *have* to talk about it and you are not *limited* to this category alone. There are plenty of other computer courses that you might have done at school (for example keyboarding, computer applications or graphic design). In that case, you would be free to choose to write about any of these to argue your point.

ACTIVITY 3

For each of the essay questions **1–5**, work with a partner to identify:

- command words or phrases
- broad and limiting terms and potential parameters
- words that add complexity to the question.

Essay questions

1. To what extent can individuals today function effectively without modern conveniences such as the internet?
2. Evaluate the impact of one social activist, one scientist or one religious leader in your society.
3. What is more important for your society to spend its money on: education, research or technological progress?
4. To what extent do human beings of all ages find technology a struggle?
5. What are the main environmental problems in your part of the world and how effectively are they being tackled by local advocacy groups?

Content-related terms

One final point to consider, in relation to deconstructing an essay question, is your range of vocabulary. While words like 'history' and 'art' are easy enough to understand, other terms, such as 'economic superpowers' or 'global sanctions', might be unfamiliar to you. These are considered *content-related* terms because they are specific to a particular topic or area of study.

The Cambridge International AS Level English General Paper syllabus requires you to write about a wide range of topics from all academic disciplines. Therefore it is helpful to learn as many of the specialist terms from these disciplines as possible. This section will help to familiarise you with a few of them. Even a basic understanding of these terms is better than none at all!

The concepts in the following list are often mentioned when discussing the global issues that this course explores. If you become familiar with these terms, you may feel comfortable enough to write about them. You are *not* required to memorise the list or study these terms in detail. Remember that the aim of the Cambridge International AS Level English General Paper syllabus is not to test your general knowledge but rather to see how maturely you can think and write about issues.

Vocabulary for discussing global issues

- globalisation
- modernisation
- conformity
- renewable and non-renewable resources
- emissions
- deforestation
- energy independence
- alternative medicine
- civil liberties
- incarceration
- economic sanctions
- dictatorship/ totalitarianism
- oppression
- military coup
- diplomacy
- small businesses and large corporations
- consumerism
- free market economy
- supply and demand
- privatisation
- outsourcing
- philanthropy
- censorship
- developing and developed countries
- infrastructure
- patriotism and nationalism
- international affairs
- foreign aid, humanitarian efforts
- gross domestic product
- immigration, migration, emigration
- travel and tourism

C Generating ideas for your essay

Now that you know what the question is asking, you can begin generating ideas which respond to it. This process – sometimes called *brainstorming* – is an essential part of the writing process. If you take time to plan and organise these ideas before drafting them, you are more likely to produce a clear and well-structured response.

Brainstorming has many benefits. It can:

- create a 'bird's-eye view' of your ideas
- help you organise ideas into more meaningful groups/chunks
- serve as a plan to refer to while you are writing
- help you create links between your ideas
- help to keep your ideas focused
- capture all your ideas in one place so that you don't forget them.

Since you will work with two different kinds of tasks – writing an essay and showing reading comprehension – you will naturally generate ideas in different ways. This chapter will first look at generating ideas to improve essay responses. Then it will cover tips for generating ideas for comprehension questions that ask for either prior knowledge *or* your own opinion.

Having a range of ideas is important because it gives you options when writing. However, as most of your writing will take place under a time limit, you will need to choose among these options and organise your thoughts quickly. In this section, we will explore strategies to help you do this effectively. You will not have time to write about every idea you note down. This section will therefore help you to narrow down the scope of your essay by selecting supporting points that are most relevant and engaging.

Using 'lenses' to generate ideas

One way to generate ideas about a particular issue is to think of the topic from different vantage points, like looking at it through different camera lenses. To help you remember the different lenses available to you, meaningfully assign each of the five (described below) to a different finger on your hand. For example, in the hand image shown, the 'social and cultural' **lens** is assigned to the fourth finger because in many cultures people wear a wedding ring on this finger to show they are married. However, you should use your own cultural references and experiences to match each lens to a finger so that you can remember the categories.

KEY TERM

Lens: a piece of glass or other transparent material on a camera which allows you to see an image in different ways, or by analogy, a way of looking at an issue from a specific perspective.

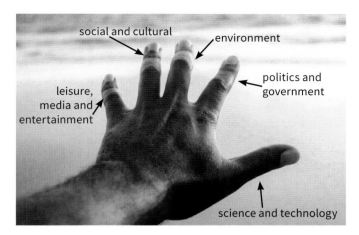

The 'hand approach'.

Reading comprehension questions may ask you to use your own knowledge in response to a text. For example, if you were asked to answer the question:

| How necessary is travelling in today's society? |

you would need to generate ideas of your own. A strategy such as the 'hand approach' could be a useful way to help you generate more specific ideas. For example, if you wanted to discuss *why* people travel, you might initially talk about travelling for business or pleasure. However, you can make your argument more engaging by going beyond the more obvious ideas.

Try using the categories of the 'hand approach' to help you think of *other* reasons why people travel. For example, what might be the *political* reasons for why people travel? A politician on a campaign might travel across the region to meet more people and experience local issues directly.

How might cultural or environmental reasons play a role in why people travel? These are the kinds of questions you might ask yourself to generate ideas quickly. This can be a useful approach when time is a factor.

Be aware that lenses may not work for every question. For example, try using lenses to generate ideas for the following prompt:

| How affordable is public transport in your country? |

It would not make sense to think about how politically or scientifically affordable public transport is.

TIP

Remember that using lenses is just *one* strategy for generating (and narrowing) ideas. If it does not work naturally with the question, avoid trying to force it. Also, some lenses might work for a particular topic, when others do not. But with five categories available, there is plenty of opportunity to come up with ideas!

From general idea to specific example

Once you have identified a lens that applies to your topic, you should provide a specific example or other evidence to prove the connection between the topic and the lens. Keep in mind that the use of specific evidence is important in an effective essay response.

For example, think again about the general point that people might travel for *cultural* reasons. To prove this, you might use as evidence a Muslim's obligation to visit Mecca at least once as part of the Five Pillars central to Islamic faith. Or perhaps you could mention that individuals or groups may travel to escape from different forms of cultural or religious persecution. In both cases, culture is the reason for travel.

In this way, using lenses to generate ideas can lead to a much deeper analysis than you may at first have considered.

89

ACTIVITY 4

Apply the five 'hand' lenses to the following essay questions. Brainstorm ideas and make a list of specific examples that link each lens to the topic.

Essay questions

1 'When crisis strikes, you never have the help you need.' Do you agree?
2 'Everything is repeated, in a circle, particularly history.' How far do you agree?
3 To what extent is breaking the law justifiable?
4 To what extent should we look forward to old age?
5 What are the benefits and drawbacks of hosting a major sporting event?

Narrowing the scope of your ideas

Once you have developed effective strategies to generate ideas more quickly under pressure, you will have completed half of the brainstorming process. The other half involves selecting the best of your ideas to include in your essay. You might have plenty of ideas, but you may not want to include them all in your response! An important rule to remember at this stage is to value *depth* of ideas rather than *breadth*. In other words, you should *develop* your ideas, rather than jump from one point to another without any detail.

Narrow the scope of your essay by focusing on a specific aspect of the issue as opposed to the entire picture. This will help you address the topic in depth (instead of skimming its breadth!).

TIP

When choosing which ideas to include in your essay, look for those that are connected or go together in some way. This can make it easier to arrange and discuss them. If you pick ideas from both the politics and government and the social and cultural categories, for instance, you might organise your essay with a socio-political or socio-economic theme in mind. This can help you write a more cohesive essay where the ideas seem like part of a 'whole'; avoid just addressing ideas at random.

ACTIVITY 5

Return to the ideas you generated in Activity 4. Complete the following steps.

1   Choose the essay topics that, in your opinion, generated the most engaging ideas.
2   Practise decision-making by picking which ideas you might include in an essay response and which you would omit.

Stakeholders, perspective and context

The 'hand approach' is one helpful strategy for thinking analytically about your essay topic. You can take this analysis a step further, however, by considering the points of view that exist *within* each category.

In this section you will learn how to generate ideas for your essay topic by considering:

• *who* is involved (**stakeholders**)
• *how* he/she/they feel about it (perspective)
• *why* he/she/they feel that way (context).

KEY TERM

Stakeholders: any persons, groups or entities affected by the outcome of a problem, situation or issue.

The diagram shows how these terms are interconnected.

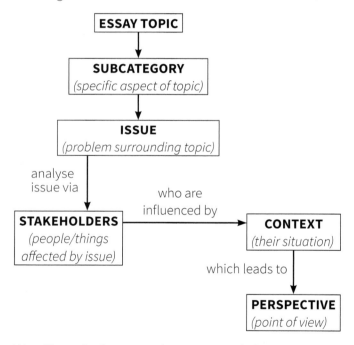

We will now look at several strategies to help you generate ideas more thoughtfully and meaningfully.

Identifying relevant stakeholders

The topics you will write about in this course concern contemporary, globally relevant issues. As you study these topics, you will consider:

• *what* is happening
• *who* it is happening to.

Those persons, groups, organisations or other entities who have an interest or concern for an issue are called stakeholders. This is because they have something 'at stake' or at risk, depending on the outcome.

Think about your own school for a moment. *What* issues exist in your academic environment? *Who* do these issues affect? (I.e. which issues affect you? Which issues affect your teachers and/or adminstrators? Which issues affect the wider community?)

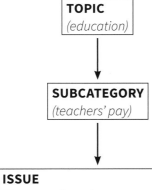

What are the issues in your school or college? How do you feel about them? What influences your point of view?

To better understand how this strategy works, let's consider the following example below:

To help you generate ideas for this essay topic *education*, ask yourself: *Who* has something at risk? Who has a relevant voice in the matter?

- The first and most obvious group would be *students*.
- *Parents* are probably upset that their children are losing valuable learning time.

- *Teachers* lose money while on strike, and they may even risk losing their jobs.

The way these stakeholders feel about the issue is their point of view, or perspective. For example, a parent's perspective might be that teachers who go on strike care more about money or themselves than they care about their students. Another perspective, held by a different parent, might be that teachers deserve better pay than they earn now. Note that just because people are categorised within the same stakeholder group, it does not necessarily mean that they hold the same opinion!

Identifying students, teachers and parents as having different perspectives on this issue is a good start. It can help you discuss the issue in more specific terms. However, to produce a more thoughtful essay, you will need to go beyond these obvious points of view. Think creatively about *who else* might be affected by the consequences of the strike. The table outlines other potential points of view.

Stakeholder	What is at risk?
students	lose out on learning opportunities and good teaching
teachers	receive no pay while striking; risk job loss or administrative and/or legal action
parents	no longer have a safe place for their children to be during working hours; may need to hire a babysitter (out-of-pocket expenses)
community	community members concerned with the well-being of students; possible increase in crime rates if youth are left without structure
the government	responsible for finding a solution to the problem; may face public criticism
teachers' unions	may spread strikes to neighbouring areas, so larger-scale disruption possible
government officials	may need to find money from their budget to improve the situation; responsible for finding a solution to the problem; may face public criticism

Identifying stakeholders helps you to consider the issue from more than one point of view, and to produce a more considerate and analytical response.

ACTIVITY 6

For each of the following issues, make a list of stakeholders whose perspective should be considered.

1 A tax on sugary foods to decrease obesity rates
2 Stricter laws regarding the private ownership of weapons
3 Making organ donations compulsory
4 Banning animal testing
5 Replacing an old building with a shopping centre

Context

Recognising multiple perspectives while you write will help you to add depth and maturity to your response. However, it is important to understand that these perspectives – including your own – are shaped by *context*, or the wider circumstances surrounding the issue and the individual.

A number of contextual factors can influence someone's opinion, including:

- geographical location
- religious beliefs
- cultural heritage
- economic or financial circumstances
- direct experience or first-hand knowledge.

KEY SKILLS

An awareness of context can help you to more fully understand the perspectives featured in reading material. For more about context, look back to Chapter 1.2 Section *E Key elements of an essay* and also at Chapter 5.2.

The example below uses the following question to demonstrate the effect of context:

Is it necessary to suspend travel during potentially dangerous health outbreaks?

STAKEHOLDER	→	CONTEXT
(international health officials, e.g. World Health Organisation)		*(no ban was issued during previous outbreaks, e.g. H1N1 flu pandemic, SARS respiratory disease)*

PERSPECTIVE
(a travel ban is unnecessary)

It may seem, at first, that allowing travel during an epidemic could be potentially disastrous for the international community. However, the opinion held by health officials is influenced by the bigger picture. These experts can use their direct experience and first-hand knowledge to make an informed decision, by referring back to previous epidemics of a similar kind and size.

It is also important to understand that because of people's individual beliefs and experiences, not all individuals within a single stakeholder group will share the same opinion. Consider the following:

International airline companies

Ban is not necessary:
Company will lose money unnecessarily

Ban is necessary:
Company is responsible for safety of passengers

Notice that within this stakeholder group, different perspectives exist, and these are based on values and experiences. The Chief Executive Officer (CEO) of a popular international airline might think it unnecessary to establish a travel ban because their company could lose money (perhaps they have seen this happen in the past). In this case, the CEO places value on money as a top priority. However, other company officials might value safety over earnings. It is therefore important to think deeply and critically about stakeholders during the planning phase to ensure a more thoughtful response.

ACTIVITY 7

1 Identify five stakeholders who might have a perspective on the question about issuing travel bans.
2 Identify reasons why each stakeholder might agree or disagree with this issue. Remember to keep context in mind while you are considering these perspectives.

Context can be understood in the following way: 'I hold X opinion *as a result of* Y background/experience', rather than just 'I hold this opinion'. As you address different perspectives in your essay – including your own – remember to keep in mind the unique circumstances which shape them.

D How brainstorming can help you

If you spend some time generating ideas, this can help you create a 'road map' for writing your essay. Once you know what input you have on the issue, you can make important decisions concerning your approach to the essay.

KEY SKILLS

Remember that you can take a position or investigate more openly, as long as you arrive at a decision at the end. Look back to Chapter 1.2 for more on essay approaches.

In completing Activity 7, you created a brainstorm of ideas by considering a variety of opinions about travel bans.

Look at the ideas you wrote down, to help you make a decision about which style to use. Consider the following:

- Do your ideas offer a range of perspectives, or are they biased toward one side or the other?
- What is your own perspective on the issue?

If you have enough information to discuss both sides of the issue, it makes sense to begin with more of an objective approach. If your notes favour one side over the other, it may be better to take a specific position. Remember, if you choose the latter, you must give consideration to opposing points of view while still supporting your own thesis.

KEY SKILLS

Chapter 3.1 Section *E Developing an effective line of reasoning* provides more guidance on writing well-reasoned arguments.

E Deconstructing questions

In this chapter, you have been learning how to understand essay questions and generate ideas for them. In this section you will work through the process of deconstructing the following question and generating relevant ideas for it:

'No man is an island.' Discuss.

Unlike other essay questions you have encountered up to now, this one requires a different kind of interpretation. The text which appears in quotation marks is taken from a poem written by the 17th-century English metaphysical poet, John Donne. Clearly, this question is not asking you literally to discuss men stranded on desert islands! You will therefore need to interpret exactly what it means before responding. You might think about:

- What does *man* refer to?

The word 'man' in this sense seems to be meant generically, referring to 'mankind' – both males and females.

- What is meant by *island*?

Think about the characteristics of an island. How do those characteristics relate to 'man'?

If you think this prompt is about 'togetherness' versus loneliness in society, you are on the right track. The assertion in the prompt that 'no man is an island' is a figurative way of saying:

- No person is alone, isolated or entirely independent of others.
- We are all connected, interdependent or tied to each other in some way.

Now that you have an initial understanding of the assertion, you will need to further identify the argument it requires. In other words, what is the other side of the claim raised in the prompt? Can you put it into words? One way of expressing it might be:

Under certain circumstances, people can live separately, isolated or independent of one another.

Is it possible to live a separate life, independent of others? Hong Kong has operated under the principle of 'one country, two systems' since 1997, when it became a special administrative region of the People's Republic of China. Hong Kong's political and economic systems stand entirely separate from China. They do, however, still share a common military.

93

Stakeholders

After deconstructing the question, you can begin generating the nuanced views surrounding it. Begin by thinking about *who* might have something to say in response to this assertion. Just as you did in Activity 7 on travel bans, take a moment to think about the varying viewpoints which surround this issue. Note your ideas on paper or discuss with a partner.

Here is a list of stakeholders who might have relevant viewpoints regarding loneliness or acceptance in society:

- residents of areas facing natural disasters
- a soldier returning from war
- foreigners who are not familiar with a local language
- countries in economic crisis
- the elderly
- citizens seeking rights, protesters for a cause or advocacy groups
- prisoners/criminals
- supporters of isolationism as a political strategy
- citizens of communist countries
- a child with a disability (physical, emotional or mental)
- alliances such as the United Nations
- groups seeking political independence from a larger nation
- societies led by totalitarian regimes.

Take a closer look at your own list. Remember: not all stakeholders think alike. Are there any stakeholders who might disagree within their own group? Based on the ideas you generate, you can then make some decisions about how you will approach the essay.

Context

Finally, consider what might influence the perspectives of the people you wrote down on your stakeholder list. What factors shape their opinion about how alone or connected we are in this world? For example, people living in regions affected by war or natural disaster might not agree with this assertion if they are not getting the aid they need to survive. In this case, politics and geographic location can certainly influence opinion.

Look at the following two examples of elderly people and consider how their views on this issue might differ based on circumstance:

- an 82-year-old American living in an assisted-living facility; her grandchildren come twice a month to visit.

- an 86-year-old Chinese woman living with her daughter; the family members have converted the basement of their house into a small apartment-style living space.

Similarly, soldiers returning from war might feel accepted or isolated, depending on what services are available to help them settle back into normal life. In each case, perspective is shaped by circumstance and experience. By looking at any issue through the eyes of another, it helps you see the issue more thoughtfully and analytically.

F Organising ideas to show comprehension

You have learnt in this chapter that lenses can be useful in generating ideas for essays, but they can also help you answer comprehension questions which ask you to use outside knowledge (see Section *C Generating ideas for your essay*). Consider, for instance, how you might apply lenses to the following comprehension question in order to generate more specific ideas:

> **In your own opinion, what are the advantages and disadvantages of migration? Explain.**

If a question asks you to use your own knowledge as part of your response, you are free to generate ideas that fall outside of the text; so lenses can help you do this quickly and systematically.

However, other comprehension questions will limit your response to what you have learnt from the text or data set provided. Even though you are using the text as the basis of your response, planning and organising your ideas is just as important for these types of questions.

When questions ask you to identify explicit information from the material, it is usually sufficient to use **annotation** to support your response. For example, if a question asks you to 'identify four reasons mentioned in the article', you can simply identify and mark these reasons as you read, then use them in your response.

The same strategy could be used for an inference question such as:

> **Explain why Paloma (a character in the reading material) might prefer option A.**

In this case, you would annotate the relevant evidence before paraphrasing the information in your response.

KEY TERM

Annotation: marks on the text which highlight important features, or written notes next to the marked text (e.g. with your questions, observations or reactions).

TIP

If a comprehension question asks you to identify different types of information from the text (e.g. reasons, options, evidence), then use a unique form of notation for each. This way, you can avoid accidentally looking at the wrong piece of information when drafting your answer.

These types of questions usually require a brief response. Other comprehension questions, however, will ask you for more, so you will need to organise your thoughts before responding to these more complex tasks.

Read the following question:

> Identify five points mentioned in the director's speech and explain how these were challenged by the development team.

This question uses two command words: identify *and* explain. In this case, you may need to do more planning than just annotation. Once you have identified the

five points, you then have to explain *how* these were challenged by the team. As the question is brief, you might be tempted to write your answer without planning. However, a simple chart such as the one below can help you get your thoughts in order and help you produce a more organised response. It will also help to ensure that you answer the question fully.

> reason → challenge
>
> reason → challenge
>
> reason → challenge
>
> reason → challenge
>
> reason → challenge

TIP

Remember: there is no need to write in complete sentences when planning!

For most other types of comprehension questions, you will need to use more elaborate planning and organisation strategies before you begin to write. The following chart shows a range of question styles you might encounter, along with a suggested strategy for planning and organising your ideas.

Comprehension question	Planning/organising strategy
Briefly explain the differences between the features of the two programmes mentioned in the article.	Create two columns and make a quick list of the features of both programmes. Then draw arrows between clear differences.
In your own words, describe what it was like to visit the sanctuary.	Find the relevant information in the text. Make a quick list of points, rewriting the original phrasing in your own words. (By doing this, you will avoid accidentally quoting the text.)
Using evidence from the reading material and from your own opinion, explain why it makes sense to accept the board's proposal to revamp the downtown area.	Create a mind map. First, include evidence from the text. Then use these ideas to generate your own. Add your own ideas to the mind map before you begin drafting your response.
Job outsourcing has become increasingly popular in the retail industry in particular. Why do you think this is so?	Create two columns. On the left side, list reasons. To the right of each reason, list evidence to support it.
Of the four options provided, which one is the best fit for Paloma's family?	Create four columns and briefly list the key points of each option. Circle the points that are strongest in each option before making your decision. Then use these notes to draft your response.

KEY SKILLS

A mind map is a visual way of note-taking. A key idea appears in a circle or square in the centre, with several smaller circles branching out around it, containing relevant points and ideas. You can find an example and more information about mind maps in Chapter 2.1 Section *B Understanding how ideas are organised, connected and ordered.*

G Practising what you have learnt

Read the list of exam-style essay questions, all of which are based on the chapter theme of *The individual and society*. Use one or more of the questions to practise what you have learnt in this chapter.

In an exam situation, you may have the option to write your essay electronically. Since typing is a very different experience from hand-writing, it is important you practise both ways of producing written responses. With this in mind, submit your essay for this chapter electronically to your teacher.

You should return to this essay to reflect on your learning experiences later in the course, once you have further developed your writing skills.

EXAM-STYLE QUESTIONS

Essay questions

1   Choose a famous person from the past and evaluate how society would perceive this figure now. **[30]**

2   'It doesn't have to be perfect to be powerful.' Evaluate whether this might be a productive way to approach business. **[30]**

3   To what extent can ordinary people make an impact? **[30]**

4   'The media pay far too much attention to insignificant matters.' What is your view? **[30]**

5   Examine the premise that power lies in the people. **[30]**

Summary

Key points to remember from this chapter:

■ Taking time to plan and organise ideas is an essential part of the writing process.

■ Taking time to brainstorm can help you make decisions about the style of your essay response.

■ Lenses are a tool that can help you narrow down ideas and issues more specifically.

■ An essay that only considers the issue from one lens may be too narrowly focused, but addressing all five lenses may make the scope of your response too wide.

■ Identifying stakeholders can help you generate ideas for writing. Their perspectives can be used as part of your essay's reasoning.

■ Perspectives are influenced by context. Thinking about *why* a person or group holds a particular point of view can therefore help you understand the complexities of an issue when reading and writing.

■ Essay questions sometimes contain broad terms, which expand the scope of your response, or limiting terms, which restrict it.

■ It is helpful to become familiar with content-related terms common to this course. You should look out for these terms in your other courses of study and outside school (e.g. in clubs, when watching the news, at community events).

■ Remember to make sure that you fully understand what the question is asking you to do. Don't read the question too quickly because you want to save time.

Chapter 2.3
Skills review and practice

This chapter will help you review the skills you have learnt so far while covering contemporary issues concerning *Technology, gender and education*.

Learning objectives

In this chapter, you will:

- apply skills you have learnt in Unit 2 to reading and writing tasks
- practise summarising and paraphrasing information
- observe the organisational structure of different texts
- strengthen writing skills by learning strategies for synthesising information and sustaining points
- work with texts to widen your general knowledge.

A Introduction

In Unit 2, you learnt some of the foundational skills of this course, such as how to:

- generate ideas using 'lenses'
- consider issues from different perspectives
- summarise text and explain ideas
- organise and develop the basic elements of an essay.

This chapter will help you to review and develop these key skills, and exam-style assessment exercises will give you the opportunity to put them into practice. These exercises will help you develop your reading and writing skills through additional practice and critical thinking.

You will work with a variety of course-related topics, each of which relate to the overarching theme of *Technology, gender and education*. These are arranged in text sets, or collections of articles, all related to similar topics within the theme. Each text set will give you the opportunity to apply the skills you have learnt so far.

B Understanding and applying information

In order to demonstrate understanding, you need to be able to identify and select important information from a text. You also need to be able to see how ideas are organised in order to understand the bigger message being communicated. This section will review the skills you learnt to help you understand information.

Texts 1-4 represent several different perspectives concerning the level of risk associated with artificial intelligence in today's world. As you read, think about the main message being expressed in each extract, and how these perspectives compare. Then answer the comprehension questions in Activity 1.

Perspective 1

While robots have been utilised in several industries, including the automotive and manufacturing sectors, for decades, experts now predict that a tipping point in robotic deployments is imminent – and that much of the developed world simply isn't prepared for such a radical transition...

While approximately two-thirds of Americans believe that robots will inevitably perform most of the work currently done by human beings during the next 50 years, about 80% also believe their current jobs will either 'definitely' or 'probably' exist in their current form within the same timeframe.

Somehow, we believe our livelihoods will be safe. They're not: every commercial sector will be affected by robotic automation in the next several years. For example, Australian company Fastbrick Robotics has developed a robot, the Hadrian X, that can lay 1,000 standard bricks in one hour – a task that would take two human bricklayers the better part of a day or longer to complete.

In a recent report, the World Economic Forum predicted that robotic automation will result in the net loss of more than 5 million jobs across 15 developed nations by 2020, a conservative estimate. Another study, conducted by the International Labor Organisation, states that as many as 137 million workers across Cambodia, Indonesia, the Philippines, Thailand and Vietnam – approximately 56% of the total workforce of those countries – are at risk of displacement by robots, particularly workers in the garment manufacturing industry.

For every job created by robotic automation, several more will be eliminated entirely. At scale, this disruption will have a devastating impact on our workforce.

Abridged and adapted from 'Robots will destroy our jobs – and we're not ready for it' by Dan Shewan in The Guardian, January 2017

Perspective 2

It's easy to imagine a post-apocalyptic future where machines take over the world. We've been watching movies, playing video games, and reading sci-fi warnings from pop-scientists about Skynet since 1985, not to mention Elon Musk.

Today, many lawyers still have negative or threatening associations with 'artificial intelligence'. Often, this sentiment is encouraged by alarmist news headlines. For example, Axios published an article titled Artificial Intelligence is Coming for Lawyers. Another study by Deloitte advertises that more than 100,000 legal jobs will be replaced in the next 20 years.

As an attorney and CEO of a company that builds AI drafting tools for thousands of lawyers, I find this recent phenomenon fascinating. While many attorneys are adopting helpful tools in order to provide better legal services, some attorneys are no doubt providing lower quality legal services than they could because they are afraid of what they 'think' artificial intelligence represents. This is like an accountant being afraid of a calculator.

By leveraging AI, lawyers have the ability to streamline repetitive tasks and reduce errors, which in turn opens up more time to spend with clients and more time for legal work. For example, we have turned all of the state and county documents in California into intelligent forms that can be easily populated, edited, signed and filed.

Our understanding of AI is at an inflection point. I propose that as attorneys, we remove our associations of AI from the dehumanizing and apocalyptic vision of sci-fi movies and alarmist headlines and instead, anchor artificial intelligence in its useful present-day applications. A word can only become meaningful when the relationship between the word and the concept it represents are agreed upon. In this sense, we should look to AI not as a threat to our future, but as a powerful set tool that can help us today to become better advocates and build more profitable businesses.

Abridged and adapted from 'Looking at Artificial intelligence from a new perspective' by Tucker Cottingham in Huffington Post, *August 2017*

Perspective 3

Let's try to remain modest and lucid about the level of maturity of AI.

Even the most powerful artificial neural networks are still a very long way from matching the capabilities of the human brain, which is much more sophisticated … and most definitely one of the most complex objects in the universe.

In fact there is a difference between 'weak AI' and 'strong AI'. Strong AI would be endowed with consciousness, like human beings; however, all the AI platforms we know today, even the most advanced, are examples of weak AI, and this is likely to be the case for a long time to come.

There is simply no evidence to prove that consciousness would spontaneously appear just because AI platforms become bigger and more complex.

For in real life, an AI platform is still a machine and, like any other machine, it needs to be kept in check if it is to be trusted. That will mean controlling the quality and integrity of the data it uses, and ensuring

that it learns in appropriate ways. It will mean taking steps to avoid the kind of dysfunctional situations reported recently, where robots started to exhibit racist behaviour simply because some of the data they were using was racially prejudiced.

That progress needs to serve the best interests of the human race, but in no way must it undermine or replace people, who need to be able to take conscious actions at every decisive moment, in situations of ever greater complexity.

However unpredictable they may be, humans with their consciousness must remain sole masters of their decisions and their destiny.

This article is part of our 'Daring to lead' series, highlighting voices from the Women's Forum for the Economy & Society Global Meeting, in Paris, on 5–6 October 2017.

Abridged and adapted from 'Artificial intelligence: the end of the human race?' by Patrice Caine in Euractiv, *October 2017*

Perspective 4

As an AI expert, what do I fear about artificial intelligence? It is a moral question, not a scientific one. As a scientist, I must follow my obligation to the truth, reporting what I find in my experiments, whether I like the results or not. Being a scientist doesn't absolve me of my humanity, though. I must, at some level, reconnect with my hopes and fears. As a moral and political being, I have to consider the potential implications of my work and its potential effects on society.

The HAL 9000 computer, dreamed up by science fiction author Arthur C. Clarke and brought to life by movie director Stanley Kubrick in *2001: A Space Odyssey*, is a good example of a system that fails because of unintended consequences. In many complex systems – the RMS *Titanic*, NASA's space shuttle, the Chernobyl nuclear power plant – engineers layer many different components together. The designers may have known well how each element worked individually, but didn't know enough about how they all worked together.

That resulted in systems that could never be completely understood, and could fail in unpredictable ways. In each disaster – sinking a ship, blowing up two shuttles, and spreading radioactive contamination across Europe and Asia – a set of relatively small failures combined together to create a catastrophe.

I can see how we could fall into the same trap in AI research. We look at the latest research from cognitive science, translate that into an algorithm and add it to an existing system. We try to engineer AI without understanding intelligence or cognition first.

Systems like IBM's Watson and Google's Alpha equip artificial neural networks with enormous computing power, and accomplish impressive feats. But if these machines make mistakes, they lose on 'Jeopardy!' or don't defeat a Go master. These aren't world-changing consequences; indeed, the worst that might happen to a regular person as a result is losing some money betting on their success.

But as AI designs get even more complex and computer processors even faster, their skills will improve. That will lead us to give them more responsibility, even as the risk of unintended consequences rises. We know that 'to err is human', so it is likely impossible for us to create a truly safe system.

Abridged and adapted from '4 fears an AI developer has about artificial intelligence' by Arend Hintze in MarketWatch, July 2017

ACTIVITY 1

1 Draw a mind map.

   a In the centre, write a short phrase or brief sentence that identifies the broader argument all four of these perspectives address.

   b For each article, write a single sentence which identifies the main idea of that perspective and add it to your mind map.

2 In a paragraph of approximately 300 words, explain the relationship between these four perspectives (where do they overlap, contrast with, or reinforce each other?).

TIP

Make sure you keep to the word limit set by the question. To avoid writing too much for reading comprehension questions, do not:
- repeat the question
- give an introduction
- include any details of the source for the text.

These use up valuable words that you could use for more important material.

Organising ideas

The way you organise your ideas in a response can play an important role in how well you communicate a point. Observing the way other writers organise ideas can help you improve your own approach. Read the following article and complete the activity that follows.

Debate over double-edged sword of technology

Technology can help drivers find their cars in a car park, make cyclists park their bikes responsibly, help parents track their children's expenses, and even identify sarcastic remarks posted online.

5   But as technology plays a bigger part in daily lives, a debate is brewing over whether Singapore should be more careful in picking the technology to adopt – with some experts warning that there are downsides to using tools to solve every problem.

10 Debates about overdependence on technology are perennial but it has assumed more relevance since Singapore's Smart Nation drive, launched in 2014, was highlighted again at Prime Minister Lee Hsien Loong's recent National Day Rally.

15 Experts warn that society needs to be constantly alive to the deep changes that technology can bring to its norms and values.

Take last month's launch of bike-sharing firm SG Bike, which is using 'geofencing', a radio-based system, to compel
20 cyclists to park in designated areas or risk fines.

But Dr Spela Mocnik, a sociologist at the Singapore University of Technology and Design's Lee Kuan Yew Centre for Innovative Cities (LKYCIC), said although the technology may help manage undesirable behaviour, it may not change the
25 mindset that causes the behaviour.

'A sense of civic-mindedness has to do with attitudes towards others, which is perhaps better addressed through education at the formal and informal level,' she added.

30 Drawing a similar dichotomy of views was another recent technology, Changi Airport's new Video-based Parking Guidance System (VPGS). About 1,000 video cameras are installed above parking spaces in the car parks of Terminals 1 to 3 to read licence-plate information that can
35 help people find their cars.

On the pro side, Associate Professor Xavier Bresson, from Nanyang Technological University's School of Computer Science and Engineering, said the technology would probably benefit large car parks, noting that finding one's car
40 wasn't a problem limited to Singapore.

He added that VPGS is an interesting application whose data can be mathematically analysed for developing other smart-city systems.

[…] sociologist Tan Ern Ser of the National University of
45 Singapore said it was important for people to 'internalise'

social values so that the use of smart devices would not make them careless, irresponsible and lazy.

LKYCIC researcher Corinne Ong noted that managers of other large car parks have used non-technological ways of solving the problem of drivers forgetting where they
50 parked, such as colour zones and animal symbols, and research should be done to find out what works most effectively.

'Using technology for problem- solving is characteristic of advanced, global societies. Application of innovative
55 technology has increasingly become a basis for assessing industry competitiveness,' said Dr Ong. 'But it is as important to ask "is it necessary?" and "are there alternatives?".'

The same issues also arise in a host of other innovations
60 that are being adopted here. For example, the push towards a cashless society recently raised concerns that the poor might get left behind or that children might not learn the lessons that come with handling physical money.

Then there is the use of technology to process human
65 language. A 'sarcasm detector' called Crystalace is being developed at the Agency for Science, Technology and Research, a computer program that classifies sentences as sarcastic or not.

While some welcomed this as a step towards more
70 sophisticated artificial intelligence, others say the software will never be accurate enough to be useful, given that sarcasm depends on context as well as tone of voice.

There are also concerns about the fragility of systems.

For example, recent reports have revealed that
75 autonomous machines like robots and self-driving cars may be vulnerable to cyber attack, which could result in them being used to spy on or harm people.

However, technology has obvious benefits to humanity, and experts have suggested ways to make the best use of it.
80

Mr Teo Chin Hock, deputy chief executive of the Cyber Security Agency of Singapore, said technology developers should consider security at every stage of development and security measures should not be an afterthought.

Meanwhile, Dr Mocnik said technology should go hand
85 in hand with social science in Singapore's Smart Nation drive, to ensure that 'technology works for society and not the other way round'.

By Lin Yangchen, **The Strait Times,**
September 2017

ACTIVITY 2

1 Identify the various perspectives addressed in the article by completing the diagram below:

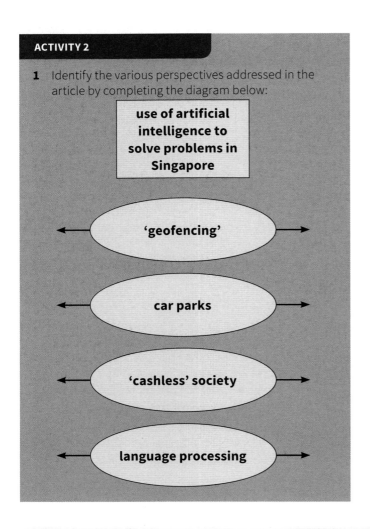

2 Which of the following transitional words or phrases would best replace the [...] in line 44?

a In addition

b Unfortunately

c Luckily

d However

Being able to identify, select and interpret evidence is an important part of reading comprehension and writing response in this course. In an exam situation, for example, you may simply be asked to identify relevant information or you might need to select *several* pieces of information which support a point you are trying to make. If the evidence you select is not relevant to the question or to your response, you risk losing marks.

In Activities 3 and 4, you will practise selecting evidence. These tasks will ask you to consider the relevance of the evidence in order to determine how well you comprehend what you are reading. In Activity 5, you will identify, select and interpret evidence in greater depth by responding to exam-style questions. You will accomplish these tasks over the course of three, related texts (labeled Texts 1–3).

To begin, read Text 1, which concerns the growing interest in STEM (Science, Technology, Engineering and Mathematics) education worldwide.

Text 1

Science advocate says, Let the children come to me

For education to fully contribute to the future success of children, schools should pay closer attention to the middle school years.

This is the idea stressed by Lorraine Hariton, senior vice-president for Global Partnerships at the Academy of Sciences, at the 'Women in STEM and Entrepreneurship' at C **Asean**, Thailand.

The STEM (Science, Technology, Engineering and Mathematics) programme should therefore be fostered in children in primary and secondary schools in order to provide them with more experimental learning related to their interests.

'We need STEM education across the entire age range,' said Hariton. 'We even started at pre-school. But the age that is most influential, especially to girls, is middle school when they start to think about gender roles. We need to make sure girls understand and can relate their passion to science and technology. One way is through experimental learning that gets not just girls, but all children, involved in science so they can see how it impacts their lives.'

Hariton, who focuses on developing partnerships for the Global STEM Alliance, said that female entrepreneurship and involvement in technology varies by country. Thailand, for instance, has different issues compared to the India or the US.

Many Asean countries, including Thailand, lag in education and research and development investment, with Thailand's investment currently at 0.6%.

To drive change, Hariton says government policies and the education system are both important. Government policy can help increase the number of women in STEM education programmes by encouraging experimental education, providing **mentoring** and online training to young people, training teachers, and other necessary aspects that excite young students to become excited about science and technology.

Hariton oversaw the launch of the Global Entrepreneurship Program, the US State Department's effort to help build an entrepreneur ecosystem around the world, expanding from three **pilot** countries – Egypt, Turkey and Indonesia – to more than 140 countries around the world.

'Thailand has less gender bias in STEM than in the US where men still largely outnumber women in this field, so female representation is better here than in the US and that's a very good thing. In India and Japan, there is a lot of gender bias, a lot of issues around women.'

The world is changing a lot culturally, partly because it's easier and less expensive to be innovative in information technology: 'The internet is making available tools that were never available before. So it's an opportunity for young innovators to change the world.'

Adapted from an article in Bangkok Post, *October 2016*

103

ARTICLE GLOSSARY

Asean: Association of South-East Asian Nations

mentor: experienced person in a company who provides training and advice to new employees

pilot: experimental, to find out if something is successful or not

ACTIVITY 3

1   According to the article, more females will get involved with technology through the help of government policies. Identify relevant details that support this.

2   This article concludes that there is an opportunity 'for young innovators to change the world'. What piece of evidence from the article is the *least* relevant in proving this point? Justify your answer.

The next text is the transcript of an interview that considers why girls do not find as much interest in the sciences as boys do. Further your practice in locating relevant information by completing the activity that follows.

Text 2

Research explores ways to overcome STEM fields' gender gap

DAVID GREENE, HOST:

When you look at fields such as engineering and technology – fields that have a lot of well-paying jobs – women are significantly outnumbered by men. And the problem is not just recruitment; it's **retention**. There's new research now into why it is often hard to retain women at tech companies and engineering schools. And here to talk about it is NPR social science correspondent Shankar Vedantam. Hey, Shankar.

SHANKAR VEDANTAM: Hi, David.

GREENE: So what is the problem you're looking at here?

VEDANTAM: Well, you know, people used to say that women were not as good at maths. But as women have started to do as well as men at science and maths, the narrative has shifted, David. And now people say, look, women really aren't as interested in these fields as men. And there's some evidence to back up this theory. Only 18 per cent of engineering majors in college are female. Lots of female students show up in college saying they're interested in science, technology, engineering and maths, but a couple of years later, they've **switched their majors**.

At the University of Massachusetts at Amherst, the psychologist Nilanjana Dasgupta told me that she had a different theory on why women might drop out of maths and tech careers.

NILANJANA DASGUPTA: The **prototype** of success in tech is very male, so I think those stereotypes get in the way of women feeling that this is the field for them. They feel good at multiple subjects, and you feel like you don't really belong in a place. Over time, you start to de-identify or move away from fields and **hang out** more in other fields where your friends are.

GREENE: So women feeling like they don't necessarily belong in a place – how did she actually test this?

VEDANTAM: Well, she invited female engineering students to join work groups that were trying to solve various kinds of problems, David. Each of these work groups had four members. What the volunteers didn't know is that three people on each of these teams were actually researchers. So only one person on each of these teams was actually a volunteer.

Dasgupta and her colleagues manipulated the team so sometimes the volunteer was the only woman on the team. Sometimes, she was 1 of 2 women. Sometimes, she was 1 of 3 women on the team. Now, by making sure the other three people did exactly the same things every time, Dasgupta was now able to tell what happened when the female students found themselves in a minority, in a group with gender **parity** and in the majority.

DASGUPTA: In teams where there's 50 per cent women or where women are in the majority, these female engineering students feel much more confident in their ability in engineering. And at the end of the team activity, they feel much more interested in pursuing careers in engineering, whereas if they are the only woman on the team, all of that sort of drops significantly.

VEDANTAM: But here's the thing that's interesting – there was not a single volunteer in the study who reported that the group had any affect on her behaviour. Every woman who was a volunteer said their participation was shaped only by their own knowledge and by their own interest. In reality, we know this is not the case. The behaviour of the volunteers was shaped significantly by their groups.

GREENE: This really feels like it's looking at sexism and bias in a very different way, looking at much more – at the thinking of the person who is being negatively affected by this in some way.

VEDANTAM: I think that's right, David. One of the implications of this work is that tech companies or engineering schools might want to ensure that when you have groups that have been historically underrepresented in certain areas – fields like engineering or fields like math – it might make sense to have a critical mass of women in work groups rather than spreading the women very thinly across, you know, your whole campus.

GREENE: Shankar, thanks for coming in to chat, as always.

VEDANTAM: Thank you, David.

GREENE: That's NPR Shankar Vedantam, who regularly joins us to talk about social science research.

From NPR News, Morning Edition, *June 2016*

ARTICLE GLOSSARY

retention: keeping employees, making them want to stay

switched their majors: changed their main subjects of study

prototype: typical model

hang out: spend time

parity: equality

ACTIVITY 4

1 What *reasons* does the transcript give for why it is hard to keep female workers in scientific fields like technology and engineering?

2 What *examples/evidence* does this transcript offer to prove that it is hard to keep female workers in the sciences? Summarise this information in your own words.

3 At the end of the interview, Vedantam concludes that 'having a critical mass of women in work groups' rather than spreading them thinly across the campus could be a solution to keeping women interested in the sciences'. Identify the single most relevant *detail* in the transcript which leads to this way of thinking.

This last article is about the impact of gender on university enrolment in the sciences. First read the article. Then practise working with exam-style comprehension questions by completing the activity that follows. For the most part, these questions are meant to assess how well you can *understand* and *apply* ideas, though some may challenge you further.

Text 3

White males now classed as a 'minority group' at university

The **move** by the Royal Veterinary College, where more than three-quarters of the intake are female, marks the first time that white men have been included in a strategy to help under-represented groups.

The huge imbalance has prompted the college, with campuses in north London and Hertfordshire, to launch a campaign, outlined in its annual report to the admissions regulator, to attract 'white males', among other under-represented groups such as pupils from poor backgrounds and ethnic minorities. Ethnic minorities of both genders together make up about 10 per cent of the UK population but only 6 per cent of the students at the college.

Professor Stephen May, Vice Principal for teaching at the college, said: 'We are not in the business of quotas, that would be discriminatory, but we hope in the long term we will see progress with white males.'

While Royal Veterinary College is an extreme case, it reflects a wider trend of women overtaking men in education. Of the 24 leading universities, only three have a majority of male students (including Cambridge, the London School of Economics and Imperial College, London).

Women outnumber men in the vast majority, including King's College, London, where 67 per cent of students are female, and Cardiff University, where the figure is 60 per cent.

Across UK universities, 984 000 female undergraduates are studying for degrees, compared to 713 000 male. The gap is expected to widen in future years as new government rules make it easier for universities to recruit students with A Level grades of AAB or better, more of whom are female.

While last week's A Level results showed boys narrowly outperforming girls at the **A* grade** for the first time, girls remained significantly more likely than boys to achieve grades in the upper range of A* to B.

30 According to Mary Curnock Cook, the chief executive of the Universities and Colleges Admissions Service, the 'very worrying gap' between male and female performance at school and university is leading to 'fundamental shifts' in society.

Figures from professions which were traditionally male **bastions** reveal the workplace gender revolution. In law, women made up to 60 per cent of individuals qualifying to 35 practise and admitted on to the **roll** of solicitors in 2010. In the same year, 56 per cent of places in UK medical schools went to women, compared to less than a quarter in the 1960s, and it is predicted that by 2017 female doctors will be in a majority.

Mrs Curnock Cook said: 'If you look at educational achievement through primary and secondary school and then university outcomes there is a very worrying gap between 40 males and females.

'Somebody needs to address what it is about our education system that is allowing females to perform overall so much better than males. If this trend continues it will start to underpin quite a fundamental sociological change.'

While women are forging successful careers on the back of superior performances in 45 school and university exams, some fear boys are being left on the scrap heap by an education system which disadvantages them.

Coursework and modular exams, less emphasis on the physical, outdoor curriculum and the lack of male teachers have all been blamed for boys' underachievement. White working class boys now do worse at school than any other group.

50 Diane Houston, a psychology professor and graduate school dean at Kent University, said that whilst boys may be disadvantaged at school, women still faced a glass ceiling in the workplace.

'But I'm not sure that at this point we should be screaming about percentage differences in attainment given the way in which women's careers atrophy through their reproductive 55 lives. There may be more women training to be solicitors, but the judges are men.'

From an article by Julie Henry in The Telegraph, *August 2012*

ARTICLE GLOSSARY

move: action
A* grade: the highest grade awarded in an A-level exam
bastions: places/things defended by a particular group
roll: official register or list

EXAM-STYLE QUESTIONS

Answer the comprehension questions **1–8**.

1   Identify three pieces of evidence from the article which prove the point that women are more represented at the university level than men. **[3]**

2   Which piece of evidence is *least* relevant in supporting the main thesis? Justify your answer. **[2]**

3   Name three reasons why boys are not performing as well as girls academically as stated in the article. **[3]**

4   Which piece of information from the article most directly supports the conclusion drawn at the end? Cite evidence in your response to justify your answer. **[2]**

5   Explain the author's likely purpose for including the story about Royal Veterinary College in the opening. **[4]**

6   In your own words, explain what is meant by the 'very worrying gap' mentioned in line 31. **[4]**

7   In your own opinion, how could the problem outlined in the article be solved? Draw a conclusion based on the evidence in the article and justify your response. **[4]**

8   In your own words, explain what is meant by the following words/phrases used in the article: **[3]**

   a   left on the scrap heap (line 45)

   b   glass ceiling (line 51)

   c   atrophy (line 54).

                                          Total marks: 25

Synthesising evidence to sustain a point

Most comprehension questions will target a specific area of the material, and require brief answers. However, in an essay response, you will be expected to extend, or **sustain**, ideas. You will need to select and apply appropriate information to your point in order to do this.

As you have already learnt in this unit, linking a reason with a specific example helps develop your point for an audience. While a single example is often sufficient, extending your thoughts further can add depth to your ideas. By combining, or **synthesising**, several pieces of evidence, you are *sustaining* your point and reinforcing it for your reader.

KEY TERMS

Sustaining an idea: the process of extending a point that you are making.

Synthesising evidence: the process of offering information from multiple sources in order to sustain a point.

Study the following mind map, and look at the paragraph plan that follows it. Notice how a synthesis of evidence from each of the texts you have read so far is used to build and sustain the main point: that the gender gap affects both boys and girls academically.

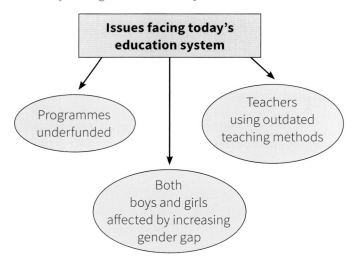

Paragraph 1

Boys are affected …

→ UK universities: 984 00 females are studying for a degree, compared to only 713 000 males; 21 out of 24 Russell Group universities have a majority of females.

Paragraph 2

Girls are affected …

→ STEM education is needed, particularly at primary/secondary level, to encourage interest in the sciences – 'We need to make sure girls understand and can relate their passion to science and technology'.

→ A study revealed that when females are the minority in science-based work groups, they are more likely to drop the subject by changing their main course of study.

Notice how the writer plans to use two paragraphs to maintain the point that the gender gap is a big issue in education for both boys and girls. There is nothing wrong with developing a single point over the course of two paragraphs. Just make sure your essay covers a range of ideas in addition to this one.

Clearly, synthesising information from multiple sources helps to sustain your ideas and deepen the points you make in your essay. Practise sustaining points by reading the Texts 1–5 and answering Activity 5, which follows.

Text 1

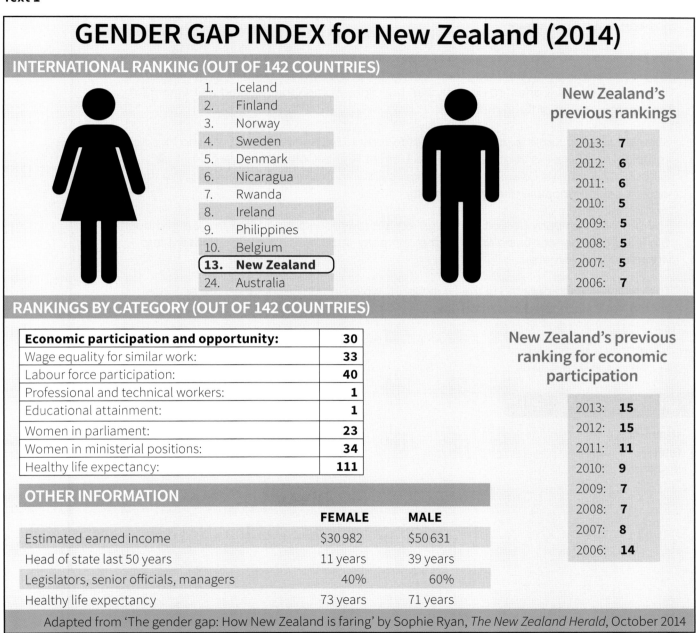

GENDER GAP INDEX for New Zealand (2014)

INTERNATIONAL RANKING (OUT OF 142 COUNTRIES)

1.	Iceland
2.	Finland
3.	Norway
4.	Sweden
5.	Denmark
6.	Nicaragua
7.	Rwanda
8.	Ireland
9.	Philippines
10.	Belgium
13.	**New Zealand**
24.	Australia

New Zealand's previous rankings

Year	Rank
2013:	7
2012:	6
2011:	6
2010:	5
2009:	5
2008:	5
2007:	5
2006:	7

RANKINGS BY CATEGORY (OUT OF 142 COUNTRIES)

Economic participation and opportunity:	**30**
Wage equality for similar work:	33
Labour force participation:	40
Professional and technical workers:	1
Educational attainment:	1
Women in parliament:	23
Women in ministerial positions:	34
Healthy life expectancy:	111

New Zealand's previous ranking for economic participation

Year	Rank
2013:	15
2012:	15
2011:	11
2010:	9
2009:	7
2008:	7
2007:	8
2006:	14

OTHER INFORMATION

	FEMALE	MALE
Estimated earned income	$30 982	$50 631
Head of state last 50 years	11 years	39 years
Legislators, senior officials, managers	40%	60%
Healthy life expectancy	73 years	71 years

Adapted from 'The gender gap: How New Zealand is faring' by Sophie Ryan, *The New Zealand Herald*, October 2014

The World Economic Forum's annual report, the Global Gender Gap Index (above), ranks countries on the gap between men and women on health, education, economic, and political indicators. The index aims to understand whether countries are distributing their resources and opportunities equitably between women and men.

Text 2

The gender gap: How New Zealand is faring

In 1999 and 2000, Motueka woman, Caitlin Lewis, worked for a seafood company as a fish **trimmer**. She was employed not long after her partner Brett Edwards – but although the pair had the same skills and background, Mr Edwards was given the more highly paid position of a trainee filleter.

Ms Lewis, now 46 and working as a labourer, said when her first pay cheque arrived, she realised she was being paid less than Mr Edwards; she felt she needed to do something about the issue as it affected not only her, but other women that worked as trimmers in the factory – many of them mothers.

She said she thought the problem should be easy to fix, so she looked up who to complain to. Ms Lewis complained to the Human Rights Commission, arguing that although she and Mr Edwards had identical skills and background, she was given the lesser paid job because she was a woman.

The seafood company denied the allegation but the tribunal found that the job had been allocated on a gender basis and that the company appointed men to be **filleters** and women to be trimmers.

The decision was appealed in the High Court, which in 2007 concluded the two jobs should not be allocated based on sex.

From an article by Sophie Ryan, *The New Zealand Herald*, October 2014

ARTICLE GLOSSARY

trimmer: someone who cuts up fish for packing

filleter: someone who prepares fish by removing the bones

Text 3

The way forward for gender equality

We all remember when the headlines, nearly half a century ago, warned of an **imminent** population explosion. Governments were **scrambling** to find the solution and their answer was to limit population growth, especially in the developing world. In 1994, we found what then seemed like an unlikely answer to dealing with changing population dynamics: women.

The International Conference on Population and Development (ICPD), held in Cairo in 1994, made news when a number of women groups were able to successfully convince governments of this proposition and shift the debate from population control to women's empowerment. They were successful because they argued that an investment in women's health and education would lead to economic development.

And they were right. During the past 20 years, **fertility rates** have generally declined as women's rights and opportunities have improved. The just-released *ICPD Beyond 2014 Global Report* notes that high fertility rates of 4 children or more per woman are now **confined** to just 45 of the world's poorest nations, down from 81 nations in the period 1990–1995. These latest statistics suggest that progress has been made, but that more work is needed.

As the new ICPD report makes clear, a nation's development potential is, in many ways, directly linked to the opportunities it offers to its poorest and most **marginalised** people, especially its women and girls. Nations that **stumble** on issues of gender equality are more likely to fall behind their neighbours in global development.

The challenge for the next 20 years, then, is clear. Nations committed to economic growth must put outdated prejudices and cultural preconceptions about the role of women behind them and embrace gender equality in both law and custom.

From an article by Phumzile Mlambo-Ngcuka and Babatunde Osotimehin, *Al Jazeera*, March 2014

111

ARTICLE GLOSSARY

imminent: likely to happen very soon

scramble: struggle to do something as quickly as possible

fertility rate: the rate at which women have children

confined: limited

marginalised: disadvantaged, treated as unimportant

stumble: do badly

Text 4

Bringing Facebook's 'She Means Business' to Pakistan

Facebook's female empowerment programme *She Means Business* is stepping into Pakistan with a collaboration with *Herself*, a similar initiative of the Punjab Information Technology Board (PITB).

Herself was launched by PITB in June 2016, after realising the low representation of women in Pakistan's startup **ecosystem**. The initiative aims to provide business training and support to expand the participation of women in the country's workforce. *She Means Business* by Facebook is a global initiative that was launched in March 2016 to empower and inspire women to become financially independent. It has been established in 14 countries, trained 7000+ women, **forged** 14 training partnerships and reached 32.5 million through its online efforts.

The aim of the partnership is to arm women with the support and resources needed for them to start their own business and participate more fully in the economy.

According to Dr Umar Saif, Chairman of PITB, 'in Pakistan, women-owned enterprises represent an insubstantial portion of existing **SMEs**. At PITB's Plan9, Pakistan's largest tech **incubator**, only 14% of start-up companies are co-founded by women. By collaborating with Facebook, we hope to be successful in further engaging women in the workforce and achieving more equal participation in the economy.'

Ritesh Mehta, Head of Economic Growth Initiatives, India and South Asia, at Facebook agrees: 'Through *She Means Business* and the support of our partners, like PITB's *Herself*, we want to shine a light on the women who start or run small businesses in Pakistan and empower them to do more – so that their families, their communities and ultimately, Pakistan's economy will benefit.'

From an article by Nushmiya Sukhera, *MIT Technology Review*, Pakistan, October 2016

112

ARTICLE GLOSSARY

ecosystem: network
forge: create
SME: small or medium enterprise
incubator: a place which provides practical support to new small businesses

Text 5

Uplift Women, Boost the Economy

Greater **integration** of women in the labour market – at all levels and in all sectors – is key to equitable, inclusive and sustainable development, and is a legitimate right of women.

Even though women constitute 50% of Asia-Pacific's total working-age population, their participation in formal employment is uniformly lower than that of men. In many countries in the region, the national female employment-to-population ratios are below 50%, which is not the case for men.

Gender-based discrimination is pervasive and goes beyond the labour force participation, as social and cultural **taboos perpetuate** discriminatory and restrictive traditional gender roles in different aspects of women's and men's lives.

There is a cost to gender discrimination and inequality. UN estimates reveal that low participation by Asian-Pacific women in the labour market bears an opportunity cost of more than 89 billion US dollars each year.

In South Asia and Central Asia, for example, the lower employment rates of women results in an average national income loss of nearly 19% and 16%, respectively. A World Bank analysis illustrates that if women's economic activity were **on par with** men's, economic growth in many Asia-Pacific countries could increase by as much as 18%.

The G20, which includes eight countries from the Asia-Pacific region, has called for reducing the gap between female and male labour force participation in their countries by 25%. Realisation of this goal by 2025 – no small **feat** – would add 100 million more women to the labour force. Asia and the Pacific could lead the way in this area.

From an article by Shamshad Akhtar, *Bangkok Post*, November 2014

113

ARTICLE GLOSSARY

integration: combining, making them become a part of

taboo: something which is prohibited

perpetuate: make something continue

on par with: equal to

feat: achievement

ACTIVITY 5

1   In your own words, explain what point the 'Gender gap index' infographic (Text 1) is trying to express.

2   Now write a one-sentence summary for each of the remaining texts 2–5.

3   If you were the lead activist for a gender equality group, what advice would you give to encourage women to demand equal pay? Use details from *more than one* text to justify your response.

4   Using evidence from two or three of the texts, and in roughly 300 words, sustain the point that gender equality can help the economy.

C Essay practice

In Unit 1, you learnt the basic elements of an essay and in Unit 2, you have begun taking the initial steps toward writing essays yourself. Specifically, you learnt several strategies for generating ideas, and you worked with reading material to observe how writers organise ideas. Unit 3 will teach you how to structure and communicate your own ideas in essay form, but now it is time to begin practice with essay writing by accessing all the skills you have learnt thus far in this coursebook.

In this section, you will practise writing essays in two ways:

- using reading material (supported)
- using outside knowledge (independent).

Essay	Details	Type
Text-based essay	• Student uses reading materials to support response • Input from articles must be summarised or paraphrased (no quotations) • Source citation is up to the teacher	Supported practice
Exam-style essay	• No reading materials are provided • Student must use outside knowledge to respond (this may or may not include information learnt from this chapter) • Students are not expected to cite sources from memory	Independent practice

Text-based essays

In an exam situation, you will *not* be given reading materials when asked to write an essay, but practising essay writing with this kind of information in front of you can be a very helpful strategy for building your own knowledge about contemporary issues. Writing about what you read also helps you remember it because you have to re-purpose the information from the text into a new format of your own. Using sources as the basis for

your writing therefore becomes an active process. As you evaluate whether or not each piece of information is relevant enough to include in your essay, you are increasing your chances of committing it to memory.

Look again at the articles provided in this chapter, several of which address equality in the modern world. Select *one* of the essay questions below and use this information to help support an essay of approximately 600–700 words:

Essay questions

1   To what extent does gender determine employment in today's society?

2   How effectively are we responding to the call for gender equality worldwide?

TIP
Return to the article, 'Debate over double-edged sword of technology'. Notice how the author sustains the first point of his argument by using multiple pieces of evidence. Use this as a point of reference as you carry out the task in Activity 6.

Here are a few points to keep in mind as you complete Activity 6:

- Spend roughly 10 minutes outlining the ideas you plan to discuss. (Think about which strategies from Chapter 2.1 might be most appropriate in helping you plan.)
- Use information from at least three to five extracts as the basis for your support.
- Draft a clear thesis that uses the language of the essay question.
- Aim to make logical, relevant connections among ideas.
- Sustain the discussion of your reasons by synthesising multiple pieces of evidence to support and reinforce them.
- Draw evidence-based conclusions that merge the evidence with your own perspective.

Exam-style essay

Notice that the content knowledge you learnt in this chapter lends itself to several of the course topics within the broad topic of *Economic, historical, moral, political and social* (see Chapter 1.1). By thinking deeply about the information you learnt and weighing it against your own perspective, you will likely feel more comfortable with these kinds of topics than you did before.

Now it is time to practise writing about these issues in a more independent way. For this next essay, you will use your own, independent knowledge to support your

argument. As this experience is more similar to an exam situation, you will work in a timed environment, and you will not be allowed to use any reading materials to help you write your essay.

ACTIVITY 7

Pick one Section 1 style question from the list below and develop an argument of 600–700 words in response to it. You will be assessed on:

- *how* you use knowledge to support a convincing and well-structured response, not on the knowledge itself
- how clearly and accurately you present the argument in written English
- your maturity of thought and appropriateness to the set task.

Essay questions

1 To what extent does education divide or unite a society? **[30]**
2 To what extent does effective learning take place outside school walls? **[30]**
3 How valuable are consumer boycotts in effecting social change in society? **[30]**
4 Evaluate how well your own country values and upholds human rights. **[30]**
5 To what extent is the health of its workers the responsibility of a company? **[30]**
6 To what extent should finding a job be a person's top priority? **[30]**

Summary

Key points to remember from this chapter:

- Sticking to word limits set by a question should be strictly regarded in this course. In an exam situation, information extending beyond these limits will probably not be read.
- Deconstructing the organisational structure of another writer's work can help you understand how to better organise your own ideas.
- Summaries and paraphrases are a way of putting the ideas of others into your own words, and should be the preferred method for writing responses to comprehension questions.
- 'Lifting' information directly from the text in quotation form, and using this as your response, does *not* show you understand what you read. Avoid doing this.
- Two strategies for sustaining a point are:
  o combining reasons with evidence
  o combining multiple pieces of evidence to reinforce a reason.

Unit 3:
Analysing and evaluating

Chapter 3.1
Argumentative writing

Dhaka, Bangladesh, 2016: A nearby industrial site is responsible for contaminating the Buriganga River with toxic waste, oil and chemicals. Residents are facing a severe water crisis. This chapter will feature information related to the key theme of *Food, water and other essential resources*.

Learning objectives

In this chapter, you will learn:

- what an argument is and how to appeal to an audience
- key elements of argumentative writing
- how to develop a well-reasoned argument
- strategies for evaluating the credibility of other sources
- how to build your own credibility as a writer.

A Introduction

In Chapter 1.2, you learnt about the basic components of an essay. The purpose of Unit 3 is to further this understanding by teaching you different ways to develop your writing.

Recall that when you write essays for English General Paper, you are required to present them in the form of an argument. Depending on how you frame your argument, your essay will vary in the way it sounds and how it is organised, so it is important to have a range of options for developing your ideas.

This chapter will introduce you to what an argument is first. Then it will teach you how to develop arguments in the most classic sense, which is by taking a clear position on an issue. Later, in Chapter 3.2, you will learn a second option for developing arguments, which is more initially objective in approach (called discursive writing).

B Understanding arguments

An **argument** uses **logical reasoning** to support a thesis (often called the **main claim** in this type of writing). When you write to argue, your goal is to convince your audience to accept, or at least to appreciate, your point of view.

Arguments are developed using varying degrees of persuasion. Imagine that you are showing different ways to present an arguable point, using a horizontal spectrum; persuasive writing would be at one end and discursive writing (as its opposite) at the other end. This is because persuasive writing feels very strongly about one side of the argument, while discursive writing does not (initially) prefer either side. In the middle of these two extremes is argumentative writing, as shown in the diagram.

DISCURSIVE	ARGUMENTATIVE	PERSUASIVE
'Hey, think this through with me.'	'Here's my side, but I'm willing to give yours fair consideration.'	'My side is the only side that matters.'

Persuasive writing offers a one-sided view of the topic or issue. Argumentative writing also favours one side, but unlike persuasive writing, it acknowledges the opposite side of the argument, too. Discursive writing eventually takes a side, but not until the very end, after every perspective has been considered. Therefore, how strongly the writer makes an argument determines where the approach will be on this spectrum.

As a writer in this course, you are expected to reason through issues logically and maturely. For this reason, you will keep away from persuasive writing because this approach does not consider opposing views reasonably. Instead, you will learn how to write argumentatively and discursively, which can help you accomplish your purpose without overstepping the bounds of logic or jeopardising your own credibility.

An argument:

- introduces the main claim (thesis) and supports it with reasons
- supports reasons with evidence
- considers the opposing viewpoint instead of ignoring or attacking it
- links evidence to claims.

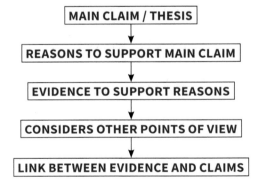

One way to look at logical reasoning is like this:

- we base reasons on evidence; we don't base evidence on reasons
- we think up logical reasons but we collect factual evidence.

In other words, reasons are your *opinion*, evidence is your *input*, and how the two connect is your *output* (commentary).

An argument should consider different perspectives, even when it supports a specific side. You will need to use logical reasoning to consider the issue and support the side you agree with, while being fair and reasonable in the process.

Context

When framing an argument, context is very important to consider. It is an important component of an argument because it has a direct effect on how the evidence is perceived.

Context can be established by explaining what is happening around or outside the issue. This can help the audience better understand the information itself and why the topic should matter to them.

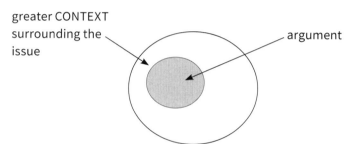

greater CONTEXT surrounding the issue

argument

For example, imagine a famous sports figure is on trial for violence. The defendant is a member of a minority group in the community because of his race and/or religion. The argument is whether or not he is guilty. How might the community's perception of his religion or race influence the outcome of his trial? Is it possible for preconceived ideas or underlying values to influence the way the jury sees the evidence in the case?

The influence of context is difficult to avoid, so it is something you'll need to consider when developing an argument.

Argumentative appeals

According to the ancient Greek philosopher Aristotle:

> Of the modes of persuasion furnished by the spoken word, there are three kinds. The first kind depends on the personal character of the speaker; the second, on putting the audience into a certain frame of mind; the third, on the proof, or apparent proof, provided by the words of the speech itself.
>
> From Aristotle's *Rhetoric*

A bust of Aristotle, who lived 384–322 BC.

In other words, there are three ways to convince, or *appeal* to, your audience to accept what you say:

- appeals to authority (*ethos*)
- appeals to emotion (*pathos*)
- appeals to logic (*logos*).

The terms *logos*, *pathos* and *ethos* come from Ancient Greek.

Appeals to authority (*ethos*)

Ethos concerns the credibility of the writer. The audience will only believe you if you appear very knowledgeable on the matter and seem trustworthy. If you are sympathetic to views that oppose your own – instead of ridiculing or ignoring them – your audience is more likely to trust you. By writing fairly, you are establishing yourself as an authority for the reader.

Your audience is also more likely to believe you if your ideas support the views of someone well-known in the field. So mentioning a public figure, expert or other stakeholder who agrees with you can be helpful in building trust in your argument.

Appeals to emotion (*pathos*)

Pathos concerns the writer's ability to understand and draw upon the emotions of the audience to gain their support. For example, arguments concerning global warming often use *pathos*, because there are few actual facts about the issues. If you change how your audience feels, it is possible to change their perspective.

TIP

You may have your own experiences which have emotions attached to them, but you should avoid using personal anecdotes unless the essay question specifically calls for it. These may be too narrow for a global audience to relate to and they are not generally acceptable in formal essay writing.

Appeals to logic (*logos*)

Logos is the structure of the argument itself and the proofs within it. To appeal to your audience's sense of logic, it is important to present your ideas in a rational order that the audience can follow, and to use reasons backed by evidence. Evidence can include numbers, statistics and other data as well as testimonial (i.e. eyewitness accounts or other 'third party' statements which serve as proof).

Additional appeal: *kairos*

One other appeal is called *kairos*, which means an appeal to timeliness (the importance of doing something at the right time). A television commercial or an advertisement that provides a limited-time offer shows *kairos* in action. In the same way, if you indicate the urgency of an argument

in your writing, you are appealing to the reader's sense of *time*. If you can create the sense that accepting your view will have a significant and immediate impact, the audience may accept it.

Use of appeals

Remember that these four appeals are not necessarily exclusive of one another. If you use statistics as evidence, you may be appealing to your audience through a combination of *logos* and *ethos*. While this information serves as evidence for your line of reasoning, it may also build your credibility by using data to support your argument.

While these appeals can be useful, you should be careful not to overly rely on just one. An essay based entirely on emotion may do little to convince an audience looking for factual evidence. However, an argument that only contains facts and data may make your reader feel detached from the issue. To be effective, the appeals should work together to achieve your purpose.

TIP

To learn more about Aristotle's ideas, watch Michael Sandel's TED Talk, 'The lost art of democratic debate'. You can search for this online.

ACTIVITY 1

Read the following speech. Identify examples of the different types of argumentative appeal.

Water security – good governance and sustainable solutions

This is what the people of Asia-Pacific are saying about water: 'The water is dirty.' 'I am not in school, my mother needs me to collect water.' 'There is **sewage** everywhere.' 'The factories use up so much water.' Four different voices with a single message – lack of access to clean water. Today, some 1.1 billion people have inadequate access to clean water and 2.6 billion lack basic **sanitation**.

Water, the foundation of life, is at the heart of a daily crisis faced by millions of the world's people – a crisis that breeds ill-health, destroys **livelihood**s and inflicts unnecessary human suffering. Overcoming the crisis in water is one of the great human challenges of the 21st century.

Water is important for our livelihood. Here the focus is on water as an economic resource shared within countries and across borders, and on the capacity of governments to manage water equitably and efficiently including across borders.

Good governance and sustainable solutions for water security have to address several issues simultaneously. Firstly, it has to deal with persistent inequalities. In high income areas of cities, people enjoy access to several hundred litres of water per day delivered to their homes at low prices. Meanwhile, poor households in both rural and urban areas of the same countries have access to less than the 20 litres of water per person required to meet basic human needs. A similar imbalance exists in agriculture and industry. These issues can be addressed by good public policies, partnerships, and investment in infrastructure. Political leadership matters in bringing these changes about.

Secondly, the Asia-Pacific region is vulnerable to climate change. Extreme weather events such as typhoons, floods and droughts threaten to wipe out much of our efforts in development and poverty reduction. Ironically while some parts of the region suffer from flooding, a greater part of the region is suffering from water shortages. We are reaching a critical stage where we do not have enough water. Countries like Tajikistan and Uzbekistan already draw more than 100 per cent of their renewable water sources, and countries like Pakistan, the Maldives and parts of Australia, China and India are close to that threshold. Even countries that have surplus water are likely to suffer short-term water insecurity because of climate change-induced droughts and floods. Given the threat of climate change we must change our development **paradigm** and adopt inclusive, green growth strategies, and other eco-efficient approaches to urban development.

The good news, ladies and gentlemen, is that water security is achievable if we address the following. The first set of issues deals with inefficient use of water. In many countries of the region some 30 to 70 per cent of drinking water is unaccounted for. Part of the

loss is due to old and **leaking** distribution systems. Moreover, much of the water that is accounted for is wasted by inefficient water use by households, industries and agriculture.

To minimise wastage and increase efficiency in water use we need to introduce progressive pricing policies that on the one hand recognise the basic need of water for human existence and on the other, progressively charge those who over-use or waste it. This would encourage households, industries and agriculturists to be more eco-efficient in using water.

The other set of issues is related to management and governance of water in an uncertain future brought about by climate change. **IPCC** reports indicate that 93 per cent of the impact of climate change will be on water-related issues. With climate change, all countries of the region are likely to face increased frequency and severity of droughts and floods. At this very moment while I am speaking to you, 2.4 million people from southern China are now suffering from severe flooding, while Vietnam is suffering from a drought. Both droughts and floods have a huge economic costs.

We need to make our water resource management more adaptive and responsive to unforeseen and rapidly changing situations. Active measures such as better **watershed** management would go a long way in this regard.

One final set of issues we need to address is waste management. As many of you know, the UN Secretary General's Advisory Board on Water and Sanitation will hold its meeting tomorrow, and I have been invited to speak on this matter.

While water security is first and foremost the responsibility of our Member Countries, we at **ESCAP** remain committed to assisting countries in addressing the issue. In our endeavour to assist countries in improving their water security we recognise the important role played by the Asia-Pacific Water Ministers' Forum and look forward to further strengthening our close collaboration.

From a speech by Noeleen Heyzer at the Asia-Pacific Water Ministers' Forum in Singapore, June–July 2010

121

ARTICLE GLOSSARY

sewage: waste water and waste from toilets

sanitation: a system for protecting people's health by removing dirt and waste

livelihood: the way a person earns money for living

paradigm: typical model

leaking: allowing water to escape when it should not

IPCC: Intergovernmental Panel on Climate Change

watershed: the area of high ground from which water flows down

ESCAP: Economic and Social Commission for Asia and the Pacific

ACTIVITY 2

Search online for the TED Talk, 'Teach every child about food' by the British chef Jamie Oliver. Make a list of the various appeals he uses to argue his point. Be prepared to present these to the class.

Recognising weaknesses in arguments

When used well, a combination of argumentative appeals can be an effective way to argue a point. What happens, however, when these strategies are used incorrectly? For example:

- an argument that relies only on emotional appeal to win your approval. Why would this be unfair?

- an argument that attacks the opponent himself/herself rather than his/her *views*. How might this change your mind about the argument?

How should we convince someone who holds a different view from ours?

In both cases, the arguments contain defects (faults) in the line of reasoning, called **logical fallacies**. It is not reasonable to make someone feel guilty in order to persuade them to listen to you, or to attack an opponent's character just because he/she has a different view. Yet mistakes like these can easily be made, especially when the writer or speaker is passionate about the issue. If the conclusion you are working toward seems obvious to you, you are more likely to just assume it is true without taking the logical steps to prove that it is. This is how fallacies are formed.

KEY TERM

Logical fallacy: a defect in the line of reasoning, which weakens the argument.

DID YOU KNOW?

The ancient Greek philosopher Aristotle was the first person to study fallacies systematically. In his work *De Sophisticis Elenchis* (Sophistical Refutations), he identified and named the first thirteen of these (though there are hundreds!). Many fallacies have Latin names since Latin was a core subject for Greek philosophers like Aristotle.

In this section, you will learn how to identify defective reasoning so you can learn to avoid it in your own writing. While there are dozens of names for the different fallacies, you will learn some of the most common ones. These are the ones you will need to be aware of – and avoid – when you are writing essays for this course. In order to fix a logical error in your essay, though, it is much more important to know *why* the reasoning is faulty rather than what it is called. Complete Activity 3 to see if you can identify logical errors. We will then learn the names of the fallacies.

ACTIVITY 3

Read the following statements. With a partner, talk about what is unfair or illogical about each of them.

1   My favourite celebrity has just tried a new diet and it worked, so I am going to try it, too.

2   If solar panels are working in remote areas in Canada, then we should obviously use them in sub-Saharan Africa.

3 According to a recent study conducted in eight European schools, learning was better in single-sex classrooms than mixed-gender classrooms. Therefore, single-sex schooling should be the international standard.

4 Supporting the death penalty means we do not respect life. If we do not care about life, we are more likely to commit violent acts ourselves, and this will lead to the end of our own civilisation. Banning the death penalty is therefore necessary.

5 The farmlands to the east have not been used for three years. Either we make the move to build a commercial site there or we will lose money altogether.

You may come across the following most common fallacies when writing to argue during this course:

Ad populum
When the arguer takes advantage of most people's desire to 'fit in' by going along with what others do, say or believe; *ad populum* is also similar to the *bandwagon* fallacy, which is an appeal to *new* ideas held by the masses.

Example: We have always done it this way, so since the group agrees it is right, well, it should be so, then.

Hasty generalisation
Jumping too quickly to conclusions before considering all the facts; hasty generalisations usually happen when the writer uses the word 'all' or 'everyone' in the statement, which leaves no room for error.

Example: Our waiter was Honduran. He was so nice! We should take our next holiday in Honduras because everyone there is going to be just as nice as he was.

Slippery slope
Presenting a series of events where one thing leads to another until the final step leads to a particular outcome; if the final outcome is unlikely to be caused by the first step, then error is present.

Example: If you skip lessons on Fridays, then you will miss important information. Next thing you know, you will be skipping lessons every day, and before you know it, you will drop out of school. You do not want to be jobless, so don't skip lessons on Fridays!

Appeal to emotion
Appealing only to the audience's emotions (*ethos*) as the main premise for the argument.

Example: I got stuck in traffic for three hours this morning, the lift broke down on my way up to my office, my dog is ill, and my poor mother can't have any food because she is having an operation tomorrow. Can I please have a pay rise?

False analogy, faulty comparison
Attempting to compare two things that are too dissimilar in nature as the basis of your point.

Example: Doctors refer to medical books all the time when they are treating patients. In the same way, I should be allowed to use a textbook in my medical exam.

False dichotomy
Leading the audience to believe there are only two choices – either this or that.

Example: Either you must eat what I am serving for dinner or you will starve.

Appeal to authority
Using a 'big name' (famous person) to persuade the audience to accept your beliefs, even though the 'big name' is not an authority on the issue.

Example: Famous actor Rod Winston thinks we should spend more money on space exploration because it could lead us to finding new resources. This is why we should invest our money in space!

Post hoc
The assumption that because B came after A, A must have caused B; hastily drawing a causal conclusion without properly identifying the link between the two.

Example: I ate sushi for lunch a few days ago, and today I had to stay home from work with food poisoning. It must have been the sushi!

DID YOU KNOW?

The literal translation for *post hoc* is 'after this', so we can use it to mean 'therefore' or 'because of this'.

Bandwagon

Suggesting that a new idea is best because of its popularity, but without regard to its validity; this fallacy is very similar to *ad populum*, where the fallacy is that 'everybody believes X, so you should believe it too'.

Example: More and more people are switching to X insurance company. You should, too!

Ad hominem

Attacking a person's character as the basis for undermining their argument.

Example: Did you read that article in *Times Today* about the dangers of drone racing? The author was only fifteen, so I doubt any of it is true.

Straw man

Oversimplifying someone else's point so that it is easy to reject it; this attempts to make your own argument look stronger.

Example: Amir thinks the whole staff should be fired for what happened last week. Clearly, Amir is not fit to be manager.

Red herring

This fallacy is named after a strong-smelling fish that can lead someone along a false trail; in a similar way, the fallacy distracts the audience away from the main point with an idea that is not relevant.

Example: The issue in question is whether or not we should raise your wages, so let's start by first discussing your concerns about sanitation.

Begging the question

The point of logical reasoning is to make progress by starting with one idea and arriving at a new conclusion. If you *beg the question*, the conclusion you arrive at is the same idea you started with, so no progress is made. Essentially, it asks the audience to believe a reason without offering evidence to support it.

Example: The athlete cannot be removed from this competition for cheating because she is an honest person!

Cherry-picking the evidence

Intentionally omitting or ignoring relevant information to make your argument appear stronger.

Example: According to Yin's book, *Solar Savings*, and two other articles I read online, switching to solar panels will save you money. (*What's left out is a study conducted by the Ministry of Energy, which proves that solar panels can be more expensive than people think*.)

DID YOU KNOW?

Fallacies can go by lots of different names. *Ad populum*, for instance, is also known as:

- *ad numerum*
- appeal to the gallery
- appeal to the masses
- argument from popularity
- *argumentum ad populum*
- common practice
- mob appeal
- past practice
- peer pressure
- traditional wisdom.

ACTIVITY 4

Now that you have learnt the names of the fallacies, go back to Activity 3 and identify the fallacy in each statement.

ACTIVITY 5

Watch Ann Cooper's online TED Talk, 'What's wrong with school lunches'. Identify some of the fallacies that appear in her argument.

C Taking a position: an argumentative approach to writing

The most common way to frame an argument is, of course, by taking a position on the issue. In this section, you will learn how argumentative writing differs from expository writing, and you will learn some strategies for effectively arguing your point.

Arguing versus explaining: key differences

In Chapter 2.1, you learnt about the importance of expository skills in this course. These can help you respond to reading comprehension questions which often require you to summarise or paraphrase information using your own words.

Expository skills can also help you explain the context of an argument and position evidence as you prepare to defend or refute it. Recall that you will not be writing expository essays at any point in this course. In this section, therefore, you will learn the key differences between expository writing and argumentative writing to ensure that you take the correct approach to writing essays for this course.

To start, think about the expository essays you may have written in the past in your English classes. This can be a helpful point of reference as we look at the subtle differences which make argumentative writing distinct from expository writing.

There are several important differences between argumentative writing and writing to explain. These differences are found mainly in:

- tone
- thesis statement development
- **counterargumentation** strategies (strategies for expressing opposite viewpoints).

These elements rely specifically on the word choice you use and the way you use language to reason through your point.

Later in this chapter, you will also learn how to develop the following in an argument:

- line of reasoning
- concluding remarks.

Depending on whether you are taking a position or investigating more objectively, you will learn how these elements can vary.

KEY TERM

Counterargumentation: a strategy of considering arguments that go against your thesis or main claim, and dismissing or minimising them (countering them) in order to strengthen your own point.

Tone

Unlike an explanation, which aims to inform, an argument seeks to convince. In writing argumentatively, there is more at stake because you are doing more than just educating the audience; you are trying to win their approval. For this reason, your tone is more commanding than if you were summarising or explaining something.

125

ACTIVITY 6

Read extracts 1–4 from an article about growing genetically modified (GM) food. For each extract, determine whether the purpose is to *explain* or to *argue* by identifying words and/or phrases that contribute to its tone.

Extract 1

Where does modern corn on the cob come from? Well-informed diners will know the answer: Latin America. But what they probably don't know is that it never grew there naturally. Humans created it. Six to 10 thousand years ago, some **innovative** Mesoamerican farmers noticed that whereas most varieties of teosinte grass produced lots of branches with a few edible **kernels** on each, others produced fewer branches. So they started breeding grass that produced good kernels with grass that didn't produce as many branches. The result: enormous, delicious, modern corn.

Extract 2

There is, so far, no good evidence that **GM** crops are unhealthy – which is striking when you consider for how long and how widely they have been used. American consumers have eaten them for decades, whereas Europeans haven't. Yet the National Academy study concludes that European and American trends for cancer, obesity, gastrointestinal tract illness, kidney disease, autism or allergies do not differ in any way that could be explained by GM crops. Something could still emerge – science rarely gives guarantees – but these **Frankenfoods** have been around longer than many powerful modern medicines that we take **with abandon**. Clearly, their ill-effects have been vastly exaggerated.

Extract 3

Over the past 30 years, GM crop use has spread from the US to most of South America, Asia and Australia. The vast majority of the plants, ranging across 14 crops from soybeans to maize and cotton, are modified to be more resistant to insects or pesticides. A few newer varieties have been created to have a longer shelf life, or not to turn brown when cut, though they are not yet widespread.

Extract 4

A new generation of GM crops is now being developed using **mind-boggling** techniques, like accelerating tiny bits of DNA-covered gold into cells. In some cases, new methods will **blur the line** between selective breeding and GM, so our regulation will have to evolve in response. But rather than **shunning** the modern wonders that help farmers feed a hungry world, we should marvel at them. And, in our shopping habits and our public policy, we should be guided by science, not superstition.

Adapted from 'We must end our superstitious objections to genetically modified food' by Juliet Samuel, The Telegraph, May 2016

ARTICLE GLOSSARY

innovative: new and original

kernels: seeds, inner parts

GM: genetically modified

Frankenfoods: a negative reference to genetically modified foods, referring to the fictional character Frankenstein who created a monster

with abandon: in a completely uncontrolled way

mind-boggling: difficult to imagine

blur the line: make the difference less clear between two things

shunning: avoiding

How can people be persuaded about the arguments for and against growing GM crops?

Argumentative thesis development

Earlier in this chapter, you learnt that the thesis statement in an argument is sometimes called a *main claim*. When discussing the elements of an argument, the phrase *main claim* is usually more appropriate. This is because when you argue, your main idea / thesis transforms into an *opinion* you want others to believe, or what you 'claim' to be true. Remember that these terms are similar and therefore perform the same function in an essay.

The purpose of argumentative writing is to argue. Your main claim (thesis) should therefore:

- be debatable (i.e. be open to other points of view)
- support one point of view.

It should also:

- focus on the key words of the question
- introduce the perspective that you will argue.

> **!**
>
> **TIP**
> It can be helpful to pose your main claim / thesis in the form of a 'because' statement. For example, 'X is beneficial/harmful *because …*'.

Take a look at the following example to see how an argumentative thesis:

- adopts a more forceful, aggressive tone
- takes a broader approach to establishing focus (i.e. does not list specific reasons)

tone is more aggressive

The sale of bottled water *should be banned* because it has serious *ethical* and *environmental* consequences.

uses lenses to introduce ideas as opposed to specific reasons

KEY SKILLS

Lenses are broader categories or themes (e.g. politics, environment) that global issues fall into. See Section 2.2 *C Generating ideas for your essay* to review lenses and how they can help you organise ideas when writing.

Read the following sample argumentative thesis statement. Based on the criteria we have discussed, evaluate its effectiveness:

If you send foreign aid to developing countries, those who receive it are more likely to suffer from inflation, fluctuations in currency, corruption and civil disorder; so it is doing more harm than good and should therefore be stopped.

What advice might you offer for revising this statement?

The writer suggests that the provision of care does not help struggling countries, so we know which side they will be arguing. When addressing the reasons (sub-claims) why, however, the thesis starts to lose its focus by listing so many individual reasons. One strategy to improve this is to use broader ideas (lenses) to group these reasons. For instance, inflation and currency fall under the broader category of 'money' while corruption and civil disorder are 'social issues'. The term 'socio-economic' could therefore cover *all* of the reasons listed:

Sending foreign aid to developing countries *is doing more harm than good because* of the negative *socio-economic* impact on those who receive it, so it should be stopped.

If you want to keep your argument clear and focused, a broader approach can be effective. Although you know from the start which side you plan to argue for, your evidence may lead you to feel more, or less, certain. It is acceptable to preview your main reasons in your thesis statement, but just make sure they are the same at the end!

KEY SKILLS

Since a discursive approach to developing an argument explores both sides of an issue, you should avoid listing reasons in the thesis because it would likely lead to a lengthy list as well. Chapter 3.2 will help you develop a discursive thesis.

ACTIVITY 7

Read the thesis statements. Determine to what extent each statement follows the guidelines for writing an argumentative thesis/claim.

1   Fast food is bad for you so fast food restaurants should be banned.
2   Urban farming is a new way of providing access to healthy food.
3   Access to clean drinking water should be a human right because of the economic and cultural complexities that come with selling it as a commercial asset.
4   Water should be commodified* because it is too expensive to control and manage it otherwise; this would allow for more equal distribution and would reduce international tensions over water.
5   In countries where access to healthy food is scarce, alternatives such as cricket farming should be pursued because this can improve the quality of life for people living there.
6   Being an ethical consumer has lots of benefits.

(*A *commodity* is a raw material that can be bought or sold. To *commodify* water means to put a price on it.)

Counterargumentation

To appear reasonable, your argument should give consideration to viewpoints other than your own. Clearly not everyone thinks the same way, so it is important to recognise that other views exist. Sensitivity to different viewpoints can build trust and credibility with a potentially sceptical audience (i.e. an audience who may not believe you). They are more likely to accept your ideas if you have taken time to consider alternative ways of looking at the issue.

If you mention an opposing viewpoint, and follow this up with reasons to either concede to or challenge it, then you are using a counterargument (also called *rebuttal*) strategy. However, it can be difficult to talk about the opposing side of an argument without sounding as if you agree with it, especially when a strong point is raised.

127

The most effective counterarguments attempt to show that the opposite viewpoint is:

- faulty
- misguided
- only partly true
- true, but with limitations.

When used effectively, this strategy can strengthen your argument, rather than weaken it. An important strategy in countering an opposing view lies in the use of tone, and careful choice of words. There are two basic elements to the wording of a counterargument:

- the opposing point
- your *counter* to that point.

KEY SKILLS

Transitions are important for establishing the tone of a counterargument. For a full list of transitional words and phrases, see Chapter 1.2 Section *F Key elements of an essay*.

ACTIVITY 8

Using the following information, write a statement which counters the opposing view presented in response to the thesis.

Thesis: The government should put penalty taxes on products like sugary drinks.

Opposing point: Lifestyle decisions should be made by the consumer, not the government.

Your counter: A local health institute reports a high cost of care for people suffering from diabetes; both patients and taxpayers suffer.

The next section will provide you with a framework for drafting counterarguments.

How to write a counterargument

First, you should acknowledge the opposing view by using an appropriate transition phrase/word, such as the following examples:

- This argument may look/sound/seem convincing ...
- Some might think/believe that ...
- Some/many/plenty of supporters think that ...
- It may be logical to assume that ...
- It may be true that ...
- The common belief is that ...
- It may appear/seem that ...
- It is easy to think/imagine/claim that ...
- Some evidence suggests that ...
- There are some who think/believe/claim/say that ...
- It is reasonable to think that ...
- Admittedly ...
- Granted ....
- Of course ...

Then shift the focus from the opposing view back toward your own by using a clear, contrasting transition, such as:

- However ...
- But ...
- Still ...
- Nevertheless ...

Alternatively, instead of using a transition in the middle of your counterargument, you could use one at the start. For example:

- While some might argue …
- Although X might seem true …
- Though X is admittedly accurate …
- Despite the perceived notion that …

Finally, introduce your evidence to undermine or dismiss the opposing view:

Faulty or misguided

- This is wrong/false/untrue/inaccurate/irrelevant because …
- This view is mistaken because …
- In reality …
- It could actually …
- This is not the case because …
- It fails to consider …
- It ignores the fact that …
- It is impractical to assume …

Partly true

- It is also possible that …
- There are other issues that …
- There remains the problem of …
- It is more practical to …
- The benefits/drawbacks outweigh the benefits/drawbacks …

True but with limitations

- It does not take into account …
- It does not consider …
- It is still worth considering …
- It encourages/discourages …
- It does not change the fact that …
- It may be the only/best/most effective/last option …

TIP

Make sure you always present your reason followed by evidence as part of your counterargument. A statement that says, 'Some believe X but that is not true', without the evidence to prove the point, is not enough to convince the reader!

129

ACTIVITY 9

1. Copy the table, adding at least six extra rows.
2. Practise organising point–counterpoint statements by creating eight or more generic counterargument sentences like examples 1 and 2 in the table.
3. Read them to a partner to make sure they sound right.

HINT: only use *one* transition per sentence (either in front *or* in the middle).

	(Transition)	Acknowledge opposing point	(Transition)	Introduce your evidence
1	_____	Some evidence suggests X	but	this is wrong because …
2	While	many claim X,	_____	they ignore the fact that …
3				
4				

D Analysing sources

In Chapter 1.2, you learnt that, especially in the digital era, not everything that is published is entirely accurate or without bias. Therefore, it is important to challenge the ideas and assumptions of others. This chapter has focused so far on judging the argument itself, but you should also challenge the *source* of the information to help you identify and disregard weak input.

When evaluating the credibility of a source, you need to consider its:

- reputation
- ability to observe
- vested interest (what it might gain from expressing a particular view)
- expertise
- neutrality.

ACTIVITY 10

Imagine you are researching a topic based on this unit's theme of *Food, water and other essential resources*. Read the information about sources 1–5. Then discuss the credibility of each (fictional) source with a partner.

Source 1

'Water, water, everywhere? I don't think so', by Merrick Gaspartes, a water rights activist whose recent speech to the United Nations was featured on the popular blog, *H2OStream*. This site specialises in the issue of global water shortages and also campaigns against the commodification of water.

Source 2

'Obesity crosses the border: Mexico's growing weight epidemic', by Jason Xiu, whose article was featured in *The Ethics of Food*, a journal for health experts and medical professionals. He has written a number of articles on issues such as subsistence farming, aquaculture, hydroponics and obesity.

Source 3

'Whoppers and westernisation: implications of fast food on Eastern nations', by Terrence Kiblin. This piece was written in March 2012 as part of a degree course in Global Health at the University of Dubai.

Source 4

'Bottled water bans, a step in the right direction,' published in February 2011 by Hans Milton. He is a writer for *Weekly Digital*, a popular mainstream Australian magazine.

Source 5

'Water won't wait', a speech presented at the World Water Summit in Nauru, April 2014. It was given by Aiman Nakayama, three-times *Peace & Progress Award* recipient, and President of the International Water Federation.

Reputation

Reputation is important when considering how reliable a source is. A source that can be considered a trusted authority on an issue is much better than a source that has been previously exposed for bending the truth. Also, if a source can prove consistently over a long period of time that it is trustworthy, then this is an important way to prove credibility.

Ability to observe

First-hand experience, or the *ability to observe* an issue directly, gives a source greater authority for reporting than a source which does not have direct contact with the issue. For example, a British journalist reporting on South African food shortages might not be as credible if he reports from another country. If the journalist is stationed in South Africa, however, this can improve his credibility. By being closer to the issue itself, this source would have more of an ability to observe the issue directly, as opposed to giving a second-hand account.

Vested interest

Having a *vested interest*, or something personally at stake, may strengthen or compromise (weaken) a source's credibility. Consider the following two scenarios:

- A start-up company selling product X notes the benefits while not mentioning the side-effects.
- A reputable law firm takes on a controversial case concerning a local celebrity.

In each of these cases, how does vested interest play a role? A company trying to profit from advertising its product, for example, might very well bend the truth to meet this aim. However, a law firm concerned with protecting its reputation may not be as likely to lie for fear of losing trust.

Expertise

The amount of *expertise* a source has about a particular issue can contribute to its credibility. Consider a medical student over a qualified doctor. The student source is not as likely to be trusted as the more senior professional, because of their educational level and experience in the field. Technical know-how is sometimes essential when determining how credible a source's opinion or evidence is. Consider, for instance, if you were asked to judge an ice-skating or gymnastics competition. While you could probably judge the skill of the performers based on general observations alone, you would not know what to look for when it came to the subtleties of technique, such as the outward turn of an ankle or the placement of a hand or finger.

Neutrality

You can learn a lot about a source's credibility by considering how *neutral* your source is (neutral = not supporting either side). As with vested interest, a source's bias will lead them to certain decisions on a particular issue. A source which is not neutral will be more likely to feel a certain way about a topic. Bias and vested interest are different, though: bias is built into the source's personality, whereas vested interest is directed by something more immediate, such as a job title or position.

ACTIVITY 11

Imagine you are responding to the following essay question:

> Can urban farming solve the issue of world hunger?

1   Find five potential sources that could be used as relevant support either in favour or against urban farming as a solution.

2   Copy the table and use it to take notes.

Source	Analysis of credibility

Record the sources you found in the left-hand column, including title, author, URL (website address), when the article was published, and any information about the author's credentials (qualifications, position, background, etc.).

3   In the right-hand column, provide a critique of the source's credibility using the criteria we have discussed so far in this section (i.e. reputation, expertise, etc.).

A neutral source does not include personal opinions or beliefs when reporting on an issue, but a biased source may let personal experiences affect objectivity. For example, if you were negatively affected by an issue as a teenager, you may be more predisposed to draw a biased conclusion about it as an adult. How you handle those predispositions in your writing can strengthen or weaken your credibility.

The initial letters of the criteria that we have considered spell out the well-known mnemonic RAVEN. (A *mnemonic* is a way of helping you to remember something more easily.)

Reputation
Ability to observe
Vested interest
Expertise
Neutrality

However, there is one other criteria that could be added to this list: cross-checking, or *corroboration*.

Corroboration

Most information sources used today are found online. When you are locating an article via a search engine, for instance, it is important to look around the website itself to ensure the source's credibility. For instance, you might go to the 'About Us' page for more information or to evaluate the worth of the source you are viewing. However, what if a bias for the topic influences the explanation of their mission or vision? If you are going to get an accurate picture of a source's credibility, you will need to look further.

One way to get a more objective understanding of a source's credibility is to corroborate it by cross-checking with the opinion of other established sources. For example, you might have found an article on a parents' organisation website which criticises the practice of sending 'fat letters' to the families of obese elementary age students (i.e. letters informing the parents that their child is overweight); it might be useful to do some additional research about this organisation to ensure their credibility. If there is any criticism about their mission, actions or the evidence they use to support their claims, you are more likely to hear about it from *other* sources than on the website itself. By 'vetting' your sources in this way, you are taking the RAVEN mnemonic strategy even further, now using (C)RAVEN to ensure credibility!

ACTIVITY 12

Read the extract from a student's essay on whether or not the government is responsible for an increase in racism. The student refers to information that he read on *The Daily Mash*, a popular website, to support his claim that the individual, not the government, is to blame:

> Research indicates that physical exertion and lack of sleep are to blame for the recent rise in racism. Medical researchers proved this claim after testing 200 people where it was revealed that those who got 6 hours or less of sleep were 80% more racist. The scientists discovered that physical tiredness releases an active chemical in the brain which results in erratic behavior. In turn, this leads to aggressive thoughts, often carried out in ways that are considered racist.

1   Using CRAVEN criteria, evaluate the source, *The Daily Mash*.

    a Visit and analyse the website for *The Daily Mash* (www.thedailymash.co.uk).

    b Cross-check its credibility to determine whether it is a valid source for this student's argument.

    c Discuss your findings with the class or in small groups.

2   Using the CRAVEN criteria, look up the following sources (using the web address or a search engine). Decide whether each is a trustworthy and reliable source for researching the stated topic. Analyse each carefully and justify your responses:

    a Environmental problems facing global society – www.dhmo.org

    b Possible tourist destinations in the United States – www.city-mankato.us

    c Body Ritual Among the Nacirema PDF

    d The health risks associated with vaccination – www.thinktwice.com

E Developing an effective line of reasoning

In Chapter 1.2 Section *F Key elements of an essay* you learnt that the body of an essay requires specific elements to support a writer's thesis:

- reasons
- evidence
- links between the two.

An *argumentative* approach to writing also relies on these to effectively argue its main claim (thesis). There is one additional element: the counterargument (see *C Taking a position: an argumentative approach to writing*).

The combination of these elements forms the basis of an effective argument, which you will explore in this section. We will also explore the more advanced elements that make an argumentative approach work.

The 'TREE' of reasoning

Arguments need care and attention if they are going to grow. When taking a position on an issue, careful use of evidence and fair consideration of the opposition are necessary. Think of the basic elements of an argument as being similar to the structure of a tree (as in the diagram). In fact, the first letter of these elements can form that word:

> **T**hesis / main claim
>
> **R**easons
>
> **E**vidence
>
> **E**xceptions, or challenges to evidence

TIP

The sunshine at the top of the tree appears when you *link evidence back to claims*. Just as a tree cannot grow without light, your argument cannot reach its full potential if you do not show your audience *why* your evidence proves your point.

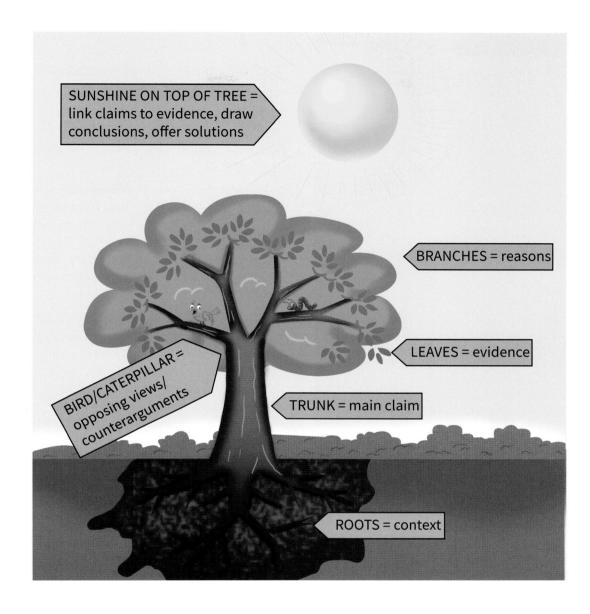

SUNSHINE ON TOP OF TREE = link claims to evidence, draw conclusions, offer solutions

BRANCHES = reasons

LEAVES = evidence

BIRD/CATERPILLAR = opposing views/ counterarguments

TRUNK = main claim

ROOTS = context

The following table further explains the tree diagram:

Tree	Argument	Similarities
roots and soil	context	rooting, basis of growth
trunk	thesis / main claim	core, strong, central
branches	reasons	extension / development of core
leaves	evidence	fullness or emptiness, determines the health of
sunshine	links claims and evidence; draws conclusions	sheds light upon, essential to growth
caterpillars or birds	counterarguments	take up residence within, part of the community, tendency to eat / attack parts of tree / argument

ACTIVITY 13

Visit the New York Times' 'Room for Debate' online and select a topic of interest, or locate an article in the op-ed section of a local news source where opinion articles are shared. Either way, be sure to select an article which presents an argument of some sort (i.e. in favour of, against, or some other nuanced view on an issue). Read the article, then complete the following activities, which will help you practise deconstructing arguments using the 'TREE' strategy.

1 Deconstruct the argument by illustrating its line of reasoning using the TREE (thesis + reasons + evidence + exceptions) strategy.

2 Answer comprehension questions **a–c**.

  a Consider the line of reasoning you illustrated in your TREE. How strong is this argument? Justify your response.

  b What kinds of appeals are present in the argument? Identify examples of *logos*, *pathos* and *ethos* as they apply (see B *Understanding arguments, earlier in this chapter*). Then form an opinion as to how fairly the authors argue their point in terms of appeal.

  c Identify any fallacies present in the argument. Be prepared to defend your observations.

Using this visual strategy for deconstructing arguments can strengthen your ability to critique:

- well-known, published arguments (a famous speech, a TED Talk, etc.)
- another student's argument (a form of peer editing)
- your own argument after it is written (a means of self-assessment).

It can also be a helpful brainstorm strategy for organising your argumentative ideas to ensure you have a good basic structure for your writing. Before you begin writing your essay, ask yourself the following questions:

- Did you plant the roots in the soil?
- Is your trunk firm?
- Do you have a range of strong branches?
- Is your tree full and healthy?
- Is your tree 'bird-/caterpillar-friendly'?
- Have you assessed the potential threat of a bird or caterpillar infestation?
- Is your tree getting proper sunlight?

Close attention to your argument will ensure good growth!

Toulmin model for well-reasoned arguments

The Toulmin model is a classic model for creating a line of reasoning that breaks down the elements of an argument more thoroughly. This approach identifies a total of six *primary* and *secondary* component parts:

Claim
Reasons/evidence ⟶ **Primary** components
Warrant   (necessary for establishing a reasonable point)

Backing
Counterargument   **Secondary** components
Qualifier ⟶ (supplement/reinforce initial reasoning)

First, a claim must be established. As you have learned, a claim must be supported by *reasons*, which should be backed by *evidence*. Toulmin's model includes both of these, collectively as its second component. This is likely because the model was originally designed to address immediate, everyday arguments (e.g. why you should not have to clean your room, or why you deserve a pay raise), which are briefer than the ones you will be writing for this course.

The last primary component involves what is called a **warrant**, which is your interpretation of the evidence to show the audience how or why it supports your reason. In other words, the warrant links evidence to reasons or claims.

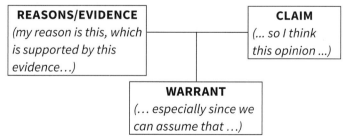

| REASONS/EVIDENCE *(my reason is this, which is supported by this evidence...)* | CLAIM *(... so I think this opinion ...)* |

WARRANT *(... especially since we can assume that ...)*

 KEY TERM

Warrant: an explanation of why or how the data supports the claim and/or reason; this can be an underlying assumption that exists but goes unstated in the argument.

KEY SKILLS

To reinforce your understanding of what a warrant is, refer back to Chapter 1.2 Section *F Key elements of an essay* where the concept of linking evidence to claims is discussed.

Writers do not always explicitly state the connection between claims and evidence, relying instead on their **underlying assumptions** about their audience. For example, if a writer argues that fast food restaurants should be banned (*main claim*) because they pose serious health risks (*reason*) such as obesity and heart disease (*evidence*) but does not offer a warrant, this is probably because they *assume* that their audience gives priority to living a healthy lifestyle (*warrant*). What happens, however, if this assumption is wrong? For example, what if the audience considers *cost* to be more important than health? Fast food might be high in calories, but since it is low in price, someone who is eating on a budget might choose it anyway. The point that fast food should be banned because of health risks no longer seems as valid, since the warrant is weak.

 KEY TERM

Underlying assumption: an unspoken value or belief about a particular issue.

TIP

Explaining your warrant clearly (i.e. recognising underlying assumptions and indicating why your evidence is valid), is a good way of checking how logical your point really is.

The Toulmin model forces you to consider the strength of your ideas. If the *primary* elements of the argument are not enough (claim + support + warrant), you can add the *secondary* elements of the model for reinforcement:

• backing for your warrant
• counterargumentation (attention to opposing viewpoints)
• qualifier (qualification of your point).

Again, since your arguments will concern the complicated issues of contemporary society (rather than simple, everyday arguments), the secondary elements will certainly be necessary. The following diagram shows how to combine the secondary with the primary elements:

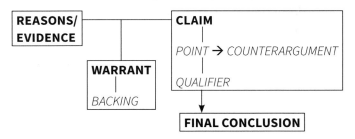

Here is one way of thinking about these components within the development of an argument:

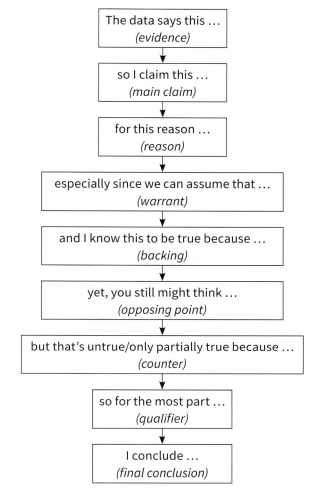

If you have an awareness of these considerations, it will help you to argue more clearly. You have learnt what happens when logical reasoning does *not* work. This model can be useful in helping you to identify weaknesses in your line of reasoning and to take appropriate action to strengthen it.

Here is an example that attempts a logical argument about fast food restaurants by employing the six elements of Toulmin's model:

Recent research suggests that sugar has particularly negative effects on the brain. According to these studies, children who consume diets high in fat and sugar are affected developmentally; specifically, results indicate that they have poorer academic outcomes than those who do not, scoring an average of 4 points below that of their peers in science (*evidence*). Based on these findings, the government should ban further development of fast food restaurants (*main claim*) because of the serious risk they pose to youth health (*reason*). It is the government's

135

job to protect the children of this country (*warrant*). In fact, programs to minimise obesity such as Michelle Obama's "Let's Move!" campaign easily reveal just how important youth health has been to the government in the past. (*backing*), so it makes sense that they play a part in banning a service linked to weight issues.

Considering these elements, and using them as a guideline, will help you to present a more stable and complete argument, and this will therefore increase the chances that your audience will believe you. Taking care to build a sound argument improves your credibility as a writer because it shows you have thought carefully about the issue before presenting it to your audience.

TIP

While this student's response fits the elements of Toulmin's model very neatly, this will not always be the case. This model should be used as a general guideline or checklist, not a strict method or formula for writing the argument itself.

ACTIVITY 14

Read the following article about eating crickets as an alternative source of nutrition. Using what you learn from the text, write a brief argument for why we should include bugs in our diet. Structure your argument using the Toulmin model.

DID YOU KNOW?

'Backing' is more likely to feature in *research* essays. For these essays, the writer has more time and resources to look deeply into the issue to find evidence to support both reasons as well as warrants.

TIP

Use the statement starters in the flow chart on page 135 to help you.

The latest buzz: eating insects can help tackle food insecurity, says FAO

While insects can be slimy, **cringe-inducing** creatures, often squashed on sight by humans, a new book released today by the Food and Agricultural Organisation (FAO) says beetles, wasps and
5 caterpillars are also an unexplored nutrition source that can help address global food insecurity. The book, *Edible Insects: future prospects for food and feed security*, stresses not just the nutritional value of insects, but also the benefits that insect farming could potentially
10 have on the environment and on addressing the rapidly increasing demand for food worldwide.

While the idea of eating a worm, grasshopper or cicada at every meal may seem strange, FAO says this has many health benefits. Insects are high in protein,
15 fat and mineral contents. They can be eaten whole or ground into a powder or paste, and incorporated into other foods.

What are the arguments for using insects as a source of food?

'Insects are not harmful to eat, quite the contrary. They are nutritious, they have a lot of protein and are considered a delicacy in many countries,' said 20

Eva Muller, the Director of FAO's Forest Economics, Policy and Products Division.

Although they are not **staples** of Western cuisine, insects currently supplement the diets of some 2 billion people and have always been part of human diets in Asia, Africa and Latin America. Of the 1 million known insect species, 1900 are consumed by humans. Some of the most consumed insects include beetles, caterpillars, bees, wasps, ants, grasshoppers, locusts and crickets.

According to the book, which was launched today at the Forests for Food Security and Nutrition conference, taking place through Wednesday at FAO headquarters in Rome, farming insects for human and animal consumption is particularly relevant at a time when population growth, urbanisation, and the rising middle class have increased the demand for food while simultaneously harming the environment that enables its production.

By 2030, over 9 million people will need to be fed, along with the billions of animals raised annually for food and as pets. Meanwhile, land and water pollution from intensive **livestock** production and **over-grazing** are leading to forest degradation, thereby contributing to climate change.

Why insects can help
'Domesticating and **rearing** insects can help sustain insect populations while also helping counter nutritional insecurity and improve livelihoods,' said Afton Halloran, a consultant for the FAO Edible Insects Programme. 'Farming insects has a huge global potential for both animal feed and food production. We are already seeing producers creating animal feed from insects and research. And development is occurring around the world in order to incorporate insects into menus and processed foods.'

The production of greenhouse gases by insect farming would likely be lower than that of livestock. For example, pigs produce 10–100 times more greenhouse gases per kilogram than mealworms.

Insects also feed on bio-waste, use significantly less water than livestock, and can be farmed more easily, the book states. Insect farming could also offer important livelihoods to people in rural areas as minimal technical or capital expenditure is required for basic harvesting and rearing equipment.

Their high nutritional value and relative ease of **en masse** production will not be enough to make insects part of people's dishes all over the world, and FAO knows this.

'Consumer disgust remains one of the largest barriers to the adoption of insects as viable sources of protein in many Western countries,' Ms Muller said in an interview. 'Nevertheless, history has shown that dietary patterns can change quickly, particularly in the globalised world.'

She added that Western countries, most notably in Europe, have also been recently expressing interest in incorporating insects into their cuisine. 'We have already seen cookbooks show up that offer recipes on edible insects, and there are a few restaurants in capital European cities that actually offer edible insects on their menus,' she said. 'I don't expect it to be something that happens very quickly, but if we remember that 20 years ago nobody in Europe would think of eating raw fish, and everybody now loves sushi, things can change, so even the cultures that are not used to eating insects may eventually develop a taste for them.'

A common misconception of insects as food is that they are only consumed in times of hunger. However, in most instances where they are a staple in local diets, they are consumed because of their taste, and not because there are no other food sources available. In fact, insect trading is **thriving** in cities such as Bangkok and Kinshasa, and there is high demand from urban consumers. In such places, insects often arouse feelings of nostalgia for the rural countryside. In other cases, insects are seen as a snack.

The book stresses that there is still a long way to go before insects can be universally incorporated into both human and animal diets. Mass-production technologies need to be perfected, potential allergies to certain species need to be explored, and legislation must be enacted on insect farming.

The food industry, including industry professionals and chefs, must also help raise awareness about insects' potential as food to increase the level of acceptance among consumers.

'Although it is unrealistic to see families in the West eating insects for their Sunday lunch within the next decade, the potential of insects is huge and we hope that slowly but surely this potential will be realised,' Ms Halloran said.

Adapted from an article in UN News Centre, *May 2013*

137

> **ARTICLE GLOSSARY**
>
> **buzz:** object of popular interest
>
> **cringe-inducing:** causing people to feel fear or disgust
>
> **staples:** basic and important foods
>
> **livestock:** farm animals
>
> **over-grazing:** allowing too many animals to feed on the grass so that the land is damaged
>
> **rearing:** breeding and looking after (farm) animals
>
> **en masse:** in a group
>
> **thriving:** developing well

F Drawing conclusions

As you learnt in Chapters 1.2 and 2.2, the conclusion is the most important part of your essay. It is when your main claim is at its strongest point, *after* your evidence has been presented.

Recall that a conclusion may include:

- a thoughtful ending / sense of closure
- a reassertion of your main claim (thesis)
- some additional insights based on the evidence you have presented.

In the conclusion of an essay, you are expected to present new insights. One approach to this is to think about the impact your topic will have on the future. In addition to the three basic elements that we have just reviewed, an argumentative conclusion may also:

- revisit opposing views and remind the audience of your counterarguments
- consider implications and consequences
- offer solutions or recommendations, and consider their limits.

These are just a few considerations that make drawing final conclusions in an argument quite different from, and more complicated than, concluding an explanation.

Revisiting opposing views and reminding the audience of your counterarguments

If you have written your argument fairly, there are probably moments where your position is challenged by an opposing viewpoint. You will want to briefly remind the reader why those challenges are minimal against the bigger picture. This will help you leave the lasting impression on your reader that your position is the more logical one.

Considering implications and consequences

In order to approach your essay topic logically and maturely, it is important to consider the consequences of accepting or denying your argument. What could potentially happen? What might be a possible outcome? This can help you persuade your audience one last time.

> **TIP**
>
> Be careful not to overemphasise the future implications or consequences of your topic. This may become an appeal to fear, which you should avoid! Try to end your conclusion on a positive point, such as what could happen if the audience accepts your views, as opposed to the negative consequences of not accepting them.

Offering solutions or recommendations and considering their limits

Since an argument is often based on a problem, it may make sense to offer your version of a workable solution. Read the extract from a student's essay, which attempts to offer a solution to the growing concerns regarding bottled water consumption:

> While bottled water is a popular luxury in society today, a closer look proves that it is harmful not only to the environment and economy, but to the very citizens it aims to help. Banning its production will be beneficial to the safety of the individual because we will be exposed to less pollution and toxic chemicals. In fact, a solution to this problem would be to simply install filters on water taps and increase access to public water fountains. With these steps in place, there is no doubt we will decrease our carbon footprint and make way for a healthier, greener planet.

Notice the phrase *a solution to this problem would be to simply…*. The word 'simply' here could be misleading because it implies that solving the problem is easy. Ask yourself: if it were so easy, wouldn't it have been solved already by experts? A remark such as this therefore oversimplifies an otherwise complex issue. While your ideas may have potential for solving real-world issues, consider the fact that experts in the field may have already tried them without success. Or perhaps they have not tried those ideas because of a particular barrier you failed to consider when you were exploring the problem.

Remember to consider the *limits* to the solutions you propose. Your ideas may be well-reasoned and therefore have potential, but they are not necessarily perfect. What barrier might there be to solving the problem in the way you suggest? What potential consequence should others be aware of if this solution is attempted?

ACTIVITY 15

Revisit the speech, 'Water security – good governance and sustainable solutions' (in *B Understanding arguments*). Identify the solutions the speaker proposes and the limits of each. Check your answers by sharing with a partner.

G Building your own credibility

Following the recommendations outlined in this chapter will help you build your credibility as a writer. In other words, if your aim is to get your audience to accept your views, you need to gain their trust. You can do this by:

- acknowledging opposing viewpoints to show you are fair and considerate
- providing plenty of evidence for your audience to consider
- choosing evidence accurately: do not attempt to deceive by suppressing important information
- considering the context surrounding your issue as this affects the evidence itself
- being fair when appealing to your audience's emotions
- addressing limits to your own ideas as necessary
- maintaining a controlled tone by selecting powerful but fair language when offering criticism.

Following this advice will help prove that you are ethical and trustworthy. Your audience is much more likely to consider you to be credible when you work with these standards in mind.

Read the article about urban farming. Then use the skills you have learnt in this chapter to complete the activity that follows.

Urban farming is revolutionising our cities

Humans are fast becoming city dwellers. Sixty-six per cent of us will likely live in urban environments by 2050. The number of mega-cities (more than 10 million inhabitants) is also skyrocketing. Currently, they are home to more than 453 million people.

The distance food travels from farm to plate is a growing concern, so there is a renewed interest in producing food closer to where people live. Urban agriculture may be the answer. Urban agriculture is the growing and distributing of local food in or near cities in a healthy way to help the environment. Examples of this kind of farming include growing plants on a balcony, backyard, rooftop, indoor and community gardens. It also includes city beehives and chicken coops as well as larger urban farms and farmer's markets. It might not solve all the food production and distribution problems, but urban farming efforts could help take pressure off rural land while providing other advantages.

And it's much more. As writer and former Vancouver city councillor Peter Ladner writes in *The Urban Food Revolution: Changing the Way We Feed Cities,* 'When urban agriculture flourishes, our children are healthier and smarter about what they eat, fewer people are hungry, more local jobs are created, local economies are stronger, our neighbourhoods are greener and safer, and our communities are more inclusive.'

Local and urban agriculture can also help reduce greenhouse gas emissions and recycle nutrient-rich food scraps, plant debris and other 'wastes'. A 2016 study from the US Johns Hopkins Center for a Livable Future found that urban agriculture has climate benefits. These include reduced emissions from transporting food; carbon **sequestration** by vegetation and crops; possible reduced energy and waste; and **enhanced** public interest in protecting green spaces.

It also noted some limitations: possible increases in greenhouse gas emissions and water use 'if plants are grown in energy- or resource-intensive locations'; less efficiency in resource use and transport emissions; and possible pollution from pesticide and fertiliser use. The study found urban agriculture to be positive overall, but concluded support from all levels of government is required to make it **viable**.

Urban agriculture isn't new. During the First and Second World Wars, Canada, the US, the UK, Australia and Germany encouraged 'victory gardens' to aid the war effort. These reduced pressure on food systems and farms. Gardens and chicken coops appeared in yards, parks, school fields, golf courses, railway edges and vacant **lots**. Sheep grazed on sports fields and kept grass **in check**.

Granted, there were fewer people and more open spaces then, but it's still possible to grow a lot of food in urban areas, especially with **composting** and enriched soil techniques. Ladner writes that Toronto plans to supply 25 per cent of its fruit and vegetable production within city limits by 2025. A study from Michigan State University concluded Detroit could grow 70 per cent of its vegetables and 40 per cent of its fruit on 570 vacant lots covering 5 000 acres of city land.

Cities needn't be wastelands of car-choked roads and pavement. Incorporating food production into ever-expanding urban areas makes cities more livable and enhances the natural systems that keep us alive and healthy.

*Adapted from an article by Dr David Suzuki in
EcoWatch, August 2016*

ARTICLE GLOSSARY

sequestration: capturing

enhanced: increased, improved

viable: capable of working successfully

lots: pieces of land for a particular purpose (e.g. for building)

in check: under control

composting: recycling plant/vegetable waste to create soil

ACTIVITY 16

Answer the questions about the text 'Urban farming is revolutionising our cities'.

Reading comprehension

1 Explain what is meant by the data used in the first paragraph (lines 1–5). **[2]**

2 Identify two reasons why urban farming is a good idea. **[2]**

3 Re-read lines 45–52. In your own words, explain the author's purpose for writing this paragraph. **[3]**

4 How would you describe the tone (i) in the beginning of the article, and (ii) at the end? Compare. **[3]**

Elements of writing

5 How does the author grab the reader's attention? Explain his strategy by referring to introductory strategies you learnt in Chapter 1.2. **[3]**

6 Identify the main claim, or thesis statement. Indicate whether it is stated or implied, and justify your answer. **[3]**

7 Identify two examples of argumentative appeals as they are used in the article. Use what you have learnt in this chapter to justify your choices. **[2]**

8 Using either the TREE of reasoning strategy or the Toulmin model, deconstruct the article's line of reasoning. **[10]**

9 Identify one counterargument strategy as it exists in the article. **[1]**

10 Using your knowledge of what an argumentative conclusion should do, critique the article's concluding paragraph (lines 62–66). What does it do well? What does it need? **[4]**

Evaluating sources and evidence

11 Identify two sources mentioned within the argument. Evaluate the credibility *and* relevance of each. Refer back to section *E Analysing sources* to help you. **[4]**

12 How does the author of the article build his own credibility? Identify two ways. **[2]**

13 In your own opinion, what is the most compelling piece of evidence used to argue in favour of urban farming and why? Using evidence from the article and your knowledge of the present day, justify your answer in 100–120 words. **[4]**

14 In your own opinion, what is the weakest aspect of the argument and why? Refer back to your line of reasoning illustration from question 8 to help you formulate and justify your answer. **[4]**

The activity that follows is based on a talk covering a similar topic to the text you have just read. This will give you an opportunity to analyse an argument in its spoken form.

ACTIVITY 17

Watch Pam Warhurst's TED Talk, 'How we can eat our landscapes'. Track her line of reasoning, then evaluate her overall approach to presenting an argument. Be prepared to share your findings with the class.

H Practising what you have learnt

Look through the list of exam-style essay questions on this chapter's theme of *Food, water and other essential resources*. Decide which essay you would like to write. Then write a well-reasoned, carefully organised essay that demonstrates your understanding of the elements of an effective argument.

You may use the knowledge you have gained from the extracts in this chapter, and/or you can use your own (outside) knowledge to support your ideas.

Remember to:

- deconstruct the terms of the essay question
- draft a working thesis
- use the strategies provided in this chapter for constructing an effective argument
- edit your work.

EXAM-STYLE QUESTIONS

Essay questions

1 'Genetically modified foods are no longer a threat in our society.' What is your view? [30]

2 To what extent do alternative forms of agriculture have a future over more traditional ways? [30]

3 How far would you agree that goverments have the right to place penalty taxes on unhealthy products? [30]

4 Can food education ever solve the growing issue of obesity? [30]

5 The concern about banning bottled water should be an international one. What is your view? [30]

6 Today, meat is more accessible than ever. To what extent is this a problem? [30]

7 'Water is a human right, not a commodity.' Discuss. [30]

8 'Wealth makes health.' To what extent do you agree? [30]

9 'The purpose of foreign aid is more political than it is humanitarian.' Analyse this statement. [30]

141

Summary

Key points to remember from this chapter:

- An argument takes a clear position on an issue and uses a logical line of reasoning to effectively communicate it. It has a more forceful tone for this reason, making it different from other approaches to writing.
- Argumentative writing is distinguishable from persuasive writing because it considers the opposition fairly through counterargumentation strategies.
- The thesis statement of an argument is often referred to as the 'main claim'.
- An argument should contain a main claim, reasons to support this claim and evidence which supports your reasons. Stronger arguments effectively link evidence back to claims.
- A variety of appeals should be used to convince your audience rather than relying on just one.
- Analysing the elements of someone's argument, or tracking those of your own, can help you identify weaknesses in reasoning.
- It is important to build the trust of your audience in order to strengthen your own credibility. You can do this by employing a variety of strategies, including fair consideration of the opposition.

Chapter 3.2
Exploring issues through discursive writing

Modernisation is a threat to tradition: to what extent do you agree? The key theme of Tradition versus modernity will be explored throughout this chapter.

Learning objectives

In this chapter, you will learn:

- what discursive writing is and how it differs from other forms of writing
- how to organise ideas using a discursive approach
- how to draw interim conclusions
- how to develop solutions as part of your conclusion.

A What is discursive writing?

What do you consider when shopping for a big purchase like a computer, a car or a mobile phone? Before spending that much money, you would probably want to compare the benefits and drawbacks of several models. At the start of this process, you have no idea which model you want to buy. But after careful consideration, you are able to make a more informed decision.

Similarly, when you are considering sensitive or complex issues, it is important that you take time to appreciate different viewpoints and weigh them fairly and thoughtfully. In this course, you have the option to develop your arguments in this way by taking a *discursive* approach.

In discursive writing, the writer considers multiple perspectives surrounding an issue in an objective way before arriving at a judgement. It is an unbiased attempt to:

- *explain* different ways of looking at a topic
- reason through the high and low points of each perspective
- arrive at a personal, *evidence-based* conclusion.

> **DID YOU KNOW?**
>
> The word 'discourse' comes from the Latin word *discursus*, which means 'going to and fro'. It sounds similar to the word 'discussion', which is your aim when writing discursively – to discuss the possibilities of both sides of an argument before reaching a conclusion.

Discursive writing is *neither formulaic nor assertive (strongly stating a point of view).*

- There is no magic formula (or fixed structure) that will successfully lead you through this style of writing. It is a logical, yet organic progression of thought, as you reason through the various perspectives.
- While you may find yourself using counterargument, your tone should remain unbiased. Remember that your purpose is to explore all possibilities before drawing your conclusions.

We think discursively all the time in our everyday lives. This is how we make decisions when we shop or judge something's value or worth. And while it is fairly easy to think in this way, it is much more difficult to express these thoughts on paper. *Writing* discursively requires a good sense of structure to effectively convey these thoughts to an audience.

Remember that discursive writing is not as unfamiliar as you might think. You are actually exposed to it every time you read a news article! Any reliable article of journalism should present all sides of an issue in an unbiased way. While the author might eventually offer a position by the end of the piece, the tone still invites readers to arrive at their own judgement based on the evidence and logic provided. In other words, good journalism is written *discursively*.

In this chapter, you will explore how journalists use this approach when writing about contemporary issues, and you will learn to apply the discursive approach to your own writing.

Read the news article on the next page, which concerns traditional print books versus modern electronic books. Then complete the task that follows. You will need a *copy* of the article for the activity.

Books vs e-books: The science behind the best way to read

While browsing the bookstore to buy a gift for that special someone (or yourself), you may be faced with a tough decision: e-books or the old-fashioned kind?

Some of the practical advantages of going digital are obvious: a portable little e-reader can carry an entire library wherever you go, which is great for travellers or those who always want a choice of reading material. On the other hand, research has been **stacking up** to show that reading on paper has a number of benefits, too. Plus, there's the **nostalgia** factor.

Each one has its pros and cons, and choosing the best option depends on a number of factors.

Perhaps the first consideration that comes to mind involves the sensory experience that reading a print book involves. Many book lovers prefer the **tactile** sensation of a bound paper book. According to researcher Åse Kristine Tveit, 'paper books are, as a rule, very well designed, they look and smell good, and they carry with them a more human touch'.

Yet as the lead author of a 2014 study published in the journal, *Library & Information Science Research*, Tveit and colleagues found that out of 143 10th grade students, most actually preferred e-readers. Boys and those who did not care much for reading also shared a strong preference for e-readers. This is likely because 'an e-reader has more in common with the electronic devices that young people use all the time,

like smartphones or iPads, than a paper book, when it comes to turning of pages, the possibilities of adjusting font size, etc.'

Therefore, while traditional books **fit the mould** for the book lover, e-books may be the more ideal option for reluctant readers, so the best choice may depend on the circumstances.

Another important aspect to consider when it comes to reading print versus electronic text concerns the way we process the information. Several small studies suggest that reading on paper instead of an electronic screen is better for memory retention and focus. For instance, *The Guardian* reported on an experiment from Norway where people were given a short story to read either on a Kindle or in a paperback book; when they were quizzed later, those who read the paperback were more likely to remember **plot** points in the right order.

According to lead researcher Anne Mangen, of Norway's Stavanger University: 'When you read on paper you can sense with your fingers a pile of pages on the left growing, and shrinking on the right.' She went on to suggest that 'the tactile sense of progress' may aid the reader in processing the text. In this sense, it appears print text may be more beneficial than its more modern **counterpart** after all.

While print can apparently help our mental capacity to understand a story, it may have some physical benefits as well. High levels of screen **luminance** from an electronic device, for instance, can contribute to visual fatigue, a condition marked by tired, itching, burning eyes.

There are also potential considerations for those reading e-books on light-emitting e-readers at night (although a number of e-readers do not use light-emitting screens). Dr Margaret K Merga, a reading and education specialist in Australia, told CBS News in an email, 'Artificial light exposure from light-emitting e-readers may interfere with users' ability to sleep, ultimately leading to adverse impacts on health.'

Moreover, a 2014 study published in the journal *PNAS* found that reading an e-book before bedtime decreased the production of melatonin, a hormone that **preps** the body for sleep. E-books also **impaired** alertness the following day.

This is not to say that e-books are entirely harmful to our health, however. In fact, individuals with poor eyesight or reading disorders like **dyslexia** can actually benefit more from e-books because they provide a range of options for changing the text size and spacing of lines. A 2013 study in the journal *PLOS One* observed reading comprehension and speed in 103 high-school students with dyslexia. The study found that people with dyslexia read more effectively, and with greater ease, when using the e-reader compared with reading on paper.

Schneps, who was the lead author on the paper, said, 'What made the difference was the ability of the device to display lines of text that were extremely short (about two or three words per line), as well as its ability to space out the text. When these people read using the modified formatting, their reading instantly improved.'

Meanwhile, in Merga's experience with students in Australia, **avid** readers still tend to prefer reading on paper. While conducting the West Australian Study in Adolescent Book Reading (WASABR), Merga and colleagues found that students preferred reading paper books. 'One student described this attitude as a preference to "own something (rather) than just use it" ', Merga said.

Evidently, there are a number of physical, mental, and emotional factors to consider when deciding whether a print book or e-book is the best fit for a reader. A younger student, empowered by owning her own books, might have to **settle for** an e-reader if she struggles with poor eyesight. Meanwhile, a reluctant, 10th grade reader might find the e-book appealing; that is, until he starts losing sleep over it. It almost seems that there's a book medium for every instance, and that it is up to us to decide what's right for the occasion. But in the end, the digital era is here to stay, and if we are going to find balance with this brave, new world around us, we must be – at minimum – willing to entertain the idea of upgrading those print textbooks to digital tablets.

Adapted from an article by Amy Kraft, CBS News, December 2015

145

ARTICLE GLOSSARY

vs: versus, compared with

stacking up: forming a large quantity

nostalgia: a feeling of happiness mixed with sadness when you think about the past

tactile: connected with the sense of touch

fit the mould: are ideal for

plot: sequence of events in a story

counterpart: equivalent

luminance: intensity of light

preps: prepares

impaired: weakened, damaged

dyslexia: a condition that makes it difficult for someone to read

avid: very keen or interested

settle for: accept something even though it is not exactly what you want

ACTIVITY 1

1   Using a copy of the article, identify the main claim/thesis of the article, and:
    - if is *stated*, underline it
    - if it is *implied*, write a one-sentence summary of it.

2   Using a (+) and (–) symbol, track the different perspectives raised around e-books and traditional books. Use the following annotations to do so:
    - EB (+) perspectives supporting e-books
    - EB (–) perspectives challenging e-books
    - TB (+) perspectives supporting traditional books
    - TB (–) perspectives challenging traditional books

3   Circle transitional words or phrases that help the writer move back and forth between the different perspectives.

4   Put an asterisk (*) where the author inserts her own views on the issue.

In Chapter 1.2, you learnt about the differences between argumentative and discursive styles, but this chapter will deconstruct these features in more depth.

There are several features that make the discursive style distinctive:

- thesis
- tone
- organisational pattern
- conclusions.

Each of these features will be explored in the following sections of this chapter.

B Writing the discursive thesis

As you learnt in Chapter 2.2, the thesis is the most important statement in the essay because it determines all the ideas and arguments within the piece. Without it, your essay would not deliver a clear, focused message.

To recap what you learnt about thesis statements:

- The thesis establishes the tone and purpose of your essay.
- It is better to stick to broader themes when addressing big ideas in an *argumentative* thesis.

A discursive thesis will not mention specific intentions. Since your response will give *equal* consideration to *multiple* points of view, it will be too complicated to list them all.

TIP

In choosing to write discursively, your purpose is to explore organically. You do not necessarily know where the discussion is going to take you. If you commit to specific intentions at the start, this may therefore force your exploration of ideas, instead of letting them develop naturally.

Here is an example of the form and shape that a discursive thesis statement may take. Note how it differs significantly from the kind of thesis statements you have learnt to write previously:

> While some believe that renewable energy will provide a promising path to a sustainable future, there are also reasons to be sceptical of these modern resources.

The neutral tone allows the writer to explore the topic without bias towards either side. It aims to gives fair

consideration to each broad position before passing judgement. Yet it still makes the writer's intentions for treatment clear to the reader. A broad approach opens up the possibilities for discussion, and gives you the flexibility to cover a range of perspectives.

The following is a list of other statement stems that you might want to use to help you form discursive thesis statements in different ways:

- While X, there is also Y.
- Although X, Y is worth consideration as well.
- … X, though not always …
- X may lead to …; however, Y …
- While X can be said, one can also argue Y.
- In some instances X, whereas in others Y.
- Depending upon the circumstances, (issue) may be accomplished through X or Y.

ACTIVITY 2

Practise writing thesis statements for each of the following discursive essay prompts. Use statement stems from the list above or create your own.

1 How necessary is it to maintain traditional crafts in today's marketplace?

2 To what extent has the mother's role evolved in today's family structure?

3 How true is the belief that today's technology makes us much more secure than technologies of the past?

4 Examine the future of family-owned businesses in a modern world.

5 How far do you agree that a college education is essential in today's society?

6 'Old buildings are no longer necessary because new designs are far better.' Discuss.

7 Evaluate the role that art galleries and/or museums play in your society.

C Maintaining an objective tone

The thesis statement establishes your intention to address an issue objectively, but the language you use in the body paragraphs is very important in maintaining that tone. When you are writing to explore, your intention is to avoid making a judgement until all evidence has been considered. It is therefore important to 'hedge' your words accordingly. **Hedging** is a type of careful language often used in academic, scientific and even political circumstances. It helps you express approximation, degree of certainty, or doubt as you discuss an issue.

KEY TERM

Hedging: the careful use of words to distinguish between fact and claim; also used to show your audience the extent to which you support the information you are presenting.

Hedging helps you to avoid overgeneralising ideas (see 'Hasty generalisation' in Chapter Section 3.1 *B Understanding arguments*). It can also improve the quality of your writing by helping you to:

- establish limits to your ideas
- protect your ideas from criticism or error
- demonstrate well-meaning when looking critically at ideas.

One of the main strategies for staying neutral as you explore an issue is to use **qualifiers** to soften the force of your claims. Qualifiers control the intensity of your tone, and help you to maintain an objective point of view. Notice the difference in the tone of these two claims:

A: Print books *help* our mental capacity to understand a story, and they *have* some physical benefits as well.

B: While print books *can apparently help* our mental capacity to understand a story, they *likely have* some physical benefits as well.

Notice that statement A is much more assertive than statement B. This is because statement B uses qualifiers to reduce the force of these claims.

KEY TERM

Qualifier: a word or phrase used to limit the meaning of a word; it maximises or minimises the value of the word.

KEY SKILLS

Many qualifiers are adverbs. See Chapter 4.2 Section *E Adverbs* to learn more about the grammatical function of qualifiers.

KEY SKILLS

Modals (e.g. *can, may, could*) are part of verb phrases and help to qualify ideas and reduce (or increase) the certainty of a statement. Chapter 4.3 Section *D Verbs* gives a more complete list of modals.

Commonly used qualifiers include:

very	nearly	extremely	barely
definitely	especially	hardly	mainly
rather	somewhat	usually	too
so	completely	really	mostly
few	some	many	most
apparently	arguably	likely	possibly

ACTIVITY 3

Return to the article 'Books vs. e-books: The science behind the best way to read'. Identify ways in which the author hedges the wording of the article to maintain an objective tone. Consider the use of qualifiers as well as modals.

147

D Organising your ideas

There is no set formula for a discursive essay, but ideas should not appear at random. As with the argumentative approach, a sense of structure is necessary to sustain a clear point. You will also need to brainstorm for discursive tasks (see Chapter 2.2 Section *C Generating ideas for your essay*), but the process of generating and organising ideas may be different. For example, you might know in advance that you want to discuss the economic implications of an issue, and you might even have a few examples in mind to support your ideas. The difference, however, is that you do not necessarily know how you feel about this information until you actually start writing about it. In a discursive exploration, most of your insights will develop as you write the essay. In this section, you will learn about strategies for organising these insights as you write.

Handling perspectives

Just like any other essay, a discursive essay contains reasons to support your thesis. But in discursive writing you are presenting reasons which represent a variety of different perspectives, such as ones that oppose one another directly, without including any bias of your own.

KEY SKILLS

A perspective is someone's point of view, or opinion. When you offer reasons that support or challenge an issue in your essay, for example, you are expressing someone's perspective. See Chapter 2.2 Section *C Generating ideas for your essay* for more about perspectives.

One of the challenges you may face when organising your ideas for a discursive essay is how to share multiple points of view without sounding contradictory or indecisive. Here is a supporting body paragraph taken from a student's essay. Read this example to see how easily this kind of error can occur.

Support paragraph 1

To what extent should handwriting still be taught in schools?

Handwriting is definitely a necessary component of education because plenty of seminal documents are often written in calligraphy. Being able to decode the loops and arcs of these artifacts is therefore key in understanding history. However, while handwriting may be pretty, it is actually not necessary to a child's education. Some people claim learning cursive handwriting helps with brain development, but there is not sufficient evidence out there to prove this. So we cannot say handwriting is academically necessary. All in all, handwriting is important to education, but other times, it is not.

Consider the following questions:

1 What is the main point this student is trying to make?
2 How does the writer organise ideas?
3 How could the writer use transitions more effectively to address these conflicting points?
4 How could the tone be adjusted to appear more objective?

In this example, the writer attempts to position two opposing viewpoints against one another in a single paragraph. This organisational approach can be called 'XYXY', because within the same paragraph the writer switches abruptly between the perspectives. While this approach is one possible writing option, it is the most

difficult. As this example demonstrates, it can easily appear contradictory.

In order to use the XYXY pattern effectively when organising your ideas, you should remember to:

• use clear transitions to show connections between sentences
• separate reasons (perspectives) into larger categories or themes to demonstrate clearer distinction between points.

How might the example paragraph look if it were revised with these points in mind? Read the revised version to see what adjustments the student has made to strengthen this support paragraph. Note the underlined and italicised phrases, which indicate improvements to the writing:

Revision

Learning handwriting has always been one of our most timeless, academic traditions, but its role in today's education system is debatable. *On the one hand*, learning cursive means that students will be able to consult seminal documents like the Constitution in their social studies classes, since these are often written in calligraphy. *On the other hand*, opponents of cursive think that while this art form is pretty, class time could be better spent on learning 21st century skills like coding, for instance. *Yet* supporters of cursive insist that writing in cursive is time well spent since it can enhance brain development and strengthen fine motor skills. Detractors, *though*, are quick to point out that very little research is available to prove this correlation. Without official evidence, it appears that while handwriting can be 'handy', it may not be necessary to youth education and development.

Notice how the student:

• uses the topic sentence to set up a debate of ideas within the paragraph
• is removed from the argument itself by mentioning the thoughts of 'supporters' and 'opponents' rather than the student's own views
• uses transitions such as 'on the one hand', 'on the other hand', 'meanwhile', 'yet' and 'though' to signal a change of direction.

Keep these points in mind to help you avoid the 'to and fro' of perspectives that can happen when discussing an issue. Later in this section we will discuss perspectives which stretch beyond merely 'for' and 'against'.

Read the following article, keeping track of the different perspectives. Then complete the activity that follows.

Kids are playing with screens more than traditional toys, survey says

Given the wealth of free and inexpensive kids' apps available on mobile devices, it's only natural that today's toddlers are growing up with touchscreens. But could mobile tech replace the traditional toy? According to a recent survey, the answer is yes.

Media research firm the Michael Cohen Group (MCG) released the results of its recent nationwide survey, which **polled** 350 parents about the play habits of their children, 12 and younger. Touchscreen devices got the most overall playtime according to the poll, with more than 60 per cent of parents claiming that their child uses a touchscreen 'often' and roughly 38 per cent claiming 'very often'.

Touchscreens beat out kids' toys that have been around for decades, such as dolls and action figures, arts and crafts, and construction-based toys, all of which had a roughly 50 per cent usage rate on the poll. Gaming consoles had a usage rate of a bit less than 50 per cent, with other children's staples such as vehicles, puzzles, and board games landing closer to 40 per cent.

Given these stats, is it safe to call a touchscreen a toy? The MCG poll reveals that 10 per cent of parents 'always' consider touch devices as playthings, while 58 per cent considered them 'sometimes' toys. The remaining 32 per cent claimed that mobile devices should never be put in the same category as physical play products.

When it comes to content, 53 per cent of parents claimed their kids played educational games. Half of parents noted that their little ones **veered** toward music-based apps, while 49 per cent reported 'free play' games with no **discrete** educational value.

The popularity of touch devices among children was evident at Toy Fair 2014, but it doesn't mean the physical toy is dead. Products like Digipuppets and Tiggly provide classic playthings such as finger puppets and shape toys, which can interact with touchscreens and include their own proprietary app. Popular mobile titles like 'Angry Birds' have **spawned** their own physical toys called Telepods, which can attach to your smartphone or tablet to add more characters to the game.

Whether a touchscreen is actually a toy is up for debate, but the two product types are becoming more closely **aligned** than ever. Just make sure that before you hand off your phone or tablet, you set up parental controls and wrap it in a **rugged** case.

By Michael Andronico, Huffington Post, February 2014

149

ARTICLE GLOSSARY

polled: recorded the opinions of
veered: moved in the direction of
discrete: separate

spawned: produced, generated
aligned: moved together
rugged: strong

ACTIVITY 4

1   Identify two perspectives raised at different points in the article.

2   Argue these two perspectives against one another in a single paragraph that responds to the following question:

> To what extent will modern technology replace traditional play?

Nuance

One of the main messages Hermann Hesse puts forth in his 1951 novelette, *Siddhartha*, is that the world is neither wholly good nor wholly evil; 'never is a man wholly a saint or a sinner.' The message he is intending for his reader, in other words, is that a grey area exists.

When writing essays, it is easy to view our topics in mere, `black and white' terms at first. In other words, you might immediately divide the perspectives of an issue into those in favour and those against. This is not a bad place to start, of course, because it grants initial access into the conversation.

However, it is important that you eventually begin to recognise the more *nuanced* perspectives out there. Take for instance, two political parties which oppose one another. Within each group, there are supporters with varying degrees of belief; not all party members believe the exact same things in the exact same way!

To present a nuanced argument, you will need to demonstrate an awareness of the many different perspectives within the overarching categories of 'in favour/against', and aim to uncover those views that stretch beyond just pro and con.

In order to achieve this level of critical thought, however, it is important to build a foundation first, which is why this next section will begin with the most basic level of discursive writing in mind. You will first learn how to organise and present directly opposing views. The ability to write a more nuanced argument will naturally follow once this organisational foundation is set.

Strategies for organising the discursive body

So far, you have learnt how to weigh one opposing view against another in a single paragraph using the following organisational structure (as in Activity 4):

> XY, XY
> Both benefits and drawbacks are mentioned within a single paragraph. (Note that the comma indicates a change of paragraph.)

When working with opposing views, there are a few other ways to organise support paragraphs to feature these perspectives. These include:

> X, X, Y, Y
> Benefits 'front-loaded' in the first body paragraphs, with drawbacks presented in the following paragraphs.
> X, Y, X, Y
> Paragraphs work back and forth between benefit and drawback.

In each of these strategies, ideas are developed in separate paragraphs. The key to using these organisational structures effectively depends on your ability to create seamless transitions between paragraphs, noting any connections such as contrasting ideas. Activity 5 will give you opportunities to practise these transitions.

 KEY SKILLS

See Chapter 1.2 Section *F Key elements of an essay* and Chapter 5.1 to revisit what you learnt about using seamless transitions.

ACTIVITY 5

1   Draft a thesis statement for the following essay:

> To what extent has the mother's role evolved in today's family structure?

2   Now generate three separate perspectives in response to the question. (This could be one perspective in favour, and two against, though for different reasons).

3   For each reason, generate ideas in the form of evidence to support and sustain these perspectives.

4   Now draft two to three body paragraphs to appear after your thesis, using transitions to move seamlessly from one reason to the next.

As you draft your support, remember to:

- make the reasons (perspectives) clear, distinguishing one from the other
- use a seamless transition in your topic sentences to move fluidly from one paragraph to the next
- provide evidence to support each reason
- link evidence back to the thesis.

Remember, there is no set formula for a discursive essay. You could use a combination of options. Consider the following essay plan, which illustrates this idea:

Introduction:	*While X, possibly Y.*
Body paragraph 1:	*X*
Body paragraph 2:	*Y*
Body paragraph 3:	*XY*
Body paragraph 4:	*XY*
Body paragraph 5:	*X*
Body paragraph 6:	*X*
Conclusion:	*Adopts X with limitations*

TIP

You do not have to use the same number of ideas on each side of the issue (e.g. three reasons in favour followed by three reasons against). This is a common misunderstanding! Your essay can have as many ideas in favour or against the issue as you wish. Points on each side do not need to be balanced, and an unbalanced essay is not necessarily a weak one. As an example, either of the following would be acceptable:

• three reasons in favour, two against
• five reasons in favour, one (sustained point) against, etc.

However you approach this, the important thing is to:

• give objective consideration to a *range* of perspectives
• sustain your points.

An essay question may not just ask you to consider the benefits or drawbacks of a contemporary topic. There are other types of value-based writing tasks that you could be asked to respond to. For example, a question might ask you to consider a specific *problem* (A) in your society, then offer several suggestions for *solving* the problem (X, Y and Z). In this case, your essay's shape will take an entirely different form:

Introduction:	*Here is problem A. Because of problem A, there are a number of potential solutions to consider.*
Body paragraph 1:	*Solution X, its impact on A*
Body paragraph 2:	*Solution Y, its impact on A*
Body paragraph 3:	*Solution Z, its impact on A*
Body paragraph 4:	*Solution Z2 (a variation of Z), its impact on A*
Body paragraph 5:	*Limits to solutions X, Y, Z, Z2*
Conclusion:	*Adopts solution Z as best option for solving problem A because …*

In this example, the essay question calls for a problem–solution approach to organising your ideas. This will produce an essay with a very different form and shape than looking at benefits and drawbacks.

Alternatively, an essay may ask you to consider *how well* something is working. Consider how you might organise your ideas in response to this question:

> How well does your society maintain cultural traditions?

Some reading comprehension questions may even ask you to 'consider the advantages and disadvantages' before arriving at a decision. Here is one example of this type of question style, which covers the same topic as the article, 'Books vs e-books: The science behind the best way to read' earlier in this chapter.

> **By considering the advantages and disadvantages, explain which option is more preferable to the reader: traditional books or electronic tablets. [10]**

With questions like this, you can organise your response in more than one way, so long as you make a decision in the end. For example, you could offer:

• four advantages and one disadvantage
• three advantages and two disadvantages.

The first option will sound more argumentative, as the bulk of points are in favour of one side. The latter option will be more discursive, since consideration is distributed more evenly across the two options. Either way, as long as you draw a conclusion at the end, you will be satisfying the requirements of this comprehension question.

TIP

Keep in mind there is no set requirement for how many paragraphs your essay should have. Instead, focus on the quality and relevance of your ideas in relation to the question, using word count limits and marks available as an indication of length.

ACTIVITY 6

1 Read the discursive essay on the next page. On a separate sheet of paper, outline the organisational structure of the points made in the essay. You should:

• use symbols to distinguish the various perspectives surrounding the issue
• note the transitional phrases used to move between opposing perspectives.

2 How does this student organise the range of perspectives in the essay? How well does the student use transitions to move between perspectives? Discuss with your class or with a partner.

151

Can renewable resources ever address our modern energy needs?

1   There are relatively easy ways people can decrease their carbon footprint, such as the simple act of switching off a light when exiting a room. Beyond this kind of individual effort, countries across the globe are increasingly seeking out ways to collectively reduce the amount of emissions being released into our atmosphere. The pursuit of alternatives such as solar and wind energy are cropping up everywhere, but being energy-efficient is not always as easy as it seems. Large-scale projects like these cost thousands, if not millions, of dollars and recent economic struggles make it harder to pay for them. Thus, the question arises as to whether or not renewable resources can ever meet our modern energy needs.

2   At first glance, solar panels seem to be quite efficient. For one thing, installing them can reduce the world's growing carbon emissions. This is because solar energy does not release any carbon dioxide, sulphur dioxide, nitrogen oxides or mercury at all, unlike other, current sources of energy do. In an effort to 'go green', the American government is willing to offer tax reductions of up to $2000 for people who adopt solar panelling. The problem is, however, that what works for the US won't necessarily work for others. Governments who are not in a position to share the financial burden of changing energy systems or regions that do not enjoy the luxury of clear skies year round make this kind of solution improbable at best.

3   Not to mention, solar energy is not necessarily the most practical alternative either. This is largely due to the cost of the panels themselves. While they effectively harness the UV rays of the Sun for most by converting heat energy into electricity, the panels are quite expensive to maintain. Efficient solar cells can cost as much as $1000, and while governments like the US are offering to fund for the panels initially, who will cover the cost for repairs when they break? With these potential obstacles in mind, solar energy may not be the answer we need.

4   Nevertheless, solar energy has been known to significantly reduce residential expenses in countries like Armenia. Almost a quarter of household energy is used for heating water in this country. World-renowned charity, Habitat for Humanity, is introducing solar panels to the houses of over a hundred Armenian families. Although long-term maintenance is still in question, it's undeniable that the country's climate is perfect for solar panels because it gets about 300 sunny days per year. This makes heating water for these families much less costly. At an average savings of at least $200 US dollars, this data suggests that solar panelling can be cost-effective, with maintenance being more affordable as a result.

5   Not every location on the map is as lucky as sunny Armenia, unfortunately, making reliability a worthy concern. The US city of Seattle, Washington, is hazy at best every day of the year, and locations like Alaska vary greatly when it comes to light and darkness. An important point supporters of solar panels raise is that UV rays still manage to penetrate even the cloudiest of days. Opponents counter, however, that even when these devices are in use, they only process approximately 15% of the heat and light that reaches them. It appears that, in theory, solar panels are promising, but upkeep and reliability for all continues to overshadow how they'll perform in practice.

6   Solar energy may have its limits geographically, but there is still hope for pursuing other modern options like wind energy. In small impoverished countries like Malawi, Africa, entire villages are taking advantage of the opportunities a mere breeze can bring. One Malawian teenager, William Kamkwamba – now part of the ever-famous TED global fellowship – wrote an autobiography about how he built a windmill to save his village from severe droughts that his region faced in 2002. He harnessed the power of wind to generate both electricity and water for crop harvesting. This also helped provide drinkable water, thereby decreasing illnesses like cholera, which arise from lack of sanitary living conditions. In this case, because of its affordability, alternative energy may be one of few means for survival in impoverished nations.

7   One trouble with wind farms worth considering, though, involves consistency. Just as the sun is not always shining, the wind is not always blowing. Back-up power plants running off natural gases would have to be created in order to keep electricity flowing in times when there is no wind. In Texas, the leading US state for wind energy, the wind blows strongest in the high plains and along its famous, arid mesas. These locations, however, are not close enough for cities like Dallas or Austin to utilise wind as energy, which means they'll need to continue to depend on non-renewable for energy.

8   Be it solar or wind energy, it is clear that while renewable resources might not meet our global needs right now, the future brings potential. As with any innovation, there needs to be a process of trial and error before a reliable product can emerge. To ignore the potential of alternative energy against more traditional, non-renewable resources like fossil fuels is equivalent to ignoring the safety of our future, since our dependence on oil not only puts our environment at risk but also our lives. There might be limits to harnessing the power of alternative energy in this era, but with a little patience and a lot of dedicated research, we just may create a brighter, greener future after all.

TIP

Notice that in Activity 6 the student limits the essay's discussion to *two* types of alternative energy, instead of discussing the full range (i.e. geothermal, biofuel, nuclear, hydro). If you narrow the scope of your essay, you can discuss the issue at a deeper level, therefore sustaining your points rather than just skimming over them.

The structure of your essay will depend on the question you pick. Recall that if you select a question that asks for solutions to a problem, this essay will be structured differently from an essay that asks you to explore the advantages and disadvantages of something. This is one of the reasons why relying on a pre-set formula for writing will not necessarily help you write an effective essay in this course. Instead, you will need to make on-the-spot decisions based on the essay topic you choose.

The importance of topic sentences

If the thesis is the key sentence in an essay, the topic sentences are also very important (see Chapter 1.2 Section *F Key elements of an essay*). Topic sentences give clear shape to the essay's structure, signalling to the reader where the discussion will go next. As with any essay, each topic sentence needs to use transitions to direct reasons or *perspectives*. For the discursive approach, effective use of topic sentences helps you avoid discussions that sound confused or indecisive.

ACTIVITY 7

Re-read the essay 'Can renewable resources ever address our modern energy needs?' and identify the topic sentences. How does the writer manage to shift back and forth between perspectives without sounding contradictory? Annotate your observations, then share with a partner.

E Drawing conclusions following a discursive approach

The process of drawing conclusions in a discursive essay is different from other approaches. In a discursive essay, conclusions appear in more than one location. In this section you will practise drawing both **final** and **interim conclusions**.

KEY TERMS

Final conclusion: the final judgement made or insight gained once all the evidence is presented in an essay; it appears at the end.

Interim conclusion: a conclusion drawn part of the way through an essay after some (but not all) evidence has been considered; such interim conclusions are not permanent: they may change as more evidence is presented.

Interim conclusions

It might be useful to think of interim conclusions as the many battles which take place in the context of a larger war. In your discursive essay, several 'battles' between opposing viewpoints will take place before you determine which one 'wins' the main argument.

An interim conclusion is the outcome of *one* particular battle. It is an inference you draw as you finish a sustained point. You may not know the final outcome at this point, but you are in a position to pass a preliminary judgement (e.g. *so far, it appears that … ; at this point, it may be that …*).

ACTIVITY 8

Re-read the essay 'Can renewable resources ever address our modern energy needs?'

1   Where does the author include interim conclusions?
2   How do these conclusions break up the text?
3   Why are these appropriate places to offer these insights?
4   In what ways does this strategy help the organisation of the essay?

Discuss your observations with a partner.

As the essay demonstrates, you may offer several interim conclusions during the course of your discursive essay. How many you include will depend on how many subsections or sustained points you raise. As the main points of your essay develop, interim conclusions can help you keep track of ideas as you head toward your final judgement. In this way, you are more likely to draw an evidence-based conclusion rather than one that is influenced by something else.

Drawing interim conclusions can help you:

- connect evidence to claims
- make sense of the evidence you have presented so far
- think of new directions and new ideas
- consider how a part of your input can affect your final conclusion.

The following flowchart presents one way of understanding how an *interim* conclusion can follow a sustained point:

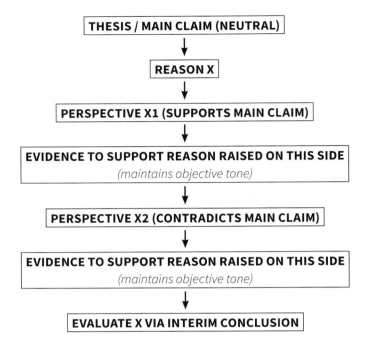

The flowchart can be applied to the issue of alternative energy as follows:

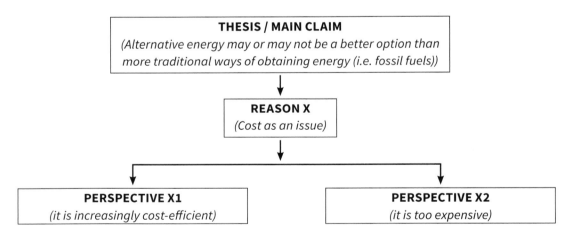

Final conclusions

Once you have thoughtfully explored all of the different points of view surrounding an issue, it is time to draw an evidence-based conclusion.

KEY SKILLS

See Chapter 1.2 Section *F Key elements of an essay* to remind yourself of the importance of evidence-based conclusions.

Remember that your conclusion is a reflection of the information presented in your essay. You should not introduce any new input or simply present a summary of the things you have already said. Instead, your concluding paragraphs should weigh the evidence presented, then judge the issue based on this evidence and your own perspective.

ACTIVITY 9

1 Review the concluding paragraph in the essay for 'Can renewable resources ever address our modern energy needs?'

2 With a partner, discuss the writer's approach to writing the conclusion. What things does it appear to do well? What kind of feedback might you offer?

Be prepared to share your observations with the class.

Evaluating the issue

So far, in the introduction and support paragraphs of a discursive argument, you have been an objective observer. Your aim has been to *report* the issue by presenting multiple perspectives along with evidence to support them. Along the way, you may have used interim conclusions to express your own logical observations about the evidence.

However, it is not enough just to present the multiple perspectives. At this point in your discursive essay, you should attempt to synthesise the information by weighing each point of view against the others before passing a final judgement.

It might be useful to ask yourself where you stand on the issue, now that you have reasoned through the arguments. Your initial reaction might be to maintain a 'middle-of-the-road' standpoint, or to continue to think that the issue depends on the circumstances (i.e. in some situations, X may apply; in other situations, it may not).

You may be inclined to leave your readers to pass judgement on their own. This is because in working through the different viewpoints with you, your readers have probably made their own decisions about what they think. However, they will still expect you to offer your position! This can validate their viewpoint or challenge them to re-think it. Not to mention, if your essay is going to qualify as an argument, you will need to assert a position at some point.

Therefore, you are expected to pass judgement at the end of a discursive essay. Making a decision means you are *evaluating* the issue, which is the highest form of critical thought and one of the main aims of this course.

TIP

If you do not offer your own judgement in the conclusion to your essay, you risk losing credibility with your audience. Sharing your position is only fair after all the effort your audience has put into following the argument with you!

How should you approach making a final judgement on your issue? A basic strategy would be to count the number of perspectives in favour versus those against, as shown in the diagram below:

Can renewable resources ever address our modern energy needs?

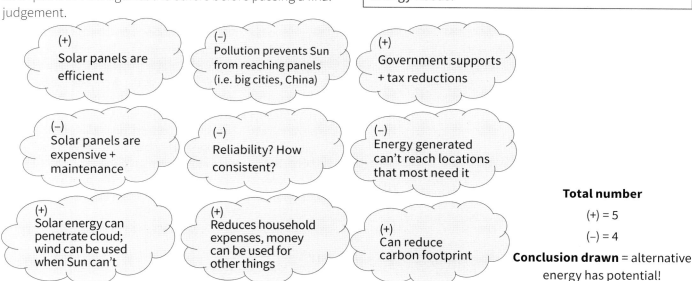

This system sounds easy enough, but reconsider the same example. Before choosing the side in favour of renewable resources, it is also wise to review the content of the points on that side. Ask yourself: are the (+) ideas strong/relevant enough? In other words, if you turned this into an argument, would you win?

Another point to consider: what if your essay presents an equal number of points in favour and against the issue? Again, consider the weight of the *contents* of the points raised: which side of the argument is genuinely more convincing? You may personally feel that alternative energy is the way to go, but just make sure that your perspective is within reason of the evidence you've shared.

You may find the following sentence stems helpful when you attempt to pass judgement and conclude your essay:

> While there are clearly some exceptions to the rule, for the most part, X is … than Y
>
> X is … but more often than not, Y …
>
> Evidently, X is … than Y
>
> Based on the evidence, it can be said that X is … over Y
>
> It appears that X is … than Y
>
> After careful analysis, X is clearly … over Y

Offering solutions

When writing the conclusion to your essay, you have learnt to briefly re-state your main points and extend these ideas by considering their impact in the future. Your conclusions up to now have primarily considered future implications based on the evidence offered. In an argumentative conclusion, this strategy can be especially helpful in convincing your audience and stirring their conscience.

There are other useful strategies to consider when drawing final conclusions:

- suggesting solutions to the issue
- offering recommendations for further research.

These options work particularly well in a discursive essay. They help to resolve any doubts your audience might still have about the negative side of your discussion.

To demonstrate what it means to suggest a solution, assume you are writing an essay on the following question:

> Evaluate the role that art galleries play in your society.

In this essay, you are invited to consider what role, if any, art galleries play in your own society. You explore the fact that they have played a powerful role in your community for many years, though just recently, this has declined. At the end of your essay, you conclude that despite the recent decline, art galleries still play an important role in your society.

Even if your audience accepts your conclusion, the input suggesting that the role of art galleries has, in fact, declined can leave the audience feeling uncertain or conflicted, despite your attempt to provide closure. One way to resolve this issue is to offer solutions for revitalising the role of these art galleries, taking account of the factors that caused them to lose status in the first place.

Consider the following student's response to this question, to demonstrate how the use of solutions can resolve any remaining conflicts that appear earlier in the essay:

> Evidently, if art is to be truly appreciated, it must be seen in person, which is why art galleries still play a significant role in our society. The sheer magnitude of a work can only be understood when the observer has the opportunity to converse with the artists themselves, an intimate interaction you simply cannot get online. One fact remains, despite this: more and more people are turning to online purchases. A potential solution to this growing problem exists, though. And believe it or not, it lies in the hands of the art gallery's biggest competitor: the internet. By using the internet to market art events more aggressively – making the appeal to buy in person stronger than filling a virtual shopping cart – we may keep this tradition alive after all. If you advertise discounts at the gallery, this can encourage buyers to purchase at the event itself; like any other advert, the more these appear in the daily social media feeds of buyers, the more likely those buyers are to be persuaded. There's no doubt these galleries are still a vital part of our community's artistic DNA, but how innovative we are willing to be will prove crucial in keeping art alive in person rather than just online.

The solution argues that if society is innovative enough, it can stop online sales from replacing the art gallery experience. This recommendation can help the audience see the potential for maintaining art galleries. Otherwise, they might just accept the fact that technology will inevitably win in a modern world, despite any general conclusions in the essay that claim art galleries can be saved.

Another option to help you think critically in your conclusion is to point out gaps in the current information available on the subject and suggest further research. For example, in an essay about whether or not cursive writing should still be taught in schools, you may point out that it can potentially help brain development, but that there is a lack of research to prove this. In your conclusion, you could recommend that further research

be conducted to find out if a strong enough link exists between the two.

F Practising what you have learnt

This section will give you further practice with key skills that you have learnt in this chapter, in different contexts: drawing evidence-based conclusions and recognising the features of discursive essay writing. Read each of the following articles (A and B), about the value of email in today's society. Then complete Activity 10.

Article A

Imagine a life free from the daily **drudgery** of deleting an Inbox full of 'unbeatable offers' and 'sales promotions'. Or worrying no more that a suspect email has broken through your multi-layered computer protection system. Or trying to pretend that you never received something, blaming it on the Web for 'losing' it, even though it is highly unlikely to have actually become 'lost in the ether'. Can you even remember the days when you actually became quite enlivened to open your email every day and wonder what fascinating messages you had received? What once used to be fun and exciting is now a dull chore, a regular necessity – trawling through the Inbox.

But perhaps there is hope for us all. First, the Twitterati are already logging off from emails because of their pedestrian nature, and soon companies may stop using them too. Some will even ban them totally from the office very soon. Although 1.8 billion email users regularly send over 107 trillion emails each year, is this then the **impending** death of our most popular form of communication? Certainly we have come a long way from smoke signals, tom tom drums, carrier pigeons, runners, the telephone, faxes and the like, but could this be a step too far?

One CEO, Thierry Breton, claims that only 10 per cent of the 200 electronic messages each of his employees receives on average every day turn out to be useful. He believes this **deluge** of unnecessary,

wasteful electronic information will be one of the most important problems a company will have to face in the coming years. It is time to think differently, out of the box, creatively, he says.

So, instead of email, his 75 000 staff will be made to use instant messaging and chat-style collaborative-service communication, inspired by social networking sites like Facebook and Twitter. Internal email will be **phased out** within the next eighteen months at his company. His staff used to spend up to two hours a day sifting emails, but now this new system reduces that work time by 20% and frees them for more productive activities.

His strategy has already been adopted by teenagers, of course, who are now shunning a middle-aged email system which was first developed as far back as 1971. As my daughter recently explained to me quite **succinctly**, 'email is for losers!' Indeed, email use is down 31% among the 12–17 year age group, with a further **slump** of 21% amongst the 18–24s. Mobile IM (instant messaging) services like Blackberry Messenger and Yahoo Messenger have **supplanted** the **ponderous** email for the tech-savvy next generation. Already 8 trillion text messages were sent around the world in 2011 by 1.5 billion mobile IM users. SMS offers the immediacy that an email cannot, and they are harder to ignore reading and responding to.

157

However, none of these present email replacements are entirely suited to the workplace, and those teenagers fortunate enough to find jobs in the next few years will still find themselves **enmeshed** in email's **spam-blighted** grip. Daily, more and more companies realise the possible potential of sending advertising messages to private customers' email, and even if millions of consumers ignore and delete their offers it only needs a minute percentage to say 'yes' for them to make a tidy profit. And everywhere around the world there is always someone who will say 'yes'. Every day 106 billion spam emails are sent out. The proportion of companies sending more than 50 000 spam emails a month has increased from 40% to 60% in four years.

Email too is still used for work by 85% of all employees even though, says Breton, 'it is disruptive, wastes a great deal of time and is miserable as a collaborative tool'. Unfortunately, email is not a beast to be easily killed; sometimes it is the most appropriate tool for communication: cheaper, quicker and more flexible than a business letter, and more of a proof than an unrecorded telephone call. But at other times people send them thoughtlessly, use them to cover their actions, to spread **specious** gossip or to try to elicit favours. In particular, emails also have a much greater propensity for future discovery of wrongdoing than instant messaging as they are held in print in the system for a very long time.

Therefore, in the workplace what could possibly replace email as a **hassle**-free, more collaborative communication tool? Yammer, a micro-blogging 'Facebook for Business', which allows groups of employees to share ideas through private communication, is now used by more than 8000 firms. Breton has introduced the Atos Wiki, which allows all employees to communicate by contributing or modifying online content, and he has also brought in Office Communicator, an online chat system which allows video conferencing, file and application sharing.

If email *is* dying therefore, it will be a **lingering demise**. It is still the most convenient way to send 'semi-business' or official mail. It still reaches a mass market for deal-a-day special-offers companies touting vouchers, reduced holidays and sale products. It has fuelled a boom in online shopping so incredible that High Street stores are not just looking over their shoulders but are even starting to go bankrupt, and the older generations still think it is better than the bad old days. But the electronic world will keep on developing and mutating and refining; that is a given. No one can dare to predict the future.

Cambridge International AS Level General Paper 8001/21
Insert Passage 3, November 2014

ARTICLE GLOSSARY

drudgery: hard, dull work

impending: about to happen

deluge: flood, huge amount

phased out: gradually discontinued

succinctly: briefly and clearly expressed

slump: steep fall

supplanted: replaced

ponderous: slow and dull

enmeshed: caught, unable to escape

spam-blighted: spoiled by too much unwanted advertising

specious: appearing to be right but actually wrong

hassle: annoying inconvenience

lingering demise: slow death

Article B

We can tweet. We can Facebook message. We can Google hangout. We can even Instagram and Snapchat. With so many social media options with which to communicate does email even matter anywhere? Actually email does still matter and it will for a long time.

Facebook has over 1.11 billion users with about 665 million of those users accessing the site daily according to company records. That's a lot of people, but it's not all the people. If you rely on Facebook as a method of communicating you are excluding people who have quit Facebook, never used it, or rarely check it.

This article cites research from the Radicati Group stating that there are about 3.4 billion registered email addresses worldwide. Sure people have email accounts, but do they use them? A survey last year revealed email to be the top activity on mobile phones and tablets. (Number two was checking news.)

One reason for email's continued significance is that it has a standard: Simple Mail Transfer Protocol or SMTP. That's why emails can be sent between people with Gmail, Yahoo, and Hotmail accounts as well as people with accounts through their employers or on personal mail servers. You can send an email to anyone regardless of what they have following the @ sign. In contrast you can't send a single message to people on different social media platforms. Sure, you can duplicate the content but then you have to duplicate your efforts to monitor responses as well.

Of course, email needs to have its own place in your communications strategy.

- Your messages can be more **verbose**, but your responses will be slower.

- Whereas a skilled community manager can post multiple times a day to social media accounts it is unlikely that multiple emails a day will be effective for anything other than getting people to unsubscribe.

- With many people feeling overwhelmed by the volume of email they receive it is important that you use meaningful subject lines that ensure your message gets opened.

'Why email still matters in a social media obsessed world'
by Kim Dale, August 2013

159

ARTICLE GLOSSARY

verbose: using more words than necessary

ACTIVITY 10

Using the various perspectives featured in Article A and Article B, draw a conclusion about whether or not email still has value in modern society. Draft a formal concluding paragraph that responds to the following prompt: *To what extent is email an outdated form of communication in today's digital society?*

The conclusion-writing skills that you have learnt in this chapter can also be applied to comprehension questions. You will find questions, when practising reading comprehension skills, which will ask you to draw conclusions about a set of data or other evidence. Study the following material and answer the past paper questions.

A

The town of Radoma (population 182 000) has been declining for years and its town centre is looking dated. The Government is to build extra housing in the town for 40 000 new residents and it has offered the town council a $180 million grant to improve the image of its town centre. Therefore, the council has decided to build a huge new indoor retail centre called The Rado in the town centre.

The Rado will have:

136 shops

12-screen cinema

15 restaurants and fast-food outlets

Parking for 3000 cars underground

Medical centre

Drop-in crèche for under-fives and an indoor playground.

B

All such retail centres need one 'flagship store' – a large, famous store to give the centre a good reputation and to attract the crowds. The town council has shortlisted four possible flagship stores:

Mola | a longstanding family department store in decline on the edge of the present shopping area, but hoping to revive its fortunes in The Rado.

Primestore | a well-known national food supermarket, branching out into clothes, gifts and other goods.

Ninani | an upmarket, medium-to-expensive fashion store.

Futurgizmo | a state-of-the-art electronics firm and retailer.

C

The town council needs to consider the following information before deciding which store will be the flagship:

1   The unemployment rate in Radoma is 10% above the national average.

2   Parking at The Rado will cost $3 an hour.

3   Futurgizmo promises to beat any competitor's price and will offer free delivery up to a 30 km radius.

4   The Rado will be built in the centre of the town on a derelict car park site.

5   90% of Mola's customers are local people, mainly over 50 years of age.

6   The average salary in Radoma is 18% below the national average.

7   The distance from the flagship's door to the nearest underground car park door is 160 metres.

8   The town council will insist that the flagship chosen must spend 3% of its annual profits on advertising itself and The Rado Centre.

9   Radoma has an out-of-town retail centre with 24 stores, easy access and free parking, just 4km from the town centre.

10   Ninani and Futurgizmo have pledged to sell all their products 3–5% cheaper than any of their other stores nationwide.

11   The Rado will be 500 metres from the bus station and 600 metres from the railway station.

12   Each flagship has placed a minimum time on when it will review its position in The Rado – Mola 3 years, Primestore 7 years, Ninani 2 years and Futurgizmo 4 years.

13   The council has insisted that all employees below middle-management level must be recruited locally.

14   Mola has promised an across-store '20% off' promotion for its first four weeks.

15   Primestore has promised $30 000 for seating and pot plants in the centre.

16   The number in the 16–30s age group of Radoma is 20% lower than the national average because they move north for better opportunities.

17   Radoma has two supermarkets and one electronics firm in the out-of-town retail centre.

18   Radoma's bus company has steadily reduced its services to the town centre every year by 12%.

19   The Rado will be located in the centre of the town's pedestrian precinct, with only one rear slip-road to the car park.

20   Consultants have advised that frequency of customer visits is often more important than spending-power.

Cambridge International AS Level General Paper 8001/21
Insert Passage 1, November 2014

PAST PAPER QUESTIONS

Answer questions **a–e**

a   The town council quickly dismissed the claims of Mola and Ninani. Choose **one** of these stores and say why you think the council believed it to be unsuitable as the flagship store. Answer in about 100 of your own words. **[10]**

b   If you were the council leader, which **one** of the two remaining stores – Primestore and Futurgizmo – would you recommend to be the flagship store? Explain your answer in about 100 of your own words. **[10]**

c Choose **one** of the points listed 1–20 in Section C and explain why you think it was the least helpful in selecting the flagship store. **[3]**

d How do you think residents living near the new Rado Centre might feel after it is built? **[6]**

e Out-of-town retail centres have become very popular compared to shopping in town centres. Why do you think this is so? **[6]**

Cambridge International AS Level General Paper 8001/21, Question 1a-e, November 2014

In this chapter you have learnt how discursive writing differs from argumentative writing. To demonstrate your understanding of the unique features of each essay style, read the following two essays and complete the activity that follows. Both essays respond to the same question:

> Should handwriting still be taught in schools?

However, they treat the issue differently. Observe the differences in purpose, tone and shape as you read.

Essay A

A rudimentary tradition in education, learning the careful loops and arcs of cursive handwriting is often viewed as a 'rite of passage' for second graders. However, as we move toward a more modernised, digitised society, plenty of schools across the globe are starting to **write off** script at the primary level, making it clear that the curriculum needs to evolve with the times. With handwriting gradually losing value in today's society, it should no longer be taught in schools as a result.

Handwriting is one of our rich and timeless traditions, but with technology becoming our primary means for communication, its decline is inevitable. While it is true that – for years – handwriting has offered us a classic, personal touch, today word-processing is the career skill future employers are seeking, not script; so schools are increasingly teaching with this in mind. In fact, according to the recently revised Common Core State Standards in America, students are expected to gain proficiency in keyboarding in order to meet national academic expectations. And while supporters of cursive argue that physically connecting letter shapes helps brain development, the truth is, there is little or no proof in the research community to validate this claim.

Since handwriting is not part of standardised testing, it's no longer a priority in most schools. In response to a push for 21st century skills, computer science classes are gaining momentum in schools all over. Initiatives like Computing the Core in the US are cropping up to support computer science education over handwriting. Scotland also finds itself in the midst of a massive curriculum **overhaul** to make computer skills a part of every child's learning experience. And with its longstanding tradition of teaching computing in schools, South Korea is set to reinforce their already sturdy approach to the subject. Meanwhile, although it is not **mandatory** in schools in India just yet, computer courses are expected to increase in the near future. Clearly, when we stop to consider which is more valuable in the workplace – cursive or code – teaching students more modern skills will prove more useful for their future than age-old traditions like handwriting.

Those who still see value in cursive argue that despite modern technology, 'signatures are always required', but this viewpoint is misguided. Rather, the gradual decline of the physical signature is happening right now. For example, most notaries use electronic notarisation as opposed to the traditional penned signature. Even home loans are largely being closed by electronic means. Since the electronic signature is just as binding as its print counterpart, cursive is no longer necessary when it comes to legal matters.

Clearly, the rich traditions of penmanship are losing popularity. Plenty of people agree that more modern skills need to be the focus of education, and real world professions also demonstrate a shift toward technology. Even if we ask the students themselves, their resounding response is that cursive is a dead end for their future. While Cursive Clubs from the US to the UK may have fun practising the art of letter-writing, or decoding the curves and loops of seminal documents, the reality is that learning handwriting is no longer a priority for the tech-savvy, 21st-century learner.

ARTICLE GLOSSARY

write off: cancel, abandon
overhaul: examination of a system

mandatory: must be done, a legal requirement

161

Essay B

From the seminal documents like the Declaration of Independence to Grandma's recipes, many of our important documents of the past have been scripted in cursive. For second graders, learning the careful loops and arcs of handwriting is a 'rite of passage', a skill that has always been a rudimentary part of many systems of education. As we move toward a more modernised, digitised society, however, schools across the globe are beginning to write off script as a requirement in elementary education. While some insist that handwriting is an essential part of learning, others argue that it is no longer relevant.

Learning handwriting has always been one of our most timeless traditions, but its role in today's education system is debatable. On the one hand, learning cursive means that students will be able to consult seminal documents like the Constitution in their social studies classes, since these are often written in calligraphy. On the other hand, opponents of teaching cursive think that while this art form is pretty, it's no longer essential to a child's education. Meanwhile, plenty of supporters claim that writing in cursive enhances brain development and strengthens fine motor skills, yet detractors are quick to point out there is actually very little research to prove this.

Thus far, it appears that while learning cursive might be nice, it may not be necessary to one's education, but for second language speakers, this is certainly not the case. Some teachers contest that writing words as opposed to typing them helps English language learners remember words better since they directly interact with the letters and patterns. Not to mention, any student struggling with manuscript is apt to feel more confident if they're good at cursive as an alternative.

With technology taking over importance in the classroom, however, handwriting still seems to be on the decline. This is because good penmanship is no longer a career skill employers are seeking, while word processing is, so schools are adjusting instruction with this in mind. One look at the recently revised Common Core State Standards in the United States reveals that nearly all states shifted away from handwriting, many opting for computer science classes instead. Scotland also finds itself in the midst of a massive curriculum overhaul to make computer skills a part of every child's learning experience. And with its longstanding tradition of teaching computing in schools, South Korea is set to reinforce their already sturdy approach to the subject.

Not all schools are necessarily on board with computer education, though. Computing is not mandatory in schools in India just yet, though it is set to increase in the near future. Over all, coding classes appear to be sweeping school curriculums across the world. With a push toward 21st-century skills, handwriting no longer appears to be a priority, so the likelihood of it lasting seems low.

From a psychological standpoint, meanwhile, there may be hope for this written form yet. Because it relies on form and balance, handwriting can almost be considered an expression of the body. There is an emotional connection rendered when writing by hand. For instance, a letter or poem written in an author's original script can be far more powerful than viewing it in the printed text of a book. And while texting may be popular, touchscreen and stylus technology gives us the comfort of this long-standing tradition yet. If emoticons were invented because of the emotion lacking in print text, then handwriting might still have a place in this world after all.

Matters of the heart keep handwriting rooted, but the needs of modern business may not. Electronic notarisation, for example, is taking over, making the 'gradual disappearance of the physical signature' all but inevitable. Many notaries now use electronic notarisation, for example, as opposed to the traditional penned signature; and home loans are increasingly being closed by electronic means. Since the electronic signature is just as legally binding as its print counterpart, handwriting is slowly losing its age-old lustre in this regard.

Evidently, it appears that the fate of handwriting teeters between two equally important desires: our need for tradition and our need for progress. The warmth and personality handwriting brings to the page is undeniably unique, but in a world that places increasing value on 21st century skills, it appears that script is losing its foothold. The skills a modern workforce needs simply do not include precision in penmanship. And with no research to prove its impact on cognitive ability, it makes sense to replace this ancient practice with a more reliable and updated approach, one that will give learners an edge as they go on to compete in an increasingly competitive, modernised society.

ACTIVITY 11

1   Which essay is discursive and which is argumentative in approach? How do you know? Annotate the essays to reflect the differences in tone and organisational structure.

2   How does the use of language affect the tone of each essay? Justify your observations.

3   How does the writer move from one point to the next in each essay? Share your observations.

Summary

Key points to remember from this chapter:

■   A discursive approach to thinking and writing is an unbiased attempt to understand the various perspectives surrounding an issue before arriving at a conclusion about them.

■   Evaluating evidence, which is a part of the critical thought process, can occur in the body of an essay, not just at the end.

■   Since you will not know exactly how you feel about an issue until the end of your essay, a discursive thesis statement should be broad, stating your general intention to explore both sides without listing specific reasons.

■   To avoid sounding contradictory or indecisive, use transitions carefully and meaningfully to move from one perspective to the next.

■   There is no set formula for a discursive essay; just remember to sustain each point and use an unbiased tone.

■   Though you are an objective observer for most of the essay, be sure to conclude your discussion by firmly evaluating the issue in the end. This is what ultimately makes your essay an argument.

163

Chapter 3.3
Skills review and practice

A government is in charge of managing the many systems that make up a society. With so many responsibilities, however, how do our leaders decide what to prioritise? This chapter will explore the theme of *Government priorities*.

Learning objectives

In this chapter you will:

- apply the skills you have learnt in Unit 3 to reading and writing tasks
- develop your critical writing skills through focused practice
- work with themed text sets to widen your general knowledge about government priorities involving the environment, education and matters of national security.

A Chapter aims

In working through Unit 3, you have learnt how to:

- recognise argumentative appeals
- identify and develop a line of reasoning
- recognise errors in logic
- objectively explore global issues
- draw interim and final conclusions
- propose solutions.

The aim of this chapter is to help you to reinforce these skills. At the end of the chapter, you will find activities to help you assess your understanding of these skills and strategies. Before attempting these assessments, you will have the opportunity to review each skill. Specifically, you will work with three text sets, which are related to the chapter's key theme of *Government priorities*.

Each text set will allow you to apply the skills you have learnt. This will help you to improve your responses to reading and writing questions.

	Text set	Skills review
1	Politics and the environment	• understanding appeals • organising ideas • analysing logic • evaluating source credibility
2	Politics and education	• analysing evidence to propose solutions and draw conclusions
3	Politics and national security	• text-based writing to practise style while expanding knowledge

B Text set 1: Politics and the environment

A text set is a collection of written sources which are all related to the same topic. The first set, *Politics and the environment*, explores a government's responsibility to maintain a healthy environment for the future. The articles put this issue in focus by exploring the progress of several governments worldwide which are trying to achieve that goal.

Understanding appeals

Remember that writers use a variety of appeals in an attempt to convince their audience to accept their point of view. Specifically, they might appeal to a reader's:

- emotional state (*pathos*)
- logic (*logos*)
- level of trust (*ethos*)
- sense of urgency (*kairos*).

KEY SKILLS

For more about argumentative appeals, see Chapter 3.1 Section *B Understanding arguments*.

ACTIVITY 1

Read Text 1 and Text 2. Both are taken from the *Pakistan Observer* and are about environmental efforts to reduce global warming and climate change in the region. The first is an editorial and the second is written by a freelance columnist. As you read:

- identify which appeals the author is using to persuade his or her audience
- analyse how effective these appeals are at convincing the reader
- evaluate which author does a better job of 'winning' the audience's approval.

Text 1

Green Pakistan

The 'Green Pakistan' initiative of Prime Minister Nawaz Sharif, Gilgit-Baltistan and Azad Kashmir conveys a shared desire of federal and provincial governments to address the challenge of environment degeneration caused mainly by **denuding** forest cover. The Prime Minister and the Chief Ministers express their resolve to make Pakistan clean, green and beautiful.

The Green Pakistan programme was approved by the PM in March last year on the pattern of the Great Green Wall Programme of China, under which 100 million **saplings** are to be planted throughout the country over the next five years. Protection and management of wildlife and reclaiming and developing forest areas are among the main aspects of the programme.

However, it took the government one year to formally launch the project, which is indicative of the priority being given to this crucial issue despite the fact that we have a **full-fledged** Ministry of Climate Change to take care of such programmes and issues. Anyhow, now that the programme has been launched and an announcement has been made to observe Feb 09 every year as National Green Day, one hopes concerted efforts would be made not only to realise this modest target of tree plantation but also surpass it with a big margin in view of serious implications of environmental issues.

We have no time to waste or indulge in just **sloganeering** as already deforestation in Pakistan is the highest in Asia while only **lip-service is being paid** to tree plantation campaigns since long. Protection of forests, increase in forest cover and conservation of wildlife would remain an elusive dream

until and unless necessary awareness is raised among citizens and they assume ownership of the drives fully realising the consequences of denuding forest cover.

We are losing more and more trees to unplanned industrialisation, housing schemes, roads and highways, runways, water reservoirs and more importantly due to felling of trees for firewood and construction material.

We can make up the loss if we sensitise local communities and involve schools, colleges, universities, government and private offices and corporate sector in tree plantation drives. Survival of saplings with proper care and protection is also a key to success of such efforts.

From Pakistan Observer, February 2017

ARTICLE GLOSSARY

denuding: stripping something of its covering, possessions, or assets; making it bare

saplings: young trees

full-fledged: fully developed

sloganeering: saying things which sound impressive, usually for political reasons

pay lip-service: say you agree with something but do nothing to support it

Text 2

The need for green Pakistan

Reducing deforestation means adopting measures to ensure reduction [of tree cutting] in areas already under forests and also attaining optimal global standards. Pakistan has only 5.2% area under forests and the sordid aspect is that it also has the highest deforestation rate in Asia. It is also the eighth worst hit country by the phenomenon of climate change. Apart from the overall global warming due to greenhouse gases emitted by the industrialised countries, one of the contributing factors also has been the **depletion** of forests in the country. The floods in 2010 and 2014 that inflicted incalculable loss on crops and infrastructure besides loss of precious human lives were the ugliest manifestations of the impact of climate change.

It is therefore our national and international obligation to raise more forests and plant as many trees around the country as possible. The PML (N) government has been very vocal at the international level in regards to dealing with global warming and climate change. Prime Minister Nawaz Sharif addressing the UN General Assembly also urged the need for concrete actions by the international community. At home the government in regards to resolving energy crisis is more focused on exploiting renewable energy resources and ensuring energy efficiency. The latest initiative known as Prime Minister's Green Pakistan Programme, is probably the biggest ever effort undertaken to tackle issues related to climate change.

This project deserves national ownership and needs to be implemented on a **perennial** basis to minimise the impact of climate change no matter which party is in power. The government has taken an initiative, which is beyond reproach. It concerns the future of the country and therefore needs unqualified support of all the segments of the society including political parties in the parliament who can make a contribution of their own in improving and expanding the scope of the Programme and further refining the implementation mechanism to achieve better results. The electronic and print media also have a national obligation to contribute towards creating awareness among the masses and playing a motivational role in this regard.

Adapted from an article by Malik M Ashraf,
Pakistan Observer, March 2016

ARTICLE GLOSSARY

depletion: reduction
perennial: lasting for a long time

Organising ideas in an argument

In Chapter 3.1, you learnt that a logical argument contains a clear line of reasoning in which the main claim, or thesis, is backed by reasons and evidence.

ACTIVITY 2

1 Watch the TED Talk debate, 'Does the world need nuclear energy?' between Stewart Brand and Mark Z. Jacobson. Work in pairs to deconstruct the arguments. Using the 'TREE' of reasoning strategy (Chapter 3.1 Section *E Developing an effective line of reasoning*), illustrate each argument's line of reasoning. Remember to identify:

- background and context (roots)
- main claim (trunk)
- reasons to support main claim (branches)
- evidence to support reasons (leaves)
- counterarguments, as they apply (birds, caterpillars)
- solutions, conclusions drawn (sunshine).

2 Once you have deconstructed each argument, discuss the strengths and weaknesses of each with your partner before deciding together which argument is stronger overall. Be prepared to defend your decision to the class.

Logical reasoning

Another strategy to determine how logical an argument is, is to identify any examples of fallacious (illogical) reasoning.

ACTIVITY 3

1 Select an article from an editorial or op-ed article found in a local or national newspaper in your region (preferably one concerning the government's role in handling climate issues). Attempt to identify any weaknesses in reasoning as they occur. (For a full list of fallacies, see *Recognising weaknesses in arguments* in Chapter 3.1 Section *B Understanding arguments*.)

2 Aim to find an article which includes at least two to three errors in reasoning, and prepare to present these to the class.

Evaluating source credibility

In Chapter 3.1, you learnt that credibility plays a crucial role in persuading an audience to believe your argument. In order to build your credibility, you need to:

- avoid faulty reasoning
- use information and sources that are credible and trustworthy when backing your claims.

This helps to make you appear as another trustworthy source, which increases the chances that your audience will accept your ideas.

TIP

Remember that when you are writing discursively, you need to weigh the different perspectives surrounding an issue before passing judgement. One strategy for evaluating the strength of a perspective is to consider the credibility of its source.

Imagine you are about to write an essay to argue whether or not global warming is a man-made phenomenon. In your research, you come across an article that cites scientist Dr Roy Spencer. Though the information appears credible enough, you are not entirely convinced, so you search the internet to check the credibility of Dr Spencer's work. Read Text 4, which is the original article citing Dr Spencer, and Texts 5–7, which are the other information sources that you gathered to corroborate the credibility of his work. Then complete the exam-style questions which follow.

Text 3

Al Gore's flat earth army

The theory, as **advanced** by **anthropogenic** global warming (AGW) alarmists, is that there's a causal relationship between manmade CO_2 emissions, and rising global temperatures during the 20th century... [but] the disconnect between actual emissions, and satellite global mean temperature data, invalidates the causality they have bitterly clung to.

One explanation climatologists like Dr Roy Spencer suggest is the increasing body of research that indicates the atmosphere responds differently to higher concentrations of atmospheric carbon dioxide, in ways that had not been recognised before. Evidence suggests that the atmosphere simply releases much more CO_2 into space than previously thought, like its own safety valve ...

Dr Spencer, a principal research scientist at the University of Alabama in Huntsville and former US Science Team Leader at NASA, reports in his peer-reviewed article two years ago, 'real-world data from NASA's Terra satellite contradict multiple assumptions

In the 2006 documentary, *An Inconvenient Truth*, former United States Vice President Al Gore urged the world to move away from fossil fuels to avoid global warming.

fed into alarmist computer models ... much more energy lost to space during and after warming than the climate models show'.

Adapted from an article by Richard Larsen, westernjournalism.com, June 2013

ARTICLE GLOSSARY

advanced: suggested, put forward

anthropogenic: caused by human activity

The following is a 'Letter to the editor', which responds to Richard Larsen's article in which he cites the work of Dr Spencer (Text 3).

Text 4

Logical fallacies and global warming alarmism

Once again Journal columnist Richard Larsen indulges his personal belief that he is a scientist by writing an article (June 23) on 'his' perception of global warming.

5 I can tolerate this based on our freedom of speech, although I must say that his idea of science leaves much to be desired.

What I cannot tolerate is his obvious misinformation by omission. I took the time to read his comments

and noted that he bases these on the work of a Dr Roy Spencer. I am a practicing scientist, but had never heard of him. So I did a literature search for Dr Spencer's works. 10

His vita from the University of Alabama is less than impressive, listing six publications of which only four are scientific papers, and I cannot attest to the quality of the journals in which he has published. 15

Upon further searching for Spencer's credentials, I found that he is an avowed **creationist**. Aha, now I understand! As one of my creationist students once said to me, 'We don't have to worry about overpopulation of the earth, if there are too many people, God will send us a war'.

It all becomes so simple, doesn't it?

Returning to Mr Larsen, he never once mentioned that Spencer was a creationist. He never once mentioned that Spencer's vita is stunningly sparse (for comparison, in my field, it is usual for an average researcher to have 50 to 100 publications). Nor did he mention that Spencer's recent interview on the website Catholic Online was thoroughly panned.

By Dennis P. Strommen, Idaho State Journal, July 2013

ARTICLE GLOSSARY

creationist: a person who believes that the world was made by (the Christian) God exactly as described in the Bible, and who does not accept Darwin's theory of evolution.

The following is an excerpt from an interview with Dr Roy Spencer for the website *Catholic Online*:

Text 5

Interview transcript

Catholic Online: Let's say tomorrow, evidence is found that proves to everyone that global warming as a result of human released emissions of CO_2 and methane, is real. What would you suggest we do?

SPENCER: I would say we need to grow the economy as fast as possible, in order to afford the extra **R&D** necessary to develop new energy technologies. Current solar and wind technologies are too expensive, unreliable, and can only replace a small fraction of our energy needs. Since the economy runs on inexpensive energy, in order to grow the economy we will need to use fossil fuels to create that extra wealth. In other words, we will need to burn even more fossil fuels in order to find replacements for fossil fuels.

Catholic Online: What should we do given the current state of affairs? Should we continue to study this issue or are we wasting resources?

SPENCER: I tell people that it is theoretically possible that Al Gore is correct. Unfortunately, the subject has become so politicised – specifically, driven by desired policy outcomes that have huge financial winners and losers – that the science has been almost hopelessly corrupted.

From a transcript published on Catholic Online,
April 2013

ARTICLE GLOSSARY

R&D: research and development

The following is part of an article reviewing the interview with Dr Spencer (Text 5).

Text 6

Scientist Roy Spencer is wrong: fossil fuels are expensive

Catholic Online interviewed Roy Spencer last week. Spencer is a climate scientist at the University of Alabama at Huntsville, and one of the few climate scientists who is considered a 'sceptic'. Like virtually all climate scientists, he acknowledges that humans are causing some global warming; however, Spencer is one of very few climate scientists who believe the human contribution to global warming is too small to worry about.

In the interview ... it was very disappointing to see a climate scientist respond to simple climate questions with factually and often glaringly wrong answers. It's something you would expect to see from a climate contrarian blogger, but any climate scientist should be able to do much better.

Spencer also made a rather perverse argument about fossil fuels when asked what he would suggest doing if he is wrong and human-caused global warming is a major threat: *Current solar and wind technologies are too expensive, unreliable, and can only replace a small fraction of our energy needs. Since the economy runs on inexpensive energy, in order to grow the economy we will need to use fossil fuels to create that extra wealth. In other words, we will need to burn even more fossil fuels in order to find replacements for fossil fuels.*

That's like telling a smoker that he should solve his addiction by smoking more cigarettes, because they're cheaper and more satisfying than nicotine patches.

From an article by Dana Nuccitelli, The Guardian, *May 2013*

171

The following article on the Drexel Univerisity website offers relevant background information.

Text 7

Not just the Koch brothers: new Drexel study reveals funders behind the climate change denial effort

A new study conducted by Drexel University environmental sociologist Robert J Brulle, PhD, exposes the organisational underpinnings and funding behind the powerful climate change countermovement. This study marks the first peer-reviewed, comprehensive analysis ever conducted of the sources of funding that maintain the denial effort.

Through an analysis of the financial structure of the organisations that constitute the core of the countermovement and their sources of monetary support, Brulle found that, while the largest and most

consistent funders behind the countermovement are a number of well-known conservative foundations, the majority of donations are 'dark money', or concealed funding.

The data also indicates that Koch Industries and ExxonMobil, two of the largest supporters of climate science denial, have recently pulled back from publicly funding countermovement organisations ...

From an article by Alex McKechnie, www.drexel.edu, December 2013

EXAM-STYLE QUESTIONS 1

Answer the comprehension questions **1–8**.

1 What is Larsen's main claim (Text 3)? Summarise it in approximately 30 words. **[1]**

2 Explain how the evidence Larsen presents links to his claim. (Hint: why is this evidence particularly relevant to his point?) **[1]**

3 In your opinion, what is strong about Strommen's response (Text 4) and what do you find weak about it? Explain your observation in approximately 300 words. **[6]**

4 Using clues from the material define the following words from Text 4: **[3]**

   a vita (line 13)

   b sparse (line 26)

   c panned (line 30).

5 Why do you think Strommen uses quotations around the word 'his' in his opening paragraph? **[1]**

6 What is Strommen's tone in paragraph 5? Explain, using information from the text to support your response. **[2]**

7 What is the main criticism Strommen has against Larsen's argument? Summarise it in one sentence. **[1]**

8 Review the extract from *The Guardian* (Text 6), which is in response to *Catholic Online*'s interview with Dr Roy Spencer. In your own words, explain what is meant by the criticisms raised against Spencer in the latter part of the extract. **[1]**

9 What do you think the extract from Drexel.edu appears to infer (Text 7)? Explain the message it is trying to convey. **[1]**

10 In what ways does the article from Drexel.edu relate to the last two sentences in Spencer's interview (Text 5)? **[2]**

11 To what extent would you find it useful to include knowledge gained from Larsen's article in your essay about global warming? Defend your decision. **[6]**

Total marks: 25

C Text set 2: Politics and education

In this set of articles, you will be asked to think again about what it means to offer workable solutions and draw worthwhile conclusions; you will also use the source material to gain knowledge about education as a government priority.

Proposing solutions in an essay conclusion

After all the evidence you have presented in an argument, it is important to bring your essay to a close in an appropriate way. Offering solutions to any outstanding issues is one way of achieving this.

KEY SKILLS

To review ways to conclude a discursive essay, including solution proposals, see Chapter 3.2 Section *E Drawing conclusions following a discursive approach.*

Read the following article about the impact of offering free college education to students in Ecuador. Then complete the activity that follows.

Text 1

Ecuador: Who benefits from free higher education?

Ecuador has become the latest testing ground for the attempt to use higher education to reverse decades of racial and social inequality through the country's prohibition, following a new constitution in 2008, of fees for all public education (including public universities).

Equity was the main reason for making education 'free' for university students. But the preliminary results of this experiment are not encouraging: so far, those who have been most rewarded by the suspension of fees are members of groups that were already advantaged and likely to attend.

The reasons are not difficult to **fathom**. Universities are expensive for families in Latin America and in much of the world, not because of the fees they charge. This was especially not a barrier for public universities in Ecuador prior to 2009, because universities used a **sliding scale** based on income.

Instead of direct fees, the biggest expense comes from the years of sacrifice by families when they encourage their children to study and eventually to pass competitive entrance exams, as opposed to working to support the household economy. In recent years, although about 80% of each birth **cohort** entered secondary schools, there was a large drop-out rate among the poor. Only about half of each cohort finishes secondary schooling and is thus eligible for 'free' university attendance.

The elimination of student fees at public universities in Ecuador expresses the ideals enshrined in the 2008 Constitution. Article 356 (unofficial translation) states:

'Public higher education will be free through the undergraduate level. Admission to public higher education institutions will be regulated through a system of evaluation defined under the law ... regardless of whether public or private, equality of opportunity in access is guaranteed, as well as equality in persistence, mobility and exit, with the exception of the fees charged by private higher education.'

But the translation of good intentions in public policy is complicated, and ideals often produce unintended consequences.

If one examines Ecuador's 2001 population census, together with more recent nationally representative household employment surveys, one can detect a growing gap in access by race, income and home language.

For example, among those born in 1990, university attainment rates were only about 5% for those self-identifying as 'black' and 8% for those self-identifying as 'indigenous'. The rates were about 20% for those who described themselves as '*mestizo*' and 25% for those who were 'white'. These gaps have not been accurately measured until now.

It is worrisome that the gaps seem to be growing, and it was to reverse this trend that the constitution declared that public higher education would be free of direct costs to students.

Despite an admirable goal, if one analyses surveys conducted a year after the suspension of user fees, it is possible to observe a widening gap in access to Ecuador's public universities, following the suspension of fees: there is a growing attendance gap between the more-**privileged** and less-privileged populations of the country.

Consider two findings from these analyses.

First, we can consider postsecondary access depending on the language spoken by a child's parents. Only 4% of college-age children whose parents spoke an indigenous language were in public universities in 2007 (before the reform), and this increased only to 5% by 2009, with 'free' tuition. By contrast, in 2007 the college-going rate was 13% for those whose parents spoke only Spanish, and their rate increased to 17% by 2009. Consequently, the gap between groups is greater now than in 2007.

Second, consider a simple indicator of family poverty. Ecuador uses a sophisticated metric of income and household welfare to define which households are qualified to receive a monthly supplement of US$38. From 2007 to 2009, one sees a slight increase in the rates (from 4% to 7%) of children going to a university whose mothers received the Human Development Bond and who thus could be considered 'poor'. This is the good news.

But the greatest beneficiaries after 2008 were not this population. There was a much bigger jump in attendance among children whose mothers did not receive the Human Development Bond: from 16% to 24%. Again, the gap between poor and middle-class children grew larger.

Those most likely to **forego** employment and finish secondary education are children whose parents do not speak indigenous languages, those who are *mestizo* or white, those with upper-income fathers, and those with highly educated mothers.

For this reason, the beneficiaries of 'free' university education will necessarily come from the most advantaged populations of Ecuador – unless the quality of primary and secondary education improves, allowing more disadvantaged children access to higher education.

From an article by David Post, www.universityworldnews.com, September 2011

ARTICLE GLOSSARY

equity: fairness
fathom: understand
sliding scale: system of gradually increasing amounts
cohort: group born in school year
privileged: having advantages (e.g. financial)
forego: miss, do without

ACTIVITY 4

1 Is a college education really 'free'? Draw a conclusion, using the points raised in the article to defend your opinion.

2 Consider the increasing gap between rich and poor learners in Ecuador. After reviewing the issues raised in the article, work in groups of three (or on your own) to propose a well-thought out, workable solution to this problem.

3 Be prepared to defend your proposal to the class by considering limits to your proposed ideas and potential opposition.

Analysing evidence and drawing conclusions

Consider the following scenario. At a recent school board meeting, citizens of the Triton Harbour School District decided it was time to adopt a new education plan. Over the next five years, they will begin implementing a new system of education in ten secondary schools across the area. If the plan works, they will increase implementation to all schools in the district over the next ten years.

Read Texts 2–4, which give information about the three proposals that the Triton Harbour citizens have to choose from when they vote next week, and read the 'Additional considerations'. Then complete Activity 5.

Text 2

Proposal A: The Renaissance Project

A skills-based environment where multiple subjects are fused together as the basis for a single project.

- Each project cycle lasts six weeks, ending in a presentation where students present and defend their projects to a 'learning panel'.

- Students meet with project directors throughout their experience and select lessons to attend based on the learning needs for their projects.

- Students are assessed against four standards in critical thinking and two standards to assess 'soft' skills.

Sample learning experience

Jacob is interested in how belief can be a driving force in bringing people together as well as driving them apart. He is currently working on the following project:

Theme: World religions

Subjects: History, literature, art

Evidence of learning:

- Interactive timeline of historical events

- Charcoal rendering of historical symbols and famous artistic images to show interrelationship as well as contrast of beliefs, morals, and values

- Interpretation of several religious texts from different points of view

Text 3

Proposal B: Ideation Institute

Students work with mentors from local businesses to solve community problems.

- Students learn the leadership and problem-solving skills to eventually launch their own business idea.

- Each learner takes part in weekly field visits to learn how a business operates and how to work through issues including: product design, marketing, budgeting, inventory, competition, etc.

- Students meet in the classroom for instructional lessons three times a week.

Sample learning experience

Deana is interested in furniture design and wants to start her own business selling her work. This term, she is working with natural wood cuts from the local area and combining them with re-purposed metals from a local factory. She has been paired with a local carpenter and has made $1200 in sales from community opportunities such as festivals and art stand events. She is currently preparing to launch an online shop in early spring.

Text 4

Proposal C: Mind Masters Online Academy

Students meet on-site but complete coursework online for an individualised, multi-level learning experience.

- Learning guides (LGs) facilitate the learning process each day while students work through various skills. Once they master a skill, students move on at their own pace to the next one. Students learn across two or more grades for two or more years.

- Traditional subjects (i.e. English, maths, history, science) are taught. Students can also choose from several options.

- LGs offer physical support through small-group instruction, project-based learning, and individual mentoring, though mentors are not allowed to instruct.

- Daily yoga 'brain breaks' and weekly field trips are part of the programme.

Sample learning experience

Farrah attends school from 9 a.m. to 2 p.m. each day and studies the same subjects as her peers attending traditional high schools in the district. She is very shy in groups but has made strides in socialising during 'brain break' activities and field trips. She is taking several more options than she could under the traditional programme because she has the ability to move at her own pace. With an interest in maths, Farrah has moved swiftly through several accounting courses so her LG has set up an internship experience for her this summer.

A fair amount of students who have success with this program tend to graduate earlier than their peers at traditional schools, and may acquire an associate's degree in add on to a diploma.

Additional considerations

District profile

Graduation rate: 72.1%

College readiness: 68.5%

Average student-to-teacher ratio: 26-1

Students eligible for a free or reduced lunch plan: 61%

Students designated as English language learners: 12%

Ethnic representation:

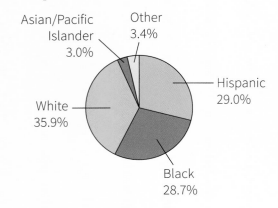

Budgeting

- District will be given the same 1% increase this autumn as they were given last year.

- Funding priorities are: (1) safety, (2) special needs and language acquisition, (3) staff salary increases.

- A proposal for a one-cent sales tax to increase school funding recently passed. The funds may only be used for 'capital' costs such as construction, technology and transport, but cannot be used on 'operating' costs such as salaries, materials and utilities.

Community

- Privately owned schools featuring an emphasis on soft skills acquisition are seeing a spike in admissions.

- Various events are held throughout the year in the local community but it is most well-known for the restaurant tasting each summer and the design festival in the spring.

- Six 'maker spaces' or 'innovation labs' are scheduled to open in early winter.

ACTIVITY 5

1   Select *one* of the proposals outlined and explain why it would be the most difficult to implement, given the considerations provided.

2   In your opinion, what is the biggest hurdle to adopting a new approach districtwide? Explain your answer using evidence from the text and from your own knowledge.

3   If you were a local business owner in Triton Harbour, which proposal would you prefer? In about 120 of your own words, explain your answer.

4   If you were a local benefactor in Triton Harbour, which proposal would you invest in? In about 120 of your own words, explain your answer.

5   Which information from the 'additional considerations' is least relevant in making a decision? Justify your answer.

D Text set 3: Politics and national security

The final text set in this chapter concerns the government's priority to keep the nation safe. As you read the texts concerning international security, think about how the issue applies to your own region or country.

After you have read each article critically, you will be asked to synthesise the information in response to the following essay question:

> Assess society's handling of the recent global migrant crisis.

As you read each article, make note of details which are relevant to the question, which you can then use to begin the writing process later.

Text 1

Sweden should remain a leader in welcoming children

I met Tabish P on a cold day in February at the group home where he lives in Gothenburg. A 16-year-old asylum seeker from Afghanistan, Tabish told me that if he could speak to the Swedish government, he would tell them he is happy here.

Tabish is one of the 35 369 unaccompanied children who sought asylum in Sweden in 2015. In a new report, published today, Human Rights Watch documents delays and difficulties these children face in getting critical care and support. The report is based on research in seven municipalities, including interviews with 50 unaccompanied children as well as with service providers and local officials.

The report recognises Sweden's leadership in providing **sanctuary** to children in need of protection. However, imperfections in the system mean children are not always getting the care they need and to which they are entitled under both international standards and Swedish law and policy. The report documents **shortcomings** in mental and physical health care, the processing of asylum claims, the guardianship system, and housing. Sweden can and should do more to ensure children are not **falling through the cracks**.

Many of the 50 children we interviewed had fled countries like Afghanistan and Syria, where they faced conflict, persecution and hardship, and travelled on their own to Sweden or became separated from their families in transit. Significant numbers experienced further traumas during their journey, including violence at the hands of smugglers and abusive authorities.

I can understand why children feel relief here. Sweden has long been a global leader in providing sanctuary to people who need protection. In many countries, Human Rights Watch has documented the detention and abuse of migrant children, and found children locked up in overcrowded detention centres where they are subject to **degrading** treatment. In Sweden, we met children living in dedicated group homes and learned about laws and practices that guarantee equal access to schools and health care.

Over the past year, people in Sweden have mobilised to welcome new arrivals. We talked with local officials, volunteers, foster parents, service providers and others. Their commitment to the well-being of these particularly **vulnerable** children is commendable.

However, international standards call for prioritising asylum claims by children, but Sweden doesn't. With the general **backlog** of asylum applications, most of the children who arrived last year face an agonising wait for a decision about their future. Extended periods of insecurity can have a particularly harmful effect on children's mental health.

Children also experienced long delays in the appointment of legal guardians. Guardians are responsible for looking after a child's best interest and act as a link between the child and the Swedish bureaucracy. Delays meant children had trouble getting information, support and education.

When we spoke, Tabish had been in Sweden for four months, but had no legal guardian and had yet to visit a doctor for a health screening or meet with a social worker. He told me he thinks about Afghanistan and feels worried and sad, but that he cannot speak with the staff at his group home about his feelings because of the language barrier.

The good news is, these shortcomings can be addressed. The government has already taken steps to understand and improve the situation, including beginning an analysis of the social services provided to unaccompanied children. The national government should enact common sense reforms to ensure children have better access to their rights. The collection of key data on health care and social services, housing, school enrollment and guardianship appointments would help identify gaps and guide policymaking.

Municipalities need increased support through training, guidelines and improved regulations to help them fulfil their responsibilities. The Migration Agency should begin making applications from unaccompanied children a priority. Sweden can continue to be a model for other countries.

From www.hrw.org/news

ARTICLE GLOSSARY

sanctuary: a place of safety

shortcomings: faults or failures

falling through the cracks: forgotten, overlooked

degrading: causing a loss of self-respect

vulnerable: able to be easily hurt or badly treated

backlog: a large number of unfinished things waiting to be completed

asylum: protection given by a state to someone who has left their home country as a refugee

---

Text 2

France and Britain pledge to solve migrant crisis together

Both countries are committed to tackling the problem together and have beefed up security to deter further bids by desperate migrants to smuggle themselves to Britain via the Channel Tunnel, the statement said – a risky undertaking it said had caused 'serious injuries and, tragically, deaths'.

'Tackling this situation is the top priority for the UK and French governments. We are committed and determined to solve this, and to solve it together,' Bernard Cazeneuve and his British counterpart Theresa May wrote in a statement published in France's *Journal Du Dimanche* and in Britain's *Telegraph* newspaper.

Hundreds of migrants have tried to make it into the undersea tunnel in recent weeks in the hopes of finding a way onto a train or lorry headed for Britain. At least ten migrants have died attempting the dangerous journey since June.

Cazeneuve met with May in London on Tuesday to discuss the migrant issue, which has been a thorn in the side of Franco-British relations for years but has taken on fresh urgency following a spike in the number of migrants crossing the Mediterranean.

Earlier this week, the British government pledged 10 million euros ($11 million) to improve fencing around the Eurotunnel rail terminal in Coquelles, outside Calais.

And British Prime Minister David Cameron, who has warned that the crisis could last all summer, promised 'more fencing, more resources, more sniffer dog teams' to aid French police in their nightly cat-and-mouse game with the migrants.

The new measures sent 'a clear message', according to May and Cazeneuve. 'Our border is secure, and there is no easy way into the UK.'

They said the world was facing 'a global migration crisis' that required a European and international response, and warned that the burden of tackling the problem should not lie with Britain and France alone.

'Many of those in Calais and attempting to cross the Channel have made their way there through Italy, Greece or other countries,' the pair wrote.

Ultimately, the crisis had to be addressed at the roots by 'reducing the number of migrants who are crossing into Europe from Africa' for economic reasons.

'Our streets are not paved with gold,' they said, adding that both governments were currently sending back around 200 migrants a month who do not qualify for **asylum**.

Separately, a French opposition MP from northern France on Sunday accused Cameron of failing to grasp the 'severity of the problem', and said the migrants should not be stopped from going to England if no stronger measures were taken.

'If he continues not to propose anything else, let's let the migrants leave and let Mr Cameron handle his politics in his own way, but on his own island,' lawmaker Xavier Bertrand, a former employment minister, told *Journal Du Dimanche*.

From http://www.france24.com/en

Text 3

Patrols to block expected 1.5 million refugees flooding across Europe

The European Commission and Turkey have agreed on a plan to stem the flow of refugees to Europe by patrolling Turkey's frontier with Greece and setting up new camps, a newspaper cited sources in the commission and the German government as saying on Sunday.

Frankfurter Allgemeine Sonntagszeitung said that, according to the plan, Turkey would be obliged to better protect the border that many migrants have crossed on perilous boat journeys to reach EU territory.

It said the Turkish and Greek coast guards would work together to patrol the eastern Aegean, co-ordinated by Frontex, the European Union's border control agency, and send all refugees back to Turkey.

In Turkey, six new refugee camps for up to 2 million people would be set up, partly financed by the EU. The EU states would commit to taking some of the refugees so that up to half a million people could be relocated to Europe without having to use traffickers or take the dangerous journey across the Mediterranean.

German authorities expect up to 1.5 million asylum seekers to arrive in Germany this year, the *Bild* daily newspaper said in a report to be published on Monday, up from a previous estimate of 800,000 to 1 million.

Bild said the German authorities were concerned about the risk of a 'breakdown of provisions' and that they were already struggling to procure enough living containers and sanitary facilities for the new arrivals.

'Migratory pressures will increase further. We now expect seven to ten thousand illegal border crossings every day in the fourth quarter,' *Bild* cited the report as saying.

'This high number of asylum seekers runs the risk of becoming an extreme burden for the states and municipalities,' the report said.

From an article by Michelle Martin,
www.smh.com.au/world

Text 4

'Rich nations' self-interest means refugee crisis set to get worse, not better'

Wealthy countries have shown a complete absence of leadership and responsibility, leaving just ten countries, which account for less than 2.5% of world GDP, to take in 56% of the world's refugees, said Amnesty International in a comprehensive assessment of the global refugee crisis published today.

The report 'Tackling the global refugee crisis: From shirking to sharing responsibility', documents the precarious situation faced by many of the world's 21 million refugees. While many in Greece, Iraq, on the island of Nauru, or at the border of Syria and Jordan are in dire need of a home, others in Kenya and Pakistan are facing growing harassment from governments.

'Just ten of the world's 193 countries host more than half its refugees. A small number of countries have been left to do far too much just because they are neighbours to a crisis. That situation is inherently unsustainable, exposing the millions fleeing war and persecution in countries like Syria, South Sudan, Afghanistan, and Iraq to intolerable misery and

suffering,' said Amnesty International Secretary General Salil Shetty.

'It is time for leaders to enter into a serious, constructive debate about how our societies are going to help people forced to leave their homes by war and persecution. They need to explain why the world can bail out banks, develop new technologies and fight wars, but cannot find safe homes for 21 million refugees, just 0.3% of the world's population.'

Refugees across the world in dire need

The report underlines the urgent need for governments to increase significantly the number of refugees they take in, documenting the plight of refugees on all continents.

Sent back to conflict zones and human rights violations

- Growing numbers of refugees in Pakistan and Iran are fleeing Afghanistan in the face of an intensifying conflict. Authorities have already forced more than 10 000 to return to their war-torn country.

- The Kenyan government wants to reduce the size of the Dadaab refugee camp's population by 150 000 people by the end of 2016. So far, they've returned more than 20 000 Somali refugees.
- More than 75 000 refugees fleeing Syria are currently trapped at the border with Jordan in a narrow stretch of desert known as the berm.

Kept in dire conditions

- In South-east Asia, Rohingya refugees and asylum seekers from Myanmar live in constant fear of arrest, detention, and persecution. In detention centres in Malaysia the Rohingya and other refugees and asylum-seekers endure a range of harsh conditions, including overcrowding, and are at risk of disease, physical and sexual abuse, and even death due to lack of proper medical care.
- The report accuses some EU countries and Australia of using 'systemic human rights violations and abuse as a policy tool' to keep people out. In July 2016, Amnesty International found that the 1 200 women, men and children living on Australia's offshore detention centre on Nauru suffer severe abuse, inhumane treatment, and neglect.

Forced to take dangerous journeys

- In 2015 more than 1 million refugees and migrants reached Europe by sea, with almost 4 000 feared drowned. More than 3 500 fatalities have already died in the first nine months of 2016.
- Refugees and asylum-seekers fleeing growing violence in Central America's Northern Triangle have faced kidnappings, extortion, sexual assault and killings during the journey through Mexico towards the US border.

'The refugee crisis is not limited to the Mediterranean. All over the world refugee's lives are at risk,' said Salil Shetty.

Countries neighbouring conflicts left to shoulder vast majority of world's refugees

The report says that unequal sharing of responsibility is exacerbating the global refugee crisis and the many problems faced by refugees. It calls on all countries to accept a fair proportion of the world's refugees, based on objective criteria that reflect their capacity to host refugees.

The report says a basic common-sense system for assessing countries' capacity to host refugees, based on criteria like wealth, population and unemployment, would make it clear which countries are failing to do their fair share.

The report highlights the stark contrast in the number of refugees from Syria taken in by its neighbours and by other countries with similar populations.

- For example, the UK has taken in fewer than 8000 Syrians since 2011, while Jordan – with a population almost 10 times smaller than the UK and just 1.2% of its GDP – hosts more than 655 000 refugees from Syria.
- Lebanon, with a population of 4.5 million, a land mass of 10 000km^2 and a GDP per capita of US\$10 000, hosts over 1.1 million refugees from Syria , while New Zealand with the same population but a land mass of 268 000km^2 and a GDP per capita of US\$42 000 has only taken in 250 refugees from Syria to date.
- Ireland, with a population of 4.6m, a land mass seven times bigger than Lebanon and an economy five times larger, has so far only welcomed 758 refugees from Syria.

'The problem is not the global number of refugees, it is that many of the world's wealthiest nations host the fewest and do the least,' said Salil Shetty.

'If every one of the wealthiest countries in the world were to take in refugees in proportion to their size, wealth and unemployment rate, finding a home for more of the world's refugees would be an eminently solvable challenge. All that is missing is cooperation and political will.'

More governments must show leadership

The report cites Canada as an example of how, with leadership and vision, states can resettle large numbers of refugees in a timely manner.

Canada has resettled nearly 30 000 Syrian refugees since November 2015. Slightly more than half were sponsored by the Canadian government, with close to 11 000 others arriving through private sponsorship arrangements. As of late August 2016, an additional

181

18 000 Syrians' applications were being processed – mainly in Lebanon, Jordan and Turkey.

Today only around 30 countries run some kind of refugee resettlement programme, and the number of places offered annually falls far short of the needs identified by the UN. If this increased to 60 or 90,

it would make a significant impact on the crisis, the report said.

The figures in the report are based on UNHCR and UNRWA figures, as well as government and NGO figures where relevant.

From https://www.amnesty.org/en/latest/news

ACTIVITY 6

Using Texts 1–4, develop an argument using a discursive approach that responds to the essay question:

> Assess society's handling of the recent, global migrant crisis.

Remember to:

- develop context
- present an objective thesis
- use topic sentences to direct points
- make perspectives clear
- where appropriate, use lenses and/or perspectives to distinguish between points
- use transitions to move appropriately back and forth between points
- where applicable, consider potential solutions or make recommendations for resolving the issue
- consider limits and consequences
- pass a final judgement on the issue by taking a side (based on the evidence you have provided!)
- end on a positive note.

E Practising what you have learnt

Use the following exam-style questions on this chapter's theme of *Government priorities* as practice for arguments featuring either approach you learned in this unit. Allow yourself no more than 1 hour 15 minutes to complete this task. If resources allow, draft your essay electronically.

EXAM-STYLE QUESTIONS 2

Essay questions

1. What is the greatest political challenge currently facing your country and how well is it being tackled? **[30]**
2. 'Protest is an important part of the democratic process.' What is your view? **[30]**
3. How well can democracy thrive when corruption is widespread? **[30]**
4. In your opinion, should education be run by private entities or the state? **[30]**
5. To what extent does your government make good use of tax revenue? **[30]**
6. Assess the least and the most important areas of government spending. **[30]**
7. Consider the consequences of forming alliances with neighbouring countries or communities. **[30]**
8. Is the money spent on prestigious events such as the Olympics or royal weddings ever justifiable? **[30]**
9. How effective are global organisations in solving the world's problems? **[30]**

Summary

Key points to remember from this chapter:

- Manipulating and re-purposing information from other sources helps you remember what you have read; this is why text-based writing activities can be particularly useful in broadening your general knowledge base.

- You can sharpen your own argumentative strategies by observing the way that others (1) appeal to their audience, (2) organise ideas and (3) reason through an issue.

- Proposing solutions to problems can help you convince your audience to accept your ideas and provide closure to your writing.

- Considering the credibility of sources helps you weigh the strength of different perspectives.

Unit 4:
Essential language skills

Chapter 4.1
Use of English

Writing a logical essay with relevant input is important in this course, but your use of English is key to effective communication. This chapter looks at the mechanics of accurate writing, in the context of the theme of *Literature*.

Learning objectives

In this chapter, you will:

- review the parts of speech
- find out why formal grammar in English is important
- learn about the most common writing errors
- edit your own written work, and the work of other students, to help improve your use of English.

A Introduction

When a teacher tells you to use good grammar, what exactly does this mean? Perhaps it means you should use complete sentences or avoid ending a sentence with a preposition. Has a teacher ever enforced a grammar rule, and then another teacher has told you to do things differently? Who should you listen to?

As students, it can be very frustrating to hear conflicting instructions about using language and grammar rules. This chapter will help you to understand why this happens. Once you understand the context of grammar rules, it will help you make your own decisions as a writer.

It can be especially helpful to understand how the various parts of grammatical speech function when you are revising and refining your written work; for example:

- When you are writing for expository purposes, such as in response to a reading comprehension question, the parts of speech that create description, for example *prepositional phrases, adjectives* and *adverbs,* can help you add detail to your writing.
- When you are expressing an argument, words that form the core of a sentence, for example *nouns, pronouns* and *verbs,* are responsible for the tone of a statement.
- When you are writing discursively, *conjunctions* can help you move back and forth between the various perspectives on an issue.

This chapter will help you to review, clarify and develop your existing knowledge of English grammar (and perhaps even challenge it!). It will focus on analysing and understanding the *function* of words and how they are used, and seeing how grammar rules are applied.

B Understanding grammar

The 'rules' of a language are based on what its speakers agree is appropriate. The important question is whether the rules come from one individual's preference or from collective social habit.

As an example of what this means, consider the following phrases. Based on what you know, pick the one you think is grammatically correct:

1	literature's finest author
2	literatures finest author
3	literature finest author

As an English speaker, you probably recognise that:

- option 1 is correct because the use of *'s* is showing *possession*, which is the aim of the phrase
- the lack of apostrophe in option 2 makes the word 'literature' *plural*, which is *not* the aim of the phrase
- the last option is incorrect grammar because without the *s*, the phrase sounds incomplete.

Because you and other English speakers accept the statements above as true, the following grammar rule is created from collective social habit:

> To form the possessive singular of a noun, use *'s*.

The majority of English speakers use *'s* when forming possessive nouns, therefore it is considered grammatically correct. Rules like this, known as **descriptive grammar**, are therefore based on a society's active use of English. In this unit, you will review the descriptive information that characterises each part of speech. This will include a brief look at the definition and function of each part of speech, before moving on to strategies for applying this knowledge to reduce errors in your own writing.

As a student, you have probably been exposed to **prescriptive grammar** rules, too. These are not really 'rules' as such. Rather, they are more like pieces of advice which tell you how you *should* (or should *not*) use language. They are based on style and preference, rather than use. In other words, prescriptive grammar is based on the *idea* of what is acceptable, rather than what native speakers actually accept.

 KEY TERMS

Descriptive grammar: rules determining appropriate language use based on how it is actually used by its speakers.

Prescriptive grammar: advice based on someone's *preference* for what is 'grammatically correct'.

An example of prescriptive grammar, which you may have heard before, is to avoid the use of *clichés* (phrases which have been used too much and are no longer interesting). When you use these, your writing does not contain any of your own fresh expression. Unlike with descriptive grammar, if you break a prescriptive rule it will not necessarily make the sentence *grammatically* incorrect.

Instead, it may have an impact on your style, or it may lead to a less formal tone in your communication. For example:

Prescriptive rule	Example where the rule is ignored
Avoid ending a sentence with a preposition	*What's up?* *What's this for?*

Clearly there are cases when ending a sentence with a preposition is acceptable, even preferable. You will notice that these examples are conversational and informal. In this course you are expected to write in a style appropriate for serious discussion, avoiding conversational style, so you will probably not break many prescriptive suggestions. (But if you do, it may not actually be 'wrong' in terms of syntax!)

More often than not, both teachers and students confuse prescriptive *suggestions* with descriptive *rules*. This often leads to classroom disputes about what is considered grammatically correct. The important thing to bear in mind is: if a 'rule' tells you there is something wrong in your writing, but the error cannot be identified specifically in the function of the word or phrase, then it is probably *prescriptive* advice rather than a grammatical error.

In your writing you should aim to use descriptive knowledge of grammar, and your best judgement, to:

- express ideas clearly
- maintain an academic register as far as possible

ACTIVITY 1

Read the following advice about using language. Decide whether you think each sentence is a *descriptive* statement (based on grammatical accuracy) or *prescriptive* advice (based on style and personal preference).

1 Avoid clichés.
2 Verbs should agree with their subjects.
3 Omit contractions.
4 Do not use double negatives (e.g. 'The library didn't have no books.').
5 Do not start a sentence with *because*.
6 Do not end a sentence with a preposition.
7 Do not split infinitives (e.g. *Mya decided to quickly run to the media centre.*).

8 Do not use a comma to split independent clauses (e.g. *This year's writing festival is quickly approaching, our group is entering one of the contests.*)
9 Use dashes in place of brackets (parentheses).
10 Use active voice, not passive.

You will learn more about these descriptive and prescriptive statements in the later chapters of this unit.

C Prescriptive grammar

The purpose of prescriptive grammar is to provide standards for language. This gives academic language its shape, and discourages an approach to language that is too relaxed for certain circumstances such as a formal essay.

DID YOU KNOW?

The word 'grammar' comes from the Greek word *gramma* which means 'writing' or 'letter'. In the Roman Empire, the Ancient Romans developed the practice of looking at patterns of words to teach Latin.

Following this kind of advice can improve the quality of your writing. Keep in mind, however, that these rules are based on someone's *idea* of what is acceptable. They are suggestions that should be followed much of the time, but they are certainly not unbreakable rules.

As an example, prescriptive grammarians William Strunk Jr and E.B. White (see Section *E Breaking the 'rules'?* later in this chapter) warn against using too many simple sentences in a row. If used appropriately, however, simple sentences can be especially powerful; some of the most classic opening lines in literature are famously simple in construction:

- 'Call me Ishmael.' *Moby Dick* by Hermann Melville
- 'All children, except one, grow up.' *Peter Pan* by J.M. Barrie
- 'It was love at first sight.' *Catch 22* by Joseph Heller
- 'Under certain circumstances, there are few hours more agreeable than the hour dedicated to the ceremony known as afternoon tea.' *Portrait of a Lady* by Henry James
- 'All this happened, more or less.' *Slaughterhouse-Five* by Kurt Vonnegut
- 'It was a pleasure to burn.' *Fahrenheit 451* by Ray Bradbury
- 'I am an invisible man.' *Invisible Man* by Ralph Ellison

Ernest Hemingway (1899–1961) is well known for his uncomplicated writing style.

KEY SKILLS

There are several types of sentence structures: *simple, complex, compound* and *complex-compound*. In Chapter 4.4, you will learn how each is formed.

Another classic example of a prescriptive recommendation tells writers not to split infinitives. Yet the famous quotation, 'To boldly go where no man has gone before', from the hit science fiction television series *Star Trek,* has made history out of this prescriptive error!

In the same way, you may use sentence fragments (incomplete sentences) in an essay to achieve a certain effect – though prescriptive rules of grammar tell you not to. Some grammar books may advise you to avoid using passive forms of verbs, but you might find that the passive voice is the better way to express a specific idea. In both cases, deviating from the rules of prescriptive grammar is not wrong. What matters is how effective your grammar decisions are, and how clearly you express your ideas.

As grammarian Strunk has said, however: 'Unless he is certain of doing well, [the writer] will probably do best to follow the rules.' As a developing writer, it might be best to stick to some of the prescriptive rules you are learning for now. As your language skills develop, you will be able to make more informed decisions about when it is appropriate to bypass advice on style.

ACTIVITY 2

1   Read the sentence written by a student in an essay, and read the teacher's feedback:

> **Student's sentence**
>
> The novel 'Things Fall Apart' by Chinua Achebe, should be read by all high school students due to the fact that it covers the timeless struggle between change and tradition.
>
> **Teacher's feedback**
>
> Avoid passive voice 'should be read by'.
> Awkward/wordy phrase 'due to the fact that'.

2   Using the teacher's feedback, revise the student's sentence.
3   Now decide: should the student follow the prescriptive advice the teacher has given? To what extent is it necessary? Justify your answer.

You can use the phrase 'due to the fact that' in your writing without being grammatically incorrect. However, the purpose of this advice is to encourage word economy. What single word could replace the student's five-word phrase?

DID YOU KNOW?

Prescriptive grammarian William Strunk (Section *E Breaking the 'rules'?*) hated the phrase 'student body' (meaning all the students at a particular school or college), insisting on 'studentry' instead. International best-selling author Stephen King (Section *E Breaking the 'rules'?*) detests adverbs and the phrase 'at this point in time'. From a descriptive standpoint, however, none of these are grammatically inaccurate.

Prescriptive guidance will only be offered in this chapter where it is most likely to affect the formal quality of your writing. As a general rule, you should keep prescribed advice in mind, but you should rely more on a combination of descriptive knowledge, word function (syntax) and your own best judgement when you communicate your ideas.

D Why grammar matters

Look back at the discussion that took place in Chapter 1.2 Section *F Key elements of an essay* regarding grammar's role in communication. Body paragraphs 1 and

2 (following Activity 4) told you that leaders like presidents and prime ministers should exercise good grammar when speaking to their audience because it builds trust and respect. When two friends are gossiping about what happened at last week's school disco, however, formal grammar probably is not as necessary. In fact, it might even be thought very strange!

Depending on the context of the situation, the use of proper grammar can be important. In this course you are writing for an academic purpose, so it is important to use an appropriate means of communication, such as choosing an appropriate register. It also requires:

- accurate grammar
- correct spelling
- proper use of punctuation.

These are collectively known as **mechanics**.

 KEY TERM

Mechanics: a collective term which refers to the various technical aspects of your writing, including grammar, spelling and punctuation.

The importance of mechanics can be seen in this way: you may have a lot of interesting ideas and opinions to share with your audience, but if you do not express them clearly, the message will never be received. Minimising *mechanical errors* is the only way to ensure you get your point across clearly!

Common writing errors

Look at the list of common writing errors in the table. In the remaining chapters of this unit, each of the **parts of speech** will be presented. Once you understand the function of words, and their role in **syntax**, you will be better able to avoid the common errors associated with each of these parts of speech.

 KEY TERMS

Parts of speech: the categories to which words are assigned based on their *syntactic* function (see **syntax**); English has the following parts of speech: nouns, pronouns, verbs, adjectives, adverbs, conjunctions, prepositions and interjections.

Syntax: the rules about the arrangement of words in phrases, clauses and sentences.

Common writing error	Parts of speech section that will address this error
Apostrophe misuse Confusing plurals and possessives	Chapter 4.3 Section *C Pronouns*
Subject–verb agreement When the subject of a sentence does not agree with the verb that relates to it	Chapter 4.3 Section *D Verbs*
Pronoun–antecedent agreement When a pronoun does not agree with its antecedent	Chapter 4.3 Section *C Pronouns*
Confusion between adjective and adverb forms	Chapter 4.2 Section *E Adverbs*
Comma splices When commas are used inappropriately to join together two independent clauses	Chapter 4.3 Section *D Verbs*
Run-ons When two independent clauses are present but do not contain proper punctuation to separate them	Chapter 4.3 Section *D Verbs*
Fragments When a thought expressed does not contain a subject and verb to complete it	Chapter 4.2 Section *C* *Common errors*
Shifting pronouns and use of 'you'	Chapter 4.3 Section *C Pronouns*
Misplaced modifiers When a description is placed too far away from the word it modifies	Chapter 4.2 Section *B Prepositions*

The parts of speech

This unit divides the parts of speech into three broad categories:

Speech parts that add detail	• prepositions • adjectives • adverbs
Speech parts that are essential	• nouns • pronouns • verbs
Speech parts that add complexity and emotion	• conjunctions • interjections

- Some *speech parts* add detail and specifics to your writing.
- Others are necessary for a sentence to be complete (subject + verb).
- There are other speech parts that extend simple sentences, make a sentence more complex, and those that add emotion and effect.

This unit assumes you will already know at least something about the parts of speech, but you will find it helpful to review these because being able to identify them will prove useful to you as a writer.

To demonstrate how identifying parts of speech can help improve your writing, look at the following sentence, taken from James Hurst's short story, 'The Scarlet Ibis':

> On the topmost branch a bird about the size of a chicken, with scarlet feathers and long legs, was perched precariously.

The scarlet ibis is a species of bird which inhabits tropical locations in South America and parts of the Caribbean. James Hurst uses the scarlet ibis as a symbol for loneliness and disconnectedness in his short story, 'The Scarlet Ibis'.

What is the subject of the sentence? Take a minute to identify it either on your own or with a partner. Is the subject 'branch', 'bird' or 'chicken'?

To find the subject, consider the following approach. Descriptive rules tells us that the subject never appears in a prepositional phrase, so get rid of those first:

> ~~On the topmost branch~~ a bird ~~about the size of a chicken, with scarlet feathers and long legs,~~ was perched precariously.

Now clear away any other non-essential words such as adjectives and adverbs:

> ~~On the topmost branch~~ a bird ~~about the size of a chicken, with scarlet feathers and long legs,~~ was perched ~~precariously.~~

Look at what remains. What is the subject? The bird! And what is the action the bird is performing? Perching (or, 'was perched' as it reads in the sentence).

If you can accurately identify the subject and verb of a sentence, you can avoid errors such as sentence fragments. This will help to improve the overall quality of your writing.

In this unit, you will learn about each of the parts of speech, and the common errors associated with them. Similar to the way this example was designed, the next chapter will begin with a review of the speech parts that add detail. Once you can identify these, it will be much easier to find the subject and verb of your sentences to ensure they are complete!

Once you have worked through the exercises in this unit, you can improve your own writing by applying your knowledge of how words function. At the start of each chapter (4.2–4.5), you will be asked to complete a themed writing activity. At the end of each chapter, you will have the opportunity to review your written work, and apply what you have learnt about the structure and function of words to your writing.

E Breaking the 'rules'?

In 1918, William Strunk Jr and E.B. White, two very influential figures in the world of grammar, published their classic guide, *The Elements of Style*. This slim edition contains both descriptive and prescriptive advice, ranging from misused expressions to matters of syntax. In 2011, *Time* magazine named it one of the 100 best and most influential books of its time. And though the advice they offer is followed in academic institutions the world over (some even appearing in this unit!), Strunk and White's prescriptive list is still a source of intense debate among grammarians and word lovers even today.

The following three extracts offer different perspectives on the advice given by grammar experts Strunk and White in their 1918 book, *The Elements of Style*. Read Perspectives 1–3 and complete the exam-style questions that follow each of them.

Perspective 1

Must you write complete sentences each time, every time? Perish the thought. If your work consists only of fragments and floating clauses, the Grammar Police aren't going
5   to come and take you away. Even William Strunk, that **Mussolini** of rhetoric, recognized the delicious pliability of language. 'It is an old observation,' he writes, 'the best writers sometimes disregard the rules of rhetoric.'
10 Yet he goes on to add to this thought, which I urge you to consider: 'unless he is certain of doing well, [the writer] will probably do best to follow the rules.'

Writer Stephen King has his own views about how far we should follow established rules of grammar.

The telling clause here is *unless he is certain of doing well*. If you don't have a rudimentary
15 grasp of how the parts of speech translate into coherent sentences, how can you be certain that you *are* doing well?

[...]

Verbs come in two types, active and passive. With an active verb, the subject of the sentence is doing something. With a passive verb, something is being done to the
20 subject of the sentence. The subject is just letting it happen. *You should avoid the passive tense*. I'm not the only one who says so; you can find the same advice in *The Elements of Style*.

Messrs Strunk and White don't speculate as to why so many writers are attracted to passive verbs, but I'm willing to … I think timid writers … feel the passive voice somehow
25 lends their work authority, perhaps even a quality of majesty. If you find instruction manuals and lawyers' torts majestic, I guess it does.

The timid fellow writes, 'the meeting will be held at 7 o'clock', because that somehow says to him, 'put it this way and people will believe *you really know*'. [Instead], throw back your shoulders, stick out your chin, and put that meeting in charge! Write, 'the meeting's at
30 seven'. There, by God! Don't you feel better?

Stephen King, *On Writing: a Memoir of the Craft*

ARTICLE GLOSSARY

Benito Mussolini: an Italian dictator and founder of the Italian Fascist Party

Answer the comprehension questions **1–6**.

1 Using your own words as far as possible, explain how King feels about Strunk and White's advice. **[2]**

2 What is meant by the term 'Grammar Police'? Explain using your own words. **[2]**

3 Provide one synonym for each of the following words as they are used in the text: **[5]**

    a perish (line 2)

    b pliability (line 7)

    c rudimentary (line 14)

    d coherent (line 15)

    e speculate (line 23)

4 What can be inferred by the phrase, 'that Mussolini of rhetoric' (line 6). Justify your response. **[3]**

5 Why does King believe you should avoid the passive voice? Explain, using your own words. **[2]**

6 What is the tone of the extract? Provide at least two examples from the extract that help develop the tone. **[3]**

7 Using your own knowledge, consider the benefits and drawbacks of breaking grammar rules and advice. Provide examples to illustrate your points. **[8]**

Total marks: 25

Perspective 2

Don't dismiss adverbs!

Not too long ago, on Facebook, aspiring **MFAs** were proudly announcing that they had spent entire revision sessions **excising** from their manuscripts every ' ord ending in -*ly*. Quoting Stephen King (who was perhaps quoting Nathaniel Hawtho ie), they assured each other that *The Road to Hell is Paved with Adverbs*. Well, with all due respect to
5   Mr King and Mr Hawthorne, it just ain't so.

To begin with, an adverb is not merely a word that happens to end in –*ly*. An adverb is one of the four content parts of speech (the others are nouns, verbs, and adjectives) which enable us to construct sentences. Every part of speech *does* something in a sentence: nouns name things, verbs provide action, adjectives and adverbs add to or limit or clarify the nouns and
10   verbs. A writer determined to eliminate adverbs will be a seriously handicapped writer, for adverbs can make more specific, add information to, not only verbs, but also adjectives and other adverbs. Adverbs, like the other content parts of speech, are essential for every writer's toolkit; they can do things that the other parts of speech cannot.

The 'death to all adverbs' crew also clearly don't understand that adverbs are not only
15   single words. Every content part of speech – noun or verb, adjective or adverb – can take different forms. That's because a part of speech is a *role* that a word, or a group of words, plays in a sentence. So the role of the adverb can be played by a

- single word: *Joe went* **home**.
- a phrase: *I'll call you* **in the morning**.
20
- a dependent cause: *We'll eat* **whenever he gets here**.

And, as in this sentence from Dickens, an adverb structure can encompass other adverbials and adjectives:

25 *He lived* in a gloomy suite of rooms in a lowering pile of building up a yard, where it had so little business to be that one could scarcely help fancying it must have run there when it was a young house, playing at hide and seek with other houses, and have forgotten the way out again.

To advise young writers to get rid of all their adverbs is like advising a **pitcher with four great pitches** to throw only three of them [...]

30 Many aspiring writers struggle, not because they don't have great ideas or wonderful stories to tell, but because they don't have the words they need to communicate those ideas or to tell those stories. They try desperately to find the 'unique voice' agents and editors want by paying close attention to their innermost selves. But these writers are looking in the wrong place: Voice is not a function of a writer's self, but of her skill with
35 words. Writers who want to create a distinctive voice on the page need to learn everything they can about how words work, about how they can be combined into sentences. Just like singers, writers who want to develop a great voice need to practice their techniques, over and over and over, so that those techniques become part of them, able to be used at will when they're drafting and revising.

And just like trained singers, writers who've mastered technique can make magic with
40 their voices, **captivating** their readers and making them turn pages. Such a writer's voice can pulse with vitality, swing like music, create all kind of effects inside readers, compel them by sheer syntactical energy to keep turning the pages. It can only do these things, though, when the writer – like all those great writers from earlier eras – has studied, practiced, and mastered the repertoire of syntactical techniques available to those of us
45 writing in English.

Including how to use – with precision, with care, with passion – the adverb.

Barbara Baig, Writer's Digest, *August 2015*

ARTICLE GLOSSARY

MFAs: students studying for their Master of Fine Arts degree

pitcher with four great pitches: a baseball reference: the pitcher is the player who throws the ball to the batter

---

EXAM-STYLE QUESTIONS 2

Answer the comprehension questions **1–6**.

1 What is the purpose of the bulleted list (lines 18–20) found early on in the article? **[2]**

2 Using your own words, explain what the author means by her analogy of young writers and pitchers (lines 27–28). Critique the strength of this comparison. **[4]**

3 How is a writer's voice formed? Explain, using your own words as far as possible. **[3]**

4 What do the following words mean as they are used in the passage?

a Excising (line 2)

b Captivating (line 40) **[2]**

5 What do Freese and King have in common when it comes to studying grammar? Use text evidence from both Perspective 1 and Perspective 2 to support your response. **[6]**

6 To what extent is the use of 'ain't' in the opening paragraph justifiable? Using 80 words or less, discuss. **[8]**

Total marks: 25

Perspective 3

50 years of stupid grammar advice

April 16 is the 50th anniversary of the publication of a little book that is loved and admired throughout American academe.

I won't be celebrating.

5 *The Elements of Style* does not deserve the enormous esteem in which it is held by American college graduates. Its advice ranges from limp platitudes to inconsistent nonsense. Its enormous influence has not improved American students' grasp of English grammar; it has significantly degraded it.

Notice what I am objecting to is not the style advice in *Elements*, which might best be described the way *The Hitchhiker's Guide to the Galaxy* describes Earth: mostly harmless.
10 Some of the recommendations are vapid, like 'Be clear' (how could one disagree?). Some are **tautologous**, like 'Do not explain too much'. (Explaining too much means explaining more than you should, so of course you shouldn't.) Even so, it doesn't hurt to lay such well-meant maxims before novice writers.

Even the truly silly advice, like 'Do not inject opinion', doesn't really do harm. (No force
15 on earth can prevent undergraduates from injecting opinion. And anyway, sometimes that is just what we want from them.) But despite the 'Style' in the title, much in the book relates to grammar, and the advice on that topic does real damage. It is atrocious. Since today it provides just about all of the grammar instruction most Americans ever get, that is something of a tragedy.

20 'Use the active voice' is a typical section head. And the section in question opens with an attempt to discredit passive clauses that is either grammatically misguided or disingenuous.

We are told that the active clause 'I will always remember my first trip to Boston' sounds much better than the corresponding passive 'My first visit to Boston will always be
25 remembered by me'. It sure does. [Similarly,] for me to report that I paid my bill by saying, 'The bill was paid by me' … would sound inane. . [Yet] 'the bill was paid by an anonymous benefactor' sounds perfectly natural. Strunk and White are **denigrating** the passive by presenting an invented example of it deliberately designed to sound **inept**.

After this unpromising start, there is some fairly sensible style advice: The authors explicitly
30 say they do not mean 'that the writer should entirely **discard** the passive voice', which is 'frequently convenient and sometimes necessary'. They give good examples to show that the choice between active and passive may depend on the topic under discussion.

Sadly, writing tutors tend to ignore this moderation, and simply red-circle everything that looks like a passive, just as Microsoft Word's grammar checker underlines every passive
35 in wavy green to signal that you should try to get rid of it.

What concerns me [most] is that the bias against the passive is being retailed by a pair of authors so grammatically clueless that they don't know what is a passive construction and what isn't. Of the four pairs of examples offered to show readers what to avoid and how to correct it, a staggering three out of the four are mistaken diagnoses. [For instance,] 'There

40   were a great number of dead leaves lying on the ground' has no sign of the passive in
it anywhere.

These examples can be found all over the Web in study guides for **freshman** composition
classes. (Try a Google search on 'great number of dead leaves lying'.) I have been told
several times, by both students and linguistics-faculty members, about writing instructors

45   who think every occurrence of 'be' is to be condemned for being 'passive'. No wonder, if
Elements is their grammar bible.

'Write with nouns and verbs, not with adjectives and adverbs,' they insist. (The motivation
of this mysterious **decree** remains unclear to me.)

And then, in the very next sentence, comes a negative passive clause containing three

50   adjectives: 'The adjective hasn't been built that can pull a weak or inaccurate noun out
of a tight place.'

Some of the claims about syntax are plainly false despite being respected by the
authors. For example, Chapter IV, in an unnecessary piece of **bossiness**, says that the
split infinitive 'should be avoided unless the writer wishes to place unusual stress on

55   the adverb'. The bossiness is unnecessary because the split infinitive has always been
grammatical and does not need to be avoided.

An entirely separate kind of grammatical inaccuracy in *Elements* is the mismatch with
readily available evidence. Simple experiments (which students could perform for
themselves using downloaded classic texts from sources like www.gutenberg.org) show

60   that Strunk and White preferred to base their grammar claims on intuition and prejudice
rather than established literary usage.

Consider the explicit instruction: 'With none, use the singular verb when the word means
"no one" or "not one"'.

Is this a rule to be trusted? Let's investigate.

65   • Try searching the script of Oscar Wilde's *The Importance of Being Earnest* (1895) for
'none of us'. There is one example of it as a subject: 'None of us are perfect' (spoken
by the learned Dr Chasuble). It has plural agreement.

• Download and search Bram Stoker's *Dracula* (1897). It contains no cases of 'none
of us' with singular-inflected verbs, but one that takes the plural ('I think that none

70   of us were surprised when we were asked to see Mrs Harker a little before the time
of sunset').

It seems to me that the stipulation in *Elements* is totally at variance not just with modern
conversational English but also with literary usage back when Strunk was teaching and
White was a boy.

75   Is the intelligent student supposed to believe that Stoker, Wilde and Montgomery didn't
know how to write? Did Strunk or White check even a single book to see what the
evidence suggested? Did they have any evidence at all for the claim that the cases with
plural agreement are errors? I don't think so.

There are many other cases of Strunk and White's being in conflict with readily verifiable

80   facts about English. Consider the claim that a sentence should not begin with 'however' in
its connective adverb sense ('when the meaning is "nevertheless"').

85 Searching for 'however' at the beginnings of sentences and 'however' elsewhere reveals that good authors alternate between placing the adverb first and placing it after the subject. The ratios vary. Mark Liberman, of the University of Pennsylvania, checked half a dozen of Mark Twain's books and found roughly seven instances of 'however' at the beginning of a sentence for each three placed after the subject. In *Dracula* I found a ratio of about one to five. The evidence cannot possibly support a claim that 'however' at the beginning of a sentence should be **eschewed**.

90 English syntax is a deep and interesting subject. It is much too important to be reduced to a bunch of trivial don't-do-this prescriptions by a pair of idiosyncratic **bumblers** who can't even tell when they've broken their own **misbegotten** rules.

By Geoffrey K Pullum, The Chronicle of Higher Education, *April 2009*

ARTICLE GLOSSARY

tautologous: unnecessarily using two words to express one meaning

denigrating: criticising

inept: unskilled

discard: throw away, stop using

freshman: student in the first year of college

decree: official statement saying that something should happen

bossiness: giving people orders

eschewed: deliberately avoided

bumblers: people who speak in a confused way

misbegotten: badly planned

EXAM-STYLE QUESTIONS 3

Answer the comprehension questions **1–7**.

1 What is Pullum's main objection to *The Elements of Style*? **[1]**

2 What is the purpose of the author's use of a bulleted list toward the end of the extract? **[1]**

3 What is the purpose of the rhetorical question on lines 75–76: 'Is the intelligent student supposed to believe that Stoker, Wilde and Montgomery didn't know how to write?' **[1]**

4 Why does the author mention Mark Liberman in the next to last paragraph? **[2]**

5 How would you describe the overall tone of Perspective 3? Provide three examples of language from the extract that support your response. **[4]**

6 If you were Strunk or White reading this, what would be your response? Respond in roughly 50 words. **[5]**

7 In your own opinion, what do you find most impressive about Pullum's argument? What causes concern? Use evidence from the text to support your claims. **[8]**

Total marks: 25

F Speech parts pre-test

The following activity aims to assess your current knowledge about grammar. However, it also includes some reading comprehension practice.

ACTIVITY 3

Read the biographical extract below, which introduces one of the 20th-century's most influential authors, George Orwell. Match each of the underlined words **1–20** in the text with the correct part of speech **a–h**.

a noun

b pronoun

c verb

d adjective

e adverb

f preposition

g conjunction

h interjection

British author George Orwell tackled hardline issues of his time (1) <u>with</u> special emphasis on (2) <u>fascism</u>, imperialism and communism. The mark he has made on the literary world is unmistakable, but his nod toward politics is equally impressive.

Arguably his best work, Orwell's novel *Nineteen Eighty-Four* is a story which (3) <u>tactfully</u> critiques Stalinism and Naziism. Winston Smith, the novel's protagonist, rebels against the government (4) <u>because</u> he despises their **callous** abuse of power. Specifically, as an employee at the (5) <u>Ministry of Truth</u>, Winston observes (6) <u>first-hand</u> how truth is easily **distorted** – deleted, even – to suit the purposes of the government's (7) **<u>figurehead</u>**, Big Brother. In his personal life, (8) <u>he</u> despises the fact that his every move is monitored by (9) <u>government</u> surveillance. Teaming up with those who he thinks are other rebels, Winston Smith endeavours to fight back against such injustices, (10) <u>and</u> he does so in the name of the future.

Orwell's storylines were **eerily** familiar to contemporary readers of the time, and they (11) <u>continue</u> to send a haunting message to (12) <u>audiences</u> today. The message he sends in each of these selections is a clear warning to beware the threat of totalitarianism, manipulation and

Images of dystopian writer George Orwell (who coined the phrase 'Big Brother is watching you') appeared on banners during recent nationwide protests in Germany against spying and surveillance.

control. (13) <u>Wow</u>, there is no doubt Orwell's ability to compose such a timeless message is nothing short of masterful! Any time society wants to express (14) <u>their</u> concerns regarding government manipulation, you just might hear the likes of 'doublespeak' and 'newspeak', phrases Orwell himself **coined**. And the next time you feel as though (15) <u>someone</u> is peering in on your privacy, you just might remind yourself of the possibility that 'Big Brother (16) <u>is watching</u> you'.

ARTICLE GLOSSARY

callous: cruel
distorted: changed, bent out of shape
figurehead: leader who has no real power
eerily: in a strange, frightening way
coined: invented

G Practising what you have learnt

Choose from the abridged list of exam-style essay questions on this chapter's theme of *Literature*. Once you have drafted your essay, set aside time to revise your work. Pay attention to the types of grammatical mistakes you make most often in your writing.

EXAM-STYLE QUESTIONS 4

Essay questions

1 'Young adults shouldn't bother reading classic literature because it does not relate to their lives.' Discuss this statement. **[30]**
2 How far would you agree that novels you read for leisure have educational value? **[30]**
3 Should traditional grammar continue to be taught in schools? **[30]**
4 To what extent is it easier to communicate through the written or spoken word? **[30]**
5 'Fiction is much more rewarding to the spirit than non-fiction.' What is your view?

Summary

Key points to remember from this chapter:

- Prescriptive rules represent an individual's idea of what is right or wrong; descriptive rules are what society as a whole deems appropriate.
- Following prescriptive rules can help you assume a more formal tone in writing.
- Breaking prescriptive rules does not necessarily make your writing grammatically incorrect.
- As a general rule, it is best that you follow prescriptive rules until you have a more thorough understanding of how breaking these rules influences style.
- When making stylistic decisions, consider your purpose and audience to help you determine what is acceptable.
- Some prescriptive advice will appear in this unit because it can improve the overall quality of your writing.
- Mechanics (spelling, grammar and punctuation) are important; if your writing is overloaded with errors, your ideas will never be communicated!
- Being able to identify the parts of speech can help you identify errors in your writing.

Chapter 4.2
Parts of speech that add detail

Literature is filled with colourful language and description. Prepositional phrases, adjectives and adverbs are the speech parts responsible for decorating the language of our favourite stories. This chapter continues the unit's focus on the theme of *Literature*.

Learning objectives

In this chapter, you will learn how to:

- identify prepositional, adjectival and adverbial phrases, and understand their function
- use descriptive parts of speech to add detail to your own writing
- identify and revise errors such as sentence fragments and misplaced modifiers
- use commas appropriately to punctuate your writing.

A Using parts of speech

In this chapter, you will have the opportunity to reinforce what you know about:

- prepositions
- adjectives
- adverbs.

As you work through the chapter, you will be asked to think about how these parts of speech play a role in the writing of others, and how you can use them to improve your own writing.

Read the following question and write a one-paragraph response to it.

- Respond as naturally as possible to the question posed.
- Do not worry about editing what you have written, other than what you notice in the moment.
- Write 75–100 words.

> Which do you prefer: fiction (e.g. short stories, novels) or non-fiction (e.g. biographies, memoirs) – and why?

ACTIVITY 1

Discuss your response to the question with a partner.

1 Swap papers and read each other's paragraph silently.
2 Taking turns, share your observations by using as many of the following statement stems as you can, or create your own:
- I am impressed by …
- Tell me what you meant by …
- What made you decide …?
- An observation I made about the content of your paragraph is …
- An observation I made about your paragraph's use of English is …
3 Try rewriting each of your paragraphs together. How can you combine your writing skills to improve the content and structure of your work?

Keep your written response. You will return to it at the end of this chapter.

B Prepositions

To help you to understand prepositions, consider the following exercise. Pick an animal of your choice. Copy the sentence model and continue the list for as long as you can:

> The (animal) is walking <u>beside</u> the mountain.
>
> The (animal) is walking _____ the mountain.
>
> The (animal) is walking _____ the mountain.

The words you chose to fill in the blanks are *prepositions*, whose job is to explain the relationship between a noun or pronoun and another word in a sentence. You may have decided your animal could be walking *on*, *up*, *around* or *through* the mountain (provided there is a tunnel!), all of which are prepositions.

A prepositional phrase can help to explain the relationship between the animal and the mountain.

Not all prepositions are used to show *physical* relationship to a noun (for instance, *during* is a preposition, but you would not say 'during the mountain'!), but thinking about a preposition's physical relationship to another word is one way of remembering this lengthy list.

The most common prepositions are listed on the next page. Note that depending on context, these words can also serve other functions.

Common prepositions		
aboard	by	outside
about	despite	over
above	down	past
across	during	regarding
after	except	round
against	excluding	since
along	following	than
amid	for	through(out)
among	from	to
around	in	toward(s)
at	inside	under
before	into	underneath
behind	like	until
below	near	up
beneath	of	upon
beside(s)	off	via
between	on	with
beyond	onto	within

! **TIP**

The list of prepositions is lengthy. While you have better things to do with your time than memorise the entire list, you should try to become familiar with it. Here are two suggested strategies to acquire a working memory of these words:

- Most prepositions involve the many things your animal can do (see the exercise earlier in this section); for example: *My goat can go above, below, around, outside, over, past, through, near, behind, beneath … the land!*
- Pair the remaining words (or all of them!) with a familiar jingle (slogan or tune) or create your own.

The function of parts of speech

One important thing to understand about parts of speech is that you should not identify them in isolation. Consider this next activity as an illustration of this point:

Identify the prepositions in the following sentence by using the Common prepositions list above.

Following the Taliban's attempt on her life, Malala Yousefzai became the youngest person ever to receive the Nobel Peace Prize for her efforts to defend a woman's right to education.

You may have identified the following words:

<u>Following</u> the Taliban's attempt <u>on</u> her life, Malala Yousefzai became the youngest person ever <u>to</u> receive the Nobel Peace Prize <u>for</u> her efforts <u>to</u> defend a woman's right <u>to</u> education.

Malala Yousefzai

Just because they are all on the list, does this make all the underlined words prepositions? If you are identifying prepositions in isolation, then the answer is yes. If you are taking into account their function, however, the answer is no. Remember that the identity of speech parts depends on their *function* in the sentence.

To properly identify prepositions, it is helpful to know about the larger word group they belong to, called a *prepositional phrase*. Think back to the prepositional phrases created in the animal example (*The goat is walking beside the mountain*, etc):

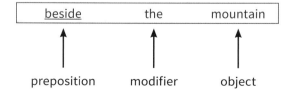

A preposition is almost always followed by a noun or pronoun, called the *object* of the preposition. The object will either answer:

- Who? or
- What?

201

As in:

> Beside ... who? (no one)
>
> Beside ... what? (beside the mountain)

Any words that *modify* (describe) the object are also included in the phrase. In this case, the article *the* acts as an adjective that modifies the mountain. Consider this next example:

> The goat walked *through the long dark tunnel.*

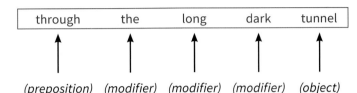

through	the	long	dark	tunnel
(preposition)	(modifier)	(modifier)	(modifier)	(object)

> Through *whom* or *what*? (through the tunnel)
>
> *What kind* of tunnel? (a long, dark one)

With all of this in mind, look back at the practice sentence about Malala. Are the words you initially identified as prepositions actually *functioning* as prepositions?

> <u>Following</u> the Taliban's attempt <u>on</u> her life, Malala Yousefzai became the youngest person ever <u>to</u> receive the Nobel Peace Prize <u>for</u> her efforts <u>to</u> defend a woman's right <u>to</u> education.

Perhaps you noticed that, though 'to' can be a preposition (as is the case with the phrase 'to education'), it is not always functioning this way in the sentence. The phrases 'to receive' and 'to defend' are not prepositional phrases because these prepositions are followed by verbs, not nouns or pronouns. When the word 'to' is followed by a verb, it becomes an *infinitive*. You will learn more about infinitives in Chapter 4.3.

Therefore, the prepositions we can identify in this sentence are:

> <u>Following</u> the Taliban's attempt <u>on</u> her life, Malala Yousefzai became the youngest person ever to receive the Nobel Peace Prize <u>for</u> her efforts to defend a woman's right <u>to</u> education.

ACTIVITY 2

Create a prepositional phrase for each of the prepositions **a–e**. Remember that each preposition should have a noun or pronoun following it that answers the question *Who?* or *What?* (Hint: challenge yourself to include words to modify the object!)

a with

b from

c without

d amid

e since

ACTIVITY 3

This activity is about famous American author Ernest Hemingway, pictured in Chapter 4.1.

1 Read sentences **a–g** and identify the prepositional phrases – identify the preposition and its object.

    a Born in 1899, Ernest Hemingway was an American writer and journalist who was known particularly for his simplified style of writing.

    b Hemingway volunteered on an ambulance unit in the Italian army during World War I.

    c Following an injury, he was decorated by the Italian government.

    d Later, as a reporter for both Canadian and US news sources, he returned to Europe to cover events like the Greek Revolution.

    e Experiences like these paved the way for some of the greatest works of literature in the US literary canon.

    f *The Sun Also Rises* is about a group of American and British expatriates in Paris and explores the notion of post-war resilience.

    g His greatest work, *For Whom the Bell Tolls*, is based on his experiences in the Spanish Civil War.

2 Re-read all the sentences straight through as if they were one paragraph; then answer the following questions.

    a Summarise the content of the sentences in no more than 45 words of your own.

    b Read these sentences *without* the prepositional phrases. What are the benefits of using prepositional phrases in writing? Explain, using your own words, and give at least one example from the activity to illustrate your point.

Why prepositional phrases matter

After all the work you have done to familiarise yourself with prepositions and understand their function in a sentence, you might still be wondering why you need to learn about them. This section will help you link the use of prepositional phrases to your own writing experience in this course.

Prepositional phrases matter for two important reasons:

- They expand the detail of your writing (*content*)
- They add variety to your sentences. (*use of English*)

The writer Edgar Allan Poe (1809–1849).

In contrast to Hemingway's minimalist approach to writing, consider the opening sentence of Edgar Allan Poe's short story, *The Fall of the House of Usher*:

> During the whole of a dull, dark, and soundless day in the autumn of the year, when the clouds hung oppressively low in the heavens, I had been passing alone, on horseback, through a singularly dreary tract of country; and at length found myself, as the shades of evening drew on, within view of the melancholy House of Usher…

This sentence, at a lengthy 59 words, can best be summed up with one word: descriptive. What would happen if the descriptive elements, such as prepositional phrases, adjectives and adverbs (including clauses), were taken out of the sentence?

> ~~During the whole of a dull, dark, and soundless day in the autumn of the year, when the clouds hung oppressively low in the heavens,~~ I had been passing ~~alone, on horseback, through a singularly dreary tract of country;~~ and ~~at length~~ found myself, ~~as the shades of evening drew on, within view of the melancholy House of Usher…~~

While nouns and verbs can be a powerful combination in expressing ideas, prepositions do much to enhance the detail of your writing. Since prepositional phrases can appear anywhere in a sentence, they can add variety to your sentence structure and style.

ACTIVITY 4

Read the extract from a literary essay.
Identify the prepositional phrases.

> In his first novel, *Lanark*, Scottish writer Alasdair Gray may have surpassed even historic local icon, Walter Scott, author of *Ivanhoe*. Gray's story, with its mix of realist and surrealist depictions which are reminiscent of his hometown of Glasgow, has earned its name as a cult classic. This author has been hailed for his extraordinary imagination and the profound message he conveys about love and persistence. With regard to his style, Gray parallels the likes of international icons like Dante, Kafka, Joyce and Carroll, making his work globally timeless.

Notice how the position and use of prepositional phrases in the extract in Activity 4 varies from sentence to sentence. Adding these phrases at the beginning, the middle or at the end of a sentence can add variety for the reader. You will learn more about sentence variety in Chapter 4.4 Section *C Structuring more complex sentences*.

C Common errors

You have seen that unpacking the details of a sentence will reveal what is at its core (centre). This is useful for two reasons. It helps you to know whether you have:

- written complete sentences
- placed descriptive phrases closest to the words they modify.

This section will show you how to check that you have done both of these things.

Sentence fragments

For a sentence to be complete, all it needs is a subject and a verb. If it does not have both, this is called a **sentence fragment**.

KEY TERM

Sentence fragment: a phrase or clause written as a sentence but lacking the essential parts of subject and verb; a fragment does not express a complete thought.

You will need to use complete sentences as part of your formal approach to writing. Being able to identify prepositional phrases can help you do this. In Chapter 4.1 Section *D Why grammar matters* you learnt that the subject of a sentence is never found in a prepositional phrase. If you can remember this rule, you can quickly identify the subject of your own sentences.

Once you have done that, all you have to ask yourself is: what action is that subject performing? If your sentence reveals an answer to that question, then you have a complete sentence!

ACTIVITY 5

Read the following extract, which is taken from a student essay evaluating the qualities that a 'good read' requires. Identify the fragments and rewrite them as complete sentences.

A good writer must transport his reader to another world. People are always drawn to the solace and entertainment of the written word. And use it to escape the mundane of everyday life. It is part of human nature to want to experience what is beyond our reach. For this reason, the intriguing plot lines of tales like George R.R. Martin's *Game of Thrones*. The twists, turns and dramatic developments keep the audience on their toes. The dragon eggs, for example. These are thought to be barren but suddenly catch fire. Hatching formidable beasts which help one of the main characters fight her adversaries for the throne. Plot twists like this make the story more dynamic, and it opens the door for future implications to emerge. Making selections like Martin's, a 'good read', indeed.

Misplaced modifiers, dangling modifiers

When you add detail to your sentences, it makes sense to keep descriptive words close to the words they are describing. If a word or phrase is too far from the word it is meant to modify, it can make the meaning of your sentence less clear. This is called a **misplaced modifier** because it appears in the wrong position in the sentence. While this can occur when using prepositional phrases, it can also take place when using other phrases, so this section will explore both.

KEY TERM

Misplaced modifier: a phrase or clause placed awkwardly in a sentence so that it appears to modify (or refer to) an unintended word.

As an example of this, imagine your classmate told you the following:

'The teacher said she will return our essays on Monday!'

Based on this statement, it appears you will receive your essays on Monday. Monday arrives, however, and the teacher does not return your essays. When you enquire, she responds with the following:

'On Monday, I told the class I would return your essays, but I didn't say when!'

Notice that the misplaced prepositional phrase caused some confusion with you and your classmate. Misplacing modifiers in your own work can have the same effect.

Consider this line from Russian writer Anton Chekhov's short story, 'The Bet', which has been rewritten intentionally here to misplace the modifier:

> He took from a fireproof safe, trying not to make any noise, the key to the door that had been unopened for fifteen years, put on his coat and went out.

Why does this sound strange? What do you think was the original (correct) wording?

The phrase 'trying not to make any noise' appears to modify the fireproof safe, but the male character in the sentence is most probably the one trying not to make any noise! To restore this sentence to its original form, you would need to move the phrase closer to the word it modifies:

> Trying not to make any noise, he took from a fireproof safe the key to the door that had been unopened for fifteen years, put on his coat and went out.

When working with descriptive phrases, you will need to be careful when using phrases to enhance the detail of your writing.

Another problem that can arise when adding description to a sentence is that the word or phrase used to modify does not relate to *any* of the words in the sentence. Unlike misplaced modifiers, a **dangling modifier** cannot be moved in order to clarify the message. An awareness of the various parts of speech used for description can help you avoid this error. For example:

> Looking toward the west, a funnel-shaped cloud stirred up dust.

Consider: was the cloud looking toward the west, or the writer?

It is obvious that a *person* would 'look toward the west', yet there is no person mentioned in the sentence; so the modifier *dangles* (hangs) without having anything to modify.

KEY TERM

Dangling modifier: a word or phrase that modifies a word which is not actually in the sentence.

Consider the next sentence:

> Having been fixed the night before, John could use the car.

In this statement, it is the car that has been fixed, not John. The sentence clearly contains an error with the modifier – but is it misplaced or dangling?

The word being modified is mentioned in the sentence, so you might call it a misplaced modifier. However, if you try to move only the phrase itself, the sentence does not make sense. You need to add words to improve the sentence:

> John could use the car, having had it fixed it the night before.
>
> or
>
> Since it had been fixed the night before, John could use the car.

This therefore categorises it as a *dangling modifier* error.

Make sure you can identify the ineffective use of modifiers in order to communicate your message more clearly.

ACTIVITY 6

Here is a student's first attempt at writing a short story. However, the student seems to be having problems with misplaced or dangling modifiers. Identify these errors and rewrite the sentences with errors to improve the story. (Hint: not every sentence will contain a modifier error.)

Jackson's trip to the indoor market today was an eventful one. And when I say eventful, I mean a series of *unfortunate* events! Shopping at the greengrocer's, the lettuce was fresh and the tomatoes were ripe, so he thought he was in luck. However, while waiting for a deli order, the lights began to flicker. Flustered, Jackson dropped the items in his hand. Oozing slowly across the floor, he watched the salad dressing. Now, feeling panic rise in his throat, the clumsy young man dashed from the stall without paying for his items. Coming out of the market, the tomatoes fell onto the pavement. He rubbed his knee, which had instantly turned red from the spill. Jackson hopped into his car and sped off. How could this day get any worse?! And that's when he saw an injured cat by the road. With his tail held high, Jackson carried the cat to the car. Next stop: the animal hospital! 'I guess dinner will have to wait!' he thought.

D Adjectives

Adjectives have one job, which is to modify – or describe – nouns or pronouns. Adjectives, like prepositional phrases, add detail to your writing. And just like prepositions, adjectives answer a certain set of questions, which can help you identify them more quickly.

Specifically, adjectives answer the following questions:

- What kind? (e.g. *classic* literature, *English* language, *sarcastic* tone)
- Which one? (e.g. *this* novel, *these* characters)
- How many? (e.g. *twenty* pages, *several* chapters)
- How much? (e.g. *some* excitement, *no* action, *enough* interest).

Those that answer 'What kind?' are considered *descriptive* adjectives because they expand the detail of the noun or pronoun. Those that answer 'Which one?' 'How many?' and 'How much?' are called *limiting* adjectives because they shrink the noun or pronoun down to specifics.

Once again, it is very important to pay attention to the *function* of a word when identifying its part of speech. For example, you might agree that the following words are nouns:

- library
- souvenir
- childhood.

However, look at these same words in context:

- Paola's stack of *library* books
- the old *souvenir* shop on Fifth Avenue
- packed with *childhood* memories.

TIP

There is sometimes a fine distinction between what is considered an adjective and what is part of a compound noun:

> Before becoming an acclaimed author, Speck was part of the *middle* class.

Technically, the word 'middle' answers 'what kind' of class, thus making it an adjective. As a strategy for making sure, cover up the adjective. Does the sentence still make sense without this descriptive word? If so, the word is better identified as an adjective. If not, it is part of a compound noun.

Now try the same test on the word 'acclaimed'. Is it an adjective modifying 'author', or is it part of a compound noun?

Adjectives can be found in two positions in a sentence:

- just before a noun: *This is <u>inspiring</u> work.*
- just after a linking verb: *This work is <u>inspiring</u>.*

An adjective which appears after a linking verb serves as a complement to the subject: it is called a **predicate adjective**. You will learn more about subject complements in Chapter 4.4 Section *B Complements*.

KEY TERM

Predicate adjective: an adjective that is connected to the subject of the sentence by a linking verb.

There are three other word groups that can perform the job of adjectives, provided that they appear *before* the noun. These are:

- articles (e.g. *a* book, *an* imagination, *the* award)
- possessive nouns (e.g. *Sandra's* book)
- determiners (e.g. *his* imagination, *their* reward).

For example, when the words 'this', 'that', 'these' and 'those' (categorised, at times, as pronouns) appear before a noun or pronoun; they can be considered adjectives because they answer the question 'Which one?'

ACTIVITY 7

Read the series of sentences on the next page about the author William Kamkwamba, whose autobiography *The Boy Who Harnessed the Wind* was published in 2009; it brought international attention to his poverty-stricken village in Malawi, Africa.

Like Malawi, other developing countries such as Costa Rica, Afghanistan, China, India and Albania are adopting renewable energy sources.

Look back at the list of questions that adjectives answer, earlier in this section, as a guide. Use this list along with your prior knowledge of nouns to identify the adjectives and the nouns/pronouns they modify in sentences 1–15.

Write your answers on a separate sheet of paper.

1 A 29-year-old Malawian native, William Kamkwamba is now famous for his recent remarkable achievements and brilliant mind.

2 His book, *The Boy Who Harnessed the Wind*, tells the autobiographical tale of how he saved his poverty-stricken village from devastating circumstances.

3 Kamkwamba was born in a poor rural community in Malawi, so his early life was difficult; his family relied on the meagre fruits of subsistence farming for survival.

4 In 2001, when Kamkwamba was just 13, a major famine ensued, claiming innocent lives and destroying entire communities.

5 At the peak of this crisis, roughly 70 per cent of the nation's farmers were considered at risk of starvation.

6 Food was scarce, and without steady income, Kamkwamba's family could not afford to send him to a proper secondary school.

7 A natural and avid learner, William felt devastated.

8 Determined to maintain a sharp mind, Kamkwamba spent many hours studying science books at the local lending library where he developed a deep passion for engineering.

9 One book concerning wind turbines attracted a lot of interest from him.

10 He was astounded to learn that wind energy could provide reliable electricity and could power irrigation.

11 A crude, Kerosene-powered generator was the only source of energy his family possessed at that time.

12 Since the engine was costly, expensive and unreliable, Kamkwamba started by fashioning a prototype windmill from an old radio motor.

13 He set about building his first real windmill, salvaging what he could from an old scrap yard.

14 Most villagers felt sceptical, but Kamkwamba continued to build his windmill with an old bicycle, one dynamo, several flimsy PVC pipes, the fan blades from a defunct tractor, and a shock absorber.

15 News of this jaw-dropping achievement spread across the country, and before long his remarkable foundation, Moving Windmills, began delivering numerous life-changing development projects across the country.

Adapted from 'William Kamkwamba, the Malawian wind tamer', www.africa-me.com

TIP

If you identify prepositional phrases first, this can help you locate adjectives, since modifiers often appear within these phrases.

Listing adjectives

Commas are usually used to punctuate when listing items in a series. But there are cases when commas are required and when they are not, particularly when dealing with lists of adjectives.

Several adjectives used in a row, to modify the same noun or pronoun, are called **coordinate adjectives**. Coordinate adjectives are separated by a comma. For example:

> Maharaj's *fast-paced, action-packed, thrill-building* plot sequences make his work stand out from any other writer in the genre.

TIP

You can tell these are *coordinate* adjectives because you can re-arrange the order of the adjectives and the description still makes sense.

KEY TERM

Coordinate adjectives: also called *paired* adjectives, are two or more adjectives that (precede and) describe the same noun; neither adjective carries more weight in describing the noun, so they can appear in any order and are separated by commas.

Cumulative adjectives, however, build upon one another to *accumulate* meaning, which means the order is much more deliberate. Therefore, commas are not typically used to separate them.

> *Several local* vendors will be pre-selling Maharaj's latest novel.

> *My favourite vintage* bookstore is hosting the book signing.

207

KEY TERM

Cumulative adjectives: two or more adjectives that build on one another and together modify a noun; unlike coordinate adjectives (whose order can be reversed), the order of cumulative adjectives is intentional, so they are not separated by commas.

TIP

If you rearrange the adjectives and the sentence no longer makes sense, then you are using a *cumulative* adjective list.

Why adjectives matter

ACTIVITY 8

The extract that follows is taken from Mark Mathabane's autobiography *Kaffir Boy*, published in 1986, about living in apartheid South Africa. Using all that you know about adjectives, identify and list those that appear in the extract and the noun or pronoun that each modifies. Write your list on a separate sheet of paper.

My parents, a generation or so removed from these earliest settlers in Alexandra, had, too, come from the tribal reserves. My father came from what is now the so-called independent homeland of the Vendas in the northwestern corner of the Transvaal. Venda's **specious** independence (no other country but South Africa recognises it) was imposed by the Pretoria regime in 1979, thus at the time making three (Transkei and Bophuthatswana were the other two) the number of these **archipelagos** of poverty, suffering and corruption, where blacks are supposed to exercise their political rights. Since 'independence', the Venda people have been under the clutches of the Pretoria **anointed** dictator, Patrick Mphephu, who, despite the loss of two elections, continues clinging to power through **untempered** repression and brutality.

ARTICLE GLOSSARY

specious: superficial, giving the appearance of being something that it is not

archipelagos: islands

anointed: chosen for an official position

untempered: uncontrolled

1970s South Africa under Apartheid, the context in which Mark Mathabane's *Kaffir Boy* is set. Signs like these were common, keeping people of different races separate in public spaces.

Think about how the author uses adjectives in the extract. Why are adjectives particularly necessary in this paragraph? What would happen if they were used less or not at all?

As the non-fiction extract illustrates, adjectives can enhance writing through the use of details. They can also communicate important details about time, type, amount and location, which help give shape to ideas. Therefore, using adjectives in your writing can mean the difference between a generalised answer and a more specific, targeted response.

E Adverbs

Unlike adjectives, which have one job, adverbs take on *several* functions. In the traditional sense, adverbs modify – or 'add on to' – verbs. But they can also be used to modify:

* adjectives
* other adverbs.

Adverbs are usually easy to spot because they end in –*ly* (e.g. *quickly, thoughtfully, certainly, gracefully, ceaselessly*).

But as you learnt with prepositions, be careful when attempting to identify a part of speech in isolation. The word 'stately' might look like an adverb at first glance, but seeing it in the context of a sentence may change that:

> The *stately* appearance of this book's cover reminds me of something from the Renaissance.

In this case, the word 'stately' tells us 'what kind' of appearance (noun), making it an adjective.

Adverbs that modify other verbs can be particularly easy to identify because they can be moved to different positions in the sentence without making it grammatically inaccurate. For example:

> *Usually*, Petro takes a book on the train to pass the time.
>
> Petro *usually* takes a book on the train to pass the time.
>
> Petro takes a book on the train to pass the time *usually*.

However, this is not the case for adverbs modifying other adverbs or adjectives, since they need to remain close to the word they are modifying. But these types of adverbs can still be easy to spot because they usually *qualify* or intensify the adjective or adverb that they modify. For example:

> This story is based on the *really* ancient musings of Rumi.
>
> Our reading group finished the book *fairly* quickly.

KEY SKILLS

A type of adverb, qualifiers are particularly useful in discursive writing. They can moderate a claim to make your point more objective. You will learn more about qualifiers later in this chapter. For a list of qualifiers, see Chapter 3.2 Section *C Maintaining an objective tone*.

One of the most effective ways to identify adverbs is a test to find out if they answer any of the following questions:

- When? (*tomorrow, later, soon, never, usually*)
- Where? (*here, there, upward, across, down*)
- How? (*gracefully, awkwardly, timidly*)
- How often / to what extent / under what circumstances? (*sometimes, always, not, rarely*)

TIP

The adverb 'not', which answers the question 'how often / to what extent?', is often wrongly identified as being part of a verb phrase:

- Mark <u>did</u> *not* <u>read</u> today.
- Mark <u>did</u>*n't* <u>read</u> today.

Remember that words like 'not' and 'never' are adverbs. They are paired with verbs to indicate 'to what extent' an action is taking place.

ACTIVITY 9

The following statements summarise the message of poems from Islamic poet Omar Khayyam's *The Rubáiyát*, which is a collection of four-line verses exploring the fleeting nature of life. Using the questions for identifying adverbs as a guide, find the adverbs in each of sentences **1–8**.

1. Enjoy the spring of your youth now because time passes rather quickly.
2. Like wine, life oozes ceaselessly from our cup; like falling leaves, life floats daintily away from our grasp.
3. There is only one way to live: graciously appreciate the present!
4. The journey of life continues forward; do not worry needlessly about the future.
5. Today you should enjoy the fruits of life: music, leisure, and love!
6. We can hardly believe what the future brings until we experience it ourselves.
7. We are quite surprised by our inability to change the past, but our actions cannot be reversed, so choose your path wisely.
8. If we could grasp our fate entirely, we could control the outcome better, but it is not our decision to make.

Common errors concerning adjectives versus adverbs

Since adjectives and adverbs both modify words, it is not always easy to identify which one should be used. In most cases, your ears may be able to detect an error. Read this sentence aloud:

> The regular scheduled writing workshop has been cancelled.

The sentence would sound much better if it read: 'The regularly scheduled writing workshop'. In this case, an adverb is needed to modify the adjective 'scheduled' to indicate 'how often'. The informal way you sometimes speak might make something *sound* grammatically correct when, in fact, it is not. Read this sentence aloud:

> Because she spoke so eloquent, the audience was mesmerised by the writer's presentation.

This sentence may not sound as if it contains an error, but it does. 'She' is *speaking*, which is a verb, so to describe the way in which she speaks, you would need to use an adverb, not an adjective. Therefore, the sentence should read, 'Because she spoke so eloquently …'.

The better your understanding of the proper function of a word in a sentence, the better you will be at picking the grammatically correct form of that word.

Why adverbs matter

Some writing experts view adverbs as unnecessary, redundant, or even lazy. Their argument is that a careful selection of specific nouns and powerful verbs is all that is needed to convey an idea. For example:

> he whispered <u>softly</u> (a soft tone is assumed when one whispers)
>
> he said <u>threateningly</u> (why not say 'he menaced' or 'he threatened'?)

In his memoir, *On Writing*, Stephen King notes: 'the road to hell is paved in adverbs'. He likens them to weeds, which fester, multiply and take over your writing.

However, while care should be taken not to overuse them, adverbs can benefit your writing when used for the right reasons (see also '50 years of stupid grammar advice' in Chapter 4.1 Section *E Breaking the 'rules'?*). Specifically, there are two types of adverbs that can enhance your writing if used sparingly:

- qualifiers
- conjunctive adverbs.

Qualifiers

Qualifiers (see Chapter 3.2 Section *C Maintaining an objective tone*) give your reader clues to how confident you are about your subject. They include words such as 'quite,' 'rather,' and 'barely,' for example.

- If you are using an argumentative approach to writing you probably will not use qualifiers as often, because this can make you sound uncertain or unsure, and may weaken your argument.
- When writing discursively, however, you will need to be more cautious about the information you are presenting, since you do not yet know how you feel about it. Qualifiers can therefore help you communicate to your audience a more thoughtful and balanced approach.

Especially since there is no sole authority on any issue, qualifiers help writers reduce the risk of unintentionally conveying an 'absolute' tone in their writing.

 KEY SKILLS

'Hedging' is a type of careful language sometimes used in academic, scientific and even political circumstances. See Chapter 3.2 Section *C Maintaining an objective tone* to review how to use qualifiers to hedge your words.

Conjunctive adverbs

While qualifiers help communicate tone in your essay, conjunctive adverbs make connections between ideas and give direction to your writing. These words are more commonly known as *transitions*.

Here are some of the most frequently used conjunctive adverbs:

also	however	nevertheless
consequently	likewise	still
furthermore	meanwhile	therefore
hence	moreover	thus

 KEY SKILLS

In addition to the conjunctive adverbs listed here, there are lots more transitions that you can use to help organise your ideas. For a full list of transitional words and phrases, see Chapter 1.2 Section *F Key elements of an essay*.

Take care not to overuse conjunctive adverbs. They can slow down your argument and confuse your reader. The following text demonstrates what can happen when conjunctive adverbs are overused.

To begin, fiction is better than non-fiction because it allows the reader's imagination to fill in the gaps of information. If a character performs a certain action, but the text does not indicate why, the reader is left to figure out why. *Meanwhile*, informational text is much more explicit in its delivery, with no parameters left undefined. *Consequently*, a reader of informational text does not experience the wonder fiction affords. *Thus*, a non-fiction reader is less empathetic to the emotions being conveyed. *Therefore*, fiction is a much better pursuit than non-fiction because it forces the reader to create meaning as opposed to having it handed to him or her.

When used appropriately, however, conjunctive adverbs can be a helpful way to organise your thoughts. They work rather like coordinating conjunctions (*for, and, nor, but, or, yet, so*), but they cannot fuse entire sentences together. For this reason, when using conjunctive adverbs to connect two independent clauses, you should use a semicolon before the adverb. The semicolon serves as a 'brace' between two complete thoughts:

The e-reader allows us to travel with twenty books in our pocket, as opposed to one or two*; consequently,* hardcopy sales at traditional bookstores have dropped.

A comma may then follow the adverb, though this is not always necessary:

E-books have largely taken the place of printed books*; nevertheless* I'll still buy the original print just for the physical experience of it.

Failure to use the semicolon when conjoining two independent clauses creates an error in punctuation called a **run-on**:

E-books have largely taken the place of printed books*,* I'll still buy the original print just for the physical experience of it.

KEY TERM

Run-on: when two or more independent clauses are joined together inappropriately, due to either incorrect or absent punctuation.

The run-on is one of the most common writing errors. You will learn about correcting this error in Chapter 4.4 Section *D Common punctuation errors.*

If a conjunctive adverb occurs anywhere else in a sentence (i.e. beginning or middle), commas may be placed on either side of it, though not always.

E-books are becoming increasingly popular, *however*, so it might be worth the investment.

E-books *however* are becoming increasingly popular, so it might be worth the investment.

Practise using qualifiers and conjunctive adverbs by completing Activities 10–12.

ACTIVITY 10

The following extract is taken from an essay about whether classic literature should be replaced by contemporary works. To offer a more reasonable discussion, rewrite the extract using qualifiers (and other terms to help you hedge words as needed) to replace absolute language. (Refer to the full list of qualifiers in Chapter 3.2 Section *C Maintaining an objective tone*.)

With the advent of e-reader technology, hardcopy texts *will fail to endure*. (absolute)

With the advent of e-reader technology, hardcopy texts *could fail to endure*. (qualifier added)

A 'Top 10' list of recommended literature for high schoolers will reveal the works of 'greats' like Shakespeare, Kafka, Socrates, Melville, among others. No one will argue that these selections are valuable, even today. Yet more and more teachers are looking to contemporary reads like *Life of Pi* and *The Kite Runner* as opposed to *Metamorphosis* or the work of Socrates. A more multicultural approach to writing is needed these days. Classic literature is never written by anyone other than dead white males, which is why the shift began in the first place. Moreover, all of the teachers blame the battle against technology to maintain students' attention. Students are always more entertained by smartphones, tablet technology and video games, making the competition to regain their interests hard. If classic literature stays in the curriculum, enticing them to love reading won't happen.

ACTIVITY 11

The following body paragraph is taken from the middle of an essay about replacing ancient traditions with modern practices. On a separate sheet of paper, list the numbers 1 to 5 and fill in the missing words for each of the blanks in the extract. Use the list of conjunctive adverbs earlier in this section to help you.

(1) _____, in an effort to re-engage students' interest when it comes to literature, a growing number of high school curriculums are swapping out tradition for a more contemporary approach to reading. Of course, star-crossed lovers still exist in literature; (2) _____they are found in the likes of John Green's best-selling young adult novel, *The Fault in Our Stars*, as opposed to Shakespeare's *Romeo and Juliet*. (3) _____, students are missing out on the opportunity to study language in different contexts. According to some research, studying the evolution of structures, trends in punctuation and speech patterns makes us better understand our current language based on this context. Teaching the classics is (4)_____ necessary if students are to gain much needed critical thinking skills. (5) _____, teachers continue to grapple with finding ways to grab the attention of a digitally-raised audience, so swapping out the old might be written in the stars, after all.

ACTIVITY 12

Depending on the position of the conjunctive adverb, decide whether the following sentences are punctuated properly. Where the punctuation is incorrect, rewrite the sentence correctly.

1 A wide-ranging variety of literature offers so many different characters, personalities and experiences with which students can identify, moreover; this helps teachers open conversations on hard issues such as race, gender and opportunity.

2 Some school districts provide a required reading list for students meanwhile others let the teachers decide on which texts to pursue.

3 Furthermore instead of grappling with ancient language, students can immerse themselves in tales they can relate to and rush head first into a love for reading.

4 It is important that students attempt to understand characters from classic literature as well; otherwise they will not see how a context outside of their own shaped that person's decisions.

F Practising what you have learnt

Return to the paragraph that you wrote at the beginning of the chapter in response to the question:

> Which do you prefer: fiction (e.g. short stories, novels) or non-fiction (e.g. biographies, memoirs) – and why?

Then complete the following tasks. (Note: you will need three different coloured pens or highlighters.)

1 Highlight/annotate the following on your answer:
   Colour 1: *prepositional phrases*
   Colour 2: *adjectives*
   Colour 3: *adverbs.*

2 Look at the presence and/or absence of the three colours on your paragraph:
   a How would you describe your use of descriptive language?
   b What effect has the use (or absence) of descriptive language had on the quality of your writing?
   c How will your knowledge of these parts of speech help your writing in the future?

Use the following exam-style questions on this chapter's theme of *Literature* for practice in essay writing.

Essay questions

1   Would you agree that fiction has little to do with real life? Discuss. **[30]**
2   To what extent do film adaptations accurately represent literary pieces such as books and/or plays? **[30]**
3   'Comic books are not literature.' How far do you agree or disagree? **[30]**
4   'Myths and legends are entertaining but of little real value.' What is your view? **[30]**
5   Can breaking the rules ever be justified? **[30]**

Summary

Key points to remember from this chapter:

- By identifying the prepositional phrases, adjectives and adverbs, you can deconstruct a statement and determine if it is a complete sentence.
- To determine the part of speech to which a word belongs, look at the function of the word in the sentence.
- Prepositional phrases can appear at the beginning, middle or end of a sentence, and can add variety to your writing.
- Coordinate adjective lists require commas; cumulative adjective lists do not.
- Qualifiers are a type of adverb that can help you achieve an objective tone in your writing.
- Conjunctive adverbs can be used as transitions from one idea to the next.
- To avoid the error of misplaced or dangling modifiers, make sure adjectives and adverbs (including their phrases) appear close to the word or phrase they modify.

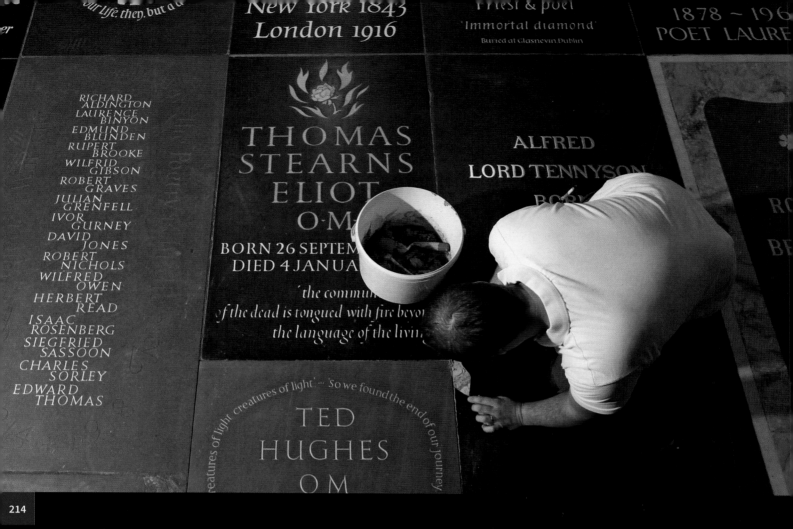

Chapter 4.3

Essential parts of speech

The photo above is of memorials to famous poets at Poets' Corner in Westminster Abbey, London. This chapter will focus on the theme of *Poetry in the modern world*.

Learning objectives

In this chapter, you will learn:

- strategies for identifying the various types of nouns, pronouns and verbs
- how to determine the function of these parts of speech in a sentence
- how to identify and avoid common errors associated with these parts of speech your writing.

A Essential parts of speech

In this chapter, you will have the opportunity to reinforce what you know about:

- nouns
- pronouns
- verbs.

As you work through the chapter, you will be asked to think about how these parts of speech affect the writing of others, and how you can use them to improve your own writing.

Before you begin your review of these essential parts of speech, read the following question and write a one-paragraph response to it. Let your response flow as naturally as possible. Structure your response as necessary in order to make your point clearly. Keep your response to under 100 words.

> What do you think makes poetry so appealing?

ACTIVITY 1

Swap your responses to this question with a partner and observe each other's approach to the same writing task. As you did in Chapter 4.2 Activity 1, use the following statement stems to share your observations, or create your own:

- I am impressed by …
- Tell me what you meant by …
- What made you decide …?
- An observation I made about the content of your paragraph is …
- An observation I made about your paragraph's use of English is …

Keep your written response. You will return to it at the end of this chapter.

B Nouns

Nouns – *persons*, *places* and *things* – are perhaps the easiest words to spot. That is because each of these are concrete entities, called **concrete nouns** for this reason.

Nouns are also ideas, however, which can be more difficult to identify. They can convey a thought or belief, an action, an emotional state, or a personal quality, and are called **abstract nouns** for this reason; for example:

> freedom (*mental state*)
> sympathy (*emotional state*)
> rebellion (*action state*)
> health (*condition*)

All of these are variations of *ideas* which – unlike persons, places or things – do not exist in the physical sense.

Sometimes, nouns can be easier to spot if they are preceded by an article (*a, an, the*):[1]

> *an* enigma
> *a* question
> *the* resistance

Another way to spot ideas is by looking at their ending, or *suffix*. A few common noun endings for *ideas* are:

> *–tion* (e.g. imagination)
> *–sion* (e.g. confusion)
> *–ion* (e.g. coercion)
> *–ment* (e.g. enjoyment)
> *–ism* (e.g. stoicism)

KEY TERMS

Concrete nouns: persons, places and things you can physically experience with the senses.

Abstract nouns: ideas which cannot be experienced directly with the senses; instead, these occur mentally or are felt emotionally.

Other categories of nouns include:

- common
- proper
- compound
- collective.

ACTIVITY 2

For each of the following poetry quotations, identify the nouns and indicate whether they are concrete or abstract.

1 The caged bird sings / with a fearful trill / of things unknown / but longed for still / and his tune is heard / on the distant hill for the caged bird / sings of freedom.

    From 'Caged Bird' by Maya Angelou

2 I stand amid the roar / of a surf-tormented shore, / and I hold within my hand / grains of the golden sand …

    From 'A Dream Within A Dream' by Edgar Allan Poe

3 The wise man is he who possesses a torch of his own; / He is the guide and the leader of the caravan.

    From 'The Marks of the Wise, of the Half Wise, and of the Fool' by Jalal ad-Din Muhammad Rumi

4 I can promise all my heart's devotion; / a smile to chase away your tears of sorrow; / a love that's true and ever growing; / a hand to hold in yours through each tomorrow.

    From 'These I Can Promise' by Mark Twain

5 The stars / Decreed that I should perish by thy hand. / I came like lightning and like wind I go.

    From 'Rustam and Suhrab' by Firdawsi

African American poet Maya Angelou writes about her experience of racial injustice in her youth. Her poem 'Caged Bird' was inspired by early African American poet, Paul Lawrence Dunbar, and was meaningful for those facing apartheid in South Africa.

Common versus proper nouns

The two types of nouns you are probably most aware of are **common nouns** and **proper nouns**.

 KEY TERMS

Common nouns: words that refer to persons, places, things or ideas of a general nature.

Proper nouns: words that identify specific persons, places, things or ideas.

To note the specific nature of the word, proper nouns are capitalised:

Common nouns	Proper nouns
white house	the White House
leader	Chancellor Merkel of Germany
book	the Book of Genesis

Compound nouns

Compound nouns require more than one word to express a single concept. These can be formed in three different ways:

Separated	air conditioner, Taj Mahal, public speaking
Hyphenated	mother-in-law, well-being, passer-by
Combined	riverboat, battlefield, greenhouse, drawback

Remember that adjective-noun combinations can sometimes be mistaken for compound nouns. The way the words are stressed can help distinguish them. Consider, for instance, the way you would emphasise:

blue <u>bird</u>   white <u>house</u>

<u>blue</u> bird   <u>White</u> House

The emphasis normally falls at the front of a compound noun, but it is the opposite for a noun plus the adjective modifying it.

Collective nouns

Collective nouns name a *group* of people or things; for example:

audience	crowd
army	jury
class	lot
committee	team

KEY TERM

Collective noun: a noun representing a group of individuals; depending on how the actions of the individuals are carried out, a collective noun can be treated as singular or plural.

When you refer to a collective noun acting as a whole group, you typically treat it as a singular noun. When referring to individual members' actions *within* the whole group, you can treat it as a plural noun. In the following instances, notice how the determiners take on singular and plural forms to match:

As a group:	The <u>jury</u> delivered *its* verdict late last night.
As individuals within the group:	The <u>jury</u> solemnly entered the room and took *their* seats.

TIP

For a sentence to be grammatically correct, the subject and verb should agree; also, pronouns should agree with their antecedents. You will learn more about agreement later in this chapter.

ACTIVITY 3

1 Read each of the poetry quotations provided. Some nouns are underlined for you in each quotation. On a separate sheet of paper and for each underlined word, identify the noun type from the list in the box below. List *all* noun types that apply to each underlined word. (Hint: a noun cannot be both common and proper, nor can it be both concrete and abstract. It can, however, be common and compound, etc.)

common	concrete	collective
proper	abstract	compound

The goddess, (1) <u>Night</u>, has drawn near, looking about on many sides with her eyes. She has put on all her (2) <u>glories</u>.

From 'Night' from the *Rig Veda*

Storm'd at with shot and shell, / Boldly they rode and well, / Into the jaws of (3) <u>death</u>, / Into the mouth of (4) <u>Hell</u> / Rode the (5) <u>six hundred</u>.

From 'The Charge of the Light Brigade' by Alfred Lord Tennyson

China marches its men down (6) <u>Po-teng Road</u> / While Tartar (7) <u>troops</u> peer across blue waters of the bay… / And since not one battle famous in (8) <u>history</u> / Sent all its fighters back again / The soldiers turn round looking toward the / border, / And think of home, with wistful eyes …

From 'The Moon at the Fortified pass' by Li Po

Season of mists and mellow (9) <u>fruitfulness</u>! / Close (10) <u>bosom-friend</u> of the maturing sun; / Conspiring with him how to load and bless / With fruit the vines that round the thatch-eaves run.

From 'Ode to Autumn' by John Keats

As he paces in cramped (11) <u>circles</u>, over and over, / the movement of his powerful soft strides / is like a ritual dance around a center / in which a mighty (12) <u>will</u> stands paralyzed.

From 'The Panther' by Rainer Maria Rilke

The clustering (13) <u>clouds</u> – / Can it be they wipe away / the lunar shadows? / Every time they clear a bit / The (14) <u>moonlight</u> shines the brighter.

A tanka (traditional Japanese poem) by Minamoto no Toshiyori

Darkness settles on roofs and walls, / But the sea, the sea in the darkness calls; / The little (15) <u>waves</u>, with their soft, white hands / Efface the (16) <u>footprints</u> in the sands, / And the tide rises, the tide falls.

From 'The Tide Rises, The Tide Falls' by Henry Wadsworth Longfellow

2 Now challenge yourself: find the other nouns contained in each line!

217

Analysing function

Lewis Carroll's poem, 'Jabberwocky', is a nonsense poem appearing in his novel, *Through the Looking-Glass, and What Alice Found There*, a sequel to another of his famous works, *Alice's Adventures in Wonderland*. Since the main character, Alice, is lost in a dreamland, it makes sense that the poem makes little sense at all! Even Carroll himself did not know the meanings of some of the words he made up. Of his own poem, he notes: 'somebody killed something: that's clear at any rate'. While the ideas may be nonsensical, their function maintains the form and structure of the English language by following standard grammatical rules.

An illustrator's impression of the Jabberwocky.

ACTIVITY 4

Read 'Jabberwocky' by Lewis Carroll. Analyse the function of the underlined words to determine if they are functioning as nouns or adjectives.

'**Twas** brillig, and the (1) <u>slithy</u> toves
Did gyre and gimble in the (2) <u>wabe</u>:
All mimsy were the (3) <u>borogoves</u>,
And the (4) <u>mome raths</u> outgrabe.

'Beware the (5) <u>Jabberwock</u>, my son!
The jaws that bite, the claws that catch!
Beware the (6) <u>Jubjub</u> bird, and shun
The (7) <u>frumious</u> (8) <u>Bandersnatch</u>!'

He took his vorpal sword in hand;
Long time the manxome foe he sought–
So rested he by the Tumtum tree
And stood awhile in thought.

And, as in uffish thought he stood,
The Jabberwock, with eyes of flame,
Came whiffling through the (9) <u>tulgey</u> wood,
And burbled as it came!

One, two! One, two! And through and through
The vorpal blade went snicker-snack!
He left it dead, and with its head
He went galumphing back.

'And hast thou slain the Jabberwock?
Come to my arms, my beamish boy!
O frabjous day! Callooh! Callay!'
He chortled in his joy.

'Twas (10) <u>brillig</u>, and the slithy (11) <u>toves</u>
Did gyre and gimble in the wabe:
All (12) <u>mimsy</u> were the borogoves,
And the mome raths outgrabe.

GLOSSARY

'**twas:** it was

ACTIVITY 5

Replace each of the nonsense words used in 'Jabberwocky' with real words that would have the same function, and keep to the aims of the poem.

Why nouns matter

What observation can you make about the short paragraph below?

Poetry is appealing because it makes a person feel things they might not otherwise experience. They might feel sadness, for example, when reading a piece by a famous person.

You may have noticed that the words are rather bland. So why is this? Mainly because the writing is non-specific in its choice of words. By adding more specific nouns to the paragraph, the writer would make their point more clearly. Consider the following questions relating to the writing:

'person': *What do we call a person who reads?*

'things': *What is a more specific word for the 'things' we feel? What are those called?*

'sadness': *Are there more specific words that could be used?*

'a piece by a famous person': *What kind of piece? A story, a poem, a novel? What proper noun could we use to be more specific? Who is the 'person'?*

Notice that the more specific your choice of words, the more alive and engaging your writing will be. Targeted choice of words is key in this regard:

> Poetry is appealing because it makes the <u>reader</u> feel <u>emotions</u> they might not otherwise experience. They might feel <u>despair</u>, for example, when reading a <u>poem</u> like '<u>The Raven</u>' by <u>Edgar Allan Poe</u>, whose main <u>character</u> is tortured by the <u>woes</u> of losing his only <u>love</u>.

An illustration for Edgar Allan Poe's poem 'The Raven'. Your choice of words can help to make your writing more interesting and engaging. What words does this image suggest to you?

C Pronouns

What observations can you make about the following extract?

> One of the greatest poets of all time, Homer is author of one of the classic works of Greek literature: the *Iliad*, set during the Trojan War. Homer is also the author of the *Odyssey,* a story that takes place after the war is over. Because of Homer, Greece's national culture is immortalised in heroic characters such as Achilles and Odysseus. Even today, Homer's influence continues to inspire art, music and literature in Western civilisation.

An obvious point is the repetitive use of the author's name. The function of pronouns is to minimise this problem, as they can take the place of nouns. By replacing 'Homer' with pronoun variations like 'he' or 'him', the repetition is avoided. The original noun to which the pronoun is referring is called the **antecedent**.

 KEY TERM

Antecedent: a word or phrase that is replaced by a pronoun.

219

ACTIVITY 6

Identify the pronouns as they are used in the following famous quotations from poetry:

1 You may forget but / Let me tell you / this: someone in / some future time / will think of us.

'You May Forget But' by Sappho

2 Midway through life's journey, I went astray / from the straight road and woke to find myself / alone in a dark wood.

From 'Inferno' Canto I from the *Divine Comedy* by Dante Alighieri

3 I am not one of those who left the land / to the mercy of its enemies. / Their flattery leaves me cold, / my songs are not for them to praise.

From 'I am not one of those who left the land' by Anna Akhmatova

4 Because I could not stop for Death – / He kindly stopped for me – / The Carriage held but just Ourselves – / and Immortality.

'Because I could not stop for Death' by Emily Dickinson

Personal pronouns, like the ones you would need to reduce repetition in the extract we considered, are probably the most familiar to you. In this section, you will learn about the following pronoun types:

- personal and possessive pronouns
- reflexive versus intensive pronouns
- interrogative, relative and demonstrative
- indefinite pronouns.

Personal and possessive pronoun case

In the 1932 film adaptation of Edgar Rice Burroughs' classic, *Tarzan of the Apes*, English explorer, Jane, wanders off into the African jungle. Tarzan, a man raised by apes who has been watching her for some time, swings down out of the trees. She faints. He carries her off to the high branches of the jungle's canopy. When she awakens, one of the most shocking scenes in grammatical history follows. Jane, realising she is in grave danger, attempts to communicate with Tarzan:

> JANE (*pointing to herself*): Me Jane.
>
> TARZAN (*pointing to himself*): Me Jane.
>
> JANE: No, no. *Me* Jane. (*Points to Tarzan*). You?
>
> TARZAN: Me Jane. You Tarzan.
>
> JANE (at a loss to explain further): No. No.
>
> TARZAN (*his face suddenly brightening*): You Jane. Me Tarzan. Tarzan. Jane.

Within just a few seconds, an English woman and her new acquaintance have committed one of the worst crimes against grammar: improper use of pronoun case!

Although she does a poor job of demonstrating it in this scene, Jane knew – and Tarzan eventually learnt – that pronouns have three cases:

- nominative
- objective
- possessive

Nominative case

When a personal pronoun appears as the subject of a sentence, or before the verb, the following forms should be used:

Nominative case *(for subject pronouns)*
I
you
she/he/it
we
they

When speaking to Tarzan, Jane could have said any of the following:

> I am Jane.
>
> You are Tarzan.
>
> We have never met before.

When working with only one pronoun, these kinds of decisions are fairly easy to make. Writers and speakers usually find it more difficult, however, when handling more than one subject. In informal conversation, for instance, you might say:

> Me and her are going to the library tomorrow morning.

Since the pronouns appear in the subject of the sentence [*Me* and *her*], these need to be in the *nominative case*:

> She and I are going to the library tomorrow morning.

TIP
When dealing with compound subjects involving yourself and others, it is often more appropriate to mention the other person before yourself.

> Me and my friends are reading the work of Victor Hugo in literature class. ✗
>
> My friends and I are reading the work of Victor Hugo in literature class. ✓

When you are in doubt, a quick way to work out which pronoun form to use is to block out the other person or group in the subject and read the sentence to see if it sounds right:

The expedition team and her travelled deep into the jungle.

<u>Her</u> travelled deep into the jungle. ✗

<u>She</u> travelled deep into the jungle. ✓

When you are writing questions, pronoun case can also be tricky to determine because of the inverted order of the subject and verb:

Did <u>him</u> and Jane finally understand one another?

The best way to handle this is to turn the question into a statement:

<u>Him</u> and Jane did finally understand one another. ✗

<u>He</u> and Jane did finally understand one another. ✓

Objective case

Meanwhile, when a personal pronoun appears in the **predicate** of the sentence, or after the verb, you should choose the appropriate form from the objective case:

Nominative case (for subject pronouns)	Objective case (for object pronouns)
I	me
you	you
she/he/it	her/him/it
we	us
they	them

KEY TERM

Predicate: the part of the sentence that contains the verb and says something about the subject.

Specifically, the objective case should be used in the following circumstances:

- direct objects (e.g. Clayton told <u>them</u> of Jane's abduction.)
- indirect objects (e.g. Clayton gave <u>them</u> the map of the jungle.)
- object of a preposition (e.g. The search team searched all around for <u>her</u>.)
- object of a verbal noun (e.g. Finding <u>her</u> was going to be a challenge.)

Once again, when dealing with more than one object, you can read the sentence with just the pronoun to see if it sounds right:

Esmeralda cheered at the sight of Tarzan's cabin, which looked like the perfect source of refuge for <u>she</u>. ✗

Esmeralda cheered at the sight of Tarzan's cabin, which looked like the perfect source of refuge for <u>her</u>. ✓

ACTIVITY 7

Apply what you have learnt so far about selecting case. Re-write the paragraph below, replacing overused nouns with a more appropriate form of pronoun in order to avoid repetitive language.

Whirling Dervishes in Turkey.

The Persian poet Rumi is regarded as one of the finest writers the world has ever known. A mystic, Rumi founded the Sufi order of the 'Whirling Dervishes', and Muslim disciples from all over the area followed Rumi's teachings. (A dervish is a performer of a hypnotic dance to bring enlightenment.) While Rumi was serving as a religious teacher, one of Rumi's closest friends was murdered by some of the disciples out of jealousy. The disciples wanted Rumi's attention, but instead of returning to the disciples, Rumi turned to poetry to mourn the loss of his companion. Today, readers know Rumi for one of his most famous works, *The Masnavi*, a long poem, demonstrating his overflowing love for God. *The Masnavi* has been translated into many languages for readers and has been analysed by countless religious leaders and literary scholars. Because of Rumi's timeless ability to define the values of society, people everywhere continue to be intrigued by him.

Possessive case

Possessive pronouns show ownership and are used in the same way as other pronouns, to replace a noun in a sentence. They are sometimes used with the genitive form 'of', but they are more often used in place of a subject or object:

> Tarzan was surprised to see Clayton because the cabin was <u>his</u>.
>
> '<u>Hers</u> are blue,' said the guide.
>
> 'This village of <u>yours</u> is hidden from the main path,' said the guide.

Possessive pronouns look very similar to possessive *determiners*, which are used before a noun to show who the noun belongs to (in place of 'a', 'an' or 'the'):

> Tarzan was surprised to see Clayton in <u>his cabin</u>.
>
> '<u>Her shoes</u> are blue,' said the guide.
>
> 'I think <u>your village</u> is hidden from the path,' said the guide.

Nominative case	Objective case	Possessive pronoun	Possessive determiner
(replaces the subject of the sentence)	*(replaces the object of the sentence)*	*(replaces a noun with its owner)*	*(used in front of a noun to determine its owner)*
I	me	mine	my
you	you	yours	your
she/he/it	her/him/it	hers/his/its*	her/his/its
we	us	ours	our
they	them	theirs	their

*'its' is very rarely used as a pronoun. It is more commonly used as a determiner in the form 'its own' (e.g. *a room with its own balcony*).

It's versus *its*

One of the most common errors that writers make concerns the possessive determiner 'its' and the use of the apostrophe.

> The <u>island's</u> vast swath of jungle made it difficult to traverse.
>
> <u>Its</u> vast swath of jungle made the island terrain difficult to traverse.

If an apostrophe appeared with the possessive determiner in the second sentence (its), the statement would have actually read:

> <u>It is</u> vast swath of jungle made the island terrain difficult to traverse.

This is because, unlike nouns, pronouns use the apostrophe to form a **contraction**:

> With the many geographic obstacles this region presents, such as jungles and high rock formations, <u>it's</u> probably one of the most difficult explorations yet.

The contraction means that '<u>it is</u> probably one of the most difficult explorations', because the sentence requires a verb.

When deciding whether to use an apostrophe, ask yourself if you mean to write 'it is'. If you need a verb to complete what you are saying, you will need 'it's'.

Note that the same rule applies to other pronouns, such as the commonly confused set of *who's* and *whose*:

> <u>Who's</u> going on this expedition? (Who is going?)
>
> <u>Whose</u> binoculars are these? (Who owns these binoculars?)

 KEY TERM

Contraction: a shortened version of a word, using an apostrophe.

Since 'who' is a relative pronoun, it uses apostrophes for contractions, not to show possession.

Another commonly confused pair is 'you're' and 'your':

> <u>You're</u> not going to believe this.
>
> <u>Your</u> backpack is over there.

Other types of pronouns

Personal and possessive pronouns are probably the ones most familiar to you and the easiest to spot, but there are other types of pronouns:

- reflexive and intensive
- interrogative, relative and demonstrative
- indefinite.

Reflexive and intensive pronouns

These pronouns are easy to recognise because they include most of the personal or possessive pronouns plus –*self* or –*selves*:

Reflexive/intensive pronouns
myself
yourself
himself/herself/itself
ourselves
themselves

Reflexive pronouns and **intensive pronouns** use the same list of words, but they serve different functions in the sentence.

KEY TERMS

Reflexive pronouns: personal pronouns which end with –*self* or –*selves*; these are grammatically necessary for the sentence to function.

Intensive pronouns: personal pronouns which end with –*self* or –*selves*; these are used in a sentence to emphasise, or intensify, a point but are not grammatically necessary for it to function.

Since they look the same, you will need to consider the function of the word to determine whether the pronoun is reflexive or intensive. A good strategy is to read the sentence without the word. If the sentence makes sense without it, the pronoun is intensive. If the sentence no longer makes sense without the word, the pronoun is reflexive.

ACTIVITY 8

For each of the following statements, identify the pronouns ending in –*self* or –*selves*. Then, using the strategy just described, determine whether each pronoun is reflexive or intensive. (Remember: reflexive pronouns are grammatically necessary, whereas intensive pronouns are not.)

1 Persian poet Omar Khayyam originally wrote the *Rubáiyát* himself, before translator Edward Fitzgerald added to and adapted it to unify both theme and style.

2 In his poem, 'Do not go gentle into that good night', Dylan Thomas urges his audience of elders not to let themselves grow old with age but instead to 'rage against the dying of the light'.

3 In his poem, 'The Negro Speaks of Rivers', poet Langston Hughes uses the pronoun I to collectively refer to all African Americans who themselves have fought racial oppression.

4 In Emily Dickinson's poem, 'Because I could not stop for death', the narrator finds herself in a personified Death's carriage, where they ride past the setting Sun and into eternity.

5 Dante's *Divine Comedy* poetically explores the consequences of sin when, as an alter ego of the author himself, the narrator travels through both Hell and Purgatory before arriving at the doors of Heaven.

6 Chilean poet, Gabriela Mistral, gained fame for her poem, 'Sonetos de la muerte', where she mourns the death of her lover, who kills himself.

7 The Duke in Robert Browning's poem, 'My Last Duchess', implicates himself as the duchess' murderer when he says he 'gave commands / then all smiles stopped together'.

Interrogative and relative pronouns

Two other types of pronouns that share a similar word list are *interrogative* and *relative* pronouns:

Interrogative	Relative
who	who
whom	whom
whose	whose
which	which
what	that

Notice that the only difference is in the last word of each list. The reason for this difference is:

- interrogative pronouns initiate questions, or 'interrogate', so the form *what* is appropriate for this purpose
- relative pronouns initiate phrases, which are part of statements, not questions, so the use of *that is* is appropriate for this purpose.

Meanwhile, the other words in the list can be used when either forming a question or making a statement. For example, look at how the pronoun *who* can be used to help form a question or a statement:

> Who wrote 'The Tyger'?
>
> William Blake, who wrote 'The Tyger', is an 18th-century poet well known for his illustrated poetry compilation, *Songs of Innocence and Experience.*

ACTIVITY 9

Pick two pronouns from the list of interrogative and relative pronouns. Write sentence pairs for each, where one uses an interrogative pronoun and the other uses a relative one.

When you see any of these pronouns, use the punctuation at the end of the sentence to help you determine which is which. If the sentence:

- ends with a question mark, the pronoun is *interrogative*
- ends with a full stop, the pronoun is *relative*.

You will learn more about relative clauses in Chapter 4.4.

Demonstrative pronouns

The demonstrative pronoun is yet another pronoun type that shares words with another part of speech. The following *demonstrative pronouns* can also function as adjectives, depending upon their function in the sentence:

Demonstrative pronouns
this
that
these
those

The easiest way to tell if one of these is working as a pronoun or an adjective is to see if the word is accompanied by a noun or not. As you learnt in Chapter 4.2, adjectives modify nouns, thefore the following rule applies:

- If the word is directly followed by a *noun*, then it is being used as an *adjective*.
- If the word is followed by a *verb*, then it is functioning as a *pronoun*.

DID YOU KNOW?

Depending upon its function, a single word can serve several different purposes. Consider the word *that* as an example:

- *As an adjective*: That poem is the best in the collection.
- *As a demonstrative pronoun*: That is my favourite poem in the collection.
- *As a relative pronoun*: Blake's poem, 'The Tyger', is one that will endure for years.

Consider these statements, regarding Ben Jonson's love poem, 'To Celia':

> 1 Penned by Ben Jonson in 1616, this *poem* tells the tale of a man in love who wishes for Celia to pledge her love to him with her eyes.
>
> 2 Penned by Ben Jonson in 1616, this *is* a love poem unparalleled by any other, whose narrator is intoxicated by the gaze of his lover.

Which use of *this* is considered a demonstrative pronoun and which is an adjective?

TIP

When identifying demonstrative pronouns, remember that:
- pronouns replace nouns, so they will *never* appear side by side
- adjectives describe nouns, so they will normally appear close together.

If in doubt, always question the *function* of the word within its context!

Since demonstratives show where an object is in relation to a speaker, this choice of language is usually reserved for demonstrations, as the word suggests.

For example, a speaker is able to say, 'I didn't ask for *these*' while also physically pointing to the antecedent of *these*.

However, keep in mind that in writing, the origin of a demonstrative pronoun needs to be clear for effective communication. You cannot physically point to the noun to which you are referring when writing, especially if more than one is mentioned:

> Increasingly, writers are creating e-books and self-publishing their work. This is a problem for their agents.

Does the word *this* refer to creating e-books, self-publishing, or both? This sentence could be revised as:

> Increasingly, writers are creating e-books and self-publishing their work. These methods are a problem for their agents.

If you use demonstrative pronouns in your writing, be sure the antecedent is clear. Complete Activities 10 and 11 to help you make decisions about when it is appropriate to use this part of speech in your writing.

ACTIVITY 10

Read the following *original statement*, which includes a demonstrative pronoun, and the revision of it. Is the revision necessary? Analyse the original statement to determine whether the antecedent of the pronoun is clear. Be prepared to defend your answer.

Original

The poems of Robert Frost are some of the most classic pieces in poetic history. These include 'Mending Wall' and 'The Road Not Taken', to name just a few.

Revision

The poems of Robert Frost are some of the most classic pieces in poetic history. These works include the 'Mending Wall' and 'The Road Not Taken', to name just a few.

ACTIVITY 11

Read the paragraph and answer the questions that follow.

> The words of Shakespeare's Sonnet 130 makes us wonder if love is as romantic as it seems. In his opening line, he notes: 'My mistress' eyes are nothing like the sun', which makes us think he does not find her gaze appealing. Later, he mentions that perfume has a far more pleasing scent than that of her breath. He then notes how poorly his love sings, how rough her hair is, and how heavy her 'tread' is upon the ground. This might seem unimpressive, but by the poem's end, the author makes it clear he will never find a love as worthy.

1   Re-read the final sentence in the paragraph. What is the antecedent of the demonstrative pronoun *This*?
2   How might the writer revise this sentence to make the antecedent clearer?
3   What purpose might an adjustment like this serve?

Indefinite pronouns

Imagine you are asked to summarise a poem you have read and really enjoyed. Without thinking too much about it, you respond:

> Well, there was this one guy who met someone from somewhere far away. He tells the narrator something. His message is basically that no one lives forever. Everyone dies and everything decays, and nothing is forever, not one's power or anything else.

You have probably noticed by now that this response is rather vague, but what is causing the problem? The problem lies in the overuse of **indefinite pronouns**.

 KEY TERM

Indefinite pronoun: a pronoun that expresses a non-specific or non-definite meaning; many indefinite pronouns end in *–body*, *–thing* or *–one*.

Indefinite pronouns		
some–	each	many
any–	either	several
no–	neither	some
–body	other	any
–thing	one	none
–one	both	all
–where	few	most

Of course, these pronouns are just as necessary as any other part of speech, but as the name denotes, they refer to unspecified persons, places, things or ideas. Because the reference is not definite, it makes it harder for the reader to grasp the meaning. Remember that using indefinite pronouns in writing is fine, but overusing them can quickly make your message unclear.

ACTIVITY 12

The vague summary that we considered, which refers to a 'guy who met someone from somewhere far away', is based on the poem, 'Ozymandias', by Percy Bysshe Shelley. Read the complete poem (you may additionally access summaries online). Then return to the inadequate summary and revise it to make it clearer and more specific.

Ozymandias

I met a traveller from an antique land
Who said: Two vast and trunkless legs of stone
Stand in the desert … Near them, on the sand,
Half sunk a shattered visage lies, whose frown,
5 And wrinkled lip, and sneer of cold command,
Tell that its sculptor well those passions read
Which yet survive, stamped on these lifeless things,
The hand that mocked them, and the heart that fed;
And on the pedestal, these words appear:
10 'My name is Ozymandias, king of kings:
Look on my works, ye Mighty, and despair!'
Nothing beside remains. Round the decay
Of that colossal wreck, boundless and bare
The lone and level sands stretch far away.

Ramesses II, also known as Ramesses the Great, held the second longest reign as pharaoh in Egyptian history. He was known for his extensive architectural projects and for the enormous statues of him all around Egypt. When the British Museum acquired a remnant of one of the statues in 1817, scholars believe it inspired Percy Bysshe Shelley's poem 'Ozymandias', which is the Greek name for Ramesses.

Common errors concerning pronouns

Earlier in this chapter you learnt about some problems to look out for with pronoun case. Pronoun-antecedent agreement is another of the most common grammatical errors. This is where a pronoun does not agree in number with its antecedent. This section will help you to understand, and to avoid, this frequent mistake.

Pronoun-antecedent agreement

You have learnt that nouns and pronouns have a similar function, but that pronouns do not specifically name a person, place or thing. Antecedents are the nouns that pronouns replace. For example:

> Rainer Maria Rilke was a Bohemian-Austrian writer who is best known for his book, *Letters to a Young Poet*. He is considered one of the greatest poets in the German language and also made significant contributions to French writing.

Rainer Maria Rilke is the noun that *he* is referring to in the second sentence.

Because the pronoun takes the place of the antecedent, it is important that the pronoun agrees *in number* with its antecedent. Therefore:

226

- If the antecedent is *singular*, the pronoun should be *singular*.
- If the antecedent is *plural*, the pronoun should be *plural*.

> *(plural)*   *(plural)*
>
> While <u>readers</u> enjoy Rilke's *Letters*, <u>they</u> also liked his *Duino Elegies*.

ACTIVITY 13

Identify any pronoun-antecedent errors as they occur in sentences **1–5**. If there is an error, rewrite the sentence on a separate sheet of paper to correct it. Note that not all sentences will contain an error.

1 One of the most prolific writers to emerge out of the Harlem Renaissance, Langston Hughes wrote about what it was like to be black in America in the 1920s and what they thought about these inequalities.

2 Hughes voiced his opinion on being black in America in poems like 'I, Too, Sing America' and 'Dream Deferred', but not all of his fellow African American peers agreed with them.

3 Specifically, many black intellectuals felt that these poems portrayed an unattractive view of black life that 'paraded' their racial defects to the community.

4 Hughes' first novel, *Not Without Laughter*, won the Harmon gold medal in 1930; he was widely praised for an authentic plot and portrayal of character experiences.

5 Hughes turned to the poetry of Paul Lawrence Dunbar, Carl Sandburg and Walt Whitman, who were were sources of inspiration to them.

There are two descriptive rules you will need to follow to make sure your pronouns always agree with their antecedents:

- When the antecedent consists of compound elements joined by 'and', the pronoun to replace it should be *plural*.

> Poets <u>and</u> playwrights alike allude to verses from religious texts in <u>their</u> work in order to connect intellectually and culturally with the audience.

- When the antecedent consists of compound elements joined by 'or' or 'nor', the pronoun will agree with the *second* of those elements.

> His novel <u>or</u> his poems make frequent reference to religious texts within <u>their</u> storyline to connect with the audience.

> His poems <u>or</u> his novel makes frequent reference to religious texts within <u>its</u> storyline to connect with the audience.

The rules for pronoun-antecedent are similar to those for subject–verb agreement, which will be covered later in this chapter.

Agreement with indefinite pronouns

Sometimes a pronoun can take the place of another pronoun. This usually happens when indefinite pronouns are involved. You may have learnt to follow rules about using words like 'everybody' and 'each'. For example:

Take singular form	Take plural form	Take either singular or plural depending on context
each	both	some
either	few	any
neither	many	none
other	several	many
one		all
–body		most
–thing		
–one		

While these rules often apply, it is important to note that considering the word *in context* will help you make the right decision about which form to use when replacing these words with other pronouns.

For example, which of the following sentences is grammatically correct?

> 1 Everybody was finishing his or her work.
>
> 2 Everybody was finishing their work.

Based on the rule, the first is correct. Yet many well-known writers use the second form, because it is commonly used in speech. Depending on your purpose, audience and context, both can be considered acceptable, though you should note the following:

- The verb phrase 'was finishing' is singular because it uses *was* instead of *were*.
- Therefore, if the verb treats the subject 'everybody' as a singular term, then 'his' or 'her' may be more appropriate in academic writing than 'their'.

227

Agreement with relative pronouns

A relative pronoun, which starts off a relative clause, modifies the word that appears directly before it. Remember that relative pronouns include:

- who
- that
- which
- whom.

A frequent error in the use of pronouns has to do with pronoun *reference*. As a general rule, the word and the pronoun it is replacing – its antecedent – should always be near to one another. Otherwise, the reader may get confused.

ACTIVITY 14

Read the following sentences and consider what is wrong (even humorous!) with the wording of each. Rewrite each sentence to connect the pronoun more directly to its antecedent.

1 If the readers don't buy the copies, put them away until the next event.
2 After putting the quill pen in his desk, George Orwell sold it.
3 Take the manuscript out of the desk and fix it.
4 The publishers told their writers they would receive a bonus.

Another common problem when using pronouns is deciding which to use when making a comparison. The use of pronouns after words like 'than' and 'as' can lead to confusion. For example, would you consider the following statement to be grammatically correct?

Lord Byron is a better writer than me.

Because the pronoun 'me' appears in the predicate of the sentence (after the verb), it seems as though the most sensible choice would be to use the objective case 'me'. This is incorrect, however. It should actually be written as:

Lord Byron is a better writer than I (am).

Even though it might not appear to be the case, there are two clauses present in the sentence, because two are needed to complete the comparison. Yet the verb in the second clause (*am,* in this example) is often omitted. The pronoun should therefore be used in the *nominative* case, since it is the inferred subject of the verb *am.*

D Verbs

When French scientist, philosopher and mathematician René Descartes wrote the Latin proposition, *cogito ergo sum* – or, 'I think; therefore I am' – he not only produced one of the most influential philosophical statements in Western thinking, he also demonstrated the power of verbs.

René Descartes wrote the famous line, 'I think; therefore I am'. What makes the construction of this sentence so complex?

Verbs are one of the most powerful of all the parts of speech because without them, we would have only fragments of thoughts. In fact, a single verb can make a complete sentence. Consider, for example: 'Read.' Believe it or not, this is a complete sentence, because as an imperative statement, the subject is assumed: (You) read.

Of course, this does not apply to every verb. 'Are' all by itself would not be considered a sentence, after all (though technically, 'be' would make sense as a complete thought on its own). When used properly, verbs can be the ultimate secret weapon for effective writing.

In this section, you will consider two types of verbs:

- linking verbs
- action verbs.

Action verbs like 'read' express an action being carried out by the subject. Linking verbs like 'are' indicate a sense of being or existing.

> **DID YOU KNOW?**
>
> Descartes' intention was to express the point that 'we cannot doubt our existence while we doubt'. In other words, as long as we can express doubt, we are alive. It was not until Antoine Leonard Thomas' revision of the statement into *dubito, ergo cogito, ergo sum* – or 'I doubt, therefore I think, therefore I am' – that this intention was more clearly expressed. This is a useful lesson – even the greatest writers need revision!

Linking verbs

Linking verbs express a form of being or existence. Often these are overlooked or disregarded because they lack the vividness of an action verb, but as Descartes' statement demonstrates, they can be just as powerful. To say, 'I am', for instance, expresses that you recognise your own identity!

The most obvious linking verb is any past or present form of *be*:

- am
- are
- is
- was
- were.

There are several linking verbs in addition to these, all of which express 'being' or link the subject to a condition. In other words, all of these verb forms essentially mean, 'X exists as ...':

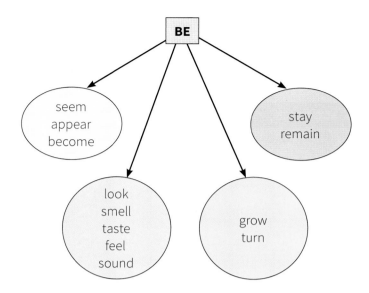

Most often, linking verbs 'link', or connect, the subject to another noun, pronoun or adjective that further identifies or describes it:

> I <u>am</u> the *master* of my fate: I <u>am</u> the *captain* of my soul.

Just like any other part of speech, though, there are times when these words are not used in the traditional sense. Sometimes they are used as action verbs, so it is important to analyse the function of the word before determining its type. The easiest way to tell if a verb is action or linking is to replace the word with an appropriate form of *be* (*am/are/is/was/were*). For example:

> The meaning of the poem remains a mystery to me.

In this case, you can take out the linking verb *remains*, replace it with 'is', and the sentence still makes sense. Therefore, *remains* is performing the function of a *linking verb*.

Now consider:

> I smell the dusty aroma of the library, and immediately I feel the nostalgia of a well-read childhood!

Here, if you replace the verb 'smell' with another form of 'be', the sentence no longer makes sense:

> I *am* the dusty aroma of the library ...!

Therefore, in this sentence, 'smell' is being used to express the physical action of smelling with one's nose. Now consider the verb 'feel', which is used in the latter clause of the sentence. Is it functioning as an action or linking verb?

ACTIVITY 15

Using the strategy just described, test the following linking verbs to see if they are being used traditionally or if they are expressing action.

1 The crowd felt spellbound by the poet's lyrics.
2 Denise turned the first page of her novel and began to read.
3 The first line of his masterpiece simply read: 'The air felt crisp.'
4 The cover of the old, leather journal felt smooth and velvety.
5 At the poetry festival, they served freshly-squeezed orange juice, but I tasted a hint of sourness.

Action verbs

Action verbs express physical, mental or emotional action. The list of possibilities is seemingly endless, so generally the rule is: if it is not one of the traditional linking verbs just discussed, it is an action verb.

Verb phrases

Verbs do not always appear as a single word. Sometimes they are expressed as a phrase.

To create tense, a **verb phrase** is needed, which may combine a main verb with one or more **auxiliary verbs**. For example:

Past	The first instalment of his poetry <u>had been published</u> in the earlier part of the century, though it is just now gaining popularity.
Present	His most recent work <u>does flow</u> much better than his past publications.
Future	He <u>will be writing</u> for a new publishing house sometime next year.

Modals can be used to express attitude and intensity toward the verb.

He <u>may be writing</u> for a new publishing house sometime next year.

In this case, 'may' expresses an attitude of possibility.

ACTIVITY 16

Read the following sentences, which have been adapted from Homer's *The Iliad*. In this famous scene, Hector attempts to fight Greece's most undefeatable warrior, Achilles. Identify the action verbs.

1 Achilles poised his spear and hurled it.
2 Hector saw it and avoided it; he crouched down, so it flew over his head and landed in the ground beyond.
3 Without Hector knowing, goddess Minerva retrieved the spear and passed it back to Achilles.
4 Now Hector returned the favour. He hoisted his spear, but it hit the centre of Achilles' shield and rebounded. In defeat, Hector admitted: 'My fate is upon me.'
5 As he spoke, Hector swiftly drew the keen blade that hung so great and strong by his side, and gathering himself together, he sprang on Achilles like a soaring eagle that swoops down from the clouds on to some lamb or timid hare.
6 Achilles in his mad rage darted towards him with his wondrous shield before his breast.
7 The brave Trojan, full of honour and glory, immediately fell upon Achilles' blow.
8 Hector, in his dying breath, then uttered his last words before death enfolded him.

231

Here is a list of modals:

MODALS		
forms of 'be'	forms of 'have'	forms of 'do'
should	may	will
would	must	shall
could	might	
can	ought	

To determine if a verb phrase is action or linking, consider the function of the *main* verb in context:

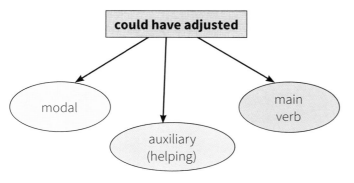

'Adjusted' is an action verb, so 'could have adjusted' is an action verb phrase.

ACTIVITY 17

Identify the verb(s) in each of the poetry extracts which follow, and any auxiliary verbs and modals.

1 Do not go gentle into that good night, / Old age should burn and rave at close of day; / Rage, rage against the dying of the light.

From 'Do Not Go Gentle Into That Good Night' by Dylan Thomas

2 Shall I compare thee to a summer's day? / Thou art more lovely and more temperate.

From Sonnet 18 by William Shakespeare

3 Gather ye rosebuds while ye may, / Old time is still a-flying: / And this same flower that smiles to-day / To-morrow will be dying.

From 'To the Virgins, to Make Much of Time' by Robert Herrick

Infinitives

As you learnt in Chapter 4.2 Section *B Prepositions*, an infinitive is a verb preceded by the word *to*. This phrase then turns into a noun, an adjective or an adverb, as shown in the following examples:

Use of infinitive	Example
Subject of a sentence	<u>To err</u> is human.
Predicate nominative (see Chapter 4.4 Section *B Complements*)	Author of *Treasure Island*, Robert Louis Stevenson's dream *had always been* <u>to write</u>.
Direct object (see this chapter Section *C Pronouns*)	In *The Great Gatsby*, main character Nick Carraway hopes <u>to rest</u> from the anxieties of his current like, but his encounters with Gatsby prove otherwise.
Adjective	Because of his clear imagery and conversational tone, the best *poet* <u>to mimic</u> is Li Po.
Adverb	In his famous poem, 'The Raven', Edgar Allan Poe tells of a raven *coming* <u>to visit</u>, which mocks at his sorrow upon losing his love, Lenore.

Like verbs, infinitives can appear in the form of phrases, too. Consider the following statement, which demonstrates this. The sentence is about poet Maya Angelou's upbringing:

> To grow up in Stamps, Arkansas, in the 1930s <u>was</u> to know great hardship.

First, identify the verb: 'was'. The phrase following the verb, 'to know great hardship' is another infinitive phrase, which serves as the predicate nominative of the sentence.

 KEY SKILLS

Remember that the word *to* plus a noun or pronoun is a prepositional phrase, not an infinitive. See Chapter 4.2 Section *B Prepositions* to review prepositional phrases.

Finding the subject and verb in questions

Questions present language in an inverted order, so it can sometimes be more difficult to find the subject and verb of a sentence; this is particularly so because the words making up verb phrases often get separated from one another. A helpful strategy for finding the subject and verb in a question is to rephrase the question as a statement, using all words from the original as far as possible:

> Will many people be attending the Classic Literature Festival in Dublin next week?
>
> Many people <u>will be attending</u> the Classic Literature Festival in Dublin next week.

With the word order restored, it is easier to see that the subject is 'people' and the action they are performing is contained in the verb phrase, 'will be attending'.

> <u>Will</u> many *people* <u>be attending</u> the Classic Literature Festival in Dublin next week?

Try this strategy on the following questions:

1 Even if you dislike the genre, will you please give the story a chance anyway?

2 Has there ever been a winner at this level of the contest?

3 Can poetry still change anything?

4 Won't you be reading the final book in her series once it hits the shelves?

Note that question 4 requires you to also break down the contraction in order to get to the essence of the question:

> Won't you be reading the final book in her series once it hits the shelves?
>
> *You* <u>will</u> (or will not) <u>be reading</u> the final book in her series once it hits the shelves.

As demonstrated, you should be careful to fully deconstruct contractions to understand the full intention of the sentence!

Common errors with subjects and verbs

Being able to recognise whether your sentences contain a verb or not will play a key role in how strong your use of English is. While sentence fragments (those not containing both subject and verb) can hinder communication and confuse meaning, complete sentences help ensure flow and clarity in your writing. As you learned in Chapter 4.1, removing descriptive language such as prepositions, adjectives and adverbs can help you see whether your sentence contains the essential components necessary to form a complete thought.

Other issues can also arise, however. This section will help you to be aware of, and to avoid, one of the most common errors: subject–verb agreement.

Subject–verb agreement

For a sentence to be complete, it must contain a subject and a verb. There is another descriptive rule, however, to ensure your sentence is grammatically accurate. Like pronouns and their antecedents, subjects must agree with their verbs:

- If a subject is singular, the verb is singular. (The *child* <u>is</u> a scholar.)
- If a subject is plural, the verb is plural. (The *children* <u>are</u> bright.)

In a verb phrase, the first auxiliary verb should agree with the subject:

> During the festival, *poets* <u>were signing</u> autographs.

232

It may *seem* simple enough, but finding the subject and verb of a sentence is not always very clear. In fact, when subjects are distanced far enough from the action they perform, it can sometimes cause agreement issues between subject and verb:

> *Poets* ~~who agree that verse can be a radical form of art and expression~~ <u>were contributing</u> to the panel.

Notice in the sentence above that a rather large clause stands between the subject 'poets' and the verb phrase 'were contributing'. Sometimes, a prepositional phrase can come between the two. At other times, a relative clause (those that begin with 'that', 'which', 'who', 'whom' and 'whose': see also Chapter 4.4) can also cause disruption. Sometimes, an appositive phrase – which is a descriptive phrase offset by commas – can stand between the subject and verb:

> One *aspect* of Felipe Alfau's novel, ~~published forty years after it was actually written~~, <u>concerns</u> the illusion of time.

If you identify and omit these words and phrases, you are in a better position to see if the subject and verb agree.

Compound subjects

Recall some of the rules you learnt about pronoun-antecedent agreement. The following rules – which concern compound subjects – are very similar:

1 Subjects containing *and* usually take a plural verb.

2 Singular subjects containing 'or' or 'nor' use a singular subject.

3 Plural subjects using 'or' or 'nor' use a plural verb.

4 When a singular subject + a plural subject contain 'or' or 'nor', the verb should agree with the nearer subject.

ACTIVITY 18

Apply the rules we have just considered to the following activity. Determine whether the subject and verb agree in each statement. Where the subjects and verbs do *not* agree, rewrite the statement so that they do.

1 Though it may use everyday words, unique sequence and order are the qualities that make poetry come alive with possibility.

2 Either the upbeat rhyme of lyrical poetry or the subtle rhythm of its pace are what make it unique to prose.

3 Transcendentalists, Romantics and the Eskimo poet has given us a unique way to perceive the world around us and experience the human mind.

4 According to the headstone of a well-known expressionist, artists and poets are the nerve endings of humanity because of the delicate sensitivity they uniquely tap into.

5 Poets who have suffered loss or the artist who has overcome near-certain death are able to access the unconscious in a way that others cannot.

As a general rule, expressions of amount such as measurements, fractions and percentages require a:

- *singular* verb when the amount is thought of as a single unit
- *plural* verb when the amount is thought of as separate parts.

To determine if an expression of amount is singular or plural, replace it with the pronoun 'it' or 'they' to find out which makes sense. For example:

> <u>Two-thirds</u> of the *Rubáiyát* collection <u>is written</u> by Omar Khayyam, whereas one third is the work of his translator, Edward Fitzgerald.

TIP

Academic subjects or areas of study often seem to be plural. However, they take singular verbs because they are considered a *single* area of study:
- civics
- economics
- gymnastics
- genetics
- linguistics.

Other items that look plural but take singular verbs include:

Titles of works	*Romeo and Juliet* is my favourite play.
Countries	*Trinidad and Tobago* is a beautiful country.
Cities	*Los Angeles* is home to a number of artists.
Organisations	The *United Nations* is an international organisation.

E Practising what you have learnt

Return to the paragraph that you wrote at the beginning of the chapter in response to the question

> What do you think makes poetry so appealing?

Then complete the following tasks. (Note: you will need several different coloured pens or highlighters for this activity.)

1 Highlight/annotate the following on your answer:

Colour 1: *proper nouns*

Colour 2: *indefinite pronouns*

Colour 3: *action verbs.*

2 Look at the presence and/or absence of the three colours on your paragraph. Consider the following:

a Proper nouns can help you point out specifics when describing. How specific is your writing?

b Indefinite pronouns, which replace other pronouns, can sound vague. How often do you use these in your writing?

c Some writers believe that action verbs are a writer's most powerful tool. How often do you use action verbs? How strong are those you use?

d How do essential parts of speech affect the quality of your writing?

e How will you use these parts of speech to improve your writing? With a fourth colour, highlight any other parts of speech you use that you feel improve the quality of your writing.

Use the following exam-style questions on this chapter's theme *Is there a place for poetry in the modern world?* for practice in essay writing.

EXAM-STYLE QUESTIONS

Essay questions

1 'A poem can be read, but to be truly appreciated, it must be heard.' Assess this perspective. **[30]**

2 'Without poetry, there is no society.' Discuss. **[30]**

3 'Rap is the most genuine form of expression in the music industry.' What is your view? **[30]**

4 Assess the intrinsic value of reading the poetry of others. **[30]**

5 To what extent does your society support and promote local poets? **[30]**

6 Assess the impact that poets from your society have had on the world. **[30]**

7 Analyse and evaluate the work of a famous poet. **[30]**

8 How far would you agree that poetry has the power to inspire real social and/or political change? **[30]**

9 To what extent can poetry change anything? **[30]**

10 'Poetry is fine, but of little use.' What is your view?

Summary

Key points to remember from this chapter:

- Nouns can be easy to spot when they are in the form of persons, places or things, but *ideas* can be harder to recognise. Remember that words preceded by an article are always nouns, and nouns can also be the object of prepositions.
- Nouns can make your writing more specific, particularly if you take advantage of concrete nouns and proper nouns.
- Words often classified as pronouns can have other functions in a sentence. Different categories of pronouns can share the same list of words. Be sure to analyse the function of a word to determine its part of speech.
- Depending on tense, verbs can take on different forms. They can appear as single words or whole phrases.
- Writing in complete sentences is a key skill in this course. Identifying the essential parts of speech (subject + verb) will improve your use of English.
- Some of the most common grammatical errors arise from misunderstanding the descriptive rules regarding the essential parts of speech, as outlined in this chapter. Agreement errors are a good example.

Chapter 4.4
Adding complexity to your writing

Online news and entertainment are quickly replacing the need for paperbacks. This chapter will explore the theme of *Media as literature*.

Learning objectives

In this chapter, you will learn that:

- adding variety to your sentences can improve your overall writing style
- complements can clarify your ideas and add detail
- conjunctions can help you structure sentences in different ways
- using punctuation properly is key in clear communication.

A Introduction

In Chapter 4.3 Section *D Verbs*, you learnt that just one word can form a sentence, so long as a verb is present and a subject is inferred. Writers like John Steinbeck, Hermann Hesse and Ernest Hemingway have used simple sentence structure to great effect:

> He unstopped the mast and furled the sail and tied it. Then he shouldered the mast and started to climb. It was then he knew the depth of his tiredness. He stopped for a moment and looked back and saw in the reflection from the street light the great tail of the fish standing up well behind the skiff's stern. He saw the white naked line of his backbone and the dark mass of the head with the projecting bill and all the nakedness between.
>
> *From* The Old Man and the Sea
> *by Ernest Hemingway (1952)*

Meanwhile, French author Marcel Proust is famously known for his labyrinthine sentence structure:

> The name Gilberte passed close by me, evoking all the more forcibly her whom it labelled in that it did not merely refer to her, as one speaks of a man in his absence, but was directly addressed to her; it passed thus close by me, in action, so to speak, with a force that increased with the curve of its trajectory and as it drew near to its target; — carrying in its wake, I could feel, the knowledge, the impression of her to whom it was addressed that belonged not to me but to the friend who called to her, everything that, while she uttered the words, she more or less vividly reviewed, possessed in her memory, of their daily intimacy, of the visits that they paid to each other, of that unknown existence which was all the more inaccessible, all the more painful to me from being, conversely, so familiar, so tractable to this happy girl who let her message brush past me without my being able to penetrate its surface, who flung it on the air with a light-hearted cry: letting float in the atmosphere the delicious attar which that message had distilled, by touching them with precision, from certain invisible points in Mlle Swann's life, from the evening to come, as it would be, after dinner, at her home, — forming, on its celestial passage through the midst of the children and their nursemaids, a little cloud, exquisitely coloured, like the cloud that, curling over one of Poussin's gardens, reflects minutely, like a cloud in the opera, teeming with chariots and horses, some apparition of the life of the gods; casting, finally, on that ragged grass, at the spot on which she stood (at once a scrap of withered lawn and a moment in the afternoon of the fair player, who continued to beat up and catch her shuttlecock until a governess, with a blue feather in her hat, had called her away) a marvellous little band of light, of the colour of heliotrope, spread over the lawn like a carpet on which I could not tire of treading to and fro with lingering feet, nostalgic and profane, while Françoise shouted: 'Come on, button up your coat, look, and let's get away!' and I remarked for the first time how common her speech was, and that she had, alas, no blue feather in her hat.
>
> *From* In Search of Lost Time, *'Volume 1: Swann's Way'*
> *by Marcel Proust (1913)*

This example, which has nearly 400 words in a single sentence, makes Edgar Allan Poe, also known for the complexity of his sentence structure, seem simple in comparison!

In this chapter, you will explore the complexities of grammatical structure, which can help you deepen your own ideas and develop your writing style. To add complexity to your writing, you will learn more about:

- adding complements to sentence predicates
- using conjunctions to create sentence variety
- using punctuation to manage sentence structure.

As a practicing writer, you have likely developed sentences that have used these approaches already, but the point of this segment is to help you build awareness as to how these choices can improve your writing. Therefore, before you learn more about these, read the following question and write a one-paragraph response to it. Remember to let your response flow as naturally as possible. Apply as little or as much structure to your sentences as you need to make a clear point. Write no more than 100 words.

> To what extent is traditional literature being replaced by online news and entertainment?

ACTIVITY 1

Swap responses with a partner and observe each other's approach to the same writing task.

As you did in Chapters 4.2 and 4.3 Activity 1, use the following statement stems to share your observations, or create your own:

- I am impressed by …
- Tell me what you meant by …
- What made you decide …?
- An observation I made about the content of your paragraph is …
- An observation I made about your paragraph's use of English is …

Keep your written response. You will return to it at the end of this chapter.

B Complements

'I am' is a powerful assertion. The subject is *I*, so we know who or what the sentence is about, and the linking verb *am* is the predicate, so we know what action the subject is performing.

But your writing will need more than this if you are going to accomplish aims like explaining, convincing and exploring the complexities of contemporary issues!

For a simple sentence to have all its component parts, it will need a **complement** following the verb.

KEY TERM

Complement: a word or group of words which appear in the predicate of a sentence in order to complete a thought.

In addition to the verb, the predicate of a sentence can include:

- a direct object
- an indirect object
- predicate nominatives
- predicate adjectives.

In this section, you will learn how to identify each of these parts of the predicate and apply them, to enhance the complexity of your writing.

Direct objects

Consider a sentence like, 'The internet introduced.' This is, technically, a complete sentence because of its 'subject + verb' structure, but it fails to communicate anything of value. What is missing?

It appears that *something* needs to receive the action of being introduced. By answering *whom* or *what* receives the action of a verb, you are establishing the direct object in the sentence. In the English language, sentences usually consist of: Subject + Verb + Object.

TIP
Remember that, just like the subject of a sentence, the direct object will never appear in a prepositional phrase (see Chapter 4.1 Section *D Why grammar matters*).

The internet introduced an alternative source of information for avid readers everywhere.

ACTIVITY 2

Read the sentence that captions the photo. Rewrite it on a separate sheet of paper. To find the object of the sentence, complete the following steps:

1. Identify the prepositional phrases by placing brackets (parentheses) around them.
2. Identify any adjectives or adverbs by circling them.
3. Identify the subject by putting a box around who or what the sentence is about.
4. Underline what action the subject is performing.
5. Double-underline the direct object, which is receiving the action of the sentence.

It is possible for a verb to be performing its action on more than one direct object, called a *compound* direct object. Conjunctions like 'and' usually indicate this:

> The internet offers quick access to information and instant updates.

What is the compound direct object in the sentence above?

DID YOU KNOW?

When a verb is followed by a direct object, the verb is considered *transitive*.

When a verb does not have a direct object, it is referred to as an *intransitive* verb.

ACTIVITY 3

Identify the direct object in the following sentences.

1 Quite literally, the internet may threaten the shelf-life of classic literature, though there may be some hope yet.

2 Scottish poet and playwright, Carol Ann Duffy, compares poetry to texting since both are short, concise expressions of thought.

3 Poetry uses language in a way that is relevant to digitally driven youth because of its brevity.

4 For instance, re-imagine the greatest lines of poetry in the form of a text or tweet!

Indirect objects

In addition to containing a direct object, sometimes a sentence will also contain an *indirect object* just before it. This is a noun or pronoun which names the person or thing *receiving* the action. Look at this example:

> Blogging expert Micha Liu will pitch her audience of aspiring writers a contest to become a featured writer on her website.

Ask yourself the following questions:

• Who or what is Liu 'pitching'? (She is pitching a *contest*.)

• *To whom* or *to what* is she pitching the contest? (Her *audience* of aspiring writers.)

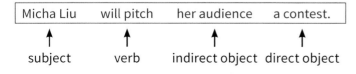

Micha Liu	will pitch	her audience	a contest.
↑	↑	↑	↑
subject	verb	indirect object	direct object

TIP

Indirect objects only appear in sentences where a transitive verb is present!

Keep in mind that the same rules already described for direct objects also apply here: indirect objects can be compound, and they will never be found as part of a prepositional phrase.

ACTIVITY 4

The Pepe the Frog meme became a right-wing icon and is used here to mock the activist movement Black Lives Matter.

Identify the indirect object in each of the following sentences.

1 Memes provide internet users entertainment through their hilarious images and trendy catch-phrases.

2 Yet as they spread virally on the web, memes can offer the world undertones of a much more sinister message.

3 In 2016, the US Anti-Defamation League handed Pepe the Frog his fate by placing him on their banned list of images.

4 Racist group Alt-right gave Pepe the Frog his infamous status as the most notorious image for spreading bigoted online memes.

5 In an era where online internet sharing runs out of control, experts give users tips for sharing responsibly.

Subject complements

Direct and indirect objects work in partnership with *action* verbs. In the follow sections, you will learn about the complements that fall after *linking* verbs to complete the predicate of a sentence:

- predicate nominatives
- predicate adjectives.

These are collectively known as **subject complements**.

KEY TERM

Subject complement: the adjective, noun or pronoun that follows a linking verb and tells us more about the subject of the sentence.

Predicate nominatives

Predicate nominatives are nouns or pronouns that are connected to the subject of the sentence by a linking verb. By simply finishing the statement *I am* with a noun or pronoun, you are using a predicate nominative:

> I am a student of English.

By removing the preposition, you can quickly identify the predicate nominative as 'student'. As with trying to identify a direct object, asking 'Whom?' or 'What?' in relation to the linking verb will lead you to the predicate nominative.

Using the strategies you have learnt so far, deconstruct the following sentence as far as you can:

> In 2012, the Kony 2012 video by Invisible Children, Inc became the most viral video in history, which exposed the injustices of child abuse in Central Africa.

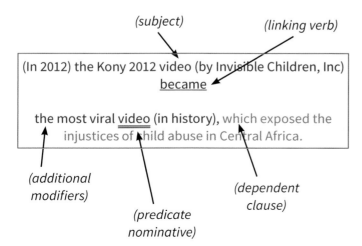

(subject)   *(linking verb)*

(In 2012) the Kony 2012 video (by Invisible Children, Inc) **became**

the most viral <u>video</u> (in history), which exposed the injustices of child abuse in Central Africa.

(additional modifiers)   *(dependent clause)*

(predicate nominative)

Activists organising a campaign to spread awareness about Joseph Kony's unjust use of child soldiers in Uganda.

TIP

Notice that after the Subject + Verb + Complement, the sentence extends further with a comma + *which* clause. This is called a *dependent clause*. You will learn more about these later in this chapter.

Predicate adjectives

Just like predicate nominatives, predicate adjectives add description and clarification to a sentence. And just like the other complements you have learnt about, these can also be compound:

> Viral videos like Psy's 'Gangnam style' are often entertaining and humorous, so they are swiftly eclipsing the age-old practice of reading for leisure.

Can you identify the *compound* predicate adjectives?

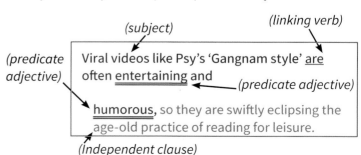

(subject)   *(linking verb)*

(predicate adjective)   Viral videos like Psy's 'Gangnam style' <u>are</u> often <u>entertaining</u> and   *(predicate adjective)*

<u>humorous,</u> so they are swiftly eclipsing the age-old practice of reading for leisure.

(Independent clause)

This is another example of a sentence which contains components that stretch beyond Subject + Verb + Complement. Starting with the comma + *so*, a whole new independent clause is formed. You will learn how to add complexity to the style and structure of your own sentences as you work through the rest of this chapter.

ACTIVITY 5

Copy the following chart onto a separate sheet of paper, allowing one row per sentence **1–7**.

	Subject	Verb	Complement	Type
1	anyone	can have	website	Predicate nominative
2				

Read the following sentences, which talk about 'spoof' (fake) websites. Complete the chart by deconstructing the Subject + Verb + Complement for each sentence. The first one has been done for you.

1 Today, anyone can have a website of their own.

2 As a result, a growing trend to create fake, or 'spoof', websites is causing problems in the online world because audiences are being fooled by them.

3 One website markets a fake product called Havidol, which apparently cures the fictitious illness Dysphoric Social Attention Consumption Deficit Anxiety Disorder (DSACDAD).

4 The parody is one artist's response to the unfair market tactics of the drug industry.

5 The website is impressively equipped with testimonials, frequently asked questions, scientific data and report abstracts, and a shop with company logos.

6 Creator Justine Cooper, an Australian artist, even offers her audience a self-assessment tool to determine whether or not they might suffer from DSACDAD and if Havidol is right for them.

7 With its professional appearance, this site has fooled plenty of viewers who think the illness is real!

241

You will now have learnt several ways in which you can add detail to your writing. Using parts of speech such as prepositions, adjectives, adverbs and complements can help you extend your thoughts and clarify ideas for the reader.

C Structuring more complex sentences

Complements can add detail and extend the range of thought in your sentences. Yet these are still relatively **simple sentences** in terms of structure, using just Subject + Verb + Complement to express an idea.

KEY TERM

Simple sentence: a sentence that contains subject, verb and complement.

There are three other, more complex options for structuring sentences, which we will look at in this section:

- complex
- compound
- compound-complex.

In order to structure complex or compound sentences, you will need to understand the importance of yet another part of speech – conjunctions. You also need to know how and when to appropriately use punctuation such as the comma and the semicolon. In fact, sentences that extend beyond the 'simple' structure require a combination of conjunctions and punctuation. Misusing these tools, however, will quickly lead to grammatical inaccuracy.

In the remaining sections of this chapter, you will learn about the correct use of:

- conjunctions
- **clauses**
- sentence types and punctuation.

KEY TERM

Clause: a unit of grammatical organisation containing a subject and predicate; clauses can stand alone as simple sentences or be part of a larger sentence.

At the end of the chapter, you will have the opportunity to apply this knowledge to your own writing to add variety and style.

Conjunctions

Conjunctions are those words that connect words or phrases together. There are three types of conjunctions:

- coordinating
- correlative
- subordinating.

You will learn about each of these in the following sections.

Coordinating conjunctions

There are seven coordinating conjunctions. You may find it helpful to remember these by using the acronym FANBOYS:

For	**O**r
And	**Y**et
Not	**S**o
But	

Coordinating conjunctions will help you join two independent clauses together to create a compound sentence. There will be more on this later in the chapter.

Correlative conjunctions

Correlative conjunctions work in pairs to connect words or phrases in a sentence. It is important to remember that each pair always works together!

The correlative conjunction pairs are:

both … and
either … or
neither … nor
not only … but also
whether … or

Knowing the patterns listed above is important for two main reasons:

- A correlative pair such as 'not only … but also' can help you to achieve a seamless transition from one essay idea to another. This not only makes ideas clear, but also logically progressive. (For a review of seamless transitions, see Chapter 1.2 Section *F Key elements of an essay*.)
- A common grammatical error involves confusion between the pairs 'either … or' and 'neither … nor': 'neither' is often used with 'or' instead of its proper partner, 'nor'. Or one is used without the other:

> Spoof websites have neither a credible domain name or a professional-looking home page. ✗
>
> Viewers want to feel not only safe but informed. ✗

How would you edit these sentences to use correlative conjunctions more appropriately?

Subordinating conjunctions

Like coordinators, *subordinating* conjunctions are also used to join together two complete ideas. The difference is that, when connected by subordinating conjunctions, one of the formerly independent thoughts is now dependent upon the other, or *subordinate* to it. For example:

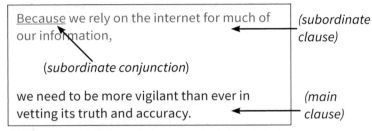

> Because we rely on the internet for much of our information, *(subordinate clause)*
>
> *(subordinate conjunction)*
>
> we need to be more vigilant than ever in vetting its truth and accuracy. *(main clause)*

Subordinating conjunctions are the words used to create dependent clauses, which you will learn more about later in this chapter.

Subordinating conjunctions			
as	before	although	so that
as if	after	even	provided that
as though	while	though	in order that
as long/	since	even though	
soon/well as	unless	even if	than
	until	if	why
when	because		
where			
whenever			
wherever			
whether			

These conjunctions are extremely important in creating variety in your sentence structure. They are used as follows:

Type of conjunction	Type of sentence
coordinating	compound
	complex-compound
subordinating	complex
	complex-compound

Read the following extract about the spread of fake news. Then complete Activity 6.

US President Donald Trump was one of the first to use the term 'fake news'.

From untrue celebrity gossip to made-up stories about politicians, fake news is on the rise in the world of social media. Since we rely on social media sites to stay informed, it is imperative that more action be taken to minimise the falsehoods in our headlines. Facebook, which was under fire for letting this happen, now allows users in America and Germany to 'flag' information whenever they think it contains questionable input. Third-party fact checkers and experts then look into each case; they either allow the story to remain or they mark it with a 'disputed' tag for readers to see. Apparently, this tag will decrease the article's visibility on the network because it gets a lower value in Facebook's algorithm. Although the company cannot prevent sharing fake news, another warning does present itself to the user to remind him or her that the information has been flagged as fake. Meanwhile, one of the biggest French newspapers, *Le Monde*, is working on a programme to help them strengthen their ability to fact-check. Because it is connected to a database that ranks sites as real, fake or satirical – called Decodex – this is supposed to lessen instances of fake news from spreading. Another popular news site, *Slate*, has not only stepped up the call to stop fake news but has also created their own browser extension to fight it, and they are calling it 'This is fake'. Progress is underway. However, until real legislation is passed to remove the fake tales that circulate, 'alternative truth' will continue to populate social media feeds all over the world.

ACTIVITY 6

On a copy of the extract about fake news:
1 Single-underline the coordinating conjunctions.
2 Circle the subordinating conjunctions.
3 Double-underline correlative pairs.
4 Write one sentence that summarises the extract.

Clauses

If you understand how clauses work in a sentence, you can learn how to improve your own sentence structure and style. Introducing variety in your writing can make the difference between a lively, engaging message and one that sounds monotonous and bland.

In the following extract, writer Gary Provost demonstrates the importance of sentence variety very effectively:

This sentence has five words. Here are five more words. Five word sentences are fine. But several together become monotonous. Listen to what is happening. The writing is getting boring. The sound of it drones. It's like a stuck record. The ear demands some variety.

Now listen.

I vary the sentence length and I create music.

Music. The writing sings. It has a pleasant rhythm, a lilt, a harmony. I use short sentences. And I use sentences of medium length.

And sometimes, when I am certain the reader is rested, I will engage him with a sentence of considerable length, a sentence that burns with energy and builds with all the impetus of a crescendo, the roll of drums, the crash of cymbals, – sounds that say listen to this, it is important.

100 Ways To Improve Your Writing by Gary Provost, 1985

As Provost demonstrates in the extract, variety can do much to empower your writing. By stringing together clauses, you can achieve the effect he illustrates here. Recall that clauses are a group of words which contain a subject and verb. This sets them apart from prepositional phrases, for instance, which do not contain a verb. There are two main types of clauses:

- **independent clauses**
- **dependent** (subordinate) **clauses**.

243

KEY TERMS

Independent clause: a clause that can stand alone as a complete sentence.
Dependent clause: a clause that is preceded by a subordinating conjunction or relative pronoun, so it cannot stand alone as a complete thought.

A simple sentence is an independent clause:

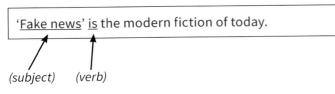

'Fake news' is the modern fiction of today.

(subject)   (verb)

When a subordinating conjunction or relative pronoun appears at the start of an independent clause, however, it becomes dependent upon the rest of the sentence to give it meaning. Otherwise, the thought is a fragment:

Because fake news is the modern fiction of today.

(subordinating conjunction)

Notice that the addition of just one word now makes the reader think: well, what of it? If this clause is left as it is, it does not express a complete thought. Subordinate clauses can only be part of another sentence. They cannot stand on their own.

independent clause ⟶ simple sentence

dependent clause ⟶ fragment

Because of this, dependent clauses usually take on the job of an adjective or adverb, where the word group modifies another word. These clauses can also serve as the subject of a sentence, functioning collectively as a noun would.

KEY SKILLS

You may have heard the advice not to begin a sentence with 'because'. This is true if the sentence stands alone as a dependent clause, but it is not true if the sentence beginning with 'because' links up with an independent clause to complete its thought.

Adjective clauses

A clause that describes a noun or pronoun in the sentence is called an *adjective* clause. These can be particularly useful in helping you define concepts for an audience who may not know as much about a topic as you do. Adjective clauses start with a relative pronoun (*that, which, who, whom, whose*). These are called *relative clauses*. For example:

Spoof websites, *which are hoax websites meant to mislead the viewer,* can be created for the simple purpose of humour or the malicious purpose of fraud.

Notice that the insertion of this clause helps the reader to understand what a 'spoof website' is without having to add a separate sentence to define it.

TIP

Always assume your reader does not know as much as you do about a subject! Use relative clauses to define content-specific terms.

In this last example, the clause is *non-essential*. In other words, if you took it out, the sentence would still make sense. At other times, adjective clauses are essential to the sentence, such as the one below:

The first YouTube star *whose content made him a celebrity* was Justin Bieber, now an international megastar in the pop music industry.

If you took the adjective clause out, it would alter the meaning of the sentence. However popular, Justin Bieber was not the first YouTube star ever!

DID YOU KNOW?

The first video ever uploaded to the popular video website YouTube was an 18-second clip by founder Jawed Karim on 23 April 2005. In the video, he is at the zoo talking about elephants.

The first video ever to go 'viral' was posted in 2006 by American vlogger Gary Brolsma, who is featured lip-synching the 'Numa Numa' lyrics made popular by Moldovan band, O-Zone.

244

YouTube sensation, Psy. On 21 December 2012, the music video for his hit single 'Gangnam Style' became the first to exceed one billion views on the website. Psy was subsequently named by the media as 'King of YouTube'.

Adjective clauses tell us *What kind?* or *Which one*? They most often appear directly after the word they are modifying. Otherwise, if separated, this can easily lead to a misplaced modifier. Remember that this is one of the most common errors that writers make, so it is important to know how it happens and how to avoid it.

 KEY SKILLS

Misplacing a modifier can decrease clear communication of your point. See Chapter 4.2 Section *C Common errors* to review how to fix these kinds of errors.

Adverb clauses

Just as adverbs modify verbs, adjectives and other adverbs, so do adverb clauses. Specifically, if you include these clauses in your writing, it will tell your audience *how, when, where, why, to what extent* or *under what condition.*

While adjective clauses start with relative pronouns, adverb clauses are initiated by subordinate conjunctions (e.g. *because, though, since, until, while*):

> *Since users can now post their own videos to websites like Facebook*, this has given everyday citizens the unique ability to share breaking news just as a journalist would.

Notice that with larger clauses, some of the smaller units of language you have already learnt about are also embedded within these (e.g. prepositional phrases).

Noun clauses

Sometimes entire clauses can perform the job of a single noun. For example, the subject of a sentence may be expressed in a clause. Noun clauses can also appear as the object of a preposition, or as a complement:

Function	Example
As the subject of a sentence	'The privilege of the platform' originally meant that very few people had access to a printing press, so spreading information was considered a privilege.
As the object of a preposition	Digital technology now extends this privilege to whomever possesses basic computer skills.
As the direct object of an action verb	We should watch what we share, however.
As the indirect object of an action verb	The media should give all citizens sharing newsworthy information some sort of credit for keeping the public informed.
As the predicate nominative of a linking verb	However, the reality of this is that not everyone shares factual information, which unfortunately does just the opposite.

Notice that noun clauses often begin with either relative pronouns or subordinating conjunctions.

Sentence types and use of punctuation

Writing with sentences of varying length and complexity can help you communicate ideas that flow for the reader. Your knowledge of clauses can help you achieve this aim because sentence types are determined by the number and type of clauses they have. Based on their clause structure, sentences can be categorised as follows:

- simple
- complex
- compound
- compound-complex.

Simple sentences

'Simple sentences' might sound like those used in children's books, and in part, this is true. However, not all simple sentences are four or five words! Though containing only one independent clause (IC), the simple sentence may also contain:

- prepositional phrases (see Chapter 4.1 Section *D Why grammar matters*)
- compound subjects (see Chapter 4.3 Section *D Verbs*)
- compound verbs.

Consider this lengthy sentence about Amazon's new role as an online publisher:

> According to an article in the *New York Times*, the e-commerce mega-company Amazon will publish over 100 books this autumn from a variety of genres in both physical and e-book form.

Can you find the subject and verb? (Hint: there is just one independent clause.)

Complex sentences

A complex sentence adds a dependent clause to a simple sentence:

> one independent clause (IC) + one dependent clause (DC)

These component parts can appear in any order, as long as the sentence flows and makes sense. Remember that the dependent clause will be led by either a subordinating conjunction or a relative pronoun:

> *While most consumers view Amazon as the central hub for online shopping*, businesses such as publishing houses see them as a threatening monopoly.

In this case, notice that the dependent clause starts the sentence, followed by the main clause.

Compound sentences

When two complete sentences are joined together, they form a compound sentence:

> one independent clause (IC) + one independent clause (IC)

Compound sentences are often formed by using a 'comma + coordinating conjunction' to fuse them together:

> Agents help writers find publishing houses to fit their style and needs, but as Amazon's publishing endeavour takes hold, this profession might see substantial decline.

Another way to join two closely-related sentences is by using a semicolon:

> Agents help writers find publishing houses to fit their style and needs; as Amazon's publishing endeavour takes hold, this profession might see substantial decline.

KEY SKILLS

When using a semicolon to join two sentences together, consider whether you need a conjunctive adverb to express the relationship between the two sentences. Review Chapter 4.2 Section *E Adverbs* to see which from the list of conjunctive adverbs might fit well in the sentence in place of *as*.

One of the most common errors that developing writers make is to use only a comma to combine independent clauses. However, the comma can only handle dependent clauses, so its usefulness is limited. For example:

> In addition to being a publisher, Amazon is a retailer, they have instant access to readers, which means a greater chance of increasing sales than a traditional publisher might. ✗

How would you adjust the punctuation in the sentence to make it grammatically correct? In the next section, you will find out about using punctuation appropriately when writing sentences that have more complicated structures.

Compound-complex sentences

The most complicated of all sentence types, a compound-complex sentence, contains at least two independent clauses just like a compound sentence, but at least *one* of these independent clauses also has a dependent clause attached to it! Keep in mind that a dependent clause can appear anywhere in the sentence:

> one independent clause (IC) + one dependent clause (DC) + one independent clause (IC)

Here is an example of a compound-complex sentence:

> To some writers, going through a traditional publisher can be a painstakingly slow process, but other writers claim the time is worth it since the support of a well-established publishing house can raise an author's authority considerably.

246

Read the paragraph about Amazon's new move toward publishing as part of its e-commerce expansion. Determine whether each sentence is simple (S), complex (CX), compound (CP), or compound-complex (CPX).

(1) For years, self-publishing carried the stigma of being the desperate alternative for authors who were rejected by major publishing houses. (2) Today, however, this is no longer the case; e-books have transformed into a billion-dollar industry. (3) One of the greatest perks is that authors get to keep up to three-quarters of sales revenue, which doubles or even triples the measly royalties earned through traditional publishing avenues. (4) They get much more creative control, too. (5) These 'independent books' have become best-sellers and blockbusters. (6) There is a lot that goes into publishing a book, though. (7) Authors need support in editing, marketing, designing, distributing and publicising their work because these are trades all of their own; a tremendous amount of time goes into each step. (8) For this reason, a growing number of digital services are now available. (9) Some of these offer assistance in every step of the process! (10) It may be an oxymoron that publishers now exist to help a writer self-publish, but this is certainly a much-needed evolution of the industry, and it marks a new era of opportunity for the writers of the world.

A map of the above sentence looks like this:

IC + comma + conjunction + IC + DC

Can you identify these component parts in the sentence above?

Taking note of how other writers structure sentences in their writing can help you make more conscious and effective decisions when you are drafting your own work. It is not enough to simply recognise good writing; you need to know *why* it is good, so you can attempt to achieve the same effect!

D Common punctuation errors

A classic example which demonstrates why punctuation matters involves the difference between the following two sentences:

Let's eat, Mum!

Let's eat Mum!

It is fairly safe to say that one comma can make a big difference!

The popular book, *Eats, Shoots and Leaves,* by Lynne Truss, demonstrates that even a single comma out of place can change the meaning of an entire message. This can cause confusion for the reader:

A panda walks into a cafe. He orders a sandwich, eats it, then draws a gun and fires two shots in the air.

'Why?' asks the confused waiter, as the panda makes towards the exit. The panda produces a badly punctuated wildlife manual and tosses it over his shoulder.

'I'm a panda,' he says, at the door. 'Look it up.'

The waiter turns to the relevant entry and, sure enough, finds an explanation.

'**Panda**. Large black-and-white bear-like mammal, native to China. Eats, shoots and leaves.'

247

If punctuation is not used properly when forming sentences, you run the risk of major miscommunication with your audience. Here are a few of the most common punctuation errors to avoid.

Run-on sentences

There are two types of **run-on sentence** errors that typically occur in writing, which can seriously affect how you communicate your message to your reader. When two or more sentences appear in succession with no punctuation to separate them, this is called a **fused sentence**. The other type of run-on sentence is called a comma splice, where a comma is used inapppropriately to join two independent clauses instead of a full stop or semicolon. (See Chapter 4.2 Section *E Adverbs* to review the comma splice.) Failing to separate ideas will lead to confusion for your readers.

KEY TERMS

Run-on sentence: two or more independent clauses joined together inappropriately, either due to incorrect or absent punctuation.

Fused sentence: a type of sentence that 'runs on' because it lacks the appropriate punctuation to separate independent clauses.

If you are fusing sentences together, consider why you are doing this. If it is because you are reluctant to split closely related ideas, for example, then try using a semicolon. Otherwise, use a a full stop (period) to remedy the error.

TIP

Try not to overuse semicolons in your writing, as too many can distract the reader.

The other type of run-on error that writers often commit is the comma splice. This occurs when the comma is used to hold together two complete thoughts. To correct this error, you have three options:

1 Replace the comma with a full stop to create two separate sentences.

> In addition to being a publisher, Amazon is a retailer. They have instant access to readers, which means a greater chance of increasing sales than a traditional publisher might have.

2 Replace the comma with a semicolon (or as an option, you can also include a conjunctive adverb).

> In addition to being a publisher, Amazon is a retailer; they have instant access to readers, which means a greater chance of increasing sales than a traditional publisher might have.

3 Add a coordinating conjunction just after the comma.

> In addition to being a publisher, Amazon is a retailer, so they have instant access to readers, which means a greater chance of increasing sales than a traditional publisher might have.

ACTIVITY 8

Using the correction strategies outlined in this section, adjust the punctuation errors in the run-on sentences **1–5**.

1 According to the Pew Research Center, roughly a quarter of teenagers are online 'almost constantly', this is made possible by the increasingly widespread availability of smartphones.

2 Nearly three-quarters of teens currently own a smartphone, just 12% say they don't own one.

3 As of 2015, Facebook is the most popular and frequently used social media platform. Although teens are increasingly diversifying their network use.

4 Photo-based social media applications that allow users to alter pictures are on the rise now that filters, icons, text and other enhancements can be applied to images.

5 According to research, girls tend to dominate social media, boys are more likely to play video games.

E Practising what you have learnt

Return to the paragraph that you wrote at the beginning of the chapter in response to the question:

> **To what extent is traditional literature being replaced by online news and entertainment?**

Then complete the following tasks. (Note: you will need several different coloured pens or highlighters for this activity.)

1 Highlight/annotate the following on your answer:

Colour 1: *simple sentences*

Colour 2: *complex sentences*

Colour 3: *compound sentences*

Colour 4: *compound-complex sentences.*

2 Look at the presence and/or absence of the three colours on your paragraph:

a How would you describe your use of sentence variety?

b How has the presence (or absence) of varied sentence structure affected the quality of your writing?

c Consider everything you have learnt/reviewed in this chapter. How will your knowledge regarding sentence structure help your writing in the future?

3 As practice, deconstruct your sentences further. Identify examples of the following:

- direct object
- indirect object
- predicate nominative
- predicate adjective
- adjective clause
- adverb clause
- noun clause.

4 Pick *two* sentences from your response to the question and deconstruct them as far as you are able. Defend your decisions to a partner or the whole class.

Use the following exam-style questions on this chapter's theme of *Media as literature* for practice in essay writing.

EXAM-STYLE QUESTIONS

Essay questions

1 To what extent would you agree that today's journalism is as much fiction as it is fact? **[30]**

2 Consider the social implications of writing about yourself online. **[30]**

3 How far would you agree that touchscreen games enhance the learning experience for children? **[30]**

4 'Online learning is a monologue, not a dialogue.' Evaluate this statement. **[30]**

5 Will e-books ever replace traditional print publications? **[30]**

6 Today's news can be transmitted by anyone with access to technology. Consider the positive and negative consequences of this. **[30]**

7 To what extent is social media good for democracy? **[30]**

8 'Traditional news sources such as newspapers and radio stations will cease to exist within the next decade.' What is your view? **[30]**

9 Other than their ability to entertain, do viral videos have any real value? **[30]**

10 'Handwritten history is no more reliable than today's digital print.' Discuss. **[30]**

Summary

Key points to remember from this chapter:

- Learning different ways to structure your sentences can help you use detail to clarify your message. It can also add a sense of style to your writing.
- To express a complete thought, most sentences will contain a subject, verb and complement.
- Direct and indirect objects can be found after action verbs, whereas predicate nominatives and predicate adjectives appear after linking verbs.
- There are four types of sentences: simple, complex, compound and complex-compound.
- Conjunctions are powerful tools in writing because they can help you coordinate ideas and structure sentences.
- Commas are not strong enough to hold two independent clauses together. Instead, you should use a semicolon or a full stop.
- Learning to identify clauses will help you avoid errors such as run-ons and misplaced modifiers.

Chapter 4.5
Reviewing, editing and revising

Ramesses II, also known as Ramesses the Great, was thought to be the greatest pharaoh of the Egyptian empire. The theme of this chapter is *What makes a person 'great'?*

Learning objectives

In this chapter, you will:

- learn what an interjection is and why it should be used sparingly
- review the parts of speech and common errors associated with these
- understand how identifying speech units can help reading comprehension
- come to know which words are most commonly misspelt and which words are most often misused
- consider style when approaching formal writing.

A Introduction

According to English writer Robert Graves, every writer 'should master the rules of grammar before he attempts to bend or break them'. In this chapter, you will review the 'rules' of grammar you have learnt in this unit, and explore some new perspectives. You will have the opportunity to not only review, but also *refresh* your understanding of the grammar you know. As you have learnt, there are rules for the English language; but there are also many exceptions to these rules. The rules of *descriptive* grammar should be followed, but *prescriptive* grammar advice should be considered in-context.

KEY SKILLS

Review Chapter 4.1 Section *B Understanding grammar* to remind yourself of the difference between descriptive and prescriptive rules.

This chapter reviews what you have learnt during Unit 4 about:

- parts of speech
- parts of a sentence
- common errors in writing.

You will do activities which ask you to use your knowledge of grammar and other mechanics to edit different types of writing. These range from the informal language used in emails and social media, to the more formal expectations of an academic essay.

Have you ever used a famous quotation as the basis for a social media post? This is an increasingly popular habit on microblogs and other media platforms. However, when the words of famous writers are quoted by others on social media, the original accuracy in grammar and spelling sometimes gets lost! The famous quotations used in this chapter have been altered on purpose to include some of the common errors addressed in Unit 4.

The chapter will also feature a list of common errors in:

- grammar
- spelling
- word choice.

Begin by reading the question that follows. Write a one-paragraph response to it, remembering to let your response flow as naturally as possible. Apply as little or as much structure to your sentence as you need to make a clear point. Write no more than 100 words.

'Build your own dreams, or someone else will hire you to build theirs.' What is meant by this quotation? Offer example(s) to illustrate your point.

ACTIVITY 1

Swap responses with a partner and observe each other's approach to the same writing task.

As you did in Chapters 4.2–4.4 Activity 1, use the following statement stems to share your observations, or create your own:

- I am impressed by …
- Tell me what you meant by …
- What made you decide …?
- An observation I made about the content of your paragraph is …
- An observation I made about your paragraph's use of English is …

Keep your written response. You will return to it at the end of this chapter.

B Reviewing the parts of speech

In order to put together clear and effective sentences to communicate your message, it is important to be aware of the individual units, or parts of speech. Sometimes, a good ear may be enough to identify a well-constructed sentence:

> I know grammar by ear only, not by note, not by the rules.
>
> *Mark Twain*

Unfortunately, not everyone has the ears of literary author Mark Twain! Therefore, learning about the rules of grammar can help you make better decisions when communicating your ideas.

In the previous chapters in this unit, you have learnt about the following parts of speech:

- prepositions
- adjectives
- adverbs
- nouns
- pronouns
- verbs
- conjunctions.

There is one other part of speech to be added to this list. The **interjection** is considered the eighth part of speech. Interjections convey short bursts of emotion, and are particularly useful in developing tone. They include the following exclamations:

Oh!	Ah!	What?!
Wow!	Oops!	Ugh …

KEY TERM

Interjection: an abrupt remark or exclamation made in speech to convey a particular emotion, and which can communicate facial expressions or body language that cannot be expressed in normal speech.

Although useful and effective, exclamations like these do not typically appear when writing for a more serious, academic purpose. Instead, interjections are typically used in narrative writing such as fiction, where they are an important feature of character development (through words, emotions and actions).

Learning to identify the function of individual words is a good starting point for understanding the purpose of larger phrases and clauses, which eventually work together to create whole sentences.

Read the following extract, taken from Andrew Lam's *Letters to a Young Refugee from Another*. Then complete Activity 2, and the exam-style questions that follow.

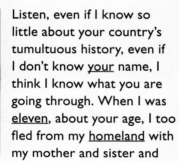

Listen, even if I know so little about your country's tumultuous history, even if I don't know <u>your</u> name, I think I know what you are going through. When I was <u>eleven</u>, about your age, I too fled from my <u>homeland</u> with my mother and sister and grandmother when the communist tanks came rolling into Saigon, <u>Vietnam</u>. We ended up in a refugee camp in Guam <u>while</u> our father was left behind.

Back then I couldn't make any sense out of what had happened to <u>me</u> or my family. History, after all, is <u>always</u> **baffling** to the young. One day I was reading my favourite book in my mother's rose garden, my dogs sleeping <u>lazily</u> at my feet, <u>and</u> the next day I was running for my life with a small backpack in which I only managed to save my <u>stamp collection</u>.

My young friend, there are <u>so</u> many things I want to tell you, so many experiences I want to share with you, <u>but</u>, most of all, I want <u>to</u> warn you that the road ahead is a very difficult and <u>treacherous</u> one, and you must be brave and strong and cunning. There are crucial things you should learn and learn quickly, and then there are things you must mull over for the rest of your life.

Indeed, life in <u>limbo</u> is difficult and humiliating, but you must remember that being robbed of what you loved does not speak to your weakness or frailty. It <u>only</u> speaks of the inhumanity and fear and hatred of those who caused you to flee and endure in <u>this</u> new dispossessed reality.

<u>By</u> the same token, I <u>implore</u> you, do not give in <u>to</u> their hatred. I know it <u>is</u> very hard, if not impossible, for someone who has just been forced out of his homeland, but you must try. Those <u>who</u> cause so much pain and suffering to you, your family, and your people are, in fact, trying to make you into their own image, even if they don't realise it <u>yet</u>. They want you to hate just like <u>them</u>, and they want you to be consumed with the fire of hatred. Don't hate. Hatred **consumes** oppressed and oppressors alike and <u>its</u> terrible expressions always result in injustice … especially for the <u>innocent</u>.

Don't hate. <u>Love</u>, instead. Love what you lost, love what you still have, and love those who suffered along with you, <u>for</u> their suffering and yours are part of your inheritance. Then, <u>when</u> you are older, tell your story … it <u>must be heard</u>.

5

10

15

20

25

30

35

40

45

50

ARTICLE GLOSSARY

baffling: puzzling, confusing
consumes: uses up, destroys

ACTIVITY 2

Analyse the function of each underlined word in the extract. For each of the underlined words, identify its:

- part of speech
- type, as it applies (e.g. proper noun, linking verb, demonstrative pronoun).

Remember: depending on the context in which it is used, the same word can have different functions!

EXAM-STYLE QUESTIONS 1

Answer the comprehension questions **1–8**.

1 Give three details to identify the author's audience. **[3]**

2 Using your own words, summarise the author's point in the second paragraph (lines 13–19). **[2]**

3 What is meant by the expression, 'life in limbo' as it is used in the extract (line 28)? Explain this phrase, using your own words. **[2]**

4 What is meant by the expression, 'mull over' as it is used in the extract (line 26)? Explain this phrase, using your own words. **[2]**

5 Using your own words, define the following words based on their use in the extract: **[4]**

    a tumultuous (line 3)

    b frailty (line 30)

    c inheritance (line 49)

    d treacherous (line 23)

6 What is the author's tone towards the end of the extract? Justify your answer by using evidence from the text. **[2]**

7 In your own opinion, what might be the consequences of writing a letter like this? (Hint: the term *consequence* includes both positive and negative consequences.) **[4]**

8 What are some other reasons why people travel? Using outside knowledge to respond, explain in roughly 300 words. **[6]**

Total marks: 25

253

You might still be wondering why it is important to be able to identify speech parts. Recall the opening stanza of 'The Jabberwocky', the nonsense poem by Lewis Carroll you read in Chapter 4.3 Section *B Nouns*. The following line from the poem has been annotated to show its structure:

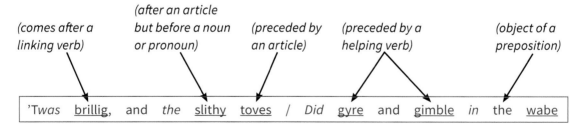

Consider the following:

- What part of speech is 'brillig'? Since ''twas' means 'it was', the word 'brillig' must be either a noun, pronoun or adjective. This is because it comes after the linking verb 'was', making it either a predicate nominative or a predicate adjective.

- The 'slithy toves' sound like a thing (noun) being described, and they *did* something, somewhere.

- You might not know what a 'wabe' is, but it is likely to be a noun or pronoun, since it is the object of the preposition *in* and is preceded by the article *the*.

Learning to identify speech parts can therefore help you improve your reading comprehension! While you might not come across any more Jabberwockies, you will need to comprehend other texts which at times might be just as hard to understand. Classic texts, such as the works of William Shakespeare, often include words that are no longer in use today, so you will need strategies to find out their meaning. If you have confidence in your understanding of the parts of speech, this can help you break down the meaning of language.

ACTIVITY 3

Read the following extract, which is from William Shakespeare's play, *The Tragedy of Julius Caesar*. In this scene, Cassius recounts a time when he went swimming in the River Tiber.

1 Identify the part of speech for each underlined word.

2 Give the meaning of each line in your own words.

The famous scene in William Shakespeare's play, *The Tragedy of Julius Caesar*, where conspirators assassinate Caesar. They were afraid that he would rise to absolute power and take away the freedom of the people of Rome.

> For once, upon a raw and gusty day,
> The troubled Tiber <u>chafing</u> with her shores,
> Caesar said to me 'Darest thou, Cassius, now
> Leap in with me into this angry flood,
> 5 And swim to <u>yonder</u> point?' Upon the word,
> <u>Accoutred</u> as I was, I plunged in
> And <u>bade</u> him follow; so indeed he did.
> The <u>torrent</u> roar'd, and we did <u>buffet</u> it
> With <u>lusty</u> <u>sinews</u>, throwing it aside
> 10 And stemming it with hearts of controversy;
> But ere we could arrive the point proposed,
> Caesar cried 'Help me, Cassius, or I sink!'

C Common errors in writing: review and practice

As you studied the various parts of speech in Unit 4, you were given examples of common errors associated with each. In this section, you will focus on the most common errors made by student writers at AS level. You will review each of these errors and practise editing your own writing and the work of others. The following checklist will help you to review earlier learning on each error:

Common error made by students	Course section where first addressed
Misplaced modifiers	Chapter 4.2 Section *C Common errors*
Confusion between adjectives and adverbs	'Common errors concerning adjectives versus adverbs' in Chapter 4.2 Section *E Adverbs*
Confusion between plural and possessive forms	(Not previously addressed)
Non-agreement of pronouns	Chapter 4.3 Section *C Pronouns*
Fragments	'Common errors concerning adjectives versus adverbs' in Chapter 4.2 Section *E Adverbs* and Chapter 4.4 Section *C Structuring more complex sentences*
Subject–verb agreement errors	Chapter 4.3 Section *D Verbs*
Fused sentences	Chapter 4.4 Section *D Common punctuation errors*
Comma splice	Chapter 4.2 Section *E Adverbs* and Chapter 4.4 Section *D Common punctuation errors*

Misplaced modifiers

A modifier *describes* another word. A modifier can be as brief as a single adjective or as lengthy as a detailed prepositional phrase. Whatever its length, when this description is placed too far from the word or phrase it modifies, it can make the meaning of the sentence very unclear!

sometimes be very different. The improper use of an adjective in speech might therefore be more acceptable to hear than to read on the page.

Consider the following quotation from Confucius. When it was rewritten in a social media post, it lost its grammatical accuracy. Can you spot the error?

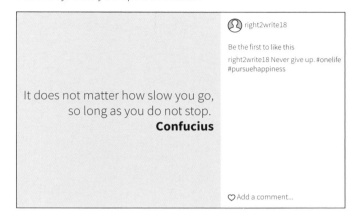

right2write18

Be the first to like this

right2write18 Never give up. #onelife #pursuehappiness

It does not matter how slow you go, so long as you do not stop.
Confucius

Add a comment…

Plural versus possessive errors

Perhaps the most classic example of misuse of plural versus possessive occurs in the so-called 'greengrocer's apostrophe'. This kind of error may have started because the greengrocers – or fresh fruit and vegetable sellers – in places like England and Australia, were often immigrants whose first language was not English; so the spelling of shop signs varied a great deal. Therefore, errors were common (e.g. *potato's, tomatoe's, carrot's, banana's*).

ACTIVITY 4

Consider the following news media headlines. With a partner, identify the misplaced modifier(s) in each and discuss how the meaning is changed as a result.

1 Security agents refuse to work after death
2 New 'smart refrigerator' holds servings for up to 24 people frozen in top compartment
3 Antique chair refurbished for man with wooden legs
4 Local celebrity walks dog in blue suede shoes and pink socks
5 Shark bites dockworker with razor-sharp teeth
6 Ex-employee comes across former factory who spent four years in prison
7 Eco-tourists stumble across rare flower hiking mountain peak

Adjective versus adverb confusion

Adjectives and adverbs can sometimes be confused, because they are both used to modify other words. Also, the way people speak and the way they write can

You have learnt that when apostrophes are used with a *noun*, they indicate possession. (An exception is when *'s* is a contraction such as in the US television show *America's Got Talent*.) With *pronouns*, an apostrophe indicates missing letters within a contraction.

Have a look at how a well-known quotation by US writer Tim Fargo has been written wrongly. Can you spot the error?

Your friend's will believe in your potential; your enemies will make you live up to it.
Tim Fargo

right2write18
Be the first to like this
right2write18 Make it count. #actions
Add a comment...

Errors with pronouns

Pronouns help avoid redundant wording because they offer an alternative to overusing a noun. However, one problem that often arises is not knowing which form of the pronoun is most appropriate to use. Can you identify the problem in the following example?

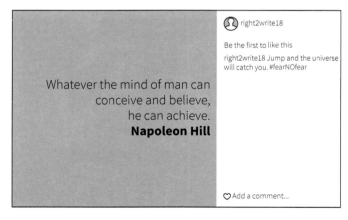

Whatever the mind of man can conceive and believe, he can achieve.
Napoleon Hill

right2write18
Be the first to like this
right2write18 Jump and the universe will catch you. #fearNOfear
Add a comment...

As you learnt in Chapter 4.3 Section *C Pronouns*, another common error is the lack of agreement between pronouns and their origin. If the pronoun that replaces a noun does not agree in number with its antecedent, you risk confusing the reader. Can you spot the deliberate error in the next example?

You must expect great things of yourself before you can do it.
Michael Jordan

right2write18
Be the first to like this
right2write18 Believe in yourself and everything else will fall into place. #knowthyself #power_of_1
Add a comment...

Fragments

For a sentence to express a complete thought, it requires a subject *and* a verb. With this in mind, what is wrong with the misquote below?

To lead people. Walk behind them.
Lao Tzu

right2write18
Be the first to like this
right2write18 Sometimes the best way to lead is to follow. #greatleaders
Add a comment...

Unlike the other quotations on this page, which were re-written incorrectly by users on social media, the 17th-century French playwright Molière's statement below includes the original version as he himself wrote it in his work, *Les Femmes Savantes*. Can you identify the error he commits?

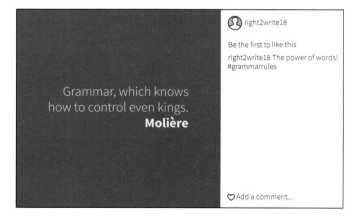

Grammar, which knows how to control even kings.
Molière

right2write18
Be the first to like this
right2write18 The power of words! #grammarrules
Add a comment...

Subject-verb agreement errors

A subject and a verb are all that are needed to make a sentence, but they must also agree. For example, if the subject is singular, the verb should match. How did this classic quotation break this rule when it was shared (incorrectly) on social media?

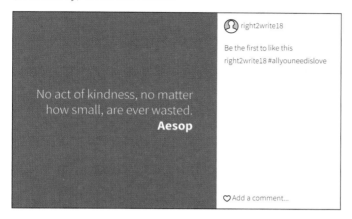

No act of kindness, no matter how small, are ever wasted.
Aesop

right2write18
Be the first to like this
right2write18 #allyouneedislove
Add a comment...

Fused sentences

It is one thing to recognise a complete sentence, but it is another thing not to recognise the difference between two sentences! Recall that a fused sentence treats two or more separate sentences as one. The fused sentence lacks the proper punctuation to indicate that more than one independent clause is present.

Remember to use either a full stop (period), a semicolon, or a comma + conjunction as the traditional means to separate independent clauses. With this in mind, how might you revise the error in the social media post below?

I am not a product of my circumstances I am a product of my decisions.
Stephen Coveney

right2write18
Be the first to like this
right2write18 You decide your fate! Make smart choices and think before you act. #thinksmart
Add a comment...

Comma splices

To avoid a fused sentence, a comma is sometimes used to separate independent clauses. But the comma is not strong enough to do this. How might you adjust the misuse of the comma in the following quotation?

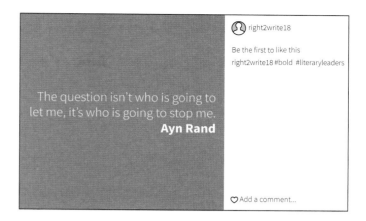

The question isn't who is going to let me, it's who is going to stop me.
Ayn Rand

right2write18
Be the first to like this
right2write18 #bold #literaryleaders
Add a comment...

ACTIVITY 5

For each of the following (miswritten) quotations, identify and correct the mechanical errors. There may be more than one error in a quotation.

1 Build your own dreams. Or someone else will hire you to build theirs. (*Farrah Gray*)
2 Wanting to be someone else are a waste of who you are. (*Kurt Cobain*)
3 Identity is a prison you can never escape from the way to redeem your past is not to run from it but to try to understand it and use it as a foundation to grow. (*Jay-Z*)
4 Whenever you see a successful person, you only see the public glories never the private sacrifices to reach it. (*Vaibhav Shah*)
5 Leadership cannot just go along to get along leadership must meet the moral challenge of the day. (*Jesse Jackson*)

D Errors in spelling and word choice

So far in Unit 4 you have reviewed a number of errors that occur in grammar and punctuation as a result of an unclear understanding of the parts of speech. However, there are other common errors made by writers at AS level. These include errors in spelling and word selection.

Commonly misspelt words

You may have heard of the spelling rhyme: '*i* before *e* except after *c*'. The word 'receive' is often misspelt, however, in spite of this maxim. Look at the following (*correctly* spelt) words. Which ones follow this rule and which ones ignore it?

*   deceive
*   believe

257

- weird
- conceive

One look at the word *weird* proves that some spelling rules you may have learnt, such as the one above, do not always apply. Therefore make sure you check the spelling of some of the most commonly misspelt words, such as the following:

irresistible	accessible
receive	twelfth
tomorrow	separate
whether	harass
definite	development
environment	recommend
necessary	desperate
countries (plural)	cemetery
soldier	calendar
weird	occasion
believe	occurrence
judgement (British English)	a lot
	accommodate
judgment (US English)	repetition
guarantee	accidentally
acquire	existence
noticeable	independent
privilege	access

ACTIVITY 6

Consider the following microblog entries, where the writer shares a classic inspirational quotation on social media. Unfortunately, the blog writer has misspelt a word or two when quoting the original words! Identify the spelling errors and write the words out correctly. There is at least one error in each quotation.

Patty Pioneer
'You cannot seperate peace from freedom because no one can be at peace unless he has his freedom.' Malcolm X

Patty Pioneer
'The value of a man should be seen in what he gives and not in what he is able to recieve.' Albert Einstein

Patty Pioneer
'Live as if you were to die tommorrow. Learn as if you were to live forever.' Mahatma Gandhi

Commonly confused words

Famous author Mark Twain once said:

> Perfect grammar – persistent, continuous, sustained – is the fourth dimension, so to speak: many have sought it, but none has found it.

In other words, writers work hard to achieve grammatical perfection, but there are plenty of obstacles standing in the way. The many **homophones** that exist in the English language, for example, cause a lot of the errors that writers commit.

 KEY TERM

Homophone: a word that sounds the same as another but has a different meaning and/or spelling.

A common example of a homophone error is the use of the word 'effect' – usually a noun – instead of the intended verb 'affect'.

Here are some commonly confused words (mostly homophones) to be aware of in your writing:

affect/effect	principal/principle
allude/elude	advice/advise
there/their/they're	accept/except
then/than	farther/further
to/too/two	its/it's

258

loose/lose	elicit/illicit
sight/site/cite	piece/peace
who's/whose	personal/personnel
whether/weather	raise/raze
lay/lie	rational/rationale
breath/breathe	right/write/rite
compliment/ complement	where/were
	your/you're
desert/dessert	

KEY SKILLS

One of the most commonly confused pairs is its/it's. To learn more about the difference between these words, see Chapter 4.3 Section *C Pronouns*.

ACTIVITY 7

Talia signs up for a social network that allows her to discover new interests by browsing and sharing images and videos. The first interest category she ticks is 'Inspirational quotes'. Here are the first posts she sees. Spot the error in each: there is at least one, but there may be more! (Note: the errors are not from the original quotations.)

> The nice thing about being a celebrity is that when we bore people, they think its their fault.
>
> Henry Kissinger, political scientist

> Big jobs usually go to the men who prove there ability to outgrow small ones.
>
> Ralph Waldo Emerson, American essayist and poet

> Never interrupt you're enemy when he's making a mistake.
>
> Napoleon Bonaparte, military leader

> It's never to late to be what you might have been.
>
> George Eliot, Victorian writer (pen name of Mary Anne Evans)

> The terrorists thought they would change my aims and stop my ambitions, but nothing changed in my life accept this: weakness, fear and hopelessness died. Strength, power and courage were born.
>
> Malala Yousefzai, children's education advocate

259

E Approaching formal writing

The examples we have looked at so far in this chapter follow standard use in English. As you learnt in Chapter 4.1 Section *B Understanding grammar*, this standard use is called *descriptive grammar*, and you should follow these rules. You should also consider *prescriptive grammar* rules, but these should only be used as recommendations, not as definite rules to be followed. The information in this section is meant to improve your approach to formal writing, i.e. the style that is appropriate for essays. However, you should also use your best judgement and consider the context.

In *Elements of Style*, Strunk and White warn:

> Think of the tragedies that are rooted in ambiguity (i.e. death on a highway caused by a badly worded road sign, heartbreak among lovers caused by a misplaced phrase in a well-intentioned letter, etc.), and be clear!

One of the rules in their text is 'clarity, clarity, clarity', and this is a useful one to follow. In order to make your point clearly, you should avoid language which is:

- figurative
- flowery (over-elaborate)
- colloquial and/or overused.

Figurative language

Some of the greatest leaders in the world have used figurative language in memorable ways. In his famous 'I have a dream' speech, African American civil rights activist Martin Luther King, Jr. used similes and extended metaphor to make particular ideas more concrete for the majority white population:

> [The Emancipation Proclamation] came as a great beacon light of hope to millions of Negro slaves who had been seared by the flames of withering injustice. It came as a joyous daybreak to end the long night of captivity … but … one hundred years later, the life of the Negro is still sadly crippled by the manacles of segregation and the chains of discrimination …

Martin Luther King, Jr.

Essentially, Martin Luther King's purpose was to inform and inspire his audience. The power behind carefully selected words like 'withering injustice', 'captivity' and 'crippled' evoke very specific feelings in the audience, while words like 'manacles' and 'chains' make clear to the audience the experience that black people faced under oppressive conditions. Keep in mind, however, that if the audience is unfamiliar with the concepts that are being compared, the message will not be conveyed.

Martin Luther King was an experienced orator. Some of the most powerful language in this famous speech was probably not scripted (not unlike the experience of an 'on-demand' writer!). As a young writer, when you are using figurative language in your writing, do it carefully and with a definite purpose.

 KEY SKILLS

Because of the strong emotions that images can evoke, you should be careful not to let figurative language lead you into the error of an *appeal to emotion*. See Chapter 3.1 Section *B Understanding arguments* to review this error in logical reasoning.

Use of over-elaborate language

Writers often believe that the larger their vocabulary, the better the impression they give in their writing, but this is not always the case. A wide-ranging vocabulary may help you select more precise language to express your point. However, controlling how often you use elaborate terms – sometimes called 'flowery' or 'fancy' language – is key. For example, if you are making a choice between the words 'use' and 'utilise', then the more straightforward term 'use' might be the better one to choose. However, if you are choosing between 'said' and 'mocked', the latter is much more specific and carries a more definite meaning. In the same way, beginning an essay with a phrase like 'since the dawn of man' would seem over-elaborate because saying 'for centuries' is just as formal.

As a further example , consider the meaning behind the following statement:

> Passageways for vehicles, humans and animals invited continuation of my journey in two highly foliated directions, and I elected to traverse the access which appeared in better repair from less traffic.

What does the above statement seem to be saying? If you have not already managed to work it out, these are the lines of a well-known poem by Robert Frost:

> Two roads diverged in a wood, and I —
> *I took the one less travelled by …*

Notice that the first version used the word 'passageway' rather than the more straightforward 'road'; and 'traverse' as opposed to 'travel'. At first glance, you may think the word choices made in the first version may seem more impressive. However, words like 'road' and 'travel' are just as acceptable in formal communication!

Therefore, when making a choice between using one word or its simpler synonym, ask yourself which would be more acceptable in a serious essay-writing context. If both would be acceptable, then choose the word that would be most suitable for reaching a wider audience.

ACTIVITY 8

Here are three famous quotations rewritten in over-elaborate language. Match these 'flowery' versions **1–3** with the correct original quotation from the list **a–e**. (Note: two of the original quotations will not be used.)

1 The entire habitable and uninhabitable regions of the third planet from the Sun symbolically embody an elevated platform, and the two varieties of carbon-based bipedal life forms appear to be merely thespians.

2 I'm unable to accurately perceive the possible directions that individuals might arbitrarily select, but given my predilection, I recognise only two viable alternatives: (1) restoring my emancipation from autocratic rule, or (2) introducing me to the grim reaper.

3 A miniscule move over a short distance to a specified location, accomplished by one individual; a forward bound of extraordinary proportions performed as a tribute to the human race.

---

a One small step for man, one giant leap for mankind.

b The more man meditates upon good thoughts, the better will be his world and the world at large.

c I know not what course others may take, but as for me, give me liberty or give me death.

d One man cannot do right in one department of life whilst he is occupied in doing wrong in any other department.

e All the world's a stage and all the men and women are merely players.

As a final thought, consider when you may have struggled with reading Shakespeare in your English class. It is easy to be intimidated by the Bard's challenging vocabulary and intricate sentence structure. Remember this as *you* write! Your reader is likely to appreciate a simply-worded message, rather than one that needs to be deconstructed!

Therefore, choose your words wisely. As Strunk and White say, 'there is nothing wrong, really, with any word, all are good, but some are better than others.'

Colloquial language

The opposite to over-elaborate language is colloquial, or informal, language. Colloquial phrases might include, 'What's up?' or 'How ya been?' This type of communication involves words or phrases used:

- in casual conversation
- in personal communication
- within a social group or wider community.

Recall (Chapter 1.2 Section *B Considering audience, register and purpose*) that the way you speak informally with friends or family can be quite different from the way you write under formal circumstances. Language considered acceptable in an informal setting may be considered too colloquial for academic writing. Academic writers often try to make their language more formal by using over-elaborate vocabulary. However, 'simple' language is often quite acceptable, and more effective, in formal circumstances. For example:

Standard expression	There are <u>many ways</u> to …
Over-elaborate expression	There are <u>a plethora of ways</u> to …

Either phrase is acceptable in a formal writing situation (i.e. when writing for a serious purpose). Remember –

don't be afraid to keep your approach simple. This will make your writing less wordy and more succinct!

KEY SKILLS

The importance of matching your language to your audience and purpose is explained further in Chapter 1.2.

ACTIVITY 9

All words have value, but a few tend to be overused in colloquial, informal language. For each of the **clichéd** phrases listed, what simpler alternative could be used which is still appropriate for a formal situation?

1   nowadays
2   this day and age
3   in a nutshell
4   better late than never
5   the calm before the storm
6   caught red-handed
7   lay down the law
8   better safe than sorry
9   scared to death
10 start from scratch
11 a wake-up call

KEY TERM

Cliché: overused phrase which makes the thought being expressed seem unoriginal.

F Finding your own voice

Over-elaborate language and colloquial language can be distracting for readers. Both rely on a contrived set of words that *someone else* has created, whether these are the 'scholarly' terms used by academics or the 'trendy' words and phrases popular in youth culture.

Consider: where, in all of this, is your *own* expression?

Writing is just as much about communicating as it is about finding your own style and identity. Therefore, it may be helpful for you to think about what wording suits your own 'voice' as a writer, rather than what words others might expect you to use. Think about how you can use language to connect with your audience while at the same time staying true to who you are as a writer and critical thinker.

G Practising what you have learnt

In this chapter, you have learnt about the various standards for grammar, spelling, punctuation and

expression. This section of the chapter gives you the opportunity to practise and apply what you have learnt to the various kinds of writing tasks you will encounter during this course.

> 'Build your own dreams, or someone else will hire you to build theirs.' What is meant by this quotation? Offer example(s) to illustrate your point.

Return to the paragraph that you wrote at the beginning of the chapter in response to the question, then complete the following tasks. (Note: you will need several different coloured pens or highlighters for this activity.)

1   Highlight/annotate the following on your answer:
    Colour 1: *agreement errors*
    Colour 2: *misplaced modifiers*
    Colour 3: *fragments*
    Colour 4: *punctuation misuse (i.e. apostrophe and comma misuse)*
    Colour 5: *misspelt words (including commonly misspelt and similar-sounding pairs).*

2   Look at the presence and/or absence of the five colours on your paragraph. Consider the following:
    a   How would you describe the frequency of each kind of error in your writing?
    b   What effect does the presence (or absence) of these errors have on the quality of your writing?
    c   How will your knowledge of these errors help your writing in the future?

You will now have the opportunity to apply your knowledge of grammar, spelling and punctuation to a sample essay and to your own reading comprehension answers. The chapter will finish with a selection of practice essay questions.

Revising essays

Part of your experience in this course requires you to write essays which demonstrate logical reasoning and the clear expression of ideas. For these essays, you will need to be able to revise your own work. Without revising, you run the risk of submitting work that could contain simple errors such as spelling. Though these may seem minor, frequent mechanical errors can quickly affect the quality of your work, and give a poor impression to your readers.

ACTIVITY 10

A fellow student has written an essay in response to one of the questions from Chapter 3.1, which targets the theme of *Food, water and other essential resources*. They have asked you to edit the work for mechanical errors including spelling, grammar and punctuation before it is submitted.

1 Read the essay below and use the questions in the margin to help you locate any mechanical errors.

2 Correct any errors you find.

3 Return to an essay you have previously drafted for this course, or select an essay question from any of the lists at the end of each chapter and write a new one. Revise your own essay to minimise mechanical errors.

There are two errors in this paragraph.

One involves a misspelling. Can you find it?

The other error concerns a pair of commonly confused words. Can you use the correct one?

1

At first glance, fast food and modern living seem like a perfect pair. To keep up with the pace of a busy schedule, consumers appreciate the conveience of getting food quickly and easily, but this industry still deserves a closer look. Therefore, while fast food should be praised for it's economic and social perks, it should be criticised for some of the health and environmental problems it causes.

2

Fast food should be criticised for some of its health problems such as obesity and other illnesses. Fast food has alot of calories, fats and sugar. If you eat too much of it, for example, you will start to gain weight until you're obese. Once this happens, you are at a higher risk of developing other problems like heart disease, diabetes and high blood sugar. These illnesses can be fatal if you don't eat right and keep your health in check, so if fast food is the cause, then it certainly deserves criticism.

There are four errors in this paragraph.

The writer is having trouble distinguishing between plural and possessive words in this paragraph. Find the error and correct it!

A fragment is an incomplete sentence. It can be attached to another sentence to make it complete. Can you locate and re-write the fragment error?

Rewrite the highlighted phrase using simpler wording.

Pronouns need to agree with their antecedents. Look at the sentence in bold and edit the pronoun-antecedent agreement error.

3

Just as fast food hurts societies health, it also hurts the environment. The higher the demand for meat, the greater the need for more space to raise livestock. Which leads to deforestation. Acres of trees are wiped out to make space for grazing ground, and as this happens, entire ecosystems are uprooted and whole cultures are displaced. The Amazon rainforest is one example of this. Indigenous tribes are being forced from their lands because the trees are being removed to make way for industrial development. **Due to the fact that the fast food industry is harming our environment and those in it, they deserve criticism for this reason.**

There are three errors in this paragraph.

Another spelling error in this paragraph. Can you identify it?

Overused phrases, (known as clichés) and colloquialisms (informal turns of phrase) are not recommended in formal writing. Get rid of the colloquialism in this paragraph by rewriting the highlighted phrase to make it more formal.

The pronoun 'you' is usually reserved for speech, so we try to avoid using it in formal essays. Help the writer replace the use of 'you'. Consider to whom 'you' is referring – what noun would work in its place? Adjust throughout the paragraph as practice, using synonyms to avoid repetitiveness.

263

4

Yet while the environment is being harmed, the average consumer's pocketbook is not, which is why fast food is often praised. Many people today are living in poverty. Since they cannot afford nutritious food from the grocery store, they turn to the Dollar Menu instead. **Even though healthier fast food items are finding their way onto the menu, items like apples as opposed to fries is still more expensive.** Meanwhile it only takes one dollar to buy more filling items like a double cheeseburger. Because of this fact, fast food can't be criticised entirely because it is making food available to those who can't afford it otherwise.

There is one error in this paragraph.

Just as pronouns must agree with their antecedents, subjects must agree with their verbs. Edit the sentence in bold to correct the subject–verb agreement error.

There are two errors in this paragraph.

Identify the two expression errors in this paragraph, one in each sentence. Add, adjust or remove words to make the meaning clearer.

5

Along these same lines, many fast food chains provide not only food but jobs for those individuals who are stuck in this cycle of poverty. By providing employment, fast food establishments can help lift society out of a financial crisis, so it is worth of praise in this case.

6

When fast food is a means of survival, it serves a purpose; but when celebrity's and commercials force it upon the customer, it becomes unfair. Today, many celebrities support fast food chains by endorsing brands and being the star in commercials. For example, Lebron James. He was in a McDonald's commercial for the new Bacon Clubhouse burger. It isn't fair to manipulate the public by associating food with celebrity status, this is decieving.

There are four errors in this paragraph.

Find and correct the plural versus possessive error in this paragraph.

There is another sentence fragment in this paragraph. Can you put this right?

Look carefully for the spelling error in this paragraph, and correct it.

Can you find the comma splice error in this paragraph and correct it?

There is one error in this paragraph.

An error with a commonly confused word can be found this paragraph. Can you identify it?

7

Another dishonest part about fast food that's worth criticising concerns the calorie count information posted on menus. In a documentary called How Many Calories, analysts took and tested food from well-known fast food locations to see how many calories were actually in the item as opposed to what was advertised on the menu. The study found that many of the items from locations like Chipotle and Subway had more calories then they actually listed. This is also unfair to the consumer who is seeking healthy food, making this option worth a second look.

8

There's no doubt fast food fits the pace of life today, but there are reasons to both praise and criticise it. If fast food production is harming something, such as a persons or an animals health, then it is worth blame; however, the conveience it offers families and the boost it gives to the economy makes this industry valuable in today's society. If fast food is here to stay, it is up to the consumer to make informed decisions to keep it in business.

There are three errors in this paragraph.

More plural versus possessive errors here. Find and correct the two errors.

There is also another spelling error in this paragraph! Find it and correct it.

Revising responses to comprehension questions

It might be obvious that your essays should demonstrate good use of mechanics, but your responses to comprehension questions should be free of errors, too. Getting into the habit of reviewing and editing these shorter types of responses with the remaining time you have can ensure that you communicate answers clearly.

Read the following article. Then answer the comprehension questions that follow. Be sure to set aside time for revision.

Scientists find evidence of mathematical structures in classic books

James Joyce's *Finnegans Wake* has been described as many things, from a masterpiece to unreadable nonsense. But according to scientists at the Institute of Nuclear Physics in Poland,
5 its grammatical form is almost parallel to a mathematical structure called a multifractal. These findings were recently published in the computer science journal *Information Sciences*.

The academics put more than 100 works of world
10 literature, by authors from Charles Dickens to Shakespeare, Alexandre Dumas, Thomas Mann, Umberto Eco and Samuel Beckett, through a detailed statistical analysis. They looked at the length and variety of sentences and found that an
15 '**overwhelming** majority' of them were constructed using a cascade, or *fractal*, format.

A fractal is a mathematical object in which each fragment, when expanded, has a structure resembling the whole. Fractals are used in science to model
20 structures that contain re-occurring patterns, including snowflakes and **galaxies**.

According to Professor Stanisław Drożdż, one author of the paper, 'nature evolves through cascades and thus arranges [itself] fractally'. As the studies
25 reveal, this applies to the way we pattern sentences. Evidently, writers like James Joyce 'had a kind of intuition, as it happens to great artists. [Their] narrative mode best reflects "how nature works" and they properly encoded this into their texts,'
30 he said.

Some works were even more mathematically complex than others, with stream of consciousness narratives being the most complex. These texts are comparable to an **irreducibly interwoven** set of

fractals called *multifractals* (or fractals of fractals!). 35
Finnegans Wake, the scientists found, was the most complex text of all.

'The results of our analysis of this text are virtually indistinguishable from ideal, purely mathematical multifractals,' said Drożdż. 40

The other works most comparable to the complex structure of multifractals were *A Heartbreaking Work of Staggering Genius* by Dave Eggers, *Hopscotch* by Julio Cortazar, The *USA trilogy* by John Dos Passos, *The Waves* by Virginia Woolf, *2666* by 45
Roberto Bolaño and Joyce's *Ulysses*. Marcel Proust's *À la recherche du temps perdu* showed 'little correlation' to multifractality, however; nor did Ayn Rand's *Atlas Shrugged*.

The academics note that 'fractality of a literary text 50
will … never be as perfect as [it is] in the world of mathematics', because mathematical fractals are infinite, while the number of sentences in a book are finite.

There are lots of genres, or categories, of literature. 55
Yet, 'ascribing a work to a particular genre is, for whatever reason, sometimes subjective,' said Drożdż, suggesting that the scientists' work 'may someday help in a more objective assignment of books to one genre or another'. Drożdż suggested today that the findings 60
could also be used to posit that writers 'uncovered fractals and even multifractals in nature long before scientists'.

Eimear McBride, whose multiple award-winning debut novel *A Girl is a Half-Formed Thing* is written in a 65
stream-of-consciousness style, said she wasn't **taken aback** by the results.

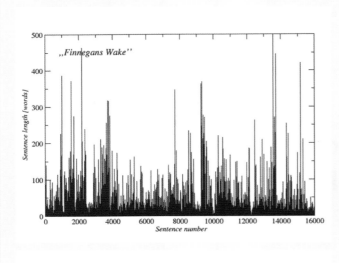

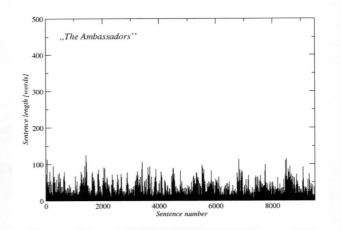

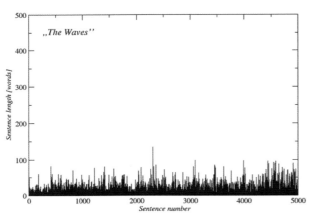

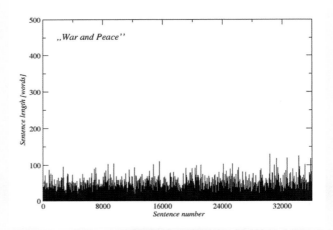

'It doesn't surprise me that works described as "stream of consciousness" appear to be the most patterned. By its nature, such writing is concerned not only with the usual load-bearing aspects of language – content, meaning, aesthetics, etc – but engages with language as the object in itself, using the re-forming of its rules to give the reader a more prismatic understanding of the subject at hand. Given the long-established connection between beauty and symmetry, finding works of literature fractally quantifiable seems perfectly reasonable.'

But she added that she couldn't 'help being somewhat disappointed by the idea that the main **upshot** of this research may be to make the assigning of genre more straightforward'.

'Surely there are more interesting questions about the how and why of writers' brains arriving at these complex, but seemingly instinctive, fractals?' she said.

*Adapted from an article by Alison Flood in
The Guardian, January 2016*

ARTICLE GLOSSARY

overwhelming: very strong, huge in amount

galaxies: systems of billions of stars held together by gravity

irreducibly: not able to be simplified or reduced

interwoven: combined so they cannot be separated

taken aback: surprised

upshot: final conclusion

Use the following exam-style essay questions on this chapter's theme of *What makes a persón 'great'?* for practice in essay writing.

EXAM-STYLE QUESTIONS 2

Answer the comprehension question **1–8**.

1 In your own words, define the following terms: **[3]**

  a multifractal (line 6)

  b fractal (line 16)

  c stream of consciousness (line 32).

2 Based on paragraphs 2 and 3, explain how writing can be similar to maths. Use your own words as far as possible. **[1]**

3 Apart from *Finnegans Wake*, name:

  a two literary works that are most similar to multifractals **[2]**

  b two that are least similar to multifractals. **[2]**

4 Explain, in your own words, one way this discovery can improve the field of literature. Use text evidence to support your response. **[2]**

5 Summarise the message expressed through the graphs measuring sentence length. **[1]**

6 Why isn't Eimear McBride surprised by these findings? Explain her perspective in your own words. **[2]**

7 What appears to be McBride's main contention with Drożdż? Justify your response. **[2]**

8 To what extent could maths be considered a 'universal language'? Discuss this, using both the material and your own knowledge. Your response should be roughly 300–400 words in length. You may want to research the issue further to find supporting evidence for your response. **[10]**

Total marks: 25

EXAM-STYLE QUESTIONS 3

Essay questions

1 Do you agree that the people from your country who have been given the title 'great' deserve it? **[30]**

2 Nelson Mandela once said that the 'real heroes' are those who are friendly and charitable to the poor. How far do you agree or disagree with this notion? **[30]**

3 When it comes to politics, to what extent does social media (e.g. Twitter, Facebook) lead public opinion? **[30]**

4 To what extent does print literature still have a place in modern society? **[30]**

5 Analyse the appeal of learning mathematics. **[30]**

6 'Leadership is a privilege to better the lives of others. It is not an opportunity to satisfy personal greed.' – Mwai Kibaki. To what extent does this statement reflect leadership in your society? **[30]**

7 To what extent do modern technologies such as e-readers, texting and the internet discourage reading? **[30]**

8 Defend the timeless popularity of memoirs. **[30]**

9 'Learning mathematics is like learning a foreign language.' Discuss. **[30]**

10 Assess the value of myths and fables in today's society. **[30]**

Summary

Key points to remember from this chapter:

- The ability to understand parts of speech can help you:
  - to avoid grammatical errors in your writing
  - to comprehend what you read.
- Make sure you are confident with the spelling of:
  - words that are commonly misspelt
  - words that sound similar to other words but are spelled differently.
- Be careful not to overuse figurative language in your writing because:
  - it can overload your ideas with emotion, which can lead to errors in logic
  - your audience might not be able to understand your message.
- Choose language that is clear and specific. Avoid using over-elaborate words as well as colloquial or clichéd language.
- No matter what kind of task you are working on for this course, take time to revise your writing.
- Minimising mechanical errors increases your chances of delivering a clear and effective response.

Unit 5:
Skills review and further study

Chapter 5.1
Reviewing your writing skills

Now that you know what is expected of you in this course, share your knowledge through peer editing.

Learning objectives

In this chapter, you will reflect on what you have learnt about writing essays for this course. Specifically, you will review what you have learnt about:

- choosing essay questions and interpreting instructions
- generating and organising your ideas
- maintaining focus on the question throughout your essay
- supporting the points you make
- expressing ideas and developing style
- considering your audience.

You will also learn strategies for:

- peer-editing and self-editing.

A Review of key points for writing

The previous units of this book have aimed to strengthen your critical approach to both reading and writing. This chapter will help you reflect on the writing skills you have learnt. It provides guidance and tips to refer to when writing for the Cambridge International AS Level English General Paper course.

The chapter ends with a section that offers guidance on self- and peer-editing. This is an important part of your learning experience. Peer-editing can help you feel confident that you are learning and developing the key skills you need for success in this course.

Question selection and interpretation

In an exam situation, for example, you may have a limited amount of time to select a question before planning, drafting and revising your response to it. Picking the right essay topic is therefore a key step in the writing process. After all, if you do not know what the question is asking, how can you expect to answer it successfully? So here are some tips:

- Only pick an essay question when you understand *all* the terms used.
- Be careful if you choose to write on topics you have very strong views about. This may lead to an unsubstantiated argument or, worse still, a biased rant!
- Do not be afraid to challenge the *assumptions* that may seem implicit in a question. In other words, avoid taking questions at face value!
- Make sure you read and respond to the *entire* question, rather than just addressing one part of it.
- Some questions will demand a stronger basis of factual knowledge than others. Make sure you choose a topic that you know enough about to provide the basis for a good essay.

KEY SKILLS

To review what you learnt about question selection and interpretation, see Chapter 1.2 Section *D Understanding the task* and Chapter 2.2 Section *B Deconstructing essay questions*.

Planning

Because your time for writing is limited, in both a class and exam situation, it may be tempting to skip the planning process. However, taking time to generate and organise your ideas is invaluable. It gives you a useful overview of the knowledge you have, which can lead to key insights when structuring the points in your essay. Having a plan of what you are going to say can speed up the writing process:

- Take time to plan your argument, even when your approach is discursive. This will help you to write a clearer, more organised discussion of the issue.
- A rough plan is all that is needed to ensure that your argument is well shaped and structured. But this does not mean a careless effort – make sure you consider your plan carefully.
- When generating ideas, think of the issue from multiple disciplines (lenses) and from multiple points of view (perspectives). Keeping your mind open to ideas outside your own will help you think on a more mature level.
- When addressing perspectives, be aware that more opinions than just 'for' and 'against' exist. Explore the various shades of these when possible.

KEY SKILLS

To review what you learnt about planning and organising ideas, including *lenses*, see Chapter 2.2 Section *F Organising ideas to show comprehension*.

Planning is an important part of the writing process because it helps you organise your ideas in a logical and intentional way.

270

Focus and organisation

The best way to stay focused when writing an essay is to keep the question in front of you and refer back to it often. Checking each idea against the question can ensure you are on the right track in offering a focused response. To make sure you stay focused on the question, remember the following points:

- Read the question carefully. Make sure you do not misread a word or overlook a phrase, as this can change the entire focus of your essay. For example, misreading 'distraction' as 'destruction', or addressing your 'region' rather than your 'country', could change the direction of your essay.

- Use the wording of the question throughout as a *signpost* for the reader. As a general rule, the language of the essay question should appear in nearly every paragraph.

- Make sure you answer the question directly, rather than simply writing everything you know about the topic! For example, if the question asks about the role of art in politics, but you merely discuss everything you know about art in *general*, your essay will not be successful in achieving focus.

Maintaining focus is important for the audience because it helps them follow your argument. But a coherent organisation of your ideas is also crucial in keeping them engaged. Therefore, to help your readers follow what you are saying:

- Use every sentence as a building block in the essay. One thought should lead seamlessly into the next in order to achieve a logical progression of ideas.

- Make sure that every paragraph, like every sentence, relates to the one before it, while also indicating what is to come next. Use seamless *transitional* strategies to achieve this.

KEY SKILLS

To review what you learnt about focusing and organising your essay, see Chapter 2.2.

Support

Evidence is a crucial component of logical reasoning. For each point raised in an argument, you should provide evidence to support it. Whether it is an example, data,

basic logic or expert testimony, evidence is necessary to illustrate your point and substantiate your claims. The following tips will help you:

- Cambridge International AS Level English General Paper essay questions are designed to provoke thought and encourage the sustained development of ideas; you can accomplish this by providing clear and appropriate examples.

- Use specific examples to minimise the likelihood of exaggerating and/or overgeneralising ideas. Exemplification is essential!

- Development of your ideas through evaluation, as opposed to description, should be a key objective.

- Do not allow a single issue or source to dominate the conversation you create in your writing.

- When using counter argumentation strategies, be sure to provide enough information to address the opposing viewpoint. Otherwise, this can quickly lead to a straw man fallacy (see Chapter 3.1 Section *B Understanding arguments*

- Give fair consideration to the opposition while supporting your main point.

271

KEY SKILLS

To review what you learnt about building support and using evidence in an essay, see Chapters 2.2, 3.1 and 3.2.

Analysing and evaluating

Being able to understand and apply the skills you have learnt in this course can make you a more *competent* writer. Being able to analyse and evaluate your own ideas as well as those of others can also help you to become a *critical* thinker. Remember to do the following:

- Analyse an issue from several relevant perspectives before judging it. To do this, use lenses to sharpen your focus on issues and think about the stakeholders involved.

- Develop your ideas through evaluation rather than description. Do not be afraid to share your own perspective in response to the evidence.

- As an option, if you note the source of information in your essay (though you are *not* required to), you can consider the source's credibility as part of your output, or commentary, on the information. Use the RAVEN strategy to help you articulate these ideas (see Chapter 3.1 Section *D Analysing sources*).

- Consider the context surrounding an issue and how it shapes the views of others as part of your analysis.

- Use evidence, not just opinion, to draw conclusions about an issue.

- Draw conclusions midway through an analysis to help you reason through an issue.

KEY SKILLS

To review what you learnt about analysing and evaluating, see Chapters 3.1 and 3.2.

Approach and style

You are writing for an academic purpose in this course, therefore it is important to use and maintain a formal register, while at the same time letting your own voice be heard. Essay questions ask you to give your own opinion, but you will need to back your viewpoints with globally relevant evidence that your audience can appreciate. Demonstrate a questioning approach by reasoning through issues and recognising that your viewpoint is not the only one! Key points to bear in mind:

- Be aware of the difference between assertion and discussion. Remember that essay questions invite debate and evaluation. They encourage genuine exploration of the topic. Use clear thinking and analysis to persuade your audience.

- When a question asks you to write from the perspective of 'you', you should offer relevant, local examples to support your ideas rather than personal anecdote. This will give your response a

more academic tone, while also demonstrating the importance of your own voice.

- A wide-ranging knowledge of topics at the general level is expected, but you should also explore your own opinions in response to this knowledge. When you give an example, don't be afraid to offer your own commentary on its relevance or value. This is the purpose of critical thought.

- Avoid responses that offer opinions but no credible evidence to support the claims being made. This will make your response appear generalised, vague and untrustworthy.

- You should aim to write a fair, well-reasoned response rather than a one-sided assertion. This will help you gain the trust of your audience.

- This course encourages discussion, *not* a mere repetition of learnt facts. Use your own opinions and natural curiosity to explore the issues!

- Try to have a genuine *conversation* with your audience rather than presenting an essay simply based on a formula.

KEY SKILLS

To review what you learnt about developing style, see Chapters 3.1 and 4.4.

Expression

The way you express your ideas plays a key role in the impact your writing has on your audience. Remember that if you cannot say clearly what you mean, your audience will not be able to understand your point.

- Write as simply and accurately as you can, while still giving attention to style and audience. Clarity is essential.

- Avoid over-elaborate or 'flowery' language. Your aim should be to demonstrate an understanding of words and how to use them appropriately in context.

- It is important to be original, so avoid using clichéd phrases. Phrases such as 'nowadays', 'kids' and 'in a nutshell' should be avoided. Instead, find your own, individual way to express your ideas.

- Avoid contrived (not natural) language, or words that you have learnt beforehand and are forcing to fit the essay question.

- Avoid the use of colloquial language and/or slang. This is generally inappropriate for an exam essay, which should be aimed at an international audience; (e.g. 'woulda' should be written as 'would have', 'for sure' as 'certainly' or 'essentially').
- When beginning an essay, avoid grand phrases such as 'since the dawn of man …'. Introducing the topic from the start of time takes your essay unnecessarily out of context. Think of when the topic has become important in more recent times.

KEY SKILLS

To review what you learnt about clear expression, see Chapters 4.4 and 4.5.

Use of English

As a writer in this course, you will not only be assessed on your ability to develop ideas in an essay, but also on how well you understand the way language is used to communicate. To demonstrate your ability to use English appropriately:

- Keep to proper usage and mechanics. If you have an effective message but your writing is full of errors, that message will not be communicated clearly! Allowing time for revision can help minimise errors.
- Make sure that any errors in your use of English do not affect the meaning of what you are saying. You can then be sure you are making your point clearly.
- Avoid the use of abbreviations (i.e., etc., e.g.) in a formal, academic essay.

KEY SKILLS

To review what you learnt about mechanics, see Chapter 4.1.

Audience

Before you begin writing, you need to consider who you are writing for. If your audience cannot relate to your message, you will not achieve your purpose. As you generate ideas, think about how your audience will receive them. Consider their values and beliefs, and show respect for them.

- Be aware of your audience. You are writing for an academic purpose, so make sure you use appropriate language.
- Remember that your audience might not necessarily agree with your ideas, so aim for a sensitive approach to the issues. While arguing your point, do so with your audience in mind.

KEY SKILLS

To review what you learnt about audience, see Chapter 3.1.

B Writing a timed essay

No matter how confident you feel about your writing skills by the end of the course, writing an essay for an assessment can still be intimidating. If you have to do an exam, you will experience less stress and anxiety if you know what to expect during the exam and feel comfortable with the exam process; this can considerably increase your chances of doing well. Here are some technical tips for when you sit your exam:

- You do not need to repeat the essay question at the top of your answer sheet. This can waste valuable time. Just give the number (e.g. 1–10) of the essay question you are answering.
- Depending on what you are writing with, you may write on both sides of the page, but make sure the writing is legible when written on both sides (i.e. some writing tools show through!).
- Essays should generally keep to the word count given in the exam instructions.
- Essays that are significantly shorter than the suggested word count are likely to be penalised. There may not be enough information to satisfy the requirements of the task.
- Whether you are typing or handwriting your essay, allow time to review and edit your work for any typographical, spelling or grammar errors.

273

To review what you learnt about the Cambridge International AS Level English General Paper course and how it is assessed, see Chapter 1.1.

C Peer-editing strategies

At first, your teacher will be the primary source of feedback for your work. As you become more confident with the objectives of the course, you will be more able to help your peers (other students in your class) to improve their writing.

This section suggests some strategies to help you give effective feedback to your peers. However, there are some myths about peer-editing which you need to be aware of first:

1 *Young writers are reluctant to be critical of their peers or do not know how to criticise constructively (i.e. with a helpful purpose).*

    Setting clear ground rules for peer-led editing activities can help you feel comfortable with the process. See Activity 1 for one way to do this; see also the list of conversation starters in the section which follows (see *Stage 1: Reading for understanding*) for appropriate language to offer respectful and constructive feedback to your peers.

2 *Peer editors tend to focus on mechanical errors but pay little attention to content and organisational structure.*

    Wrong! If you use an effective system such as split-column annotations, this can help you balance the kind of feedback you give. (See '*Peer-editing Stage 2: Annotating the essay*' later in this chapter.)

3 *There is little reason for one writer to want to spend time reading another's work if it is not benefiting them directly.*

    Assessing the work of others can help you improve your own writing practice. Whether you are reading good work, or work that needs improvement, assessing the work of others helps you to see which strategies work and which ones do not.

4 *Young writers do not know enough about the writing process to guide their peers.*

    Effective peer-editing can be helpful for both you and your fellow students. Discussing your intentions and working through problems with someone else can enrich your learning. It can be more helpful than working it out on your own. Your teacher is there to advise when you are unsure!

ACTIVITY 1

As a class, set ground rules for peer-editing. What kinds of things need to be clear before you begin commenting on each other's work? Write a collective list of five to eight rules and display these during the activity. Here are two to get you started:

- Be considerate towards the other person's feelings.
- Writing does not have to be perfect to be good!

If you use an effective system for editing, you are less likely to focus on just one thing (such as mechanics) and more likely to give honest and balanced feedback. Just as you read a poem more than once to understand it, you will need to read someone else's work more than once in order to analyse it. It is helpful to see the peer-editing process in three separate stages.

Peer-editing Stage 1: Reading for understanding

Before you look at the details, take time to look at the 'big picture' of your partner's work. Read the essay from start to finish to get familiar with the:

- style
- content
- points raised.

For this first reading, focus on what your partner is trying to say. Are the points clear? Does the overall argument fit together and flow logically? Make some notes to help you understand the overall message of the essay.

During this stage you might consider the following questions. Does your partner's essay:

- stay focused on the essay question?
- offer a thesis statement and refer back to it frequently with points raised in the body?
- use an organisational pattern that is easy to follow?
- lead to a conclusion that relates to the points made in the essay?

You may want to ask your partner a few clarifying questions before moving on to the next stage.

Here are a few useful phrases to help you better understand your partner's intentions:

Conversation starters

I like how you …

Tell me what you meant by …

Did you mean to …?

Why did you …?

How will this …?

I am unfamiliar with …

Tell me more about …

TIP

Imagine how you might feel when someone else is reading *your* essay! Remember that your partner(s) might feel self-conscious about having you comment on their work. Starting a conversation with a phrase such as 'I like how you …' can help your partner feel more comfortable and confident. This may lead to an easier conversation as you begin the peer-editing process.

Talking through ideas with someone else is a great way to sort them out. Discussing points through conversation can help you both see the purpose more clearly. Conversations like these often lead to key insights, which may help you reword or reorder essay ideas more effectively!

Peer-editing Stage 2: Annotating the essay

It may be difficult to sit on your hands (i.e. not to start marking) during your first reading of the essay, but Stage 1 prevents you from over-marking your partner's paper. Otherwise, too many marks could look overwhelming and make your partner feel defeated.

For example, you are reading your partner's first body paragraph. You notice that it lacks evidence to support the point raised. So you make a note in the margin only to find that the *next* paragraph provides an example to illustrate that point! If you are too quick to mark an essay, you may *mis*mark it! You should read the work through once before giving written feedback.

For this stage in the peer-editing process, use the following two-column annotation system to make comments on your partner's essay:

1 Reasoning, support, organisational structure	2 Mechanics (use of English)
Comments/suggestions/questions regarding: • strength of topic sentence • use or lack of examples/evidence • organisational structure and transitions • ideas to enhance approach	Recommended adjustments to mechanics, including: • spelling • grammar • punctuation • style • awkward or unclear wording • redundancy (text that is unnecessary)

Separating content and structure from mechanics gives a visual reference of what kind of feedback you are giving. If you notice you are giving a lot of comments in the right-hand column (mechanics), this will prompt you to give more attention to content and structure.

When you offer written feedback on your peer's work, remember to be specific. On the next page you will find some points to help you give quality feedback in writing.

Instead of writing ...	try letting your partner know ...	like this ...
'Good!' or 'I like this!'	... <u>what</u> you like	'This topic sentence makes your first reason very clear!'
'Unclear point' or 'What do you mean?'	... <u>what</u> is wrong	'How does this example relate to your thesis?' or 'Connect this evidence to your thesis.'
'Work on your transitions'	... ways to strengthen connections between ideas	'Use a transition here to show how these two ideas are similar (e.g. "similarly" or "likewise").'
'Needs an example'	... concrete ideas that could help support the point	'Have you ever heard of Maslow's Hierarchy? This might help you prove your point about "needs" versus "wants". (I learnt about it in Psychology, so I can tell you about it or let you borrow my book!)'

Balancing strengths and weaknesses when giving feedback helps your partner feel more confident, and more receptive to constructive criticism. It is also helpful to use a friendly and informal tone in your feedback as long as this does not distract from the point you are making.

Peer-editing Stage 3: Using a checklist

Finalise your observations using a checklist. This can help you communicate to your partner what key elements of the essay may be missing. It is best to do this last, when you have had time to look closely at the details both in conversation and in written feedback. You can then return to the overall picture by looking at strengths and weaknesses.

There are two ways to complete a checklist for your partner's essay:

- Fill it in *with* your partner, locating and colour-coding the various components with them as you go (e.g., thesis = yellow, reasons = green, evidence = blue, arrows show connections, etc.)

- Fill in the checklist *on your own*, then review it with your partner afterwards.

The first option is a good way for both you and your partner to strengthen your understanding of the essay's

components, working together to identify and evaluate them. As you become more confident during the course, you can move on to the second option, identifying the elements on your own, then discussing them with your partner.

On the next page is a checklist which reflects the essay components you have learnt about this course. Use a checklist like this to give feedback to your partner during Stage 3 of the peer-editing process. (Depending on the task, style and topic of the essay, not all the components of the checklist will be needed.)

Essay introduction

- Your introduction engages the audience! It grabs the reader's attention because you indicate *why* the issue matters. Specifically, you show that the issue is:
  - important in modern society.
  - relevant both locally and globally.

- Your introduction informs the audience! It assumes the reader is new to the topic, so you take a moment to provide important information before moving forward, by:
  - defining broad or unknown terms as necessary
  - setting limits / narrowing the scope of ideas to be addressed
  - showing them how outside influences further shape its circumstances.

- Your introduction directs the audience! It lets the audience know what to expect by:
  - using a formal register / setting an academic tone
  - indicating your purpose for writing via a thesis statement
  - previewing the big ideas you plan to address as necessary.

Essay body

- The body of your essay organises your ideas! Your topic sentences:
  - establish your reasons to support your thesis, making clear the point of the paragraph
  - use transitions to appropriately guide and connect ideas.

  Your ideas:
  - are ordered logically/intentionally/ meaningfully (clear line of reasoning)
  - are relevant to the question
  - use language from the question to maintain focus.

- The body of your essay convinces/engages the audience! Your support paragraphs:
  - use evidence to support your reasons
  - sustain points through evidence and elaboration (rather than just 'skimming' or listing ideas)
  - consider a range of perspectives.

- The body of your essay enlightens the audience! Your support paragraphs:
  - counter opposing points of view by conceding to, minimising or dismissing them
  - link evidence back to your thesis / main claim
  - offer interim conclusions to manage individual sections of information at a time.

Essay conclusion

- Your essay conclusion reminds the audience what has come before! The concluding paragraph:
  - *briefly* summarises points raised in the body
  - revisits any concerns the audience may still have (i.e. valid, opposing views), and alleviates these.

- Your essay conclusion enlightens/energises/ challenges the audience! The concluding paragraph does any of the following:
  - draws conclusions based on evidence from the essay
  - considers what will happen if people agree/ disagree with your perspective (consequences)
  - considers the impact of agreeing or disagreeing with the conversation surrounding the topic (implications)
  - calls your audience to action
  - offers solutions to solve any remaining problems associated with your topic
  - recommends further research to clarify remaining gaps in your topic
  - considers limits to any of the conclusions you draw or the recommendations you offer.

Use of English

- Your use of English makes the message clear and easy to understand! The essay:
  - uses complete sentences
  - places modifiers close to the word/phrase being described
  - shows agreement between subject and verb
  - shows agreement between pronoun and antecedent
  - observes proper spelling
  - uses punctuation appropriately
  - varies in sentence structure

277

- o uses your own language / word choice
- o has generally good grammar.

Overall approach

- ■ Your overall approach respects the audience! It:
  - o considers the issue from multiple perspectives
  - o shows sensitivity to opposing views

- o builds trust
- o avoids personal bias
- o uses appropriate language
- o offers relevant and informed input to back claims.

To summarise, here are a few basic rules for effective peer-editing:

- Be respectful, but also be *honest*. Give the same help you would like to receive from others.
- The main focus of a peer-editing session is to check that your partner has produced a clear, readable *and* logical argument. Grammar is not the only feature that you should comment on!
- Remember that you are both working with the same objectives in mind – to help each other develop the key writing and thinking skills to succeed in your course!

> **TIP**
> You (or your teacher) might want to standardise your annotations for marking the checklist. For example, you might:
> - highlight areas that your partner did well
> - use a pen to circle, underline or make notes about things that need work.

Peer editing can help both you and your partner to feel confident that you *are* learning and developing the key skills for this course.

D Self-editing strategies

Peer-editing allows you to observe how other writers approach the writing process, which can lead to improvements in your own approach. This kind of practice can be helpful because eventually you will need to be able to assess your *own* work when other people are not there, such as during an exam situation. The following strategies provide you with different approaches to self-editing:

Read your writing back to yourself

When you read your own work, you tend to see the words as you *intended* them to be. Because of this, you can easily miss errors while your brain fills in what you *wanted* to say:

a To help you spot errors, read your work aloud to yourself. Hearing your ideas as you have actually written them can help you spot errors in grammar as well as logic.

b Correct mechanical errors by reading your essay *backwards*. This can help you identify errors more effectively than reading forwards (i.e. the way you intended it to be read).

Deconstruct your ideas using colour coding

Colour code the basic elements of your writing as follows:

Colour	Elements
Yellow	thesis / reasons to support your thesis (another option is to *circle* the reasons)
Blue	evidence to support reasons
Green	your own voice, where you link evidence to claims, or offer interim/final conclusions or other insights based on evidence, etc.
Orange	context to inform/interest/educate the reader about the topic
Red	organisational strategies (i.e. transitional words or phrases)
Purple	opposing views (another option is to *underline* your counter-argument in the same colour)

You might create your own system as a class to identify relevant elements. Use the peer-editing checklist to guide your analysis.

Use the 'TREE' of reasoning

See Chapter 3.1 Section *E Developing an effective line of reasoning* to deconstruct the elements of your writing. This works for any style of essay, as there are always reasons and evidence present, along with conclusions drawn from these.

Chapter 5.2
Reviewing your reading comprehension skills

Learning objectives

In this chapter, you will reflect on the reading skills you have developed and the strategies for reading comprehension you have learnt in this course. Specifically, you will review what you have learnt about:

■ reading critically and actively
■ using hints in the text to determine the meaning of words in context
■ key words in comprehension questions and tips for responding
■ organising and developing ideas in your response
■ keeping to word limits, and the importance of following instructions
■ accurate and appropriate use of English in communicating your answers.

A Review of key skills in reading comprehension

Reading comprehension can help you to navigate the world around you – for example, when you need to understand what a news headline suggests or to interpret the tone of an email. The tips and strategies in this chapter will help you reflect on the things you have learnt about how to respond effectively to reading.

Reading carefully

Careful readers can also become effective writers, so the two assessments in the Cambridge International AS Level English General Paper course are linked. If you interact carefully with the ideas and language of the material, you are more likely to understand what you are reading. This is an important objective for the course, but also a necessary skill for life.

Remember to keep the following points in mind as you read for comprehension:

- Before you begin reading the material, spend some time previewing the questions that accompany it. This will help you set a *purpose* for your reading.

- Pay attention to key words in comprehension questions, which will affect the focus and intentions of your response.

- Actively read each question; when possible, such as in an exam situation, circle and/or underline key words and instructions.

- Actively read prose material, jotting notes as you read (such as observations, connections to what you already know, reactions or questions); when possible, such as in an exam situation, circle/underline/bracket important information (such as main points/reasons, key details, structure).

- Break prose material into smaller, manageable sections, identifying the key purpose and/or message conveyed in the beginning, middle and end of each section.

- Use arrows to make connections between related information in the material. For example, there might be information in one paragraph that exemplifies a point made earlier. Actively connecting information in this way can help you to understand the material.

- Sometimes, data such as statistics can be overwhelming. For example, if percentage increases in energy efficiency were listed in several regions of a country, you could draw a simple pie chart to help you interpret the data:

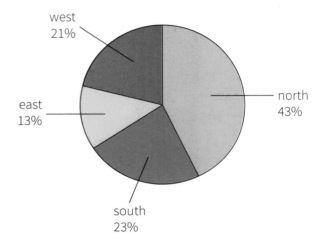

- Pay attention to the source of specific evidence, or the source of the whole extract, when it is given. This can help you form judgements about the information and it can aid your interpretation of the material. Note quick observations about the strength of these sources using strategies like RAVEN (see Chapter 3.1 Section *D Analysing sources*).

🔗 KEY SKILLS

To review what you learnt about skills for close reading, see Chapter 1.3 Section *C Strategies for close reading*.

Words and phrases in context

A wide-ranging vocabulary can help you develop your reading comprehension. If you come across a word that is unfamiliar to you, there are strategies to help you get a sense of its meaning:

- Thinking about the context can help you determine the word's meaning. Pay attention to clues, which can appear before and/or after the word, or within the sentence.

- Before you begin reading material, scan the comprehension questions to find any vocabulary tasks. As you read, write down synonyms in the margin for each vocabulary term or phrase you come across.

- When a comprehension question asks you to provide a synonym for a word, make sure the grammatical form matches the original (i.e. replace a noun with a noun, replace an adjective with an adjective, etc.).

- Before writing a sentence using a vocabulary word, which is a type of comprehension question, briefly review the original context in which the word was used. Then aim to use the word in the same *context*. For example, if the word is *pool* as in 'pool your resources', your sentence would not mention a swimming pool!

- However, when you are asked to write sentences using words from the material, make sure you apply the words to a different *subject*. For example, if the original uses the vocabulary terms in material about volcanoes, *do not* use them in sentences about volcanoes! Instead, you might use the same words in sentences about *tsunamis* or any other topic. Make sure they are used appropriately and in the same sense that the words were originally used.

- When you are writing sentences using vocabulary words, make sure you demonstrate the meaning of the words by constructing appropriate context clues.

KEY SKILLS

To review what you learnt about the meaning of words and phrases in context, see Chapter 1.3 Section *D Essential reading comprehension skills*.

Responding to questions

As with essay questions, every word counts in comprehension questions. It is therefore important to read each question carefully and understand it fully before attempting to respond, otherwise, your answer might not meet all the requirements of the task. Bear in mind the following:

- When a question explicitly asks that you use *your own words* to respond, *do not* include quotes from the material in your response. Lifting information directly from the material does not demonstrate that you understand it!

- Questions may include more than one task. Make sure you address *all* parts of the question!

- Questions that ask you to explain or summarise something are usually limited to a particular section, as opposed to all of the material. You might be asked, for example, to 'summarise X's point in paragraph 5', or to 'explain paragraphs 3 and 4 using your own words'.

- Be aware that several variations of a question might exist, so it is your job to read carefully. One question, for instance, may ask you to consider the advantages *and* disadvantages of something. When responding to this type of question, make sure you do both. At other times, you may be asked to consider *only* the advantages, which means you would not mention disadvantages at all.

- As part of the logical reasoning task, you are likely to be asked to consider several options before judging them. Pay careful attention to the question's wording in these cases, too, which may ask you to choose:

  o the *most* suitable option
  o the *least* suitable option.

  Normally, questions that ask you to pick the 'most' or 'least' suitable option *restrict* your discussion to mentioning only the one you choose.

- Check whether a question wants you to use explicit details from the material to support your response, or whether it allows you to use some of your own, outside knowledge and/or reasoning. Look at the following examples.

  1 Use the material to form the basis of your response when you see phrases like:

  > Using information from the material, …
  >
  > Use evidence from the material to …

  2 Use both the material *and* your own knowledge and/or reasoning to formulate your response to questions such as:

  > Based on what you read, do you think …
  >
  > In your own opinion, do you think … Justify your answer.
  >
  > If you were (stakeholder X), how would you respond / what would you do/think/decide …

281

3 Questions may ask you to use your own wider knowledge and/or reasoning:

> Using evidence from the material or your knowledge of the present day, …
>
> In your own opinion, … (*provided that the question is unrelated to information in the material*)

Once you understand the question, keep the following strategies in mind when responding:

- Attempt to answer all questions. Remember there is no penalty for trying!

- Logical reasoning tasks often present you with a number of options before asking you to pick the 'best' or 'most suitable' one. As mentioned above, you will probably be asked to consider both advantages *and* disadvantages of your choice. Since you are discussing the 'best' option, you should naturally provide more benefits than drawbacks in order to maintain your decision that it is the 'best' overall.

- If you are asked to provide advantages *and* disadvantages, these do not need to be equally balanced. For example, you could mention *four* advantages and only *one* disadvantage. Make sure you develop (sustain) each point rather than merely listing them.

KEY SKILLS

To review what you learnt about understanding and responding to comprehension questions, see Chapter 1.3 Section *D Essential reading comprehension skills*.

Generating and organising ideas

Setting aside time to organise your response is as important for comprehension questions as it is for essays. Logical reasoning tasks, in particular, require careful planning. For these questions, you are often asked to look at several sources of information and to combine ideas from them all. The following advice may be helpful:

- When you are asked to choose the 'best' or 'most suitable' option, use a table layout to list the qualities of each option. Then analyse the

information in each column by marking the qualities as advantages (+) or disadvantages (–) before making your choice.

- When you are giving your opinion, you will need to support this with either text-based justification or examples from your own knowledge. Use mind-mapping strategies to help you outline reasons and examples.

KEY SKILLS

To review what you learnt about generating and organising your ideas, see Chapter 2.2.

Developing ideas

When you *develop* an idea, you are expanding your thoughts on it, not just listing it and moving on. Sustaining your point like this helps the reader understand not only *what* your point is; it also gives them a deeper sense of *why* you think that way, or even *how* you arrived at that idea. Bear in mind the following:

- When asked to provide reasons, use the subordinating conjunction 'because' to help extend your thoughts. Avoid simply giving lists of reasons, unless the question specifically asks for this.

- Another way to develop your ideas is to connect the reasons you offer and the evidence used to support these reasons. By linking the two, you are sustaining your point by justifying *why* your evidence is relevant.

- When a comprehension question asks you to 'justify your answer', use specific examples from the text rather than vague or generalised explanations.

- When a comprehension question asks you to identify the 'least relevant information' in a text, you will need to justify your choice. If you leave your audience to assume why the input is not relevant, you will have only half-answered the question!

- A 'perceptive' response is one that uses a 'what + why' combination to substantiate claims or reasons you have identified. For example, when you are asked to give advantages and disadvantages of something (with 10 marks available), you would need to provide the following to ensure a perceptive response:

Advantage 1 + why it is advantageous	2 marks
Advantage 2 + why it is advantageous	2 marks
Advantage 3 + why it is advantageous	2 marks
Advantage 4 + why it is advantageous	2 marks
Disadvantage 1 + why it is disadvantageous	2 marks
	|
	10 marks total

KEY SKILLS

To review what you learnt about developing your ideas, see Chapter 2.2.

Organisation and style in your response

While your response to a comprehension question will be much shorter than a full-length essay, it still needs to be well organised. This will help you to communicate your answer clearly and effectively.

- As in an essay, use topic sentences to make your main point clear. Then offer evidence and exemplification to further develop and support your point.

- The use of transitions in your response can help you organise, and show connections between, your ideas.

- Carefully worded answers can help you avoid making generalisations or unsupported claims. To write a nuanced response (i.e. to express a precise meaning), remember to incorporate:
  o modals (to indicate possibility)
  o comparatives (to analyse)
  o superlatives (to express judgement).

KEY SKILLS

To review what you learnt about strategies to organise and style your response, see Chapter 1.3.

B Writing within the set limit

In addition to assessing your reading skills, comprehension questions are also designed to assess your ability to write concisely. If your response goes beyond the limit that is set, the excess writing may not be included when awarding marks. Therefore, it is very important that you remember to write *within the word limits set by the question*.

When responding to comprehension questions which specify a word limit, avoid repeating the question, giving an introduction, or citing individuals. For example, 'According to astrophysics enthusiast and Nobel prize winner Herbert McGinner from the International Aerospace Studies Institute, …'. These unnecessary elements waste valuable words, leaving fewer available for information that could gain you credit.

Offering more information than the question requires can lead to contradictory or inaccurate answers. If a question asks for:

- a synonym for a word, provide *only* one
- a sentence using a word from the text, provide *only* one
- two reasons that support a claim, provide *only* two
- an 80-word response, do not *exceed* this limit.

When you are writing a response, you may not arrive at your greatest insights until the end. Keep in mind that if your response exceeds the limit set, your best ideas will not be credited!

C Use of English

You may have excellent ideas, but if you cannot use English well enough to communicate them effectively, your ideas will suffer. While use of English is not credited in the same way in comprehension answers as it is in essays, it still plays an important part in the success of your responses. To help communicate your answers clearly, remember the following points:

- Use articles (*a*, *an*, *the*) appropriately. Omitting them can make the meaning less clear and your writing less fluent.

283

- Edit your work to correct any spelling errors. Make especially sure that you have not misspelt any words that appear *in the materials*!

- When you make a *comma splice* error, you write two sentences when you should only write one (see Chapter 4.2 Section *E Adverbs* and Chapter 4.4 Section *D Common punctuation errors*). Be aware of this when asked to respond to a question using just one sentence.

- Disagreement between pronouns and their antecedents can confuse the reader and make the point you are trying to make less clear (see Chapter 4.3 Section *C Pronouns*). Therefore, make sure your pronouns and antecedents always agree!

- The quality of students' responses, and in particular their use of English, often deteriorates if they write more than the specified word count. This is another good reason to keep within the limit that is set!

Glossary

The number in brackets at the end of each definition refers to the chapter where the term is used.

abstract nouns: ideas, which cannot be experienced directly with the senses; instead, these occur mentally or are felt emotionally (4.3)

annotation: marks on the text which highlight important features, or written notes next to the marked text (e.g., with your questions, observations or reactions) (2.2)

antecedent: a word or phrase that is replaced by a pronoun (4.3)

argument: the process of using logical reasoning to convince an audience to accept your point of view (3.1)

argumentative: a type of essay that asks you to *argue* something by developing a line of reasoning in order to arrive at a logical conclusion; the aim is to convince your audience either to accept your position or even to take action (1.2)

audience: the person/people that you are speaking to or writing for; for example, in a writing competition your audience would be the competition judges, while your audience in this course is usually your teacher (1.2)

auxiliary verb: another name for a helping verb (4.3)

biased: having a tendency to believe one side of an argument more than the other as a result of one's personal opinions and/or prejudice (1.2)

broad terms: any words in an essay question that can be broken down into more specific sub-categories; these terms *broaden* the possibilities of the essay's scope (2.2)

clause: a unit of grammatical organisation containing a subject and predicate; clauses can stand alone as simple sentences or be part of a larger sentence (4.4)

cliché: overused phrase which make the thought being expressed seem unoriginal (4.5)

close-reading: a thoughtful, critical analysis of a text which focuses on both structure and meaning to develop a deep, precise understanding (1.3)

collective noun: a noun representing a group of individuals; depending on how the actions of the individuals are carried out, a collective noun can be treated as singular or plural (4.3)

comma splice: the faulty practice of using a comma to join together two independent clauses; instead, either a semi-colon or full stop should be used (4.2)

Command words: terms that indicate how you are expected to respond to a question (1.2)

common nouns: words that refer to persons, places, things or ideas of a general nature (4.3)

comparatives: adjectives or adverbs used to compare differences between the two objects they describe (1.3)

complement: a word or group of words which appear in the predicate of a sentence in order to complete a thought (4.4)

concrete nouns: persons, places, and things you can physically experience with the senses (4.3)

connotation: the underlying emotion produced by a word or phrase (1.3)

context: the circumstances and information you need to know in order to fully understand an issue (1.2)

context clues: information surrounding an unknown word, which help you understand its meaning (1.3)

contraction: a shortened version of a word, using an apostrophe (4.3)

coordinate adjectives: also called *paired* adjectives, are two or more adjectives that (precede and) describe the same noun; neither adjective carries more weight in describing the noun, so they can appear in any order and are separated by commas (4.2)

counterargumentation: a strategy of considering arguments that go against your thesis or main claim, and dismissing or minimising them (countering them) in order to strengthen your own point (3.1)

cumulative adjectives: two or more adjectives that build on one another and together modify a noun; unlike coordinate adjectives (whose order can be reversed), the order of cumulative adjectives is intentional, so they are not separated by commas (4.2)

dangling modifier: a word or phrase that modifies a word which is not actually in the sentence (4.2)

deconstruct: break down, analyse (2.2)

dependent clause: a clause that is preceded by a subordinating conjunction or relative pronoun, so it cannot stand alone as a complete thought (4.4)

descriptive grammar: rules determining appropriate language use based on how it is actually used by its speakers (4.1)

discursive: a type of essay that asks you to *explore* an issue by considering objectively various points of view before arriving at an evidence-based conclusion (1.2)

effective communication: using language accurately to express your thoughts or opinions about a topic while remaining sensitive to your audience's feelings and experiences (1.1)

evidence: the factual information that supports your reasons; evidence may appear in the form of examples, data (i.e. statistics), case studies, expert opinions or logic (1.2)

exemplification: using concrete examples to illustrate your point; exemplification is one of several ways for providing evidence (2.2)

expository writing: a type of essay that asks you to *explain* something to the reader by presenting it clearly and sharing details and facts, to educate and inform your audience (1.2)

final conclusion: the final judgement made or insight gained once all the evidence is presented in an essay; it appears at the end (3.2)

foreshadowing: a technique in which the writer (or film director) gives clues to the reader (audience) about what is going to happen (1.2)

fused sentence: a type of sentence that 'runs on' because it lacks the appropriate punctuation to separate independent clauses (4.4)

hedging: the careful use of words to distinguish between fact and claim; also used to show your audience the extent to which you support the information you are presenting (3.2)

homophone: a word that sounds the same as another but has a different meaning and/or spelling (4.5)

indefinite pronouns: a pronoun that expresses a non-specific or non-definite meaning; many indefinite pronouns end in *–body*, *–thing* or *–one* (4.3)

independent clause: a clause that can stand alone as a complete sentence (4.4)

infer: to draw conclusions from evidence given (1.3)

intensive pronouns: personal pronouns which end with *–self* or *–selves*; these are used in a sentence to emphasise,

or intensify, a point but are not grammatically necessary for it to function (4.3)

interim conclusion: a conclusion drawn part of the way through an essay after some (but not all) evidence has been considered; such interim conclusions are not permanent: they may change as more evidence is presented (3.2)

interjection: an abrupt remark or exclamation made in speech to convey a particular emotion, and which can communicate facial expressions or body language that cannot be expressed in normal speech (4.5)

key details: specific information to support the main idea (1.3)

lens: a piece of glass or other transparent material on a camera which allows you to see an image in different ways, or by analogy a way of looking at an issue from a specific perspective (2.2)

limiting terms: any words in an essay question that restrict the response; these terms *shrink shrink* the possibilities of the essay's scope (2.2)

logical fallacy: a defect in the line of reasoning, which weakens the argument (3.1)

logical reasoning: expressing a point of view by offering reasons to support your main thesis (3.1)

main claim: the thesis, or primary point, of your argument (3.1)

main idea: the writer's central message (1.3)

mechanics: a collective term which refers to the various technical aspects of your writing, including grammar, spelling and punctuation (4.1)

misplaced modifier: a phrase or clause placed awkwardly in a sentence so that it appears to modify (or refer to) an unintended word (4.2)

modal: a type of auxiliary verb used to express attitude toward the main verb (4.3)

objective: not influenced by personal feelings or opinions when presenting an argument (1.2)

parameters: key terms in the essay question which make the scope of the question wider or narrower (1.3)

paraphrasing: maintaining the *idea* of someone's thoughts, observations or ideas, but putting them into your own words (2.1)

parts of speech: the categories to which words are assigned based on their *syntactic* function (see **syntax**); English has the following parts of speech: nouns, pronouns, verbs, adjectives, adverbs, conjunctions, prepositions and interjections (4.1)

perspective: a point of view or opinion about a problem, situation or issue (1.3)

predicate: the part of the sentence that contains the verb and says something about the subject (4.3)

predicate adjective: an adjective that is connected to the subject of the sentence by a linking verb (4.2)

prescriptive grammar: advice based on someone's *preference* for what is 'grammatically correct' (4.1)

prompt: a question or instruction which encourages you to respond (1.1)

proper nouns: words that identify specific persons, places, things or ideas (4.3)

purpose: your reason for writing/speaking; for example, your purpose may be to persuade someone to agree with you about something (1.2)

qualifier: a word or phrase used to limit the meaning of a word; it maximises or minimises the value of the word (1.2)

quoting: using the exact words from the text (verbatim) to express a thought, observation or idea (2.3)

reflection: a thought, idea or opinion formed after careful consideration of information or experience (1.2)

reflexive pronouns: personal pronouns which end with *–self* or *–selves*; these are grammatically necessary for the sentence to function (4.3)

register: type of language used for a particular purpose, or in a particular setting (2.3)

relevant: directly related to the issue being discussed (1.2)

run-on: two or more independent clauses joined together inappropriately, either due to incorrect or absent punctuation (4.4)

scope: the extent or range of possible ideas; 'defining scope' refers to determining how broad or narrow your essay's coverage will be (2.2)

seamless transition: a movement from one idea to another without the use of standard transitional words or phrases (2.2)

sentence fragment: a phrase or clause written as a sentence but lacking the essential parts of subject and verb; a fragment does not express a complete thought (4.2)

shape: the way the writer organises their writing to develop their point or provide information (1.2)

signal words: words or phrases that recommend what style of essay you should write (1.2)

simple sentence: a sentence that contains subject, verb and complement (4.4)

stakeholders: any persons, groups or entities affected by the outcome of a problem, situation or issue (2.2)

subject complement: the adjective, noun or pronoun that follows the linking verb and tells us more about the subject of the sentence (4.4)

summary: a short, clear description that gives the main points or facts from material (2.1)

superlatives: adjectives or adverbs used to describe an object which is at the upper or lower limit of quality (1.3)

sustaining an idea: the process of extending a point that you are making (2.3)

syntax: the rules about the arrangement of words in phrases, clauses and sentences (4.1)

synthesise: create new ideas or understanding by combining knowledge from different sources in fresh ways (1.1)

synthesising evidence: the process of offering information from multiple sources to sustain a point (2.3)

thesis: a summary of the main idea, which makes the intentions of an essay clear to the reader; this idea should be supported by evidence during the course of the essay (1.2)

thesis statement: the main idea that guides the direction of your essay;. all ideas should reflect directly back to this statement (2.2)

tone: the attitude of the writer towards their subject or audience (1.2)

topic-specific terms: words that may not be familiar to your audience because they relate to a particular subject (e.g. technology) (1.2)

topic sentence: a sentence that identifies the main idea of the paragraph (1.2)

transitions: words or phrases that connect one idea to another; examples include: *however, in addition, likewise, for example* and *in fact* (1.2)

underlying assumption: an unspoken value or belief about a particular issue (3.1)

verb phrase: contains the main verb, and its direct or indirect object, and may also have one or more helping verbs (4.3)

warrant: an explanation of why or how the data supports the claim and/or reason; this can be an underlying assumption that exists but goes unstated in the argument (3.1)

Index

A

ability to observe, 130
abstract nouns, 215
action verbs, 230
active reading, 37
adjective clauses, 244–245
adjectives, 206
    adverbs *vs.,* 209–210, 255
    coordinate, 206
    cumulative, 206–207
    importance of, 208
    predicate, 206, 240–241
ad populum, 123
advanced, 169
advent, 61, 62
adverb clauses, 245
adverbs, 208–211
    adjectives *vs.,* 209–210, 255
    conjunctive, 210–211
    importance of, 210–211
afforded, defined, 67
A* grade, 107
aligned, 149
ample, 69, 70
angst, 67
animated fantasy film, 67
anime, 67
annotation, 94, 95
anointed dictator, 208
antecedent, 219
anthropogenic, 169
AOs. *see* assessment objectives (AOs)
appeals to authority, 119, 123
appeals to emotion, 120, 123
appeals to logic, 120
archipelagos, 208
argumentative appeals
    appeals to authority, 119
    appeals to emotion, 120

appeals to logic, 120
    kairos, 120
argumentative thesis, 21
    development, 126–128
argumentative writing, 15, 118
    appeals to authority, 119
    appeals to emotion, 120
    appeals to logic, 120
    conclusions, 138–139
    counterargumentation, 125, 127–129
    credibility building, 139–141
    expository writing *vs.,* 124–127
    kairos, 120
    purpose of, 126
    reasoning. *see* reasoning
    tone, 125
arguments
    and context, 119
    defined, 118
    organising ideas in, 167
    Toulmin model, 134–136
    weaknesses in, 122–124
Aristotle, 119, 122
articles, 206, 215
ASEAN (Association of South-East Asian Nations), 102, 103
assessment criteria
    comprehension questions, 11
    essays, 8–9
assessment objectives (AOs), 3–4
asylum, 179
audience, 13–14, 273
author's purpose, identification of, 50
auxiliary verbs, 230, 231
avid readers, 145

B

backlog, 178
baffling, 252

bandwagon fallacy, 123, 124
bastions, 107
biased, 15
blur the line, 126
body, of essay, 23–27
    features of, 25
Bollywood, and fashion, 40–41
books *vs.* e-books, 144–145
bossiness, 195, 196
brainstorming, 72, 88, 93
broad terms, 85
bumblers, 196
by-product, 70

C

callous, 197
canvas, 69, 70
Carroll, Lewis, 218
checklist, usage of, 276
choli, 41
clauses, 241, 243–245
    adjective, 244–245
    adverb, 245
    dependent, 243, 244
    independent, 243, 244
    noun, 245
close-reading
    defined, 37
    strategies, 37–42
cohort, 173, 174
coined, 197
collective nouns, 216–217
colloquial language, 261–262
combo, salwar, 40, 41
comma, 211, 257
command words, 15–17
common nouns, 216
communication
    effective, 4, 12
    language, 13

comparatives, 55–56

complements, 238
 direct objects, 238–239
 indirect objects, 239
 subject, 240–241

complex sentences, 246
 clauses, 241, 243–245
 conjunctions, 242–243

composting, 140

compound-complex sentences,
 246–247

compound nouns, 216

compound sentences, 246

compound subjects, 233–234

comprehension questions, 6–7, 94–95
 assessment criteria, 11
 material for, 8
 responses to, 14–15

comprehension skills. *see* reading
 comprehension

conclusions, 27–29
 argumentative writing, 138–139
 discursive writing, 153–157
 features of, 28
 final, 153, 154–157
 interim, 153–154

concrete nouns, 215

condemnation, 61, 62

confined, 111

confused words, 258–259

conjunctions, 242–243
 coordinating, 242
 correlative, 242
 subordinating, 242–243

conjunctive adverbs, 210–211

connotation, 51

consumes, 252

content-related terms, 87–88

context, 19, 20, 92, 94
 arguments and, 119

context clues, 54

contraction, 222

coordinate adjectives, 206

coordinating conjunctions, 242

core knowledge, 13

correlative conjunctions, 242

counterargumentation, 125, 127–129

counterpart, 144, 145

crave stories, 67

creationist, 170

cringe-inducing creatures, 136, 138

critical reading, benefits of, 30

crop up, 70

cumulative adjectives, 206–207

D

dangling modifiers, 205

data analysis, 60–62

deconstruct, essay questions, 84–88,
 93–94
 complexity, 86–87
 content-related terms, 87–88
 scope of topic, 84–86

decree, 195, 196

degrading, 178

deluge, 157, 158

demonstrative pronouns, 224–225

denigrating, 194, 196

denuding, 166

dependent clause, 243, 244

depletion, 167

Descartes, René, 228

descriptive grammar, 186

determiners, 206, 222

dictating art, 69, 70

direct objects, 238–239

discard, 194, 196

discourse, 143

discrete, 149

discursive thesis, 21, 146

discursive writing, 15, 118, 143–163
 body, strategies for organising,
  150–153
 conclusions, 153–157
 defined, 143
 handling perspectives, 147–150

thesis, 21, 146
tone, 146–147

dissent, 39

distorted, 197

drudgery, 157, 158

dyslexia, 145

E

e-books, 211
 books *vs.*, 144–145

Ecuador, 172–174

eerily, 197

effective communication, 4, 12

English, usage of, 14

enhanced public interest, 139, 140

en masse production, 137, 138

enmeshed, 158

equity, 172, 174

errors, grammar, 204–205

ESCAP (Economic and Social
 Commission for Asia and the
 Pacific), 121, 122

eschewed, 196

essay elements, 19
 body, 23–27
 conclusion, 27–29
 introduction, 19–23
 review of, 30
 thesis statement, 21–22

essay ideas, generating, 88–92
 context, 92, 94
 general idea to specific
  example, 89
 lenses and, 88–89
 scope of, narrowing, 89–90
 stakeholders, 90–91, 94

essays
 annotating, 275–276
 assessment, criteria for, 8–9
 elements of. *see* essay elements
 exam-style, 114–115
 ideas, generating. *see* essay ideas,
  generating

questions, deconstructing. *see* deconstruct, essay questions
    text-based, 114
    topics selection for, 5–6
    travel, 61–62
    writing, 4–6, 114–115, 273
ethos, 119, 123
evictions, 38, 39
evidence, 19, 23–24
    linking to claims, 27
    and logical reasoning, 271
    reflection of, 28
    relevant, 28
    synthesising, 108
exam-style essays, 114–115
expertise, 130
expository writing, 15
    argumentative writing *vs.,* 124–127

F

façade, 69, 70
Facebook, 112
falling through the cracks, 177, 178
fantasy film, 67
fashion, Bollywood and, 40–41
fathom, 173, 174
faux pas, 41
favelas, 70
feat, 113
feedback, peer-editing strategies, 274–278
fertility rates, 111
figurative language, 260
figurehead, 197
filleters, 110
final conclusions, 153, 154–157
fit the mould, 144, 145
forego, 174
foreshadowing, 28
forged, 112
formal writing, 259–260
    figurative language, 260
    over-elaborate language, 260–261

fostered, 39
Frankenfoods, 125, 126
freshman, 195, 196
full-fledged, 166
fused sentence, 247, 248, 257

G

galaxies, 265, 266
gender equality, 111
Gender Gap Index, 109
GM (genetically modified), 125, 126
grammar, 186–187
    adjectives. *see* adjectives
    adverbs. *see* adverbs
    descriptive, 186
    errors, 204–205
    importance of, 188–190
    meaning of, 187
    parts of speech. *see* parts of speech
    prescriptive. *see* prescriptive grammar
    writing errors, 189
'Green Pakistan' initiative, 166–167

H

'hand approach,' 89, 90
hang out, 104, 105
hassle-free, 158
hedging, 146–147
Hemingway, Ernest, 237
Hesse, Hermann, 237
highest-grossing film, 67
holistic designing, 41
homage, 67
homophones, 258

I

ideas
    brainstorming, 72
    connecting, 68–71
    development, 282–283
    essay, generating. *see* essay ideas, generating

generating, 282
    main, 46–48
    order of, 72
    organising, 66–68, 100–107, 147–153, 167, 282
    paraphrasing, 75, 78
    scope of, 89–90
    summarising, 73–74, 78
    sustaining, 108–113
illicitly, 69, 70
imminent, 111
impending, 157, 158
in check, 140
incubator, 112
indefinite pronouns, 225–226
    agreement with, 227
independent clause, 243, 244
indirect objects, 239
inept, 194, 196
inferences, 48–49
    images and, 48–49
    skimming headlines, 48
infinitives, as verbs, 231–232
information
    source of. *see* information sources
    understanding, 98–100
information sources, 129
    ability to observe, 130
    expertise, 130
    neutrality, 130–131
    reputation, 130
    vested interest, 130
innovative, 125, 126
in tandem, 41
integration, 113
intensive pronouns, 223
interim conclusions, 153–154
interjection, 252
interrogative pronouns, 223–224
interwoven, 265, 266
intransitive verb, 239
introduction, essay element, 19–23
    features of, 19
    topic, 22

IPCC (Intergovernmental Panel on Climate Change), 121, 122
irreducibly, 265, 266

J

'Jabberwocky' (Carroll), 218
Jonson, Ben, 36

K

kairos, 120
kameez, 41
kernels, 125, 126
key details, 46–48
   identification of, 47–48
knack, 67
knowledge, 13
kurtas and churidars, 41

L

language, 13
lapped up, 41
leaking, 121, 122
left a mark, 41
lehnga, 41
lenses, and ideas generation, 88–89
Lilesa, Feyisa, 38
limiting terms, 85
lingering demise, 158
linking verbs, 229–230
livelihoods, 120, 122
livestock, 137, 138
logical fallacy, 122
logical reasoning, 57–60, 118, 168
   evidence and, 271
lots, 140
luminance, 144, 145

M

main claim, 118, 126
main ideas, 46–48
mandatory, 161
marginalised people, 111

masses, 41
mechanics, 189
mentoring, 103
MFAs, 192, 193
mind-boggling, 126
mind mapping, 70, 71, 96
misbegotten, 196
misplaced modifiers, 204–205, 254
misspelt words, 257–258
modals, 230, 231
modifiers
   dangling, 205
   misplaced, 204–205, 254
move, 106, 107
Mussolini, Benito, 191

N

the NBA, 69, 70
neutrality, 130–131
Nietzsche's abyss, 62
nominative case, pronouns, 220–221
nostalgia, 14, 144
noun clauses, 245
nouns, 85
   abstract, 215
   collective, 216–217
   common, 216
   compound, 216
   concrete, 215
   importance of, 218–219
   possessive, 206
   proper, 216
nuance, 150

O

objective case, pronouns, 221
on board, 70
ongoing trends, 41
on par with, 113
outlandish, 41
Outsider Art Fair (OAF), 76–77
over-elaborate language, 260–261

overgrazing, 137, 138
overhaul, 161
overwhelming, 265, 266

P

paired adjectives, 206
paradigm, 121, 122
parallel structure, 21
paraphrasing, 75, 78
parity, 105
parts of speech, 189, 190, 196
   functions of, 201–202
   nouns. *see* nouns
   prepositions, 200–203
   pronouns. *see* pronouns
   reviewing, 251–253
   verbs. *see* verbs
patches, 70
pathos, 120
pay lip-service, 166
peer-editing strategies, 274–278
Pepper (robot), 86
perennial, 167
perpetuate, 113
personal pronouns, 220–222
perspectives, 17, 18
   handling, 147–150
persuasive writing, 118
phased out, 157, 158
phrases, 53–54
pilot countries, 103
pitcher with four great pitches, 193
plot, 144, 145
plural verb, 233
Poe, Edgar Allan, 203
Politics and education, 172–176
Politics and national security, 177–182
Politics and the environment, 165–171
polled, 149
ponderous, 157, 158
possessive nouns, 206
possessive pronouns, 220–222

pragmatic, 54
predicate, 221
predicate adjectives, 206, 240–241
predicate nominatives, 248
prepositional phrases, 203
prepositions, 200–203
preps, 145
prescriptive grammar, 186, 187–188
    example of, 186–187
prima facie, 23
privileged, 173, 174
problem-solving, logical reasoning
    and, 57–60
prompt, 4, 5
pronoun-antecedent agreement,
    226–227
pronouns, 219–228
    demonstrative, 224–225
    errors concerning, 226–228
    errors with, 258
    indefinite, 225–226, 227
    intensive, 223
    interrogative, 223–224
    nominative case, 220–221
    objective case, 221
    personal, 220–222
    possessive, 220–222
    reflexive, 223
    relative, 223–224, 228
proper nouns, 216
prose analysis, 60–63
prototype, 104, 105
Proust, Marcel, 237
psyche, 67
punctuation errors, 247–248
purpose, message, 13

Q
qualifiers, 17, 147, 209, 210
questions
    comprehension. *see*
        comprehension questions
    essay, deconstructing. *see*
        deconstruct, essay questions

responding, 281–282
selection/interpretation, 272
quoting, 75

R
rage, 41
R&D (research and development), 170
reading
    active, 37
    challenging ideas and
        assumptions, 42
    comprehension. *see* reading
        comprehension
    critical, benefits of, 30
    purpose-setting for, 36
    re-reading, 39–40
    and text connection, 37
reading comprehension, 42–57, 280
    author's purpose, identification
        of, 50
    comparing ability, 55–56
    emotions, 50–51
    inferences, 48–49
    key details, 46–48
    logical reasoning, 57–60
    main idea, 46–48
    phrases, 53–54
    prose analysis, 60–63
    tone, 50–51
    typs of, 57–62
    words, 53–54
rearing, 137, 138
reasoning, 132–138
    logical, 57–60, 118, 168
    'TREE' of, 132–134, 278
rebuttal, 127
redefined, 41
reflection, of evidence, 28
reflexive pronouns, 223
register, 13
relative pronouns, 223–224
    agreement with, 228
relevant evidence, 28
repression, 39

reputation, 130
retention, 104, 105
rogue state, 54
roll, 107
rugged case, 149
run-on, 211
run-on sentences, 247–248

S
salwar combo, 40, 41
sanctuary, 177, 178
sanitation, 120, 122
saplings, 166
sari, 41
scope, of topic, 84–86
scrambling, 111
seamless transition, 27
self-editing strategies, 278
sentence fragments, 204
sentences
    complex, 246. *see* complex
        sentences
    compound, 246
    compound-complex, 246–247
    fused, 247, 248, 257
    run-on, 247–248
    simple, 241, 245–246
    topic. *see* topic sentences
sequestration, 139, 140
settle for e-reader, 145
sewage, 120, 122
shortcomings, 177, 178
shunning, 126
signal words, 16
simple sentences, 241, 245–246
singular verb, 233
skills development, 4
sliding scale, 173, 174
sloganeering, 166
slump, 157, 158
SME (small or medium enterprise), 112
social media, 50
spam-blighted grip, 158
spawned, 149

specious, 158, 208

speech, parts of, 189, 190

sported, 41

stacking up, 144, 145

stakeholders, 94
    defined, 90
    identification of, 90–91

staple, 67

staples, 137, 138

Steinbeck, John, 237

STEM (Science, Technology,
    Engineering and Mathematics)
    programme, 102–103

street art, in Rio de Janeiro, 69–70

Strunk, William, Jr, 190

stumble, 111

subject complements, 240–241
    predicate nominatives, 248

subjects
    compound, 233–234
    and verbs, 232–234

subject-verb agreement, 232–234
    errors, 257

subordinating conjunctions, 242–243

succinctly, 157, 158

suffix, 215

summarise, 73–74, 78

superlatives, 55–56

supplanted, 157, 158

sustaining, ideas, 108–113

switched their majors, 104, 105

sycophant, 41

syllabus, aims/objectives, 3–4

syntax, 189

synthesise, 7, 8

synthesising evidence, 108

T

taboos, 113

tactile, 144, 145

tagging, 69, 70

taken aback, 265, 266

tautologous, 194, 196

technology, 101

text-based essays, 114

thesis, 19
    argumentative, 21
    defined, 19
    discursive, 21

thesis statement, 21–22
    drafting guidelines, 21

thriving, 137, 138

time limit, to writing, 84

tone, 15, 50–51
    argumentative writing, 125
    discursive writing, 146–147
    registers of, 51

topics, scope of, 84–86

topic sentences, 26–27
    importance of, 153

topography, 69, 70

touchscreens, 149

Toulmin model, arguments, 134–136

transitions, 25, 210
    seamless, 27
    topic sentences and, 26–27

transitive verbs, 239

'TREE' of reasoning, 132–134, 278

trimmer, 110

tsunami, 67

U

ubiquitous, 69, 70

underlying assumptions, 135

untempered repression, 208

upshot, 266

utopian, 70

V

veered, 149

verbose, 159

verb phrase, 230, 231

verbs, 228–234
    action, 230
    auxiliary, 230, 231
    infinitives as, 231–232
    intransitive, 239
    linking, 229–230
    subject–verb agreement, 232–234
    transitive, 239

vested interest, 130

viable, 140

vulnerable, 178

W

waning, 40, 41

warrant, 134, 135

watershed, 121, 122

whim, 41

White, E.B., 190

with abandon, 125, 126

words, 53–54

wrath, 38, 39

write off script, 161

writing
    argumentative. *see* argumentative
        writing
    discursive. *see* discursive writing
    errors, 189, 254–257
    essays, 4–6, 273
    expository. *see* expository writing
    formal. *see* formal writing
    persuasive, 118
    time limit, 84

Y

yarnbombing, 80–81

yesteryear, 41

Your Name (fantasy film), 67

Acknowledgements

The authors and publishers acknowledge the following sources of copyright material and are grateful for the permissions granted. While every effort has been made, it has not always been possible to identify the sources of all the material used, or to trace all copyright holders. If any omissions are brought to our notice, we will be happy to include the appropriate acknowledgements on reprinting.

Chapter 1.2 'Why we must save dying tongues' by Rachel Nuwer, published on bbc.com/future, adapted and used by permission of the author and publisher; Chapter 1.3 'An Ethiopian Runner Makes a Brave Gesture of Anti-Government Protest at the Olympic Finish' by Ndesanjo Macha in De Birhan, originally appeared on *Global Voices* on August 24, 2016; 'Bollywood influence on fashion trends waning', India Today, adapted and used with permission from IANS agency; 'Travel essay: Selfies – are they ruining travel?' by Ute Juncker, adapted and used with permission from the author; Chapter 2.1 'Animated fantasy film charms Japan and soars to the top of the box office' by Justin McCurry, September 2016 (adapted), copyright Guardian News & Media Ltd 2017; 'But I'm not artistic' by Gai Lindsay in The Conversation, January 2015 (adapted); 'The legalization of Brazilian street art in Rio de Janeiro, Brazil' by Michelle Young (3 Sept 2012) Huffington Post, adapted and used by permission of the author; Excerpt from 'Art makes you smart,' By Brian Kisida, Jay P. Greene, and Daniel H. Bowen, New York Times Nov 24, 2013, used with permission; Excerpt from 'The story of an art fair whose work was never meant to be sold' by Priscilla Frank, Huffington Post, Jan 2017, used with permission; 'S'porean artist is keen enthusiast of unique art of yarnbombing' By Phyllicia Wang, The New Paper © Singapore Press Holdings Limited, reprinted with permission; Chapter 2.3 'Robots will destroy our - jobs and we're not ready for it' by Dan Shewan (adapted), copyright Guardian News & Media Ltd 2017; 'Looking at artificial intelligence from a new perspective' by Tucker Cottingham, CEO of Lawyaw (www.lawyaw.com) an A.I. powered document automation platform for attorneys, adapted and used by permission of the author; 'Artificial Intelligence: the end of the human race?' by Patrice Caine, Oct 10 2017, adapted and used with permission; '4 fears an AI developer has about artificial intelligence' by Arned Hintze, Jul 23 2017, MarketWatch, adapted and reproduced with permission of Marketwatch, Inc. via Copyright Clearance Center; 'Debate over double-edged sword of technology' by Lin Yangchen, The Straits Times © Singapore Press Holdings Limited - permission required for reproduction; 'Science advocate says, 'Let the children come to me'', Oct 2016, adapted and used with permission from Bangkok Post; Transcript from NPR news report titled "Research Explores Ways To Overcome STEM Fields' Gender Gap" was originally broadcast on NPR's Morning Edition on June 15, 2016, and is used with the permission of NPR, any unauthorized duplication is strictly prohibited © 2016 National Public Radio, Inc.; 'White males now classed as a minority group at university' by Julie Henry, August 2012 © Telegraph Media Group Limited 2012; 'The gender gap: How New Zealand is faring' by Sophie Ryan, Oct 2014, with permission from The New Zealand Herald; 'The way forward for gender equality' by Phumzile Mlambo-Ngcuka and Babatunde Osotimehin in Al Jazeera; 'Bringing Facebook's 'She Means Business' to Pakistan'

By Nushmiya Sukhera, Oct 2016, used with permission from MIT Technology Review Pakistan; 'Uplift Women, Boost the Economy' by Shashad Akhtar, Nov 2014, Bangkok Post; Chapter 3.1 'Water Security - Good Governance and Sustainable Solutions', a speech by Noeleen Heyzer given at the Asia-Pacific Water Ministers' Forum in Singapore, © 2010 United Nations, reprinted with the permission of the United Nations; 'We must end our superstitious objection to genetically modified food', by Juliet Samuel, May 2016 (adapted) © Telegraph Media Group Limited 2016; 'The latest buzz: eating insects can help tackle food insecurity, says FAO' © United Nations [2013], adapted and reprinted with the permission of the United Nations; 'Urban farming is revolutionizing our cities' by David Suzuki, adapted and reprinted with permission from Greystone Books Ltd; Chapter 3.2 'Books vs. e-books: The science behind the best way to read' by Amy Kraft, December 2015 (adapted), CBS News; 'Touchscreens versus Toys' by Michael Andronico, February 2014, adapted and used with permission from Huffington Post; 'Why e–mail still matters in a social media obsessed world' by Kim Dale, 29 Aug 2013, reprinted with permission from Social Media Week; Chapter 3.3 'Green Pakistan', Feb 2017, from Pakistan Observer; 'The need for green Pakistan', by Makik M Ashraf, March 2016, adapted from Pakistan Observer; 'Al Gore's Flat Earth Army', by Richard Larsen, June 2013 in westernjournalism.com (adapted); 'Logical Fallacies and Global Warming

Alarmism', by Richard Larsen, July 2013 in westernjournalism.com; 'Catholic Online interviews Dr. Roy Spencer', by Marshall Connolly, April 2013, reprinted with permission of Catholic Online www.catholic.org; 'Scientist Roy Spencer is wrong: fossil fuels are expensive, by Dana Nuccitelli, May 2013, copyright Guardian News & Media Ltd 2017; 'Not just the Koch brothers: new Drexel study reveals funders behind the climate change denial effort', by Alex McKechnie, December 2013, reprinted with permission from the author; Excerpt from 'Ecuador: who benefits from free higher education?' by David Post, February 2017, used with permission from the writer and University World News; 'Sweden should remain a leader in welcoming children' by Rebecca Riddell, June 2016, posted on Human Rights Watch; Excerpt from 'France and Britain pledge to resolve migrant crisis together' (2015) published by france24.com; Excerpt from 'Patrols to block expected 1.5 million refugees flooding across Europe', by Michelle Martin published in Sunday Morning Herald, reprinted with permission from Reuters; 'Rich nations' self-interest means refugee crisis set to get worse, not better' October 2016 © Amnesty International 2017; Chapter 4.1 extract from *On writing: a Memoir of the Craft* by Stephen King, Scribner, p120-123; 'Don't dismiss adverbs' by Chris Freese, August 2015 © Copyright Barbara Baig, 2015; Excerpt from '50 years of stupid grammar advice' by Geoffrey K. Pullum, from The Chronicle of Higher Education, The Chronicle Review, Volume 55, Issue 32, Page B15, used with permission; Chapter 4.2 points adapted from 'William Kamkwamba, the Malawian wind tamer', www.africa-me.com; Chapter 4.3 "Caged Bird" from SHAKER, WHY DON'T YOU SING? by Maya Angelou, copyright © 1983 by Maya Angelou, used by permission of Random House, an imprint and division of Penguin Random House LLC, all rights reserved, and with permission from Little, Brown Book Group; 'Do not go gentle into that good night' by Dylan Thomas, from THE POEMS OF DYLAN THOMAS, copyright © 1952 by Dylan Thomas, reprinted by permission of New Directions Publishing Corp; Chapter 4.5 Extract from 'Letters to a Young Refugee from Another' by Andrew Lam, used with permission of the author (Andrew Lam is the author of Perfume Dreams: Reflections of the Vietnamese Diaspora and other books); 'Scientists find evidence of mathematical structures in classic books' adapted and used with permission, Copyright Guardian News & Media Ltd 2017. Graphs in the article are reprinted with permissions from IFJ PAN.

Past paper examination questions are reproduced by permission of Cambridge Assessment International Education.

Thanks to the following for permission to reproduce images:

Cover Colormos/Getty Images; Chapter 1.1 Katerina Griniezakis/EyeEm/Getty Images; D. Corson/ClassicStock/Getty Images; Jacqui Hurst/Getty Images; NIKLAS HALLE'N/AFP/Getty Images; Chapter 1.2 Harry Hook/Getty Images; Corbis/VCG/Getty Images; © All Rights Reserved to Sarin Soman. www.sarinsoman.com/Getty Images; Carl Court/Getty Images; Jurgen Schadeberg/Getty Images; De Agostini Picture Library/Getty Images; Jacob Maentz/Getty Images; Chapter 1.3 DISCIULLO/Bauer-Griffin/GC Images/Getty Images; Buda Mendes/Getty Images; Santosh Harhare/Hindustan Times via Getty Images; Jakubaszek/Getty Images; Digital Vision/Getty Image; A: Thomas Barwick/Getty Images; B: Justin Case/Getty Images; C: Owen Franken/Getty Images; D: Marcelo Endelli/LatinContent/Getty Images; Left: Owen Richards/Getty Images; Right: Richard Drury/Getty Images; Centre: Jamie Garbutt/Getty Images; Top right: TeeJe/Getty Images; Centre left: JACQUES Pierre/hemis.fr/Getty Images; Centre right: Martial Colomb/Getty Images; Bottom left: by Susan Blick/Getty Images; Chapter 2.1 In Pictures Ltd./Corbis via Getty Images; Kyodo News via Getty Images; paul mansfield photography/Getty Images; Luiz Souza/NurPhoto via Getty Images; LimeWave - inspiration to exploration/Getty Images; Top left: Chris Mellor/Lonely Planet Images; Top right: Paolo Cordelli/Lonely Planet Images; Centre right: Erik Isakson/Blend Images; Centre left: wrangel/Getty Images; Bottom left: uniquely india/Getty Images; Jenny Anderson/Getty Images; David Scherman/The LIFE Picture Collection/Getty Images; gvidal/Getty Images; Chapter 2.2 Norman Kent / Barcroft Media via Getty Images; Luis Martinez/Getty Images; RubberBall Productions/Getty Images; JOHN THYS/AFP/Getty Images; jaminwell/Getty Images; Photography taken by Mario Gutiérrez/Getty Images; Caiaimage/Sam Edwards/Getty Images; Stephen J. Boitano/LightRocket via Getty Images; Chapter 2.3 Tessa Bunney/ In Pictures Ltd./Corbis via Getty Images; LeoPatrizi/Getty Images; Wang HE/Getty Images; GUILLAUME SOUVANT/AFP/Getty Images; Chapter 3.1 Zakir Hossain Chowdhury / Barcro / Barcroft Media via Getty Images; DEA/G. NIMATALLAH/Getty Images; MANJUNATH KIRAN/AFP/Getty Images; Wolfgang Flamisch/Getty Images; Justin Sullivan/Getty Images; MARWAN NAAMANI/AFP/Getty Images; George Rose/Getty Images; Leisa Tyler/LightRock via Getty Images; Chapter 3.2 Ábel Polesz/EyeEm/Getty Images; Klaus Vedfelt/Getty Images; Education Images/UIG via Getty Images; Chapter 3.3 Jeremy Sutton-Hibbert/Getty Images; Francis Dean/Corbis via Getty Images; Education Images/UIG via Getty Images; JANEK SKARZYNSKI/AFP/Getty Images; Blend Images/Alamy Stock Photo; Anthony Asael/Art in All of Us/Getty Images; Education Images/UIG via Getty Images; JONATHAN NACKSTRAND/AFP/Getty Images; Chapter 4.1 Wodicka/ullstein bild viaGetty Images; Earl Theisen Collection/